# MENU
## PLANNING
## &
## MERCHANDISING

RICHARD J. HUG and M.C. WARFEL

# SECOND EDITION

### McCutchan Publishing Corporation
P.O. Box 774, 2940 San Pablo Ave., Berkeley, CA 94702

ISBN 0-8211-0734-8
Library of Congress Catalog Card Number 97-74244

Printed in the United States of America

# Contents

# Exhibits

# Tables

# Preface

Since the first edition of *Menu Planning and Merchandising* was published in 1991, the food service industry has experienced a slowing in growth from the rapid expansion of the 1970's and 1980's. The quick service retaurants (known as fast food restaurants in 1991) have surpassed the full dining group in total volume. Casual has become important in restaurants as well as in dress and in life style. This move to more casualness is evident in comparing the representative menus in this new edition with those in the old edition.

Irrespective of the changes, the menu is still an important part of a successful food operation, but it is not the only or even the most important part. This new edition examines menu writing and merchandising in relation to the entire food service operation. The procedures are adapted to an approach to menu planning and merchandising that food service managers use and that I and Mr. Warfel, who co-authored the previous edition, have successfully used.

In this revised edition, the principles necessary to produce successful menus and restaurants are used as a basis for procedures but adapted to accommodate the changes in technology, demographics, and lifestyles that have been developed in this age of the information superhighway.

I wish to thank those who have granted permission to use their materials as exhibits in the text.

I wish to dedicate this edition to my mentor, Mr. M.C. "Mike" Warfel, who died since the publication of the previous edition.

I would like to express my thanks to John McCutchan, the publisher of this book, and to Kim Sharrar, the editor.

Richard J. Hug

# 1 Profile of the Food Service Industry

**Purpose**: To present the current state of the food service industry and to describe the changes during the past five years.

We have been bombarded by news of the changes and progress in telecommunications during the past few years, and indeed they have been truly great. Many changes in other industries have been related to the telecommunications revolution, and while these have not been so extensive, they have been substantial.

## A Perspective on Food Industry Sales Volume

Exhibit 1–1 shows the Gross Domestic Product (personal consumption expenditures) for 1996 and its divisions into durable goods, nondurable goods, and services expenditures. From 1991 to 1996, the gross figure grew by 25.8 percent. Considering the growth of the information-related industries, it is not surprising that the increase in services was 33.5 percent while durable goods and nondurable goods grew less, with increases of 16.6 percent and 17.7 percent, respectively.

Exhibit 1–2 shows the relationship between the food service industry sales and the total nondurable goods sales, and the portions of the total food service volume contributed by the commercial (for profit) and industrial (nonprofit) segments.

### Projection for the Year 2000

The food service industry had high growth in the 1960's, 1970's, and 1980's. The sales volume doubled from $115 billion to $231 billion during the 1980's. The prospects are for a sales volume of $392 billion in the year 2000, or an increase of only 70 percent versus the 100 percent seen during the previous decade. These figures do not take into consideration the inflation factor, which reduces the real growth factor to between 2.5 percent and 3.5 percent annually.

### Food Service Volume Overall

From 1991 through 1996, food service spending as a percentage of nondurable goods grew from 18 percent to 22 percent. The commercial volume increased by 40.5 percent, while the industrial volume increased by only 24.7 percent. Decreasing volume in hospitals, the military, and transportation was only partially offset by a substantial increase in food volume in correctional institutions in the industrial segment.

1

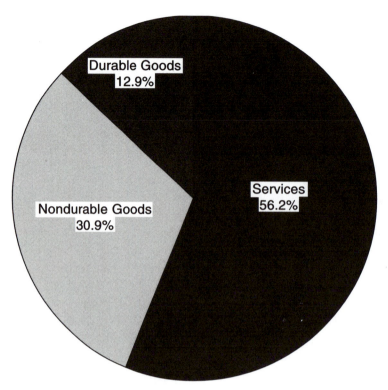

**Exhibit 1-1**
**Personal expenditures by U.S. consumers in 1996**
*Source*: U.S. Department of Commerce.

## Commercial Operations

Table 1–1 lists the segments of the commercial operations in the order of their volume and their percentage growth over the past five years. The most prominent change in the volume was the move into first place of the quick-service operations. The recreation and catering segments increased in volume to move ahead of the department/discount stores.

### Quick-Service Restaurants

Quick-service food operations have been the fastest growing segment of commercial food service operations, which is not surprising in view of the recent proliferation of these units throughout the country. In addition to young consumers being attracted to these restaurants, tourists have found that the quick service meets their desires to spend more time driving and less time eating. However, the international expansion of these chain operations has been the largest contributing factor to their growth, pushing their sales volume above the full-service restaurants between 1991 and 1996. The current primary international targets of quick-service operations are Asia, the Pacific Rim countries, and South America. Operators look to Russia and China for long-term potential, but unpredictable currency fluctuations have led operators to be cautious in planning more units.

Table 1–2 shows a breakdown of the quick-service segment by type of restaurant.

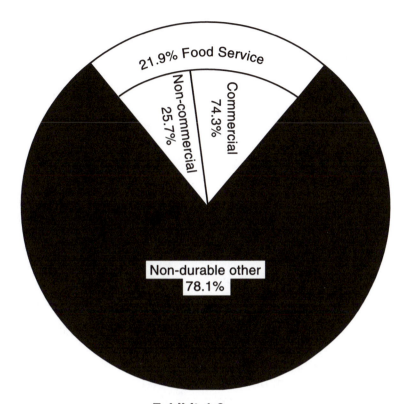

**Exhibit 1-2**
**Food service as part of nondurable expenditures and breakdown by percentage between commercial and noncommercial segments**

*Source*: U.S. Department of Commerce and *Restaurant and Institutions*.

**Table 1–1**
**Volume and percentage growth of commercial food service operations from 1991 to 1996**

| Commercial Segments | Volume (in billions) | Five-year Growth (percentage) |
|---|---|---|
| Quick service | $105,000 | 64.8 |
| Full service | 96,073 | 21.8 |
| Lodging | 14,457 | 62.4 |
| Supermarkets | 4,934 | 57.1 |
| Recreation | 3,428 | 19.4 |
| Caterers | 3,165 | 30.8 |
| Convenience stores | 3,093 | 21.8 |
| Department/discount stores | 1,151 | −49.8 |
| Other | 2,354 | 54.1 |
| Total volume | $233,658 | 40.5 |

**Table 1–2**
**Sales volume and growth of quick-service restaurants**

| Type of Restaurant | Current Volume (in billions) | Five-year Growth (percentage) |
|---|---|---|
| Burgers | $52,352 | 77.5% |
| Pizza | 17,462 | 40.8 |
| Chicken | 12,509 | 95.3 |
| Sweets | 8,054 | 29.9 |
| Sandwiches | 6,534 | 45.2 |
| Mexican | 6,081 | 90.0 |
| Seafood | 2,011 | 34.1 |
| **Total** | **$105,003** | **64.8%** |

During the past five years there has been no change in the sales volume of these restaurant types. The burger restaurants have increased their lead over pizza restaurants, and posted the largest dollar volume gain.

The chicken restaurants almost doubled their volume by adding new chains of restaurants as well as by expanding units in existing chains and widening their selections.

The quick-service Mexican restaurants have followed the expanded popularity of Mexican food in large northern and West Coast cities both in full-service and quick-service units.

The rapid expansion of sweets units before 1991 has slowed considerably during the past five years. The accent on health and diet foods and cholesterol warnings are adverse to this type of unit, but $8 billion in volume and a 30 percent increase during the past five years indicates that not all consumers are intimidated by what sometimes seems an extreme emphasis on health.

### Full-Service Restaurants

During the past five years full-service restaurants have lost their prime position of attractiveness for the dining-out people of the United States. However, their 41 percent market share added to the 44 percent volume of the quick service units still accounts for about 95 percent of the total volume of for-profit operations.

Table 1–3 shows the four types of full-service restaurants and their current annual volume and growth over the past five years.

**Table 1–3**
**Sales volume and growth of full-service restaurants**

| Type Restaurant | Volume (in billions) | 5-Year Growth (percentage) |
|---|---|---|
| Casual/theme | $46,149 | 32.9% |
| Family | 38,391 | 19.2 |
| Fine dining | 7,027 | −13.8 |
| Cafeteria | 4,506 | 12.2 |
| **Total** | **$96,073** | **21.8%** |

The *casual/theme* restaurants presently control 48 percent of the volume in full-service restaurants and are also the fastest growing group. They have retained their rapid growth in volume despite less emphasis on entertainment to attract customers.

The *family* group of restaurants are continuing a small but steady growth. They and the casual/theme restaurants control 88 percent of the market in the full-service segment.

The *fine dining* restaurants have continued to lose their appeal to the eating-out populace. Their volume has decrease 13.8 percent during the past five years. This is certainly understandable given the observable decreased formality in our daily lives, including dress, the conduct of business, speech, and manners.

When adjusted for inflation, *cafeterias* gain less than one percent per year, and have actually lost a bit of their market share.

### Lodging

The trend in this section of commercial food and beverage operations is to be a profit center rather than a necessary service to room guests. This trend is reflected in an accounting change that separates the food and beverage budget from the rooms; the two segments now operate as independent units. In addition, many hotel food and beverage operations are leased to chain operators of restaurants.

After a hiatus of several years, hotel building has had something of a resurgence. This return of activity has been in the smaller but growing U.S. cities rather than in the large cities where the population is static or actually declining. The proliferation of delis and coffee houses in the neighborhoods of hotels have attracted many of the hotel guests.

## Supermarkets

The changing lifestyle of Americans has positively affected the supermarket segment. As the number of families with both parents working continues to rise, so does the demand for already prepared meals. The "to-go" sections of the supermarkets have broadened the choices available, which means more trips to the supermarket for an increasing variety of take-out meals.

## Recreation

This segment of the commercial food service industry includes food sales at theme parks, sporting events, movie houses, and bowling alleys. This group has turned the tables on the predictions that the 1990's would see a decline in the rate of growth. The opposite has been true.

In spite of some closings in theme parks, attendance at the remaining parks are breaking records year after year, and the accompanying food sales have witnessed the same growth.

The professional baseball leagues added teams in 1992 and are scheduled to add more in 1997. The taxpayers are funding new stadiums in several cities and upscale sections have been added to some older facilities.

Since most homes in the United States have VCRs, the popularity of movie houses has declined somewhat. Now offerings through the Internet can be expected to give more competition to movie houses. Plus, some analysts go so far as to predict the demise of the retail chains selling and renting video tapes. However, this seems unlikely in the near future.

## Convenience Stores

The number of convenience stores (C-stores) has continued to climb. The number is expected to exceed 100,000 by the year 2000, up from less than 60,000 in 1990. The methods of purveying prepared food have undergone many changes over the years. Some buy prepared foods for warming in microwave ovens. Others have food prepared at a central commissary and delivered to the individual units. Most are operated with gas stations.

The next move is likely to be a combination of an oil company, a quick-service chain, and a convenience store group.

## Department Store/Discount Store

The reported volume for this segment is down about 50 percent from five years ago. However, these figures are apple-and-orange comparisons because this segment has tie-ins with quick-service chains. Their food volume is reported with that of the commercial segment; for example, Burger King/Woolworth and Little Caesar/K Mart.

## Caterers

Despite the increased competition from supermarkets and hospitals, this segment has experienced substantial gain during the past five years. Caterers have made their service more attractive by offering a more complete service. In addition to furnishing linen, china, glassware, and silverware (both flatware and holloware), they furnish tents for outside activities, decorate for parties, and arrange for musical and other entertainment.

## Institutional Operations

Table 1–4 shows the institutional segments, their current volume, and their percentage growth during the past five years. The most dramatic increases have been in the correctional institutions and elder care segments, which grew 200 percent and 136 percent, respectively. On the downside, military feeding was down by 15.2 percent.

**Table 1–4**
**Sales and growth rate of institutional segments**

| Industrial Segments | Volume (in billions) | Five-Year Growth (percentage) |
|---|---|---|
| Business and industry | $19,365 | 19.6% |
| Schools | 16,972 | 28.0 |
| Hospitals | 11,993 | 11.4 |
| Colleges | 8,533 | 18.2 |
| Corrections | 5,457 | 200.0 |
| Nursing homes | 4,998 | 31.9 |
| Military | 4,726 | −15.2 |
| Transportation | 3,696 | 17.3 |
| Child care | 2,494 | 3.0 |
| Life/elder care | 2,214 | 135.5 |
| **Total** | **$80,687** | 23.2% |

### Business and Industry

The business of employee feeding during the past few years has been characterized by mergers, meaning fewer but larger operators in this segment. The segment has become internationalized, with the London-based Compass group and the Paris-based Sodexho prominent among the large feed-

ers, along with American-based Marriot and Aramark.

Another recent development has been the broadening of services among most of the large operators to include cleaning floors, washing uniforms, removing trash, and so on.

### Schools

Next to business and industry, this is the largest of the not-for-profit food operators. Together they represent nearly 50 percent of the total industrial food volume. A late development in this segment is the privatizing of student feeding operations. The Hartford Connecticut School System has contracted with a commercial food operator for the total feeding operation.

### Hospitals

Health care has been a frequent, if not daily, item in the newspapers and on radio and television news programs. The mergers among hospitals, HMOs, and large chains of for-profit hospitals has had an effect on all phases of hospital services. Food service is no exception. Although Table 1–4 shows an increase in volume over the past five years, in most recent years the decreasing number of days a patient stays and the changes mentioned above have resulted in declining food service volume in hospitals. It appears that there will be continuing changes and the possibility of governmental regulations, so any future estimates are at best tentative.

### Colleges

The zero growth in this segment of food service in the late 1980's revived in the early 1990's. While a gain in volume (not adjusted for inflation) during the past five years is reported in Table 1–4, there is currently zero growth again. As a result, more colleges are contracting food services to private companies; vending machines have become more prominent in some areas, and some food courts have appeared that offer a variety for every taste. Perhaps an accent on imaginative management in these operations requires upgrading of the position of food service director, which would be another kind of employment opportunity for those in the food service business.

## Correctional Institutions

The reasons for the sharp increase in this segment are clear. New prisons have been built to accommodate the rising crime rate and consequent convictions, and some states have mandated that greater portions of sentences be served before parole can be considered.

Prisons have been pressured to more humanely treat prisoners, which includes serving healthier food. Some prisons are offering the same diets as hospitals. Also, some private operations have contracted to provide food service in correctional institutions.

## Military

The decline in food service volume in the military is consistent with the decline in military personnel since the end of the "cold war." One change in this segment is that the many old-fashioned Officers Clubs are being replaced by high-energy nightclubs and other food and beverage outlets open to all. Irrespective of such changes, the volume of feeding will rise and fall with the number of personnel in the services.

## Transportation

The early forecasts that this segment will grow steadily through the 1990's with slower growth in the latter years than in the early years of the decade have been accurate to date and will most likely be as we near the year 2000. The airlines will be the reason for the slower growth. Competition among the airlines requires management to decrease costs, and food service is the area most likely to be revised. However, airlines have shown some imagination in economizing. Rather than merely cutting back, some have initiated ethnic dishes, especially Mexican and fruit platters and vegetable dishes. These reduce costs but are not apparent cost-cutting measures to the consumers.

# 2 What Makes a Successful Restaurant?

**Purpose:** To review the many factors needed to make a restaurant successful and to illustrate the menu's role in achieving success.

The success of a restaurant *can* be guaranteed. Although the formula to achieve success is not magical, it is available to people who are willing to meet the requirements that we will describe in this chapter. The ingredients of this formula for success must be applied continuously; they are "the six g's":

- Good environment
- Good friendly service
- Good food and beverages
- Good value
- Good sales programs
- Good management

Thousands of successful restaurants can be found from coast to coast in the United States. In Europe and Asia, Africa and Australia, there are thousands more. But many restaurants in all these areas have failed, usually shortly after opening their doors for business; others have prospered for a time, and then failed. The successes have several things in common. Those that prospered for a while and then failed had the essential ingredients for success but then lost one or more ingredient. Maybe somebody erroneously reasoned that cheating a little would increase profit—it does not work! The restaurants that opened and shut in short order *never* had the stuff of success. What the successful ventures have in common are simple ideas, but ideas that are faithfully and continuously followed. We have a combined experience of ninety-nine years in hotel and restaurant operations from which we have created a formula using these ingredients—the "six g's"—that will guarantee success from the outset.

## Good Environment

### Location

This may be a trite expression but it is worth repeating once more: The three most important factors in running a successful hotel or restaurant are location, location, and location. This statement forcefully emphasizes the importance of location, which is a central element in this first of our "six g's"—good environment.

In order to determine what constitutes a good location for a restaurant, management must conduct a rather elaborate feasibility study. We will not discuss feasibility studies in depth at this point, but we provide the following outline to illustrate the complexities involved in merely establishing a base for estimating sales volume.

*Type of neighborhood*
- residential
- retail
- wholesale
- manufacturing

*Traffic pattern*
- automobiles
- parking potential
- pedestrian

*Potential customers at this location*
- families
- business people
- young adults

*Customers' income level*
- executive
- middle management
- blue collar

After analyzing these factors that contribute to a restaurant's patronage at a particular location, one can, with reasonable accuracy, estimate how many people are available to become customers of a restaurant at the different meal periods, and the amount of money they can afford to pay and are willing to pay for meals. Similar factors must be considered when planning a menu.

## Lighting

Location is only the first ingredient in creating a good environment. We must consider environment as perceived by the customer. He or she, perhaps especially she, is immediately aware of a restaurant's lighting. Is the room glaring with light, or is it so dark that one must pause a bit to allow the eyes to adjust to the dimness of the place? Customers have been heard to remark more than once in ill-lighted restaurants, "I should eat more carrots." Lighting should be sufficient to highlight the fine points of the decor, and garner customers' approval, but not so bright that it makes guests feel as if they are entering a fish bowl. Incidentally, the size and boldness of the menu type must be coordinated with the lighting in the restaurant. One restaurant, as a gimmick, furnished the waiters with flashlights, but it proved more of an inconvenience than an amusement for the customers.

## Decor

Decor is another vital item that makes up the first ingredient for success (good environment). This is especially true in a signature or theme restaurant. The food served in ethnic restaurants must be supported by an ambience characteristic of the nationality. There must be consistency in decor even in a family restaurant or fast food operation. Note that serving ethnic foods as part of the bill of fare in, say, a steak house can create a discordant image in what may otherwise be a good operation. Italian dishes are perhaps an exception because they are often served in many U.S. homes.

An important principle to remember when choosing restaurant decor is that it be consistent. In addition to consistency in theme and design among the walls, ceiling, floor, and various artifacts that make up a particular decor, there must be consistency among the uniforms of service personnel, dishes, and furniture. Designers must consider all these things to create a pleasing environment, and they must also think about function. Unfortunately, decorators sometimes do not consider the restaurant's operational needs. For example, some uniforms have ruffles or sleeves that encumber service; others are so heavy they trap perspiration. The color and design of the menu also must create a suitable vehicle for an excellent selection of appropriate food items.

## Physical Plant

Environment naturally affects the customers' satisfaction with their dining experiences. The location of a restaurant is of prime concern to the owners or operators of the establishment. The lighting and decor are certainly the operators' concern because they can affect customers' satisfaction. But customers are unaware of some elements of good environment because these features touch them only indirectly. An example is the physical plant.

The basic physical plant and the features it comprises are prime factors in the successful operation of an eating place, and from the operators' viewpoint form part of the environment. For example, the overall size of a restaurant, which includes the dining room, kitchen, and storage areas can, if properly apportioned, greatly contribute to a smooth operation.

Conversely, if the kitchen area, for example, is not large enough to support the number of guest seats, service will suffer. However, if the kitchen is disproportionately large, chances are that too much equipment will be bought and overstaffing will balloon labor costs. An efficient layout in a properly sized kitchen will create an orderly flow of service personnel traffic and eliminate wasted motion by the preparation staff. In such a kitchen the different kinds of cooking equipment are balanced and the supporting refrigeration is well placed. The proper distribution of work among stations in the kitchen depends on a menu that produces guest orders in a well-balanced manner. This balance will be studied in depth in Chapter 14.

The dining room layout is certainly a part of the environment. For example, a compartmented room has the advantage of giving guests the impression that they are a part of a lively clientele even when business is slow. Customers are not aware that there are empty areas beyond their vision. From management's viewpoint such an arrangement allows parts of the dining room to be closed and consequently not staffed. This flexibility adds to payroll control but does not affect the guest in any way. Such an arrangement is particularly valuable in hotel operations that have varying levels of occupancy on different days of the week and in different seasons. Coffee shop restaurants in hotels especially depend on the hotel's occupancy for a good portion of their volume.

### Storeroom

The last area to discuss in our consideration of good environment is the storeroom.

The storeroom is commonly considered a source of overhead expense. However, if of proper size and run efficiently, it is more an operating function. Rather than being an expense, it is a place to make money by saving money. A properly sized storeroom allows for a small reserve stock of nonperishable merchandise. This reserve makes it unnecessary for the buyer to purchase under the pressure of need, which in turn helps maintain favorable price levels.

The cost of making deliveries has been growing rapidly during the past twenty-five or thirty years. Naturally, the fewer the deliveries, the lower the delivery costs. This saving is reflected in the price of the goods. Sufficient storage makes possible weekly and monthly deliveries of some items. A good buyer can always negotiate for better prices on large-quantity deliveries and can avoid buying when an item is in short supply.

So good environment, although seemingly a simple concept at first glance, involves a number of vital features and functions that contribute to the first step in creating a successful food operation. Sometimes taking that first step is the hardest. The professional consulting business is built on the premise that the first step in solving a problem is recognizing what the problem is. To keep a restaurant successful, you must learn what it takes to build that success.

## Good Friendly Service

To define this second ingredient in the formula for a successful restaurant, we must consider three elements:

1. Many restaurants have good food, and often the service decides whether the store survives or fails.
2. Service might be good and efficient but not particularly friendly.
3. Although the waiter may be friendly, he might not seem to do anything right.

A brief and to-the-point definition of good friendly service is, "anticipating guests' needs and wishes before they have to ask."

## Appearance

One of first things guests notice as they sit down at a table or a counter is the appearance of the server. To give good and friendly service, one must look presentable to the guests. The personal appearance of the service personnel, including the bus boy or bus girl, can suggest attractiveness and cleanliness or it can cause guests concern about whether the food is sanitary. Courtesy and efficiency do not compensate for poor appearance. Personal cleanliness, good posture, and proper grooming are essential for good guest relations.

## Preparation

Louis Nizer, a brilliant trial lawyer, said that the key to conducting a successful trial is 90 percent preparation and 10 percent execution. This is also true for service personnel in the food service industry. Before the beginning of a meal, the preparation in the kitchen and in the dining room can make or break the operation. While the cooks make their *mise en place* (set up), the waiter or waitress undertakes the preservice and side-work duties. Preservice generally refers to making the guest tables ready. Side-work is making sure the service stand equipment and supplies are in place, and cleaning and filling salt and pepper shakers and sugar bowls. The latter is done not only before the meal but also during the meal period when the waiter is not busy with guests. Whether the food outlet is a classical dining room, family restaurant, or fast food operation, premeal preparation must be done to allow good service. This prep varies by menu, of course. In later chapters we discuss the many details and variety of data and their sources needed to build a successful menu.

## Know Your Menu

The proper approach by waiters and waitresses in using the menu is to remember that they are salespeople. Maybe waiters and waitresses should be called meals salespeople as a constant reminder of their primary function. The first requisite is that they know the product—the menu selection. Briefly, this means knowing about the menu items: what they are, the methods used to cook them, the proper pronunciation of the foreign words that appear on even the simplest menus, the cooking times in order to advise guests of the times required for preparing a la carte foods, and accompaniments to the different entrées. Servers must also sell. Sell appetizers. Sell drinks. Sell desserts.

## Organization

Service requires organization. "Who is the lamb chop?" This type of question has been heard by anyone who regularly eats in restaurants with a group of other people. It is excused by most people (customers are basically compassionate) who probably think it is difficult to remember who ordered what. But food service operators know that service personnel need not rely on memory to properly serve the orders. Keeping track of orders is not difficult; it merely requires a system for taking the orders. The most common system calls for identifying seats by number, beginning with an identifying object—say, the kitchen door. If all the service people are using the same system, any waiter can pick up any tray and check, then serve the proper foods to each guest without asking questions. If orders are handled in this manner, guests need not have compassion for forgetful servers. If they are not familiar with the ploys used by waiters, they may very well think, "What a remarkable memory that waitress has." By all means we do not want to hear, "What an attractive person. Too bad he doesn't know anything about food service."

## Cooperation

To do just about any job, a person requires the cooperation of others. This is especially true in the restaurant business. The waiter must work with the kitchen staff, with other waiters, and with the bus help. What does this have to do with good friendly service? To be a friendly waiter or waitress and pleasant with guests, one must be happy and relaxed. Such an attitude on the job begins with getting along with others. If after the meal preparation one is tense and testy because of poor relationships with fellow workers, this tension will be passed on to the guests.

How does one build good relationships with fellow workers? The first and all-inclusive principle is that the cooperation of others is earned by cooperating with them. This is the Golden Rule expressed in rather a self-interested way, but it is still golden.

## Special Groups

Good friendly service requires giving special attention to special groups of people. For example, serving children in a restaurant presents an excellent opportunity to use some commonsense psychology. Parents are pleased and encouraged to dine out more often if special attention is given to their children. Use all the facilities provided by the restaurant: high chairs, booster chairs, bibs, small glasses for ease in handling milk or other drinks. Especially helpful is a children's menu. In addition to having special items adapted for children, with special prices, it very likely will have a coloring book or game to occupy the child during the wait for food. Avoid a common mistake made by many people when speaking to children, especially strangers: you must not talk down to them.

Today, being elderly or disabled does not confine people to home as it did a few years ago. Such people will be part of the clientele in most restaurants and often require special attention. They may need extra time for both ordering and eating. Being alert to their needs for help pays good dividends, and it is part of that good friendly service.

## Complaints

We know a very good restaurant, one that truly appreciates its guests and makes every effort to gain guests' appreciation, that has this message on the back of its menu:

> Thank you for allowing us to serve you. Our goal is to provide a quality, bountiful meal with good service in a pleasant atmosphere. If we succeeded, tell others; if we failed, please tell us. Have a wonderful day.
> —The Staff of Benedicts

Like any fine restaurant, Benedicts welcomes complaints from guests. Complaints can provide an opportunity to improve an operation. Even the best of us make an occasional mistake on the job. Accept it and freely offer genuine apology. If the service staff's reaction to complaints is surly and unapologetic, very likely the guest will not return. A reputation for such guest treatment leads to a "closed" sign hanging in the window.

## Tips for Providing Good Friendly Service

Serving good food is certainly important. Equally important is good friendly service. The service people are the most direct representatives of the restaurant. Their contact with guests can either increase or decrease patronage. Mechanical efficiency is not everything. The human touch, a note of cordiality, adds a little glow, and the response of the guests can be amazing. Benjamin Franklin put it very well: "The taste of the roast is often determined by the handshake of the host." Here are thirty-three points of good service to attend to:

1. Pleasant greetings for everyone
2. Assist in seating women customers

3. Assist women with coats
4. Properly set tables with silver, glasses, and napkins
5. Provide full salt and pepper shakers
6. Have sugar bowls full
7. Provide sugar substitutes
8. Serve from correct side
9. Always say, "Pardon me, sir" (or madame) when appropriate
10. Remove chipped china and glassware and bent silver from service
11. Pour coffee carefully to avoid spillage into saucer
12. Properly carry side towel
13. Speak to all guests with respect and courtesy
14. Waiters and waitresses stand observing at stations
15. Always subdued conversation among service personnel in dining room
16. Quietly remove dishes and silverware from tables and dining room
17. Remove litter from floor immediately when dropped or noticed
18. Keep water glasses full
19. Fill water glasses and coffee cups to level for easy handling by guests
20. Clean ash trays in smoking area
21. Correct and instruct waiters and waitresses out of the range of customers
22. Replace guest napkins and silverware when they are accidentally dropped on the floor
23. Pay close attention to the details of orders—gravy, sauce, and so on
24. Present menus when suggesting desserts
25. Hot food on hot plates—cold food on cold plates
26. Remove plates promptly after *all* guests are finished eating
27. Present checks promptly
28. Place check on table face down
29. Always thank guests when they get ready to leave
30. Assist guests as needed when they are leaving
31. Remember to say "good-bye" to guests
32. Care in personal appearance—uniform, shoes, fingernails, and so on
33. Respond to guest's call from another waiter's station

## Good Food and Beverages

This third "g" necessary to a successful restaurant might certainly be called a truism. Nevertheless, it is well to discuss some guidelines that will ensure that this simple ingredient for success is realized.

The first step in serving good food is to buy good food. There is an old adage, "One cannot make a silk purse out of a sow's ear." In modern computer terms, "Garbage in, garbage out." Do not expect a cook to produce good-quality meals out of inferior raw materials. Steps must be taken to ensure that good products are purchased and carefully received. Your insurance policy is in a practical testing program and in a complete, up-to-date set of food purchase specifications. If a testing program is to prove effective and worth the time and expense involved, a few basic ground rules must be observed. The most important is that the decisions of the testing group be accepted by all its members. Another necessary part of the testing procedure is that testing be done in a suitable environment. Of course, products should be tested using "blind" testing procedures. The last ground rule that must be observed is that testing be done often. This ensures that the purchase specifications are kept current.

The three secrets of good French cooking are:

1. Everything that goes into a dish must be of good quality; the butter, the eggs, the meat, the vegetables—in short, everything.

2. One must have a taste for and love of cooking.
3. Butter, butter, and more butter.

In this health-conscious age, many may frown on the third secret of good French cooking. A successful and prominent chef in a popular New York restaurant proudly admits to following these three secrets, and has been dubbed "Cholesterol Queen of New York."

Appendix A includes two forms that add to efficiency in testing: butcher test and cooking test cards. Appendix B includes a taste test–score sheet. Also included is a sample table showing food purchasing and receiving specifications.

## Good Beverages

The second part of this third key to success relies on a few basic considerations. First, only good brands of liquor, beer, and wine should be purchased; second, serve a generous drink and employ personnel qualified to prepare good drinks; and third, follow the recommendations for good and friendly service discussed in the previous section.

## Good Value

In a way, this fourth ingredient for a successful restaurant venture is the end result of all the "six g's" working together. However, a substantial element of this ingredient is price, although prices have very little to do with the overall concept of good value. In a coffee shop in the suburbs, the price for a dinner may be $5.95, and people return often and pay the $5.95. In other restaurants, meals costing $10.00, $15.00, and $25.00 can be good values too. The patrons of these eating establishments are looking for a combination of food and service that justifies the price paid. When they find it, they feel they are getting good value at these higher prices. If the food and service are not good, even the low price of $5.95 will not be a good value for the coffee shop customers.

## Repeat Business

If customers continue to come back to a restaurant and the business is growing, you can be sure that the restaurant gives good value. Growth as a result of word-of-mouth advertising is evidence that the message being relayed is that good value is given at that food operation. It is great to have the reputation of being the most beautifully decorated restaurant in town, or for offering the greatest selection of exotic dishes, or for having the speediest service. But the best reputation—one that leads to real endurance—is the reputation for good value.

## Beverage Service

The service of drinks is very important in gaining that most valuable "good value" reputation. As mentioned above, drinks should be generous, and only first-label brands should be poured. And there is another dimension to gaining guest satisfaction in drinks: the quality of service. Unfortunately, the so-called club service is forgotten or ignored in many bars and restaurants today, even those commanding top prices. Perhaps you have witnessed or had the experience of ordering an expensive scotch and soda. The price may have been $3.50 or more. In return for your $3.50 you are handed a full glass of liquid. This liquid has a faint amber tint, evidence that scotch whisky is in the glass. The slight effervescence suggests club soda. The bartender splashed some scotch in an iced glass and filled it to the brim with soda from a "gun" dispenser. You may not want that much soda, but you were not given a choice. In club service the customer is served a glass containing ice and a shot glass or small decanter containing the scotch. One can see that it is a generous drink. A split bottle or small pitcher holds the soda. The server pours the scotch over the ice and adds a little soda. The customer can then add the amount of soda that satisfies taste. It is rather obvious which beverage service would contribute to good value and which would create a desire to go somewhere else—the next time.

## Good Sales Program

A good sales program is important for every operation from the mom and pop restaurant to the Persian Room at the Plaza or the Pump Room at the Ambassador East. The first point to remember is that a good sales program and advertising are not the same thing. Newspaper, radio, television, and magazine advertising can attract first interest in a restaurant, but many very successful operations never buy one piece of advertising.

A certain restaurant in a rather small community in New England devised a plan to "buy" advertising without buying advertising. We will explain why this is not a contradiction. A special credit card was issued to a few key persons in radio work. They had the privilege of "charging" up to $300.00 per month for meals, but they never received a bill. The 30 percent food cost and lower beverage cost meant that the restaurant's expense was less than $100.00—hardly enough to buy one ad. But in this small community it was difficult to turn on the radio in the morning and not hear good reports about this particular restaurant. Very often it was about what new things were going on. That is one way to "buy" advertising without buying advertising.

We mentioned in our discussion of good friendly service that perhaps waiters and waitresses should be called salespeople. Their selling efforts are crucial to the volume of a restaurant. Some old and successful food operations spend money on incentive programs for the service personnel rather than on buying advertising. In other words, they keep the money in the family. This builds sales and contributes to the development of employee loyalty. Feedback from servers to management on the customers' reactions to all phases of the restaurant from decor to menu to cooking styles to operating hours is vital to managerial decisions. Such programs also tend to slow down turnover of personnel, which is an added cost savings.

In a free-standing restaurant or in a food outlet in a hotel, reputation is often built around the personality of the manager or principal customer contact person. Part of a sales program can be geared toward members in associations like the Rotary Club, Sertoma, Lions or any number of other clubs that hold weekly luncheon meetings. Most members of these clubs frequent restaurants—consider them potential customers.

What is a restaurant known for or what is different about it? Persons return again and again to restaurants that offer something different each visit. Interest must be kept alive in order to develop a regular clientele. What represents a restaurant better than its menu? The Sunday newspapers have page after page devoted to telling about what the different merchants are selling and the specials for the week. The menu has the same function in a food operation. The menu is not the end result of the sales program, but it is a strong part of the overall result. The restaurant's strategy must be built into the menu.

## Good Management

Charles Schwab, who was Andrew Carnegie's right-hand man, said, "A person cannot be successful at a job that he does not like." To succeed in the food business, managers must not only like the business but be curious about it. Every day that they go to work, they *really* want to go to work. They are constantly looking for something new and different for their customers in order to add and improve service. If it takes controls, they learn about controls. They will learn enough to ensure that the proper controls are in place. As an example, a particular restaurant was running a food cost of six points below what the controllers established as the potential cost. The manager was not cheating. To achieve this low cost, each day after lunch the manager sat down with the chef and reviewed the sales analysis. How many orders of the several items were sold? They projected how many covers were to be served on the following day. Food supplies were issued to the kitchen on the basis of these projections. The keys to the supply room were in the manager's pocket—perfect control. As the meal period was coming to an end, small amounts of food were issued to fill the need. At the end of the meal there rarely were leftovers to be sold at a reduced price and a lesser profit. This is an excellent example of a manager seeking ways to improve profit—and succeeding.

If managers approach their jobs as described above, you can be sure that they will be *on* the job. It requires long hours and hard work to be a good restaurant manager, but nobody said that the job is easy. The food business requires "hands-on" management. It is well to remember that workers usually do not do what they are *expected* to do, but what they are *inspected* to do. This suggests two important points: employee supervision and control. Dozens of good books are available that discuss management. Most of them can be condensed into one sentence: Good management entails a proper, productive relationship between the boss and the employees. The vice president for personnel of a large organization said that by sitting in a hotel lobby and observing the facial expressions of guests and employees, he could characterize the management of the operation.

## Employee Selection

It takes considerable thought and study, however, to discover how such relationships between management and employees are developed. A few guidelines must be followed. The first consideration is that potentially good employees be hired. The expense of and time-consuming paperwork required by today's employees' benefits and the costliness of employee turnover have focused attention on the importance of care in the selection of personnel. Good managers school themselves in how to conduct successful interviews of prospective employees.

## Training

After a qualified person is selected, it is not enough to show him or her the dining room or kitchen and say, "That is where you will work, go to it." This sounds facetious, but it has been done, and is still being done. It costs money to train employees, but not nearly as much as the cost of lost business, which will inevitably happen if you turn untrained people loose in a restaurant job. Taking the trouble to train personnel after carefully selecting them is sensible.

## Organization

Organization is another key to good relationships between management and employees. In restaurants with many employees, which is the case in nearly every establishment, good relationships among them are important and do not happen automatically— good relationships among employees must be fostered and nurtured by management. The service personnel especially must be aware of the importance of this concept. As we mentioned before, getting along with your fellow workers is an important part of good friendly service. So, after having hired and trained people, the manager must help them become a smooth-working unit.

## Information

To keep this well-oiled machine in good working order calls for a continuing application of management skills. Keeping employees informed is essential. Everybody wants to know what is going on in the company for which they work. In fact, it is absolutely necessary if a person is expected to maintain a high degree of interest and enthusiasm. Such qualities dim if the employees get the feeling that they are "on the outside."

## Control

Leadership is another point often overworked and mentioned prominently but seldom analyzed in discussions of management. Boiled down to its essence, leadership is control. The boss calls the shots, the workers respond, and an effective job results. When discussing their profession, many managers shy away from the word "control" because it suggests accounting. Control by management is usually what the word "leadership" connotes.

## Compensation

The last important concept in good relationships between management and workers is compensation. Adequate pay for a job well done is really an effective management tool.

Good value is the relationship of monetary and nonmonetary units. In a meal it is the quality and presentation of the food, the quality of service, and the price paid. This same analysis must be made of the job done by employees and the pay they receive. To strike the proper balance there must be good value for management and good value for the employee.

## Conclusion

In all of the ingredients in our formula that not only contribute to but guarantee the success of a food operation if they are followed faithfully, the menu plays an important part. As we discussed, all the inquiries that need to be made to choose a restaurant's location are the same as those needed to plan a menu. And what better sales tool is there than an exciting menu? The menu brings the guest and the waiter together in a friendly manner. The details of the menu are remembered by customers who have found good value in a restaurant, and it is this memory that leads them back to enjoy again.

As you study menu planning and merchandising, you must remember that a good menu is needed for success, but it is not the only or most important factor. A good menu must be an integral part of an operation that is well managed by adherence to the "six g's."

# 3  Know Your Restaurant

**Purpose:** To examine the different types of restaurants and their particular characteristics. To consider the unique operating approaches required by each type.

Restaurants can be grouped into several classifications, such as fast food operations and classical restaurants. The differences between the different groups are obvious to any observer. But each classification has subdivisions. As we discussed in Chapter 2, good value is not characterized by huge portions at low prices. Good values can be found at many price levels and at various portion sizes. To know your restaurant means to know the market "niche" that your operation should aim to serve.

The first consideration in planning a menu is the type of restaurant that will be using it as a selling tool—the menu is the principal link between the customers and the kitchen. Many of the same foods are served in all restaurants, from gourmet to fast food. All serve from the same list of beef, veal, pork, lamb, poultry, fish, eggs, and the accompanying vegetables, fruits, and a few prepared items such as soups and bakery goods. What distinguishes the food selections among restaurants is the product quality, how foods are prepared, and how they are served. The prices reflect the differences, but prices are also determined by geographical location (which leads to higher or lower costs of doing business), ambience, and, to some extent, reputation.

## Classical Restaurants

This general classification includes several types, but they have in common full service, "white tablecloth," and traditional foods—both American and Continental. The subclassifications are distinguished by different types of service.

Below are features to be found in classical restaurants. No classical restaurant includes all of these features, but they all will have one or more.

1. A "European" atmosphere—the environment is warm and dark, but lighting is not as dim as in many lounges and supper clubs.
2. Some kind of display, including an hors d'oeurves table, a wine display, or a dessert cart.
3. A special emphasis on appetizers and soups. Seldom would salads be served as appetizers. More often they would follow the main course, so that guests do not consume vinegar, which is part of most salad dressings, while they are drinking the wine.
4. Prominently feature lobster, shrimp,

breast of capon, lamb, and beef.

5. French service, characterized by table-side cooking and service. The salads are likely to be tossed tableside.
6. Elegant table-top service, including crisp linen, hand-blown glassware, fine china, and silver-plated flatware. There may be a profusion of silver holloware.
7. Large drinks dramatize the fine glassware.
8. Leisurely service. A person in a hurry should not choose one of these restaurants. Businessmen entertaining clients are frequent patrons. Reservations are encouraged.
9. Normally staffed by waiters. If the service is French, personnel will work in teams. Russian service and American (plate) service are the more common services.
10. High prices, credit cards accepted, and the waiter collects the check.
11. Usually found in metropolitan cities, often in hotels.

## American Service

Many excellent restaurants that have the features to qualify as fine classical restaurants have modified service, best described as American or plate service. In this type of service all the hot food is prepared in the kitchen and is also plated there. It is delivered by the waiter or waitress, ready to be eaten. However, it is quite common in American service establishments to prepare the salads at tableside. Most successful plate-service restaurants are known for something a bit different from the ordinary. Special salads can give the restaurant an opportunity for an unusual presentation. Don Roth's Blackhawk restaurant in Chicago featured excellent foods of all kinds but caught the fancy of the public with its "Spinning Salad." Its simple presentation consisted of the waiter spinning the salad bowl in a bed of shaved ice while adding ingredients and tossing them. A singing sound was produced as the salad bowl whirled about in the ice.

Other special features in plate-service restaurants are desserts and exotic coffees prepared at tableside. Crepes suzette, cherries jubilee, and Irish coffee are common examples. Baked Alaska served with a procession is especially eye-catching. Such presentations are entertainment for the guests and something for which a restaurant is easily remembered. This type of restaurant offers unlimited potential in menu preparation. With a well-equipped kitchen, the range of items can be as wide as the menu writers' imaginations can conceive and the chefs' skills will permit.

Exhibit 3–1 is the menu of a popular chain of restaurants that features food selections that would seem favored by today's young people, but their clientele includes businessmen, retirees, and women's groups, along with youths. It is typical of a casual restaurant of the 1990's that serves good food appealing to a wide market. Note at the bottom of the center panel the section provided for "Specials," which change daily.

## French Service

French service is the most demanding on the service personnel, but the hard work is compensated by the great opportunity this type of service offers for guest entertainment. The personal attention given helps the guests feel that they are participating in a very special meal. In this service guests feel very important as they are given the royal treatment.

A unique characteristic of French service is that the food is served from a cart in the dining room. Food partially prepared in the kitchen is carried into the room on platters by a waiter, who then places it on the cart's heater to be kept warm until the final cooking is commenced. The final cooking is done by the waiter at tableside while the guests watch.

French service requires two waiters to work as a team. The leader of the team is called the *chef de rang*. The second waiter, who assists, is called the *commis de rang*. The *chef de rang* asks the guests for their orders; the *commis*

## MUNCHIES

**BUFFALO CHICKEN WINGS**    $4.99
Spicy wings with celery sticks & Bleu cheese dressing.

**MOZZARELLA STICKS**    $4.99
Mozzarella deep-fried with our marinara sauce.

**SUPREME NACHOS**    $5.99
Tortilla chips with chili, Cheddar, jalapeños, lettuce, tomatoes, sour cream & fresh guacamole.

**QUESADILLAS**    $4.99
Two cheeses, bacon, tomatoes, onions & jalapeños grilled between tortillas with guacamole, sour cream & salsa.

**BEER BATTERED ONION RINGS**    $2.99

**ONION PEELS**    $3.99
Crispy battered onion strips served with our Creamy Horseradish dipping sauce.

**BAJA POTATO BOATS**    $5.49
Crisp potato skins under Jack Cheddar, bacon bits & pico de gallo served with sour cream & salsa.

**VEGGIE PATCH PIZZA**    $4.59
A super-thin crisp crust topped with artichoke hearts, mushrooms, spinach, fresh tomatoes & a blend of Italian cheeses & herbs.

*Blackened Chicken Salad*

**BLACKENED CHICKEN SALAD**    $6.49
A spicy combination of blackened chicken breast on a bed of mixed greens with eggs, tomatoes & Cheddar served with hot bacon mustard dressing & garlic bread.

**GRILLED CHICKEN CAESAR SALAD**    $6.49
The classic combination of crisp romaine, garlic croutons & fresh grated Parmesan, all tossed in a tangy Caesar dressing. Topped with a char-broiled chicken breast.

Classic Caesar without chicken    $4.99

## Salads

**FRIED CHICKEN SALAD**    $6.49
Bite-sized chicken fingers on a bed of salad greens surrounded by Cheddar, diced tomatoes & eggs. Great with honey mustard dressing. Served with garlic bread.

**ORIENTAL CHICKEN SALAD**    $6.49
Crisp Oriental greens topped with chunks of crunchy Chicken Fingers, toasted almonds & crispy rice noodles tossed in a light Oriental vinaigrette.

**SANTA FE CHICKEN SALAD**    $6.49
Strips of char-broiled Fajita chicken breast with guacamole & sour cream on a bed of greens tossed with two cheeses, pico de gallo, tortilla strips & our Mexi-Ranch dressing.

**MEDITERRANEAN STEAK SALAD**    $6.99
Grilled marinated steak tossed with sautéed mushrooms & onions on a bed of salad greens. Topped with crumbled Feta cheese, tomato wedges, red onion rings, cucumber slices, Kalamata olives & grilled Pita bread. Served with olive oil balsamic vinaigrette.

**LOW-FAT VEGGIE QUESADILLA**    $4.99
Fresh mushrooms, red peppers, onion, broccoli & carrots smothered in non-fat shredded Cheddar/Mozzarella blend & sandwiched between two wheat tortillas. Served with fat-free sour cream & shredded lettuce. Less than 10 grams of fat.

**LOW-FAT BLACKENED CHICKEN SALAD**    $6.49
Our non-fat Honey Mustard dressing & non-fat Cheddar/Mozzarella blend give this Blackened Chicken Salad the same great taste as our original & less than 5 grams of fat.

**LOW-FAT LEMON CHICKEN PASTA**    $6.99
Thin slices of grilled lemon-marinated chicken breast, fresh cauliflower, broccoli, carrots & zucchini over angel hair pasta tossed with a light lemon herb sauce with mushrooms & sprinkled with Parmesan cheese. Just 12 fat grams.

**LOW-FAT & FABULOUS BROWNIE SUNDAE**    $3.29
Too good to be true! Your favorite dessert in a low-fat version. A brownie wedge with fat-free frozen vanilla yogurt & non-fat hot fudge make it all happen with only 2 grams of fat.

 Applebee's Signature Items

## Exhibit 3-1
## Typical casual restaurant menu with wide appeal
*(Applebee's Neighborhood Grill and Bar menu reprinted with permission from Applebee's International)*

*House Sirloin*

*Enjoy one of the following: a bowl of Today's Soup, House Salad or Small Caesar Salad with any food item for only $1.99*

**APPLEBEE'S HOUSE SIRLOIN**    $8.99
A 9 oz. choice sirloin steak served with your choice of potato & vegetable.

Smothered with sautéed onions, mushrooms & green peppers    $9.49

**STEAK OR CHICKEN FAJITAS**    $7.99
Strips of marinated steak or chicken breast char-broiled, & served on a sizzling platter with sautéed onions & green peppers, fresh guacamole, shredded Cheddar cheese, pico de gallo & sour cream with soft hot flour tortillas served on the side.

**GRILLED SALMON & ALFREDO PASTA**    $7.99
Char-broiled salmon fillet served with creamy Garlic Alfredo fettuccine & steamed vegetables.

**SMOTHERED CHICKEN**    $7.99
Our char-broiled, marinated chicken breast topped with Monterey Jack, sautéed mushrooms, green peppers & onions & served with your choice of potato & vegetable.

Without cheese, mushrooms, green peppers & onions    $7.49

**RIBLET PLATTER**    $8.99
Over a pound of slow hickory-roasted rib tips in our spicy Bar-B-Que sauce served with French fries & cole slaw.

**BROILED CAJUN TROUT**    $7.29
A char-broiled fillet of Rainbow trout seasoned with Cajun spices & served with your choice of potato & vegetable.

**STUFFED SHELLS FLORENTINE**    $5.99
Ricotta, Mozzarella & Romano are blended with sautéed spinach & stuffed into jumbo pasta shells. Served 'al Parmigiano' with side salad & garlic bread.

**SIZZLING STIR-FRY BEEF OR CHICKEN OR COMBO**    $6.99
Your choice of teriyaki chicken breast or spicy sirloin steak served on a bed of sizzling rice or spicy Szechuan noodles & stir-fry vegetables with our special stir-fry sauce. Choose both for a Combo.

**BOURBON STREET STEAK**    $8.99
A 10 oz. sirloin steak marinated in Cajun spices, char-broiled with sautéed mushrooms & onions & served with fried new potatoes.

ENJOY
APPLEBEE'S
FANTASTIC
FOOD
AND DRINK
SPECIALS

*Exhibit 3-1, continued*

### *Just Right* BITES

**RIBLET BASKET** $6.49
A hearty portion of slow hickory-roasted rib tips basted in our spicy Bar-B-Que sauce & served with fries.

**CHICKEN FINGERS BASKET** $5.79
Breaded chicken tenderloins, fried & served with French fries & honey mustard sauce.

**RIBLET & CHICKEN FINGERS BASKET** $6.49

**FAJITA QUESADILLAS** $6.29
Your choice of our famous beef or chicken fajita meat folded into crisp cheese, tomato, onion, jalapeño & bacon quesadillas. Served with guacamole, sour cream & picante sauce.

**CHICKEN PESTO PRIMAVERA** $6.99
Char-broiled Italian chicken breast & fresh garden vegetables steamed with garlic on a bed of fettuccine tossed with basil, tomatoes, walnuts, Parmesan & olive oil.

**CHICKEN POT PIE** $5.99
Tender chicken chunks simmered in a rich creamy sauce with potatoes, carrots, peas & pearl onions topped with a freshly-baked pastry crust & served with a small salad.

**CHICKEN ENCHILADA** $6.49
Char-broiled fajita chicken breast with onions & peppers in a spicy ranchero sauce wrapped in a soft flour tortilla under a blanket of melted cheeses & mild sour cream sauce.

### • Sandwiches •

*Add Fries to any Sandwich...$.99*

**BACON CHEESE CHICKEN GRILL** $5.89
A char-broiled, marinated chicken breast with bacon strips & Monterey Jack on a multi-grain bun with lettuce, tomato & onion.
Without bacon & cheese $5.39

**GRILLED PASTRAMI SANDWICH** $5.99
Warm pastrami with sautéed onions, tomato slice & melted Provolone cheese piled high on grilled thick-sliced rye bread.

**PHILLY CHEESE STEAK** $5.89
Thinly sliced roast beef with grilled mushrooms, green peppers, onions & melted Provolone on a toasted hoagie roll.

**CALIFORNIA VEGGIE ROLLUP** $5.99
Carrots, Bell peppers, zucchini, yellow squash, mushrooms & red onions steamed & stuffed into a warm wheat tortilla with diced tomatoes & avocado slices. Spiced up with chipotle mayonnaise & melted Jack/Cheddar cheeses & served with French fries.

**"RIBLET STYLE" BAR-B-QUE SANDWICH** $5.69
Lean pork shoulder, cooked "Riblet" style, chopped & piled high on a toasted roll. Served with sides of Bar-B-Que sauce & cole slaw.

*Club House Grille*

**CLUB HOUSE GRILLE** $5.89
Applebee's signature hot club sandwich with warm sliced ham & smoked turkey, Cheddar, tomatoes, mayonnaise & Bar-B-Que sauce on thick-sliced grilled French bread. Served with a side of cole slaw.

**CHICKEN FAJITA ROLLUP** $5.99
A flour tortilla topped with melted Jack & Cheddar, fajita chicken breast strips, shredded lettuce & pico de gallo, then rolled, sliced & served with French fries & Mexi-Ranch dipping sauce.

**FRENCH DIP & CHEDDAR CROISSANT** $5.99
Lean roast beef with melted Cheddar, creamy horseradish sauce & au jus for dipping; served warm with your choice of French fries, onion rings or cole slaw.

**SALAD & STEAMED VEGETABLES PLATE** $5.99
Our dinner salad or small Caesar salad followed by a plate of fresh steamed broccoli, carrots, cauliflower, new potatoes & zucchini.

**CHILI & HALF SANDWICH** $4.99
A mildly spicy mix of ground beef & sautéed onions topped with Cheddar & jalapeños, served with your choice of a half Club Sub or a half Chicken Walnut Salad Sandwich.

**SOUP & HALF SANDWICH** $4.99
Our soup of the day & your choice of a half Club Sub or a half Chicken Walnut Salad Sandwich.

**SALAD & HALF SANDWICH** $4.99
Our dinner salad or small Caesar salad with your choice of a half Club Sub or a half Chicken Walnut Salad Sandwich.

**SOUP & SALAD COMBO** $4.99
Our soup of the day with a dinner salad or small Caesar salad.

*Exhibit 3-1, continued*

*de rang* then takes the orders to the kitchen and places the orders with the cooks. He delivers the food to the *chef de rang* for its final cooking and placement on plates. The *commis de rang* places the food before the guests.

Cocktails ordered prior to the meal are handled by the *chef de rang*. He also pours the wine during the meal.

There are disadvantages to French service. From the brief description above you can see that service is rather slow. It requires more service personnel than other types of service and is consequently more expensive. The service from carts in the dining room requires space to roll the carts about, which reduces the number of seats a dining room can accommodate. Meal prices must reflect the costlier features of this type of service.

Exhibit 3–2 is the menu from the Bistro de Paris restaurant at the French Pavilion at Epcot Center in Florida. Note the items in the Appetizers, Soups, Fish, Meat, and Dessert sections featured by three leading French chefs.

## Russian Service

Russian service is perhaps the most popular kind of service in U.S. classical restaurants, both in hotels and as free-standing operations. It dates back to the early nineteenth century, and may be described as a modification of French service. Russian service does not require a team of waiters, although teams are sometimes used. In Russian service the food is fully prepared in the kitchen and carried into the dining room on large platters. The food is then transferred from the platters to plates that have been previously placed before the guests.

Russian service is widely used in banquets in many of the large cities of the United States and Canada. It has the advantage of personalizing the service while at the same time being a fast service. Because one waiter can work alone at each station, Russian service is less expensive than French service. Portions among guests at a table are more uniform than

is usually found in French service. This service is also less wasteful. Dining room areas can afford more seats. Nevertheless, there are some disadvantages. The last guest to be served sees his food taken from a nearly empty tray, which can be a bit unappetizing. If each guest at a table orders different foods, a great number of platters are required to carry the food into the dining room, and this can be quite cumbersome. Russian service also requires a large investment in platters, which are ordinarily silver in elegant restaurants. In today's air-conditioned restaurants, keeping the food hot presents a problem because the platters are not provided supporting heat after they leave the kitchen.

## Buffet Service

Buffet service can be found at all price levels. It is sometimes used to economize on service personnel and permit low prices. At the other end of the scale, the banquet buffet in a fine restaurant or hotel can be the top offering of the establishment. Buffets traditionally are identified with classical restaurants in room ambience and food selections. Today buffets are common in family restaurants and at breakfast in hotels and motor inns.

This method of presenting food to guests provides the caterer with an opportunity to merchandise the menu visually. For many people in and out of the food business one of the most memorable scenes in the cinema operetta was the lavish buffet tables usually set in the palaces of the Hapsburg Empire of the late nineteenth century. They delighted the eye with a profusion of silver trays—oval, round, and rectangular—displaying vividly colored cold foods and highly polished, steaming chafing dishes of vegetables and meats. The dessert table was of equal elegance.

Exhibit 3-3 shows a variety of eight dinner buffets offered at a Florida resort hotel. The several selections include what might be called standard buffets (i.e., Prime Rib buffet and Seafood buffet), but also offer theme selections based on the geographical

# Bistro de Paris
## Dinner

*The Chefs of France*
*Paul Bocuse · Gaston Lenôtre · Roger Vergé*
*Thank you for visiting with us during our*
*25th Anniversary Celebration*
*Bon Appetit*

## Préludes
### Appetizers

**Gratin d'escargots de Bourgogne**
Casserole of snails in a herb butter and a hint of garlic                                    8.25

**Bouquet de crabe et homard à l'estragon,**
**sauce de petits pois au curry à la façon de Roger Vergé**
Timbale of crab and lobster with tarragon,
served with a sauce of peas flavored with curry, featured by Roger Vergé          13.75

**Magret de canard fumé et sa salade gourmande aux coeurs d'artichauts**
Breast of smoked duck, with fresh greens and artichoke hearts
tossed with walnut dressing                                                                 12.00

**Feuilleté au Roquefort**
Baked Roquefort and Brie Cheese in puff pastry, served with selected greens         6.75

## Soupes
### Soups

**Double consommé de volaille et boeuf en croûte**
Double consommé of chicken and beef with vegetables topped with puff pastry         5.95

**Soupe à l'oignon gratinée, à la façon de Paul Bocuse**
Onion soup topped with Gruyere cheese, featured by Paul Bocuse                       3.95

**Bisque de homard**
Cream of lobster soup                                                                        5.25

## Salades
### Salads

**Salade maison**
Salad of selected greens, house dressing                                                    3.50

**Salade de chèvre chaud**
Baked goat cheese served on a bed a spinach, lettuce and mushroom                    8.25

Taxe et service non compris
(Sales tax and gratuity not included)
Margarine and salt substitute available on request.

## Exhibit 3-2
## The Bistro de Paris dinner menu
*(Reprinted with permission from Chefs de France, Lake Buena Vista, Florida)*

## Poissons
### Fish and Seafood

**Filet de bar sur une fondue de tomate confite au fenouille**
Filet of grouper flavored with fresh rosemary and oregano,
served on a bed  of  tomato compote and braised fennel                    21.95


**Marmite du pêcheur parfumé au safran à la façon de Roger Vergé**
Mediterranean seafood casserole of grouper, scallops and shrimp flavored with saffron,
served with garlic sauce and croutons featured by Roger Vergé              24.50


**Saumon grillé aux Agrumes**
Grilled salmon served on polenta cake with  mixed greens
and a warm citrus vinaigrette                                             22.50


## Viandes
### Meat and Poultry

**Le filet de boeuf grillé avec sa fricasée de champignons, sauce au poivre vert**
Grilled tenderloin of beef with mushrooms and a green peppercorn sauce
served with a potato gratin                                               23.95


**Le filet de veau Basquaise**
Veal loin sautéed with onions, peppers, and tomatoes
served with semolina and vegetables                                       22.95


**Suprême de canard aux pêches à la façon de Paul Bocuse**
Roast duck garnished with peaches, raspberry vinegar sauce,
served with vegetables, featured by Paul Bocuse                           21.25


**Carré d'agneau persillé à la fleur de thym sur son tian de légumes**
Roast rack of lamb roasted and flavored with herbs,
served with mushrooms tart and potato gratin                             26.00


A 15% service charge will be added for parties of 8 or more.
Menu Pour Les Enfants
Children's Menu Available                                        9/96

*Exhibit 3-2, continued*

## Délices et Gourmandises
### Desserts

**Tulipe de fruits frais et de sorbets avec son coulis de framboise**
Fresh fruit and sherbet served in a crispy tulip shell with raspberry sauce    5.95

**Coulant au chocolat, sauce vanille**
Chocolate soufflé filled with melted chocolate served with a vanilla sauce    5.95

**Crème brulée**
The traditional way of vanilla cream baked with brown sugar    3.95

**Soufflé glacé au grand-Marnier, Gaston Lenôtre**
Ice cream soufflé with Grand-Marnier, featured by Gaston Lenôtre    4.95

**Millefeuille de crème légère au caramel à la façon de Gaston Lenôtre**
Light puff pastry with vanilla cream topped with caramel sauce,
featured by Gaston Lenôtre    4.25

**Tarte fine aux pommes et sa glace caramel flambée au Calvados**
Fresh baked thin apple tart served with caramel ice cream and flambeed calvados    5.25

**Gâteau d'anniversaire pour deux**
Our birthday or anniversary cake for two    5.95

**Crèpe suzette flambée**
Hot crepes glazed with orange sauce, flambeed with Grand Marnier    5.95

**Matignon au chocolat avec sa crème Anglaise**
Light chocolate mousse cake surrounded with chocolate leaves    4.95

## Boissons
### Beverages

**Café**
100% Colombian coffe,
regular or decaffeinated    1.75

**Café Grand-Marnier**
Coffee with Grand-Marnier
and whipped cream    5.25

**Café express**
Hearty coffe    2.25

**Lait, thé, thé glacé**
Milk, tea, Nestea iced tea,
caffeine-free tea    1.75

**Eau Minérale**
Mineral Water    2.25

**Jus d'orange**
Orange juice    1.95

**Bière Française**
French beer - Bottle    3.50

*Coca-Cola* Classic, Sprite,
Caffeine-free diet coke,
Minute maid orange soda    1.75

Refills on all above non-alcoholic beverages other than Café express and mineral water

*Exhibit 3-2, continued*

# WINE LIST

## Aperitifs

| | |
|---|---|
| Dubonnet White or Red | 4.25 |
| Lilet White or Red | 4.75 |
| Kir au Cassis | 4.25 |
| Vermouth Cassis | 4.50 |
| Pernod | 5.25 |
| Sparkling Burgundy Cassis | 5.75 |
| Champagne Cocktail | 8.50 |
| Coupe de Champagne | 8.25 |

## House Wines

| | | |
|---|---|---|
| Vin Blanc, Paul Bocuse | Glass  3.75 | Carafe 8.75 |
| Vin Rouge, Paul Bocuse | Glass  3.75 | Carafe 8.75 |

## Carte des Vins

| | | Glass | Bottle |
|---|---|---|---|
| **Vins Blancs** | | | |
| 20 | Chardonnay, Chefs de France | 5.75 | 23.00 |
| 21 | Bourgogne, Gaston Lenôtre | | 27.75 |
| 23 | Bordeaux, Sauvignon Blanc, B&G | | 23.25 |
| 25 | Vouvray, Blanc, B&G | 7.50 | 30.00 |
| 28 | Puligny-Montrachet, Laboure Roi | | 52.00 |
| 26 | Pouilly Fuissé, Paul Bocuse | 8.75 | 36.00 |
| 27 | Viognier, Chefs de France | | 32.00 |
| **Vins Rosés** | | | |
| 46 | Côtes de Provence, Roger Vergé | 5.75 | 23.00 |
| 47 | Tavel Rosé, Domaine de Longval | | 29.00 |
| **Vins Rouges** | | | |
| 33 | Beaujolais, Paul Bocuse Vineyards | 5.75 | 23.00 |
| 32 | Merlot, Chefs de France | 4.50 | 18.50 |
| 34 | Bourgogne, Gaston Lenôtre | | 26.50 |
| 37 | Cabernet Sauvignon, Chefs de France | 4.75 | 19.50 |
| 35 | Gevrey-Chambertin, B&G | | 51.00 |
| 36 | Châteauneuf du Pape, B&G | | 32.00 |
| 39 | Côtes du Rhône, Roger Vergé | | 24.50 |
| 40 | Fonset Lacour, Bordeaux B&G | 5.25 | 21.00 |
| 41 | St. Emilion, B&G | 7.50 | 30.00 |
| 42 | Château Magnol, B&G, Cru Bourgeois | 11.25 | 45.00 |
| 43 | Château Larose-Trintaudon, Cru Bourgeois | | 33.00 |
| 44 | Château Gruaud-Larose, Grand Cru Classé | | 85.00 |
| **Sparkling White Wine** | | | |
| 45 | Crémant de Bourgogne, Paul Bocuse | | 36.75 |
| **Champagnes** | | | |
| 50 | Mumm-Grand Cordon, Prestige | | 160.00 |
| 48 | Mumm-Cordon Rouge, Brut | | 63.00 |
| 49 | Half Bottle | | 32.00 |

Tous nos vins sont disponibles au Palais du Vin
(All of our wines are available at the Palais du Vin)

*Exhibit 3-2, continued*

# Dinner Buffets

*(Minimum 50 Guests)*

## AMERICAN BUFFET

Marinated Vegetable and Penne Pasta Salad        Green Bean, Tomato and Red Potato Salad
Fresh Garden Salad with Choice of Dressing

*– Choice of Two Entrees –*

Boneless Breast of Chicken        Seafood Newburg or Seafood Creole
Roast Pork Loin        Beef Stroganoff with Noodles

Seasonal Fresh Vegetables        Choice of Potato        Rolls and Butter
Selection of Dessert and Beverage

## PRIME RIB BUFFET

Fresh Garden Salad with Choice of Dressing        Red Potato Salad
Tropical Fruit Salad        Marinated Vegetable and Penne Pasta Salad

Carved Prime Rib of Beef with Horseradish Sauce

*– Select Second Entree from the following –*

Breast of Chicken Dijon        Chicken Cordon Bleu        Roast Pork Loin        Seafood Newburg        Shrimp Etoufee

Seasonal Fresh Vegetables        Choice of Potato        Rolls and Butter
Selection of Dessert and Beverage

## ROAST BEEF BUFFET

Marinated Vegetable and Penne Pasta Salad        Green Bean, Tomato and Red Potato Salad
Fresh Garden Salad with Choice of Dressing

Carved Roast Beef, Au Jus

*– Select Second Entree from the following –*

Baked Breast of Chicken        Roast Pork Loin        Chicken Cordon Bleu
Seafood Newburg or Seafood Creole        Broiled Red Snapper with Chive Butter

Seasonal Fresh Vegetables        Choice of Potato        Rolls and Butter
Selection of Dessert and Beverage

## SEAFOOD BUFFET

Fresh Garden Salad with Choice of Dressing        Fresh Fruit Salad        Bay Shrimp and Crabmeat Salad
Tortellini with Pesto and Marinated Vegetable Salad

*– Choice of Three Entrees –*

Scallops St. Jacques        Broiled Red Snapper        Shrimp Scampi        Oysters Rockefeller
Seafood Newburg or Seafood Creole        Broiled Grouper Fillet

Fresh Carrots with Honey Glaze        Parsley Buttered Potatoes        Fresh Seasonal Vegetables
Rolls and Butter
Selection of Dessert and Beverage

**Exhibit 3-3**
**Buffet dinners from a resort hotel**
*(Reprinted with permission from Radisson Suite Resort on Sand Key, Clearwater Beach, Florida)*

# Dinner Buffets

## TEXAS BARBECUE BUFFET

Fresh Garden Salad with Choice of Dressing     Mexican Salad
Black Bean, Corn and Red Pepper Salad

*– Choice of Three Entrees –*

BBQ Beef     BBQ Chicken     BBQ Spareribs
Beef Fajitas     Chicken Fajitas

Corn-on-the-Cob     Baked Beans or Mexican Rice
Corn Bread     Fresh Watermelon     Rolls and Butter
Kentucky Pie or Blackberry Cobbler and Beverage

## HAWAIIAN BUFFET

Oriental Cucumber Vinaigrette     Tropical Fruit Salad
Fresh Garden Salad with Choice of Dressing

*– Choice of Three Entrees –*

Sliced Tenderloin Teriyaki     Broiled Mahi-Mahi with Lemon Chive Sauce
Boneless Breast of Chicken with Island Stuffing     Roast Stuffed Pork Loin

Fresh Island Vegetables     Oven Roasted Potatoes     Rolls and Butter
Islander Key Lime Pie and Beverage

## ITALIAN BUFFET

Tomato and Fresh Mozzarella with Basil Olive Oil
Chilled Rotini Salad     Caesar Salad

*– Choice of Three Entrees –*

Shrimp Scampi     Chicken Parmesan     Lasagna
Seafood Fettuccine     Veal Scaloppine with Lemon Sauce

Fresh Zucchini and Tomato Concasse     Basil Potatoes     Pasta Selection
Sliced Italian Breads

*– Choice of One Dessert –*

Almond Amaretto Mousse Cake     Black and White Espresso     Chocolate Truffle Mousse Cake

Beverage

**1201 Gulf Boulevard Clearwater Beach, Florida 34630 (813) 596-1100 Fax (813) 595-4292**

*Exhibit 3-3, continued*

location of the resort. These are particularly attractive to the guests from northern cities who come to enjoy the warmth of the sun, the sea, and the sand.

## Family Restaurants

The prosperity that followed World War II has continued to the present, with only brief periods of recession. It has produced in the United States and many other countries a new life-style that much of the population enjoys. The basic element of this life-style is affluence. This affluence has created widespread demand for all types of consumer goods, with a heavy accent on the trappings of sport and leisure. The restaurant industry has adapted to this change in life-styles by creating food operations that meet customers' new desires. The family restaurant is one example.

Following are some of the identifying features of family restaurants:

1. Found in suburban neighborhoods and as coffee shops in hotels and motels. They are, most prominently, chain and franchise operations in large and medium-sized cities.
2. Neat and often inexpensive environment. The owner or manager can nearly always be found on the premises.
3. Feature simple, friendly service. American service (plate service) is used. The food is of good wholesome quality and at a medium to low price level.
4. Food selections are on the light side— lots of chicken. Family dinners are commonplace and children's menus are available. Exhibit 3-4 is the menu from a Bob Evans restaurant, a very large and successful chain of family restaurants.

## Buffet Family Restaurants

The American people's desire to eat out has spurred most of the types of restaurants into a period of expansion that began in the 1950's and continues today. The buffet family restaurant, which is an adaptation of the cafeteria concept, has found a niche in providing the young family of limited resources an inexpensive way to eat out. Buffet family restaurants differ from the classical idea of a cafeteria in that they charge one price that entitles the customer to eat any and everything served. Many of these operations have adopted a promotional gimmick in their pricing policies. They might charge one price for adults, which includes everyone thirteen or fourteen years of age and older. Beginning at twelve or thirteen years of age, a discount off the adult price is given—35 to 50 cents–and an additional discount in this amount is given for each lesser year of age down to three. Children two years or younger eat free of charge.

A promotional ploy to encourage repeat business among senior citizens is a card sold for one dollar. The card entitles the senior citizen to a fifty-cent discount at each visit. Two visits pays for the card. The customer gets a real discount on additional visits.

Another deviation from the regular cafeteria operation is that the customers serve themselves for most of the food offered. A chef carves one or two higher-cost items, such as roast beef or ham. Beverage dispensers include the soft drinks that are very popular among children. A soft ice cream dispenser and a variety of syrups and toppings challenge the customer to concoct exotic desserts. Children from eight to eighty willingly accept the challenge.

The buffet family restaurant differs significantly from the cafeteria in the number of items available, particularly entrée

# SANDWICHES
### SALADS & SOUPS

## SALADS

*Served with fresh baked bread and your choice of dressing:*
*Bob Evans Colonial, French, Buttermilk Ranch, 1000 Island, Blue Cheese, Oil & Vinegar,*
*Honey Mustard, Reduced Fat Italian, or Fat-Free Ranch.*

**Tuna Salad Plate**
All white meat Albacore tuna mixed with
our special dressing and penne pasta.
Served with tomatoes and seasonal fresh
fruit .............................................................. $5.69

**Frisco Salad**
Fried tender chicken strips, bacon bits,
American cheese, green onions and diced
tomatoes served on a bed of salad
greens ......................................................... $5.39

**Grilled Chicken Salad**
Tomatoes, green onions, green peppers and
Swiss and American cheeses, topped with
marinated grilled chicken strips and served
on a bed of lettuce ................................... $5.69

**Fruit Plate**
Seasonal fresh fruit served with two Country
Morning muffins .......................................... $5.59

## CLASSIC SANDWICHES & BURGERS

*Add coleslaw and French fries to your meal for $1.99.*

**Pot Roast Sandwich**
Tender pot roast with onions and carrots.
Served on grilled sourdough bread ........ $3.89

**Tuna Salad Sandwich**
Chunks of all white meat Albacore tuna
mixed with our special dressing and served
on grilled sourdough bread ................... $2.99

**Grilled Chicken Sandwich**
Served on a grilled bun with honey mustard
dressing, lettuce and tomato .................. $3.89

**Chicken Monterey Sandwich**
Topped with melted Monterey Jack,
tomato, green peppers and green onions.
Served on a grilled bun ......................... $3.89

**Turkey Bacon Melt**
Grilled turkey breast with bacon, American
cheese, and tomato served on grilled
sourdough bread .................................... $3.89

**Fried Chicken Sandwich**
Boneless breast of chicken on a
grilled bun with lettuce and tomato ...... $3.89

**Grilled Cheese Sandwich**
American cheese melted on Texas toast .... $1.79

**Perch Sandwich**
Seasoned and topped with American
cheese and served on grilled sourdough
bread ....................................................... $2.99

**Sausage Sandwich**
Sold at state fairs as our Farm Boy. Served
with onion on a grilled bun ................... $2.99

**5-Star Double Decker**
Two patties, cheese, lettuce, tomato and
Bob Evans special sauce ........................ $2.99

**Turkey Burger**
Served with lettuce, tomato and fat-free
Ranch dressing on the side ................... $2.99

**Deluxe Hamburger**
Served with lettuce and tomato .............. $3.19

**Deluxe Cheeseburger**
With American or Monterey Jack cheese,
lettuce and tomato ................................. $3.39

**Bacon Cheeseburger**
Topped with American or Monterey Jack
cheese, bacon, lettuce and tomato ........ $3.99

## SOUPS & MORE

*Potato Soup, Bean Soup, Beef Vegetable Soup,*
*or our original recipe Sausage Chili with beans.*

Crock .................................................. $2.29        Cup .................................................. $1.69

**Loaded Baked Potato**
With cheese, bacon bits, green onions and
sour cream ............................................. $1.79
Served with salad and bread ............... $3.89
Served with a cup of soup and bread ... $4.29
Available after 11 a.m. daily

**Soup & Salad**
Our side garden salad served with a cup of
soup and fresh baked dinner rolls ........ $3.79

**Soup & Sandwich**
A cup of soup with one of
these great sandwiches:
• Pot Roast
• Turkey Bacon Melt
• Fried Chicken
• Grilled Chicken
• Chicken Monterey
• Bacon Cheeseburger
.................................................. $4.99

*Tuna Salad*

*Pot Roast Sandwich*

**Kids Tender Chicken
Strips & Fries**

KIDS MENU FOR
**$1.99**
Free Activity Sheet For Kids

## BEVERAGES

FREE REFILLS on these selected beverages:

| | |
|---|---|
| Coffee | $.99 |
| Fresh-brewed **Sanka** | $.99 |
| Hot Tea, regular or decaffeinated | $.99 |
| Hot Chocolate | $.99 |
| Fresh-brewed Iced Tea | $1.09 |
| Lemonade | $1.09 |
| Cherry Kool-Aid | $1.09 |
| Coca-Cola, Coke, Sprite, Barq's | $1.09 |

Milk
(chocolate or 2% white)        Tomato, Orange
or Apple Juice

Regular Size ..... $.99        Regular Size ..... $.99
Large Size ..... $1.39        Large Size ..... $1.39

**Exhibit 3-4
Popular family restaurant menu**
*(Bob Evans restaurant menu reprinted with permission)*

*Sirloin Tips & Noodles*

*Barbecued Boneless Ribs*

*Chicken Vegetable Pasta*

*Apple Barbecued Chicken*

# ENTREES

*All entrees are served with complimentary buttermilk biscuits or yeast-raised dinner rolls.*

## HOMESTEAD CLASSICS
### $4.99

**Vegetable Stir-Fry**
Served on long grain & wild rice. *7 grams of fat* _____ $4.99
Add a side dish for 99¢

**Vegetable Harvest Dinner**
Your choice of any four side dishes ___ $4.99

**Legendary Chicken-N-Noodles**
A Bob Evans Special Recipe. Served with a garden salad _____ $4.99

**Tender Chicken Strips**
Served with barbecue sauce and two side dishes _____ $4.99

## HOMESTEAD SPECIALTIES

**Chicken Stir-Fry**
Served on long grain & wild rice. *11 grams of fat* _____ $6.29
Add a side dish for 99¢

**Chicken Vegetable Pasta**
Topped with Alfredo sauce. Served with a fresh garden salad and grilled garlic bread _____ $6.79

**Fried Perch**
Two flaky lemon pepper seasoned fillets with two side dishes _____ $6.29

**Homestyle Meat Loaf & Gravy**
Topped with beef gravy and served with mashed potatoes and green beans _____ $6.69
*Available after 4 p.m. daily and 11 a.m. Sunday.*

**Spaghetti with Meat Sauce**
Made with our own Bob Evans Italian sausage. Served with a garden salad and grilled garlic bread _____ $5.69

**Country Fried Steak**
Served with mashed potatoes and green beans and topped with country gravy _____ $6.69

**Open-Faced Roast Beef**
Fork tender choice beef served with mashed potatoes and a garden salad _____ $6.99

**Turkey & Dressing**
Served with mashed potatoes and gravy, cranberry relish, and a garden salad ___ $6.99

**Barbecued Boneless Ribs**
Pork ribs cooked in our special sauce. Served with a baked potato° and a garden salad _____ $7.29

**Sirloin Tips & Noodles**
Served with a garden salad _____ $6.79

**Grilled Chicken**
Two marinated boneless chicken breasts, *7 grams of fat*. Served with two side dishes __ $6.99
One piece dinner _____ $5.29

**Chicken Pot Pie**
Chicken and vegetables in a rich sauce, topped with a flaky crust and served with a garden salad _____ $5.59

**Country Fried Chicken**
Two boneless chicken breast fillets, served with two side dishes. Add country gravy at no extra charge __ $6.99
One piece dinner _____ $5.29

**Chicken Monterey**
Topped with Jack cheese, tomatoes, green peppers and green onions. Served on long grain & wild rice with grilled vegetables __ $6.99
One piece dinner _____ $5.29

**Stuffed Pepper**
Two green pepper halves filled with a blend of Bob Evans sausage, ground beef, rice and spaghetti sauce. Served with grilled vegetables and a garden salad _____ $5.39

## FROM THE CHARGRILL

*Served with your choice of two side dishes. Available after 4 p.m.*

**Cajun Catfish**
Two catfish fillets seasoned for a mild Cajun flavor _____ $7.39
One piece dinner _____ $5.39

**Top Sirloin Steak**
A seasoned and aged 8-ounce USDA Choice Top Sirloin with A-1® Bold steak sauce on the side _____ $8.99

**Apple Barbecued Chicken**
Two skinless breasts with our own special apple barbecue sauce. *8 grams of fat* _____ $7.39
One piece dinner _____ $5.39

## SIDES
### $1.19

Fresh Coleslaw • Fresh Garden Salad • Long Grain & Wild Rice, *4 grams of fat*
Grilled Vegetables • Bread & Celery Dressing • Applesauce • Cottage Cheese
Fresh Home Fries • French Fries • Mashed Potatoes with Gravy • Buttered Sweet Corn
Glazed Baby Carrots • Green Beans, *1 gram of fat* • Baked Potato°
*°Loaded baked potato available for an additional 60¢*
*°Available from 11 a.m. daily*

SI 9/96
2

*Exhibit 3-4, continued*

items. The usual fare in addition to the items served by the carver includes chicken quarters, a meat stew, a fish fillet, and a pasta. The cafeteria will usually have ten or twelve entrées plus cooked-to-order steaks and individually prepared sandwiches.

Cafeteria menus are the topic of Chapter 12.

## New Entries in Food Service

During recent years, new specialty shops have entered the restaurant picture, most prominently the bagel shops and the coffee houses. Some operate during the breakfast and luncheon periods only, others through early dinner.

### The Bagel Shop

The number of bagel shops is growing nationwide, and most offer a variety of bagels and an equal variety of flavored cream cheeses, which can range from walnut raisin to chocolate chip. Many bagel shops adapt the bagel for both breakfast and luncheon: ham and egg on a bagel for breakfast and roast turkey on a bagel for lunch, for example. One bagel franchise even offers bagel party platters for home entertainment.

### The Coffee House

Exhibit 3-5 is a menu from a type of operation that has developed during the past several years. Coffee houses, of course, are not new, but have developed considerably to present a more rounded food and beverage service. In addition to the multiple coffee choices, the operation illustrated has a variety of herbal and blended teas, full bar service, fancy desserts, and three meals of food selections. Note also the invitation to show creativeness in preparing your own sandwiches and salads, cappuccinos and lattes. They also provide a delivery service for which one can order by telephone or fax.

## Fast Food Operations

The proliferation of these restaurants is evidence of a trend in the eating habits of people worldwide. McDonald's restaurants are the premier example of this type of food outlet. They are found in Europe, the Soviet Union, Asia, Japan, and Australia as well as throughout the Western Hemisphere. Perhaps this is why a bus driver guide leading a tour of Sydney, Australia, referred to a McDonald's restaurant as the "American Embassy." Such restaurants certainly can be described as an American mission abroad undertaken unofficially by unaccredited ambassadors. These restaurants cater to a hurried world.

The identifying items of these restaurants are familiar to all of us. They provide

1. Good food at a low price.
2. Fast service for both eat-in and carry-out orders.
3. Limited menus featuring foods especially favored by young people, such as hamburgers, pizza, fried chicken, sandwiches, sodas, dairy drinks, finger foods, salads, and salad bars.
4. No liquor. Beer is available in some outlets.
5. Young, part-time employees.
6. Clean and colorful environment. There is always plenty of parking space.

The menu selections in these operations, as in the chain and franchise family restaurants, are controlled by the parent company. This is a great advantage for travelers because they know what to expect of the food offered in restaurants with the familiar identifying signs. Nonetheless, these are well-managed operations and, as mentioned above, one can expect new food offerings on any visit, in addition to the known items. Although the check average is comparatively low, the fast food operations generate over $100 billion annually and command over 40 percent of the commercial market.

# INSOMNIA
## A Coffee House Lounge

Kick Back with a Funky Monkey

Take a Magic Carpet Ride

Bask in Strawberry Fields

See a Turtle Shake

Share a Naked Latte...

*Always Serving Hot Breakfast, Lunch and Dinner*

### HOURS:

Monday-Thursday 7:30 am-Midnight
Friday 7:30 am-2:00 am
Saturday 10 am-2:00 am
Sunday 10 am-Midnight

32884 U.S. Hwy 19 N. • Palm Harbor, FL 34684
Palm Lake Shopping Center
(NW Corner of US 19 & Tampa Road - Next to Shapes)

*We Deliver! Call or Fax us your order!*
Tel: 789-3771 • Fax: 789-2939

---

Soup .................................................... $2.00
Fresh selection daily - served in a 16 ounce gourmet mug
(with salad) $3.25

## Colossal Sandwiches

All of our soon to be famous sandwiches are served on a warm foccacia bread, piled extra high, exactly how you want it! We serve only the highest quality of meats and cheeses, including **Kosher** products.
(All sandwiches are served with your choice of chips, pasta salad or fruit.)

|  | Sandwich | Salad |
|---|---|---|
| BLT Stack .................................... | $4.50 | $3.50 |
| Bacon, lettuce and tomato dressed with honey mustard - great with avocado. | | |
| Classic Club ............................... | $4.95 | $3.95 |
| Smoked turkey breast, bacon, lettuce and tomato piled high with honey mustard dressing. | | |
| Hamlet ....................................... | $4.95 | $3.95 |
| Ham, Swiss cheese, lettuce and tomato grilled then dressed with special mustard. | | |
| Pastrami Stack (Kosher) ............. | $4.95 | $3.95 |
| Pastrami and cheese, any way you like it! Grilled and dressed with our special mustard. | | |
| Roast Beef Stack ........................ | $4.95 | $3.95 |
| Lean roast beef, provolone cheese, lettuce and tomato dressed with mayonnaise, salt and pepper. | | |
| Veggie Stack .............................. | $4.50 | $3.50 |
| Lettuce, tomato, cucumbers, carrots, sprouts, onion and avocado dressed with light ranch, Caesar or creamy Italian and sweet basil! | | |
| Caesar Salad .............................. | $4.50 | $3.50 |
| Romaine lettuce, parmesan cheese, croutons and pepper - a delicious sandwich! | | |
| Greek Salad ................................ | $4.50 | $3.50 |
| Lettuce, feta cheese, ham, tomatoes and cucumbers, dressed with a light, creamy dressing. | | |
| Light Pasta Salad ............ $2.50/cup | $3.50/meal |  |
| Tri-colored rotini tossed with parmesan, pepper, garlic and a light dressing. | | |

**Stack Your Own** - Choose from any combination of deli meats, cheeses, vegetables and dressings - hot or cold! Sandwiches and Salads made to order.
· Smoked Turkey, Ham, Roast Beef, Pastrami, Hard Salami & Bacon
· American, Provolone & Swiss Cheese
· Lettuce, Tomato, Cucumber, Sprouts, Carrots, Avocado & Onion
· Mayonnaise, Honey Mustard, Special Mustard, Ranch, Italian, Caesar & Blue Cheese

---

Sunshine Shake .................................... $3.25
Vanilla frozen yogurt and orange juice blended then topped with whipped cream - it's a dreamsicle shake!

☆ Turtle Shake ..................................... $3.75
Ice cream or frozen yogurt blended with creamy peanut butter, Hershey's and caramel syrups then topped with crushed graham crackers and whipped cream.

Yellow Submarine ................................. $3.75
Your choice of frozen yogurt or ice cream over top fresh bananas then smothered with Hershey's chocolate, whipped cream and your favorite flavored syrup.

Brownie Sundae .................................. $3.95
One of our fresh baked cream cheese brownies, warmed then topped with ice cream, Hershey's and whipped cream (and peanut butter on request).

## Munchies & Meals

### Breakfast

Cereal ................................................ $2.00
Choose from oatmeal, grape nuts or granola.

Yogurt, Granola & Fruit ....................... $2.75

Bagel or Croissant Sandwich ............... $3.00
With a variety of cream cheeses, eggs, bacon, cheese - however you like it (with only cream cheese). $1.75

Ugly Omelette ..................................... $3.50
They may not be pretty, but they're delicious! Three eggs with anything you want: vegetables, ham, turkey, bacon, cheeses...served with your choice of toast.

iNSOMNiA Pancakes ............................ $3.50
Stacked high then buttered and topped with whipped cream. The syrup is up to you...choose from hazelnut, Irish cream, caramel, strawberry, vanilla, B-52, chocolate or maple. (May we suggest chocolate chip pancakes w/B-52.)

French Toast ....................................... $3.50
Four slices of challah bread, battered then cooked sweet, topped with whipped cream and syrup.

### Light Munchies

Peanut Butter Jam ............................... $3.25
Two sandwiches with crunchy or creamy peanut butter, strawberry or grape jam on your choice of bread - try it toasted!

Grilled Cheese .................................... $3.50
Your choice of breads and cheeses grilled golden and dressed with honey mustard.

---

### Exhibit 3-5
### Coffee house menu

(Insomnia Coffee House Lounge menu reprinted with permission)

# iNSOMNiA!

## Coffee & Espresso Menu

All Specialty AuLaits, Cappuccinos and Lattes are served with a dipping cookie.

**Insomnia Brew** .................... $1.75
Daily selection of straight, flavored or decaf coffees served in a 16 oz. gourmet mug.

☆ **Java the Hut** .................... $2.50
Your choice of brewed specialty coffee topped with whipped cream, cinnamon.

**Caffe au Lait** .................... $2.50
Your choice of brewed specialty coffee topped with steamed milk.

**Signature au Lait (create your own)** .................... $2.75
Blended with your favorite flavored syrup and topped with whipped cream.

**Brown Cow** .................... $3.00
Your choice of brewed specialty coffee blended with Hershey's chocolate and steamed milk, topped with whipped cream and chocolate.

**Espresso** .................... $1.50
Insomnia's own espresso blend brewed dark and full. Enjoy your espresso short (Ristretto) or tall (Americana).

**Cuban Coffee** .................... $1.50
Brewed from Cuban Coffee Beans, this espresso-sized beverage is rich, full-bodied and sweetly acidic (bitter) Ask for it SWEET!

**Con Panna** .................... $2.00
A shot of espresso topped with whipped cream.

**Macchiato** .................... $2.00
A shot of espresso topped with frothed milk.

**Mocha Espresso** .................... $2.25
A shot of espresso blended with Hershey's syrup and topped with whipped cream.

☆ **Magic Carpet Ride** .................... $3.00
Triple shot of sweet espresso topped with frothed milk, whipped cream and nutmeg.

**Liquid Lava** .................... $3.00
Triple shot of espresso topped with whipped cream, cinnamon. Also comes with a glass of ice cold water.

**Cappuccino** .................... $2.50
A shot of espresso layered with equal parts of steamed and frothed milk.

**Mocha Junkie** .................... $3.00
A shot of espresso layered with Hershey's chocolate milk and velvety chocolate, topped with whipped cream and more chocolate.

**Carmalot** .................... $3.25
Our classic cappuccino blended with caramel syrup then topped with whipped cream, nutmeg and cinnamon.

☆ **B-52 Moo** .................... $3.25
Our classic mocha cappuccino blended with Mexican Kahlua, Grand Marnier, and Creme DeCocao syrups, topped with whipped cream and chocolate.

**Nilla Haze** .................... $3.25
Our classic cappuccino blended with vanilla and hazelnut syrups then topped with whipped cream and nutmeg.

**Nutty Irishman** .................... $3.25
Our classic cappuccino blended with hazelnut and Irish cream syrups, topped with whipped cream and nutmeg.

☆ **Sugar Daddy-O** .................... $3.25
Our classic cappuccino blended with hazelnut and caramel syrups then topped with whipped cream and nutmeg.

**Breve** .................... $3.25
Our classic cappuccino with a twist! We steam sweet half-n-half instead of milk for a thicker, fresher cappuccino - sweet and creamy.

**Caffe Latte** .................... $3.00
A shot of espresso blended with steamed milk and a touch of velvety frothed milk - 10 oz.

**Con Leche** .................... $2.50
Rich Cuban Coffee and steamed sweet milk (much like a sweet latte).

**Mocha Latte** .................... $3.50
A Latte with steamed Hershey's chocolate milk then topped with whipped cream and chocolate.

**Naked Latte** .................... $3.25
Our classic Latte light! Steamed skim milk and a light froth over espresso.

☆ **Strawberry Fields** .................... $3.75
A shot of espresso blended with steamed Hershey's chocolate milk and strawberry syrup, topped with whipped cream and more strawberry.

☆ **Funky Monkey** .................... $3.75
An AMAZING Latte: steamed Hershey's chocolate milk blended with hazelnut syrup and topped with whipped cream and chocolate. Ask for it with extra funk!

**Signature Cappuccino or Latte** .................... $3.25/$3.75
Topped with whipped cream and your favorite toppings.

**Honey Bear** .................... $2.75
Steamed half-n-half blended with honey then topped with whipped cream and your favorite toppings.

**Hot Chocolate (Flavored)** .................... $2.50

**Hot Herbal & Hand Blended Teas** ...... $1.50/cup - $3.00/pot
Enjoy a variety of teas from China, Japan, Russia or sip on Orange Blossom Spice or any of our Fruit Teas (ask at the counter for our tea list).

## Chillers

**Iced Coffee** .................... $1.50
Choose from the daily ice brews.

**Flavored Iced Tea** .................... $1.50
Brewed fresh and sweet daily.

**Ice Cream Float** .................... $2.25
Ice cream or frozen yogurt, choose your soda

**Iced Cappuccino** .................... $2.50
A sweet blend of espresso and cream, chilled then topped with whipped cream.

**Iced Mochaccino** .................... $3.00
Our delicious iced capp blended with Hershey's chocolate and topped with whipped cream and chocolate.

**Hazelnut Freeze** .................... $3.00
Iced capp blended with hazelnut syrup, topped with whipped cream (or try a Mocha-Haze).

## Shakes & Sundaes

**Fresh Fruit Shake** .................... $3.25
Frozen yogurt and fresh fruit, you choose the fruit.

☆ **Space Shake** .................... $3.25
Your choice of a shot of espresso or iced cap blended with ice cream or frozen yogurt, topped with whipped cream and chocolate (or add any flavored syrup $.50).

**Strawberry Truffle** .................... $3.25
Frozen yogurt or ice cream, Hershey's chocolate and strawberry syrup blended then topped with whipped cream, strawberry and chocolate.

Exhibit 3-5, continued

A new dimension in the fast food business is delivery service. Speed in delivery has become a competitive aspect among a segment of this classification.

## Signature Restaurants

Most signature restaurants are full-service operations. However, because of the wide disparity in their menu selections, presentations of food, and direction of merchandising efforts, they deserve to be described as a separate entity. A few years ago, discussions of this segment revolved around the various themes represented by these restaurants. In fact they were usually referred to as theme restaurants.

The early 1950s saw many post-war changes in American life-styles as consumers sought new pleasures. For example, the number of golf players moved from rather few at country clubs to many thousands enjoying the game at public and semipublic courses. Arnold Palmer caught the fancy of television viewers, and professional golf was on its way to an unpredicted popularity, offering prize money that has produced scores of millionaires in the golfing ranks. Tennis followed the same pattern. Motels for travelers and fast food operations for those in a hurry were growing in geometric proportions to meet the needs of many consumers' new life-styles. Specialty restaurants, later called "theme restaurants" and now called "signature restaurants," were provided by the food service industry to amuse and feed this consuming public. Just as the designation for these restaurants changed from specialty to theme to signature, the character of many restaurants changes as new owners assume management or because alert management recognizes that the tastes of the public are changing and so redesigns the restaurant to accommodate the public's new demands.

Calling this type of restaurant a "new concept," however, is a great overstatement. Restaurants with characteristics of the signature group have existed for centuries. In Europe some signature restaurants date back to the seventeenth century and are still operated by the same family and feature the same food that made them famous and successful three hundred years ago.

Several items characterize signature restaurants:

1. Known for an item or group of items served (e.g., Barbecued Back Ribs).
2. A theme that is carried out in both the decor and food served (e.g., Trader Vic's exotic tropical isle atmosphere and food).
3. Built around the reputation of a celebrity (e.g., Don Shula's Steak Houses).

Exhibit 3-6, a three-panel dinner menu, perfectly portrays the signature restaurant of the 1990's. The layout and artwork make dining at the restaurant an evening's entertainment, and together with an attractive list of menu items, contribute to providing the customers a high-quality, satisfying meal. Exhibit 3-7 is the back of the menu. It carries on the idea of the restaurant as a source of entertainment. The menu layout is also a good example of how to locate items on a menu, which will be discussed in length in Chapter 13, "Menu Mechanics."

Individuality is a key to the continuing popularity and financial success of these restaurants. Certain dishes are immediately identified with a signature restaurant, which produces repeat business built on word-of-mouth advertising. Krebs restaurant in upper New York had such a reputation for Sunday dinner that it is said anyone within one hundred miles on a Sunday headed for Krebs. They featured one price and served family style. There were about five items on the menu—chicken, turkey, and roast beef cooked in beer were standards. They had one dessert—apple pie—that *everybody* ordered. Something as simple as a basket of breads can become special, but it must be the best. *Then* it becomes special.

Perhaps the most unusual signature res-

## APPETIZERS

Black Bean Soup
  Cup .................. 2.50
  Bowl ................. 2.95
Soup of the Day
  Cup .................. 2.50
  Bowl ................. 2.95
Chips and Salsa ........... 3.95
  With Guacamole
Chile Relleno ............. 4.95
  With a green chile and cactus salsa
Fire-Roasted Green Chile and
Corn Fritters ............. 3.95
  With pineapple-orange-cilantro dip
Escargots ................ 5.95
  Truly authentic- as found in recent Pueblo
  excavations
Gazpacho Salad ............ 3.95
  Medley of refreshing yellow and red toma-
  toes, cucumbers, sweet peppers and onion,
  celery and a bold gazpacho dressing

Tangy Corn .............. 5.95
  In shuck canoe with jalapeño jack cheese and
  grilled shrimp kabobs
Almond Crusted
Chicken Tenders .......... 4.95
  Honey Mustard dip
Santa Fe Trail Bites ....... 5.95
  Riblets, cheddar-stuffed jalapeño pepper,
  chile relleno and green chile stuffed with
  barbecued beef
Shrimp Cocktail ......... 5.95
Santa Fe Grilled Shrimp ... 5.95
Black -n- Blue Sirloin .... 5.95
  Thinly sliced, served with Wasabi horserad-
  ish sauce, pickled ginger and soy sauce

Please check blackboard for
daily changing of pasta
and additional selections.

## LIGHT DINNER SALADS

All salads
served with
freshly
baked bread.

Sandwiches
and burgers
served with
tostitos and
cole slaw.

Southwestern Caesar .............. 5.95
  Steak Caesar                    add 2.95
  With grilled shrimp             add 3.50
  With grilled breast of chicken  add 2.95
  With almond-crusted chicken tenders  add 2.95

Kokopelli's Salad ................ 8.95
  With grilled breast of chicken, crisp bacon, blue cheese, guacamole,
  red onion, sweet red peppers with a tasty gazpacho vinaigrette

Crabmeat Salad ................... 8.95
  With fresh fruit and avocado. We couldn't leave this one behind!

## SIZZLING FAJITAS AND SUCH...

Marinated Chargrilled Breast
  of Chicken ............... 9.95
Steak Fajita ............... 9.95
Shrimp Fajita .............. 9.95
Grouper Fajita ............ 10.50
  Grilled or blackened
Combination of any two ....... 10.50

Howlin' Coyote Burger ........ 5.50
  With jack cheese and our green chile
  cactus salsa
Almond Crusted
Grouper Sandwich ............ 8.50
  Always fresh, served with lettuce, tomato
  and a zippy remoulade sauce (or grilled
  or blackened)
Crabmeat Quesadillas ........ 7.95
  With jalapeño jack cheese
Chicken Quesadilla .......... 6.95
  With onion and cheddar cheese
Veggie Quesadilla ........... 5.95
  Grilled veggies, wild mushrooms and
  jalapeño jack cheese

Above quesadillas served with veggies, sour
cream and cactus salsa. (Ask your server for
jalapeños if you like it spicy!)

**Exhibit 3-6**
**Signature restaurant menu**
*(E & E Stakeout Grill menu reprinted with permission)*

## STAKEOUT DINNERS

Tenderloin of Beef and Vegetable Kabobs .............. 8.95
Brushed with our Poblano Tequila BBQ Sauce

Chicken on the Bluffs .............................. 10.50
With artichokes, tomatoes, avocado and jalapeño jack cheese

Applewood Smoked Bacon Wrapped Chicken ............. 10.50
With garlic mashed potatoes and caramelized onions

The Mixed Grill ................................... 13.50
Pork chop, petite filet mignon, and tender breast of chicken
With grilled shrimp, add ... 2.95

The Trail Chop .................................... 10.50
A half pound pork chop marinated and chargrilled, with chile-fried
onion straws and garlic mashed potatoes.           Add a chop... 2.95

From the Skillet .................................. 10.95
Beef tenderloin, boneless pork chop and breast of chicken with sautéed
onions and topped with cheddar cheese

Ribs, Full Slab ................................... 13.25
Ribs, Half Slab ................................... 9.95
With our special Poblano Tequila BBQ sauce

Rack of Lamb ...................................... 20.50
Roasted with garlic, Dijon mustard and rosemary (Please allow 20 minutes)

## STAKEOUT STEAKS

Stakeout Steaks are of the highest quality available; we use special steak seasoning with cracked black pepper. Ask for our smoked Chipotle-Adobo Sauce if you like it a bit spicy.

Filet Mignon, 6 oz. ............................... 13.75
Filet Mignon, 9 oz. center cut .................... 19.50
Filet Mignon, more than 9 oz., cut to order, add per oz. ...... 2.50
The most tender cut of beef, corn fed from Iowa, served with Sauce Bearnaise

Center Cut Sirloin ................................ 12.95
12 oz. lean and tasty

Certified Angus N.Y. Strip, 10 oz. ................ 15.50
Certified Angus N.Y. Strip, 12 oz. ................ 17.50
America's Signature Steak

14 oz. Delmonico .................................. 16.00
Corn fed by Eugen by hand in Idaho!

Rodeo Steak ....................................... 14.95
14 to 16 oz., STAKEOUT SPECIAL

T-Bone ............................................ 20.50
20 oz. - The stuff of legends!

The Big Chief, 24 to 28 oz. ....................... 24.75
The Big Chief, 28 oz. and over .................... 25.75
BE HUNGRY! (Please allow 20 minutes)

Prime Rib, 10 oz. ................................. 12.95
Prime Rib, 12 oz. ................................. 14.95
Prime Rib, 14 oz. ................................. 16.95
Tempting, slow-roasted cut. (We roast a limited number of Prime Ribs each
night, please bear with us if we sell out early occasionally)

Dinners are served with our **southwestern Caesar salad**, freshly **baked bread**, fresh **vegetables** and your choice of **garlic-mashed** potatoes, **baked potato**, **french fries** or our daily changing **pasta**.

**Gazpacho salad**, in place of Caesar, add 1.95

**Skillet Potatoes**, add 1.95

**Fat free Gazpacho vinaigrette available.**

*Exhibit 3-6, continued*

KOKOPELLI WON'S FISHING

## SEAFOOD

**Filet of Black Grouper** ........................ Market Price
Fresh from the Gulf, baked with grilled peppers and a medley of vegetables
with white wine and olive oil

**Filet of Salmon** ............................... 10.50
Sweet pepper-pesto grilled with avocado-lime cucumber salsa

**Shrimp Tempura** ............................... 9.95
Lightly battered and fried, served with sweet-n-sour orange-pineapple dip

**Grilled Shrimp**
Marinated and Santa Fe grilled on a skewer        Nine Shrimp ... 12.95
                                                  Five Shrimp .... 9.95

**Surf and Turf** ................................ 24.50
6 oz. Filet with 8 oz. Florida Lobster Tail

> For your convenience,
> a suggested gratuity of 15%
> will be added to your check.

## SIDES

Skillet Potatoes ................. 1.95

Sauce Bearnaise ................. 1.00

French Fries .................... 1.75

Pasta du jour ................... 1.00

Wild Mushrooms .................. 2.00

Tangy Corn in Shuck Canoe ....... 3.00

## DESSERTS

**Upside Down**
**Apple Walnut Pie** .............. 3.95
Ala mode, add .99

**Million Dollar Cake** .......... 3.50
Chocolate pear fudge cake
Ala mode, add .99

**Chocolate Torte** .............. 3.50
**Key Lime Pie** ................. 2.95
**Raspberry Flan** ............... 3.50
**Fresh Fruit** .................. 2.95
**Ice Cream** .................... 2.95

## BEVERAGES...

Coffee, Hot and Iced Tea ........ 1.50

Espresso ........................ 2.00

Cappuccino ...................... 2.95

## LITTLE BIG CHIEFS

**Almond-Crusted**
**Chicken Tenders** ............. 2.95
With pasta or fries and honey-mustard dip

**Little Big Burger** ........... 2.95
With fries

**Oodles of Noodles** ........... 2.95
Our daily pasta with dreaded veggies

**Dinosaur Bones** .............. 2.95
Riblets with dreaded veggies

**Shrimp Tempura** .............. 3.95
With french fries and orange-pineapple dip

*Exhibit 3-6, continued*

THE ATMOSPHERE OF THE E&E STAKEOUT IS CHARGED NOT ONLY BY THE TERRIFIC FOOD AND THE ENERGY EMANATING FROM OUR STAFF. BUT IT ALSO EMBODIES A SPIRIT- AN ANCIENT SPIRIT. THERE IS A LEGEND AMONG THE BELIEVERS OF KOKOPELLI. CASANOVA OF THE ANCIENT ONE. THE HUNCHBACK FLUTEPLAYER. KOKOPELLI IS A PERSONALITY. AN ETHEREAL PRESENCE. A BENEFICENT GOD TO SOME. AND A CONFOUNDED NUISANCE TO OTHERS. GOOD. SASSY. UNPREDICTABLE. BELIEVED TO BE A GOD OF LUCK AND OF FERTILITY. KOKOPELLI MEANS MANY THINGS TO DIFFERENT PEOPLE. NOT ONLY WILL YOU F E E L KOKOPELLI THROUGHOUT THE ROOM- HE HAS INSINUATED HIMSELF INTO OUR MENU!

TAKE A LOOK AND ... E N J O Y !

**Exhibit 3-7**
**Back panel from signature restaurant menu**
*(E & E Stakeout Grill menu reprinted with permission)*

taurant in the world was the Cow and I in Venezuela. On the hour, a cow walked through the restaurant. The customers put lumps of sugar on the corner of their tables, and the cow wended her way through the dining room, eating the lumps of sugar. That was the show. Incidentally, the restaurant had excellent food and service. Because of its multiple artifacts that amuse the guests, one particular restaurant has been described as a "cheap vacation." It is a characteristic of the signature restaurants that they create an enjoyable, sometimes exotic experience along with serving good food, especially the dishes for which they have become well known.

Special china and glassware, sometimes following a theme and sometimes as attractions on their own, are features found in this group of restaurants and are remembered favorably by customers.

The good manager of a restaurant is always thinking of something new to keep the interest of customers. This may seem to contradict the paragraph in this part where we mentioned that three-hundred-year-old restaurants in Europe are serving the same foods today as they served in the seventeenth century. Today they attract customers because they are known for this tradition. But the patrons always go away remembering something they did not expect to find. As has been often said, "The only real constant is change."

## Ethnic Restaurants

Many of the ethnic restaurants, like those in the signature group, can be considered full-service operations. Nevertheless, they are a distinctive group and require special discussion. Some of these, such as Italian and Chinese restaurants, are found in abundance across the United States. Others—such as Russian, Slavic, or Indian—are rarely located outside large cosmopolitan areas. What these restaurants have in common, of course, is that they all feature the foods and atmosphere of a particular nationality.

Only a few years ago ethnic restaurants were operated by a family or families from the country represented by the restaurant's cuisine. Today franchise and chain restaurant operators have entered this field, most often with Mexican, Italian, and Japanese outlets.

### Italian Restaurants

The ethnic restaurant most familiar to Americans throughout the country is the Italian. Pasta dishes have been adopted by most families as part of American home cooking. One of the advantages of the Italian restaurant is the variety that the menu can offer, in both food selections and prices. The menu can include a long list of pasta dishes without putting an undue burden on the kitchen because the items build on a single base. Many pasta items can be quite profitable at reasonable prices.

At the other end of the price scale, typical Italian dishes of veal and poultry can take on gourmet dimensions and lend themselves to showmanship in tableside cooking service. The pizza fast food operations, both carry-out and table service, can be classified as ethnic restaurants, but they are usually not thought of as such because they have become so familiar.

Exhibit 3-8 is the dinner menu from the Cucina Italian restaurant in Kohler, Wisconsin. This is a classical restaurant, but note the inclusion of pizza—a popular favorite in fast food operations—presented in a manner consistent with the other menu selections.

### Chinese Restaurants

Along with Italian restaurants, Chinese restaurants have been familiar to most Americans. "Send out for Chinese" is a familiar line in television sit-coms as well as at lunch time in large eastern cities where the pace of life often borders on the

## DINNER

### ANTIPASTI

**Antipasti Misti**
a selection of Italian cheeses, meats and marinated vegetables.................................$9.00

**Gamberi**
smoked gulf shrimp, roasted garlic remoulade,
tomato horseradish sauce, grated parmesan .................................$7.50

**Cozze Della Casa**
fresh mussels with white wine, garlic and parsley, lemon herb broth .................................$6.50

**Ravioli Fritti**
fried ravioli stuffed with a medley of Italian cheeses, served with sauce marinara ...........................$5.50

**Calamari Fritti**
small squid breaded and fried, served with marinara and roast garlic mayonnaise...........................$5.00

### ZUPPE

**Zuppe del giorno**
cup .................................$2.50
bowl.................................$3.50

**Minestrone**
a traditional soup of fresh vegetables, beef and pasta
cup .................................$2.50
bowl.................................$3.50

### INSALATA

**Insalata Semplice**
a mixed salad of seasonal baby greens, toasted pine nuts, sundried tomatoes,
feta cheese, balsamic mustard dressing.................................$5.00

**Insalata Mozzarella**
sliced roma tomatoes, topped with basil vinaigrette
fresh mozzarella and ground pepper .................................$5.50

**Insalata di Caesar**
a Cucina classic.................................$5.00

**Insalata con Spinaci**
spinach salad with oranges, red onions, fennel and basil vinaigrette .................................$4.50

### PIZZA

Our pizzas are made from a homemade crust and tomato sauce prepared daily.  We use Wisconsin's
finest provolone, mozzarella and romano cheeses.  Now this is pizza!

|  | 9" | 12" |
|---|---|---|
| **Pizza Traditional**<br>fresh basil and tomato sauce, topped with sundried tomatoes,<br>roasted Italian sausage and mozzarella cheese | $9.50 | $12.00 |
| **Quattro Stagione**<br>sundried tomatoes, basil pesto, fresh spinach, red onions, black olives,<br>feta and skim mozzarella cheeses, tomato sauce | $9.50 | $12.00 |
| **Cucina Classico**<br>a blend of herbs and mayonnaise, sundried and roma tomatoes,<br>artichokes, romano and parmesan cheeses | $9.50 | $12.00 |
| **Pizza Quattro Formaggio**<br>a blend of fontinella, mozzarella, parmesan and romano cheeses,<br>fresh herb pesto sauce | $9.50 | $12.00 |
| **Pizza con Carne Mista**<br>roasted Italian sausage, capicola ham, pepperoni, mozzarella<br>and provolone cheeses, tomato sauce | $9.50 | $12.00 |
| **Pizza Sante**<br>a low fat pizza of fresh and sundried tomatoes, mushrooms,<br>red onions, fresh spinach and tomato sauce<br>with a sprinkle of parmesan | $9.50 | $12.00 |

## Exhibit 3-8
## Italian restaurant menu

*(Cucina Italian Restaurant menu reprinted with permission from Kohler Company, Wisconsin)*

# DINNER

## PASTA

**Lasagna**
pasta sheets layered with ground beef,
Italian sausage and cheeses in a rich tomato sauce ................................................................ $11.00

**Capelli con Pesto**
angel hair pasta, smoked chicken,
pine nuts and tomatoes, tossed in a pesto cream ................................................................ $10.50

**Penne con Caponata Rustica**
tube shaped pasta with eggplant,
zucchini, tomatoes, fennel, bell peppers
and onions, in a rich tomato broth ................................................................ $10.00

**Ravioli ai Quattro Formaggio**
ravioli of four blended Italian cheeses with rock shrimp,
roasted tomatoes, brandied shrimp cream ................................................................ $13.00

**Tortellini alla Forestierra**
asiago cheese tortellini, roasted mushrooms, caramelized onions,
light porcini cream, toasted pine nuts ................................................................ $13.50

**Spaghetti alla Bolgonese**
spaghetti with our own meat sauce
and grated parmesan cheese ................................................................ $10.00

**Linguine Milano**
Italian sausage, roasted tomatoes, leeks, pepperoncini,
rosemary vermouth sauce ................................................................ $10.50

**Capelli d' Angelo con Frutti di Mare**
angel hair pasta with gulf shrimp, scallops,
calamari, tomatoes, garlic olive oil,
white wine and herbs ................................................................ $14.00

**Linguine ai Gamberi di Golfo**
gulf shrimp with linguine, fresh leaf spinach,
sundried tomatoes and garlic basil,
olive oil and cracked pepper ................................................................ $13.50

**Farfalle di Vitello Rustica**
butterfly shaped pasta with ribbons of veal,
zucchini, roasted tomatoes, peppers,
black olives and herbs, rich tomato broth ................................................................ $12.00

**Capelli alla Gamberi**
angel hair pasta, gulf shrimp,
prosciutto ham and black olives,
tossed in a romano cream sauce ................................................................ $13.50

**Fettuccine Alfredo**
flat pasta noodles with prosciutto ham and roasted tomatoes,
tossed in a rich parmesan alfredo sauce ................................................................ $9.50

## PIATTI DELLO CHEF

**Scalloppine di Vitello**
scalloppine of veal with porcini mushroom,
marsala jus, lemon garlic, soft polenta ................................................................ $16.50

**Risotto con Frutti di Mare**
shrimp, scallops, fresh clams, mussels and calamari, tomatoes,
Italian cheeses and herbs ................................................................ $16.50

**Piccata di Maiale**
seared pork piccata, roasted wild mushrooms,
artichoke hearts, capers, white wine,
lemon and herbs, soft polenta ................................................................ $13.50

**Cottollette Arrosto**
oven roasted veal chop, marsala jus, caramelized onions,
braised fennel, soft polenta ................................................................ $19.00

*Exhibit 3-8, continued*

frantic. Chinese food can be easily packaged for carry-out service, and since it comes bite-sized, it is convenient to eat almost anywhere. Many households, especially among the young, have woks in their kitchens along with the microwave oven.

Chinese restaurants are still largely owned and operated by a Chinese family or families. The reason is that few cooks of other ethnicities have learned the art of Chinese cooking, and there are no serious efforts to change this situation. Exhibit 3-9 is the menu from the China Jade restaurant in Holiday, Florida. It includes everything one expects from a Chinese restaurant: the breakdown of items in sections of poultry, beef/pork, seafood, house specialties, combination platters, and the very popular family dinners.

## English Restaurants

Perhaps it was an "ugly American" who characterized English food as fish and chips, overdone roast beef, and the world's worst coffee. The truth is that there is no universal sense of taste. The basic raw materials used in English cookery are the same as in France and the United States, but different products are produced. One might just as well shout, "*Vive le difference.*"

Some favorite English foods and beverages include thick soups, hot potted shrimp, lamb and lamb chops, roast beef and potatoes, game and game pies, fresh seafood, short breads and pastry, coffee, gin, and beer and ales.

## Mexican Restaurants

In the 1950's the United States was "invaded" by pizza parlors. On a somewhat lesser scale the 1970's and 1980's witnessed a surge in the number of Mexican restaurants. This proliferation was principally accomplished by chain and franchised operations that moved into two areas of the food industry: fast food and family restaurants.

The staple foods of Mexico allow for very filling meals at quite low prices. Refried beans and rice accompany practically all dishes. The tortilla, similar to the pancake, is made from corn and is the base for tacos and enchiladas. Beef and chicken are the popular meats, although turkey and fish are offered on some Mexican restaurant menus. The principal characteristic of Mexican food is usually that it is spicy, although Mexican restaurants in the United States have modified this for the tastes of those who do not care for "salsa picante."

Exhibit 3–10 is the menu from the Mexican restaurant El Zarape (zarape is a variable of *sarape*, which is a blanket that is used in several different ways) in Dunedin, Florida. It is owned and operated by a family from Mexico.

## French Restaurants

There are many French restaurants in the United States, especially in the large cities. But the classical restaurants that advertise Continental cuisine are mostly modified French restaurants. It is rather common to see French cooking terms on the menus of family restaurants.

European chefs, whether from France, Germany, or Italy, still dominate the American restaurant business and are well versed in French cooking. The culinary schools, for the most part, base their instructional curriculum on the French style of cooking. Julia Childs, a charming American chef, has been a leading influence in introducing French cooking to Americans through her popular shows on public television.

It was French genius that popularized sauces in cooking. The purpose of sauces, in the beginning, was to enliven and give flavor to otherwise rather dull-tasting foods. The need for such additives has diminished through the years with raw products improved through scientific breeding of animals and better vegetable production. Refrigeration and

# Appetizers

| | |
|---|---|
| Egg Rolls (1) | 1.00 |
| Barbecued Ribs | (3) (Small) 3.25 (6) (Large) 5.95 |
| Fantail Shrimp (6) | 5.15 |
| Fried Wonton (12) | 2.25 |
| Chicken Wings (6) | 3.50 |
| Beef Sticks (4) | 4.50 |
| Dim Sum (4) | 3.95 |
| Dumplings, Pan Fried or Steamed (6) | 4.75 |
| Pork Strips | 4.50 |
| Chicken Fingers (6) | 2.95 |
| Cold Noodle with Sesame Sauce | 3.95 |
| Cold Sliced Chicken with Sesame Sauce | 4.95 |

**Pu Pu Platter** (Per Person)
*Rib, Chicken Wing, Fried Shrimp,*
*Beef Stick & Egg Roll.*
**- $3.95 -**

# Soup

| | |
|---|---|
| Egg Drop Soup | 1.00 |
| Wonton Soup | 1.20 |
| Chicken Rice Soup | 1.25 |
| Subgum Wonton Soup (Per Person) (Min. For Two) | 2.25 |
| Hot and Sour Soup (Per Person) (Min. For Two) | 1.75 |
| Noodle Soup (Per Person) (Min. For Two) | 2.25 |
| Wonton Egg Drop Mixed Soup | 1.45 |

# Combination Platters

| No. | 1. | Chicken Chow Mein, Fried Rice and Egg Roll | 6.50 |
|---|---|---|---|
| No. | 2. | Pepper Steak & Onions, Fried Rice & Egg Roll | 7.25 |
| No. | 3. | Sweet & Sour Pork, Fried Rice and Egg Roll | 6.95 |
| No. | 4. | Pork Egg Foo Young, Fried Rice and Egg Roll | 5.95 |
| No. | 5. | Bar-B-Q Spare Ribs, Fried Rice and Egg Roll | 7.50 |
| No. | 6. | Shrimp with Lobster Sauce | 8.75 |
| No. | 7. | Kung Bo Chicken | 7.50 |
| No. | 8. | Beef with Broccoli | 7.50 |
| No. | 9. | Pork Lo Mein | 6.75 |
| No. | 10. | Moo Goo Gai Pan | 6.95 |

*All Combination Plates Include*
*Wonton or Egg Drop Soup, Ice Cream and Hot Tea.*

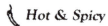 Hot & Spicy

**Exhibit 3-9**
**Chinese restaurant menu**
*(China Jade Restaurant menu reprinted with permission)*

# Poultry

| | | |
|---|---|---|
| 腰果雞丁 | **CASHEW CHICKEN** | 7.25 |

腰果雞丁 **CASHEW CHICKEN** ............................................ 7.25
*Diced chicken breast, sauteed with crispy cashew nuts in a tasty sauce.*

蘑菇雞片 **MOO GOO GAI PAN** .......................................... 6.25
*Sliced chicken with mushrooms and Chinese vegetables.*

杏仁雞 **BONELESS CHICKEN (Wor Shu Gai)** ................. 6.50
*Tender boneless fried chicken in a tantalizing sauce garnished with shredded almonds.*

檸檬雞 **LEMON CHICKEN** ................................................ 6.50
*Deep fried chicken, garnished with a delicate lemon flavored sauce.*

雞球 **CHICKEN KEW** ......................................................... 6.75
*Chicken pieces dipped in egg batter and deep fried, then sauteed with Chinese vegetables.*

蠔油雞脯 **HO YU GAI PO** .................................................. 7.75
*Tender chicken meat fried to a golden brown then sauteed with roast pork, snow peas, mushroom and bamboo shoots.*

雞片鍋巴 **SIZZLING CHICKEN WOR BAR** ....................... 7.25
*Sliced chicken breast with a variety of Chinese vegetables served over crispy rice on a sizzling plate.*

宮保雞丁 **KUNG BO CHICKEN** ........................................ 6.95
*Hot! Chicken breast diced and sauteed in rich brown sauce with red peppers and peanuts.*

四象豆雞丁 **CHICKEN WITH STRING BEANS** ................. 6.75

木須雞 **MOO SHU PORK OR CHICKEN** ......................... 6.95
*Shredded pork or chicken sauteed with Chinese vegetables and eggs, wrapped in thin Chinese pancakes with plum sauce.*

爆雙丁 **SHRIMP & CHICKEN W. BROWN SAUCE** ..... 7.95
*Shrimp and diced chicken stir-fried with Chinese vegetables in our delicious brown sauce.*

芝麻雞 **SESAME CHICKEN** ............................................... 8.95

左宗棠雞 **CHEF'S SPECIAL CHICKEN (General Tao's Chicken)** 7.50
*Special tender chicken with snow peas, mushrooms and water chestnuts. Served with our chef's special sauce.*

蜜汁雞 **HONEY CHICKEN** ................................................. 7.50


# Classic Favorites

| | | | |
|---|---|---|---|
| 炒麵 | Chow Mein | | Chicken .......... 4.95 |
| 什碎 | Chop Suey | with | Roast Pork ..... 4.95 |
| 芙蓉蛋 | Egg Foo Young | | Beef ............... 5.25 |
| 炒飯 | Fried Rice | | Shrimp .......... 5.75 |
| 揚州炒飯 | Yung Chow Fried Rice | | ........................ 5.75 |
| 本樓炒麵 | House Special Chicken Chow Mein | | ........................ 5.50 |

*(All Subgum Dishes Add 50 cents to the Above Prices)*


# Lo Mein

| | | |
|---|---|---|
| 炒麵 | Chicken, Pork or Vegetable | 5.25 |
| | Beef | 5.95 |
| | Shrimp | 6.50 |
| 本樓炒麵 | House Special Lo Mein | 6.95 |

*Exhibit 3-9, continued*

## Seafood

| 蝦 龍 糊 | SHRIMP WITH LOBSTER SAUCE | 7.95 |

*Jumbo shrimp sauteed in a delicately spiced meat and egg sauce.*

| 清 炒 大 蝦 | SAUTEED JUMBO SHRIMP | 7.95 |

*Jumbo shrimp sauteed with selected Chinese vegetables in a delicate white sauce.*

| 蝦 球 | SHRIMP KEW | 7.95 |

*Fried shrimp covered with mixed Chinese vegetables in a delicious sauce.*

| 宮 保 蝦 | KUNG BO SHRIMP | 7.95 |

*Hot! Whole prawns, shelled and sauteed with peanuts and red peppers.*

| 蝴 蝶 蝦 | BUTTERFLY SHRIMP | 8.50 |

*Jumbo shrimp pressed with bacon and egg, pan fried and served with bean sprouts and pea pods in our special sauce.*

| 廣 東 龍 蝦 | MAINE LOBSTER CANTONESE | 11.95 |

*Maine lobster, chopped in shell, sauteed in our secret spiced meat and egg sauce (in season).*

| 海 鮮 鍋 巴 | SEAFOOD WOR BAR | 11.95 |

*A combination of fresh lobster, shrimp and crabmeat with Chinese vegetables, served over crispy rice on our special broiler.*

| 干 貝 蝦 仁 | SHRIMP WITH SCALLOPS | 8.95 |

*Fresh scallops delicately sauteed with fresh shrimp and selected vegetables in a delicate white sauce.*

| 雪 豆 蝦 | SHRIMP WITH PEA PODS | 7.95 |
| 雪 豆 牛 | BEEF WITH PEA PODS | 7.25 |
| 雪 豆 雞 | CHICKEN WITH PEA PODS | 6.75 |

*The chefs are liberal with the use of Chinese snow peas.*

| 黑 尾 川 蝦 | SHRIMP REUNION SZECHUAN STYLE | 9.95 |

*Bay shrimp sauteed in chef's special Szechuan sauce, surrounded with fantail shrimp.*

## Vegetables

| 素 什 錦 | BUDDHIST DELIGHT | 5.75 |

*Fresh seasoned Chinese vegetables, sauteed in light sauce.*

| 魚 香 芥 蘭 | BROCCOLI WITH GARLIC SAUCE | 5.25 |

*Fresh broccoli in hot spicy garlic sauce.*

| 雪 豆 馬 蹄 | SNOW PEAS WITH WATER CHESTNUTS | 5.25 |
| 麻 婆 豆 腐 | MA POU BEAN CURD (Tou Fu) | 5.25 |

*Hot braised Chinese bean curd and minced pork.*

| 家 常 豆 腐 | HOME STYLE BEAN CURD | 5.25 |

*Mixed vegetable and bean curd.*

## Sweet and Sour

| 甜 酸 雞 / 肉 | Chicken or Pork | 5.95 |
| 甜 酸 大 會 | Shrimp or Combination (Chicken, Pork & Shrimp) | 6.95 |

Hot & Spicy

*Exhibit 3-9, continued*

# Beef • Pork

| | | | | |
|---|---|---|---|---|
| 蒙 | 爆 | 牛 | **MONGOLIAN BEEF** .............................. 7.25 |
| | | | *Sliced tender beef sauteed with green onions.* |
| 青 | 椒 | 牛 | **PEPPER STEAK AND TOMATO** ............... 6.95 |
| | | | *Sauteed beef sliced with fresh tomatoes, green peppers and onions.* |
| 蠔 | 油 | 牛 | **BEEF WITH OYSTER SAUCE** .................. 6.95 |
| | | | *Sliced beef blended with oyster sauce, bamboo shoots, mushrooms and water chestnuts.* |
| 湖 | 南 | 牛 | **HUNAN BEEF (Mild or Hot)** ................... 7.50 |
| 湖 | 南 | 鶏 | **HUNAN CHICKEN (Mild or Hot)** .............. 6.95 |
| | | | *Hot! Thin slices of chicken sauteed with fresh Chinese vegetables in hot pepper sauce.* |
| 牛肉四季豆 | | | **BEEF WITH STRING BEANS** ................. 6.95 |
| 叉燒四季豆 | | | **ROAST PORK WITH STRING BEANS** ......... 6.45 |
| 麻辣四季豆 | | | **MINCED PORK WITH STRING BEANS** ....... 5.95 |
| 牛 | 肉 | 球 | **STEAK KEW** ...................................... 10.95 |
| | | | *Prime cut of tenderloin cubes marinated in sherry wine and oyster sauce, mixed with Chinese vegetables.* |
| 芥 | 蘭 | 鶏 | **CHICKEN WITH BROCCOLI** ................. 6.95 |
| 芥 | 蘭 | 牛 | **BEEF WITH BROCCOLI** ...................... 7.25 |
| 芥 | 蘭 | 蝦 | **SHRIMP WITH BROCCOLI** ................... 7.75 |
| 火 | 山 | 牛 | **VOLCANO STEAK** ............................. 10.95 |
| | | | *Beef tenderloin set aflame with rum and served on a bed of Chinese vegetables.* |
| 白 | 菜 | 牛 | **BEEF WITH CHINESE VEGETABLES** ......... 6.95 |
| 白 | 菜 | 肉 | **ROAST PORK W. CHINESE VEGETABLES** ...... 6.95 |

## Senior Citizen Special

**All Senior Citizen Combination Plates Include**
**Pork Fried Rice, Egg Roll, Wonton or Egg Drop Soup,**
**Hot Tea and Fortune Cookies.**

SN 1.   Chicken Chow Mein ................................. 4.95

SN 2.   Sweet and Sour Chicken ........................... 5.15

SN 3.   Shrimp with Lobster Sauce ....................... 5.95

SN 4.   Pork Lo Mein ....................................... 5.25

SN 5.   Pepper Steak with Onion ........................... 5.75

*** For Customers 60 and Over ***

Hot & Spicy

*Exhibit 3-9, continued*

# House Specialties

陳 皮 牛 🌶 **ORANGE BEEF** ............................................... 10.95
Marinated beef tenderloin slices, pan-seared to perfection with diced orange peels and flecked with garlic and ginger.

四 川 牛 🌶 **SZECHUAN BEEF OR CHICKEN** ....................... 7.50
Tender slices of beef or chicken, blended together with water chestnuts, bamboo shoots, and carrots.

炒 三 鮮 🌶 **THREE'S COMPANY** ........................................ 8.35
Large shrimp, sliced b-b-q pork and breast of chicken, cooked with sliced mushrooms, scallions and bamboo shoots.

全 家 福 **SIZZLING HAPPY FAMILY** ........................... 9.50
Fresh shrimp, scallops, beef and chicken, cooked with mixed Chinese vegetables on a hot plate.

檀 島 五 寶 **HAWAII FIVE "O"** ......................................... 10.50
Fresh lobster meat, jumbo shrimp, chicken, roast pork and tender beef, sauteed with imported mushrooms, baby corn, choice vegetables and a pineapple ring.

七 星 伴 月 **SEVEN STARS** ............................................... 14.95
A mixture of chicken, roast pork, Maine lobster meat and vegetables, topped with butterfly shrimp and breaded chicken.

本 樓 牛 排 🌶 **JADE SIZZLING STEAK** ................................ 10.95
A tender prime sirloin steak, broiled to perfection, cut in thick, juicy slices, topped with assorted Chinese vegetables in our chef's special sauce.

陳 皮 鶏 🌶 **TANGERINE CHICKEN** ................................ 8.95
Marinated chicken meat, pan-seared to perfection with diced orange peels and flecked with garlic and ginger.

帝 王 鴨 **IMPERIAL DUCK** ......................................... 9.95
The crispy boneless duck has tantalizing aromatic flavor surrounded with tender fresh vegetables.

龍 鳳 鶏 球 **PHOENIX AND DRAGON** ............................. 8.25
Fresh shrimp with white chicken meat, broccoli, bamboo shoots, snow peas and water chestnuts in a special garlic sauce.

北 京 鴨 **PEKING DUCK** .................................... (Whole) 29.50
Crispy roasted duck served with mandarin pancakes, scallions and imported HoiSin sauce.

北 京 蝦 **PEKING SHRIMP** ......................................... 10.50
Jumbo shrimp marinated in egg white, fried and covered with our special sauce and served with broccoli.

三 冠 鍋 巴 **TRIPLE CROWN WOR BAR** ......................... 7.95
Slices of beef, chicken, b-b-q pork, bamboo shoots, snow peas and Chinese greens, served sizzling hot over crispy rice.

大 千 鶏 🌶 **TA-CHIEN CHICKEN** .................................... 7.50
Chunks of chicken meat w. Chinese vegs. & broccoli in hot & spicy sauce.

華 王 鶏 **JADE PAN-BROWN CHICKEN** ..................... 7.50
White meat chicken breast, pan-seared to golden brown and crispy, in a tangy brown sauce, surrounded with fresh broccoli.

華王龍鳳配 **PAN-BROWN CHICKEN VS. SHRIMP** ............ 8.95
Jumbo shrimp w. boneless white meat chicken pan seared to golden brown.

芝 蕙 鶏 蝦
煎 麵 底 **CHICKEN & SHRIMP CANTONESE** .............. 10.95
White meat chicken, jumbo shrimp served in a mild garlic sauce on a bed of pan fried noodles.

本樓炒米粉 **HOUSE SPECIAL RICE NOODLES** ..................... 6.95

 🌶 Hot & Spicy

Exhibit 3-9, continued

# Family Dinners

DINNER FOR (2) .................. 1 FROM A AND 1 FROM B
DINNER FOR (3) .................. 1 FROM A AND 2 FROM B
DINNER FOR (4) .................. 2 FROM A AND 2 FROM B
DINNER FOR (5) .................. 2 FROM A AND 3 FROM B
DINNER FOR (6) .................. 3 FROM A AND 3 FROM B

*Choice of Wonton or Egg Drop Soup, Served Individually with Family Dinners.*

*Our Family Dinners are Based on Estimated Costs, Any Change of Selection From B to A, Necessitates a Charge of $1.50 to the Original Price of Dinner.*

*Egg Roll (1) Per Person, Pork Fried Rice and Ice Cream, Served with Family Dinners.*

## $8.75 Per Person

| Group A | Group B |
|---|---|
| Hunan Beef | Sweet & Sour Chicken |
| Shrimp with Lobster Sauce | Bar-B-Q Pork Chow Mein |
| Sweet & Sour Shrimp | Subgum Chicken Chow Mein |
| Ho Yu Gai Po | Beef Chop Suey |
| Almond Chicken | Curry Chicken |
| Almond Beef | Chicken Egg Foo Young |
| House Special Lo Mein | Shrimp Egg Foo Young |
| Boneless Chicken | Beef Chow Mein |
| Cantonese Chicken Chow Mein | Beef or Pork w. Chinese Vegs. |
| Lemon Chicken | Minced Pork w. String Beans |
| Ta-Chien Chicken | Buddhist Delight |

*Please Ask The Management For Details Regarding Our Party Facilities and Catering Service*

## "For Weight Watchers"

The Following Dishes are Cooked with Lean Meat or Seafood and Mixed Vegetables, with No Salt, No Sugar, No M.S.G.

1. **CHICKEN WITH MIXED VEGETABLES** .................. 6.95
   Slices of white meat chicken steamed with mixed vegetables.

2. **BEEF WITH MIXED VEGETABLES** .............................. 7.95
   Lean slices of beef steamed with mixed vegetables.

3. **JUMBO SHRIMP WITH MIXED VEGETABLES** ...... 8.95
   Fresh jumbo shrimp steamed with mixed vegetables.

4. **VEGETABLE DELIGHT** ................................................. 5.95
   Steamed mixed vegetables.

5. **SEAFOOD WITH MIXED VEGETABLES** ................. 10.95
   Lobster meat, jumbo shrimp, scallop, steamed w. mixed vegetables.

6. **SHRIMP & CHICKEN W. MIXED VEGETABLES** ... 8.95
   Jumbo shrimp & sliced white meat chicken steamed w. mixed vegetables.

*Exhibit 3-9, continued*

# APPETIZERS

**NACHOS – 4.50**
Tortilla chips covered with melted cheese.

**QUEZADILLA – 4.50**
Melted cheese on two flour tortillas with your choice of meat.

**NACHOS with BEAN DIP – 4.50**
Tortilla chips covered with cheese, bean dip on the side.

**NACHOS with GUACAMOLE – 4.75**
Tortilla chips covered with cheese, with guacamole dip on the side.

**NACHOS ESPECIALES – 4.95**
Tortilla chips smothered with beans, meat and cheese.

**NACHOS EL ZARAPE – 5.25**
Tortilla chips smothered with beans, meat and cheese, topped with lettuce, tomatoes, cheese and jalapeños.

# DINNER SELECTIONS

All dinner selections include beans and rice. Choice of meat includes ground beef, shredded beef and chicken.

**1   TWO TACOS - CRISPY** ...... 6.50
Two folded crisp corn tortillas with meat, lettuce, and cheese.

**2   TWO TACOS - SOFT** ...... 6.50
Two folded soft corn tortillas with meat, lettuce, and cheese.

**3   TAQUITOS** ...... 6.50
Two corn tortillas rolled with your choice of meat, topped with lettuce, guacamole and sour cream.

**4   TOSTADA** ...... 6.50
A crisp corn tortilla with beans and meat, covered with lettuce, cheese, guacamole and sour cream.

**5   FLAUTA** ...... 6.95
Meat rolled into a flour tortilla with lettuce, and cheese, with guacamole & sour cream on the side.

**6   BURRITO ROJO** ...... 6.95
Rolled flour tortilla with beans and meat inside, topped with red sauce & cheese.

**7   BURRITO RANCHERO** ...... 6.95
Rolled flour tortilla with beans and meat inside, topped with ranchero sauce and cheese, guacamole & sour cream on the side.

**8   CHIMICHANGA** ...... 7.50
A deep fried burrito topped with our enchilada sauce and cheese, with guacamole & sour cream on the side.

**9   BURRITO - VERDE** ...... 7.50
Rolled flour tortilla with beans and meat inside with choice of red or green tomatillo sauce and cheese.

**10   GORDITA** ...... 7.50
Delicious deep fried corn dough, soft tortilla smothered with beans and meat, topped with lettuce, cheese, guacamole & sour cream.

**11   TWO TAMALES** ...... 7.50
Seasoned pork wrapped in a corn dough, steamed in a corn husk, topped with red sauce and cheese.

**12   CHILES RELLENO** ...... 7.50
Two green chiles stuffed with cheese, then dipped in a fluffy egg batter, cooked until golden brown, covered with ranchera salsa & cheese.

**13   TWO ENCHILADAS ROJAS** ...... 7.25
Two corn tortillas rolled with meat inside topped with red sauce and cheese.

**14   TWO ENCHILADAS VERDES** ...... 7.25
Two corn tortillas rolled with meat inside topped with green tomatillo sauce and cheese.

**15   TWO ENCHILADAS RANCHERAS** ...... 7.25
Two corn tortillas rolled with meat inside topped with ranchera sauce and cheese.

**Exhibit 3-10**
**Mexican restaurant menu**
*(El Zarape menu reprinted with permission)*

# COMBINATION DINNERS

*Include beans & rice. Choice of meats is ground beef, shredded beef or chicken.*

**16 ENCHILADA & RELLENO** ...................................................................................**7.25**
*One enchilada with choice of meat topped with red sauce and cheese, one relleno topped with ranchera sauce and cheese.*

**17 BURRITO & TACO** ..........................................................................................**7.25**
*One burrito with beans and meat inside topped with red sauce and cheese, one taco with meat, lettuce, and cheese.*

**18 TACO & TAMALE** ...........................................................................................**7.25**
*One taco with meat, lettuce, and cheese, one tamale topped with red sauce and cheese.*

**19 TAMALE & RELLENO** ....................................................................................**7.25**
*One tamale topped with red sauce & cheese, one relleno topped with ranchera sauce & cheese.*

**20 ENCHILADA & TACO** .....................................................................................**7.25**
*One enchilada with choice of meat topped with red sauce and cheese, one taco with meat, lettuce, and cheese.*

**21 TOSTADA & ENCHILADA** ..............................................................................**7.25**
*One tostada with beans and meat covered with lettuce, cheese, guacamole and sour cream, one enchilada with choice of meat topped with red sauce and cheese.*

**22 ENCHILADA, BURRITO & TACO** ...................................................................**7.95**
*One enchilada with meat topped with red sauce, one burrito with beans and meat inside topped with ranchera sauce and cheese, one taco with meat, lettuce, and cheese.*

**23 RELLENO, TACO & TAQUITO** .......................................................................**7.95**
*One relleno topped with ranchera sauce and cheese, one taco with meat, lettuce, and cheese, one taquito topped with lettuce, and cheese.*

**24 TOSTADA, TAMALE & FLAUTA** ...................................................................**7.95**
*One tostada with beans and meat covered with lettuce, cheese, guacamole and sour cream, one tamale topped with red sauce and cheese, one flauta with meat inside with lettuce, with cheese on the side.*

**25 ENCHILADAS SUPERIORES** .........................................................................**7.95**
*Three enchiladas one each with red, green and ranchera sauce, choice of meat and sauce.*
*Three enchiladas one*

# ORIGINAL MEXICAN DISHES

*Include beans and rice.*

**26 CHILE VERDE** ................................................................................................**8.25**
*Chunks of pork cooked in a green tomatillo sauce and spices (with 3 tortillas).*

**27 CHILE VERDE CON NOPALES** .....................................................................**8.25**
*Chunks of pork cooked in a green tomatillo sauce with Mexican cactus (with 3 tortillas).*

**28 CHILE COLORADO (Hot)** ..............................................................................**8.25**
*Chunks of pork cooked in our special hot red sauce (with three tortillas).*

**29 STEAK ACAPULCO** ........................................................................................**8.25**
*Tenderloin, sliced & cooked with fresh tomatoes, onion, green pepper, mushrooms (with 3 tortillas).*

**30 POLLO RANCHERO** ........................................................................................**8.25**
*Two pieces of chicken cooked in a ranchera sauce (with 3 tortillas).*

**31 POLLO EN MOLE** ............................................................................................**8.25**
*Two pieces of chicken cooked in our special semi-sweet mole sauce (with 3 tortillas).*

**32 LENGUA RANCHERA** .....................................................................................**8.25**
*Slices of beef tongue cooked in a ranchera sauce (with 3 tortillas).*

**33 LENGUA EN MOLE** ........................................................................................**8.25**
*Slices of beef tongue cooked in a special semi-sweet mole sauce (with 3 tortillas).*

**34 MACHACA** ......................................................................................................**8.25**
*Shredded beef cooked with fresh tomatoes, onion, green pepper and spices (with3 tortillas).*

**35 CAMARONES RANCHEROS** ..........................................................................**8.75**
*Fresh shrimp cooked in our special ranchera sauce (tortillas).*

**36 CARNE ASADA** ..............................................................................................**8.75**
*Two slices of beef, grilled and then served with special picadillo sauce.*

**37 FAJITAS (Beef, Chicken, or Mixed)** ............................................................**8.95**
*Grilled tender strips of meat with slices of cooked onions, tomatoes, and green peppers.*

**38 FAJITAS (Shrimp)** .........................................................................................**10.25**
*Grilled shrimp with slices of cooked onions, tomatoes, and green peppers.*     Gratuity is not included in prices.

*Exhibit 3-10, continued*

# MUCHO MAS ALA CARTA

Burrito Deluxe.............................4.95
Burrito Ranchero .........................4.95
Burrito Verde ..............................4.95
Chimichanga ..............................4.95
Flauta.........................................4.95
Tostada (corn) ...........................4.95
Gordita ......................................4.95
Tacos (2) ...................................3.25
Enchiladas (2) ............................3.95
Tamales (2)................................4.25
Chiles Rellenos (2) .....................5.50
Taquitos (3) ...............................4.95

# SOFT

# DRINKS

Minutemaid Orange
Root Beer
Coke
Diet Coke
Sprite

# SIDE ORDERS

Chips & Salsa.................................................2.50
Guacamole .....................................................1.75
Sour Cream ..................................................... .85
Refried Beans .................................................1.50
Mexican Rice ..................................................1.50
French Fries....................................................1.50
Tortillas (3) ..................................................... .85
Jalapeños ....................................................... .85

# KID'S MENU

K1 One Enchilada with rice & beans .3.50
K2 One Taco with rice and beans ...3.50
K3 Quezadilla with rice and
       beans .............................................3.50
K4 Flauta with beans ......................3.50
K5 Burrito with rice ......................3.50
K6 Beans and Rice ............................2.75

| | |
|---|---|
| Mexican Cheeseburger ...........4.25 |
| Reg. Cheeseburger ..................3.75 |
| Hamburger ..............................3.50 |
| Hot Dog...................................3.25 |
| *Include French Fries or Salad* |

# DESSERTS

Deep Fried Ice Cream ...........................2.50
Sopapilla ............................................3.00
Flan - Custard .....................................2.50
Regular Ice Cream ...............................1.50
*Vanilla, Chocolate, Strawberry*

*Exhibit 3-10, continued*

transportation have also contributed to these changes. Nonetheless, hollandaise, béarnaise, and bordelaise sauces appear on menus from coast to coast in the United States.

## Nouvelle Cuisine

*Nouvelle Cuisine Francaise* is the title of a book published in the eighteenth century. In the mid 1970's, nouvelle cuisine was presented as a "new" type of "lighter cooking" by the French as something of a reaction to the "heavy" sauces that play a great part in classical French cooking. There was a stress on fresh, high-quality ingredients and minimal cooking time, which are bits of good advice. But the big emphasis and principal feature of nouvelle cuisine was on light sauces. This was to be accomplished by a reduction in the use of butter, eggs, and flour as thickening agents. This cooking technique was like the term *nouvelle cuisine*— really not new.

## Japanese Restaurants

The introduction of the Japanese restaurants on a nationwide scale coincided with the influx into the United States of myriad products from Japan. A principal attraction of these restaurants is the showmanship in the cooking procedures. The menus are usually quite limited but have grown somewhat in recent years. Unlike the Chinese restaurants, there are few family-owned properties, except in areas with large Japanese populations. Several large chain and franchise operations account for the bulk of the Japanese restaurants.

Exhibit 3–14 is the menu from the Arigato restaurant. The menu is quite colorful, very readable, and laid out effectively to highlight the different presentations. Arigato is a small chain of five Japanese restaurants.

## Other Ethnic Restaurants

The above are the most popular ethnic restaurants in the United States, but many other nationalities are represented by restaurants that feature their countries' typical foods. German restaurants with heavy foods and big portions are common in midwestern areas. Swedish smorgasbords are fairly widespread, but the Scandinavian communities in the dairy states are more often associated with this ethnic variety. Jewish restaurants are numerous in areas with a large Jewish population. Their food is best described as a combination of German, English, Kosher, and American foods. The Jewish people have very discriminating tastes, so it was not much of an exaggeration when a food editor described the Jewish restaurants as having the best food in the world.

## Cafeterias

This type of food service is widespread in both the commercial restaurant business and the institutional field. Chapter 12 is devoted to cafeteria menus and operations. Suffice it to say at this point that the cafeteria menu is a visual display, and the order and arrangement of the foods are of utmost importance.

# Frozen Drinks

Strawberry Daiquiri, Margarita,
Strawberry Margarita,
Pina Colada  3.95

# Specialty Drinks

 **Ho Tei Dream -** A mug full of luck and Oriental splendor. A mixture of tropical fruit juices, rum and a splash of almond.     **4.00**
Drink and Mug  6.00

 **Maneki Neko -** A zesty sensation blending plum wine and vodka with a hint lemon.     **4.00**
Drink and Mug  6.00

 **Tokyo Rose -** A mysterious blend of passion fruit juices, rum, lemon and a touch of cherry.     **4.00**
Drink and Mug  6.00

 **The Geisha -** A unique blend of spirits and exotics to entice your delicate palate. Curacao, pineapple, lemon and rum.     **4.00**
Drink and Mug  6.00

**Hari Kari Nut -** If he or she is a hard nut to crack, this Oriental concoction will soften the shock. Coconut milk and pineapple juice blended with rum.     **4.00**
Drink and Mug  6.00

# Japanese Drinks

**Saketini -** A Martini with sake instead of vermouth. If you like martinis this is a must.     **3.95**

**Sake -** Hot rice wine served in a decanter. Your trip to Japan is not complete if you have not experienced this nectar of the gods.     **3.50**

**Plum Wine -** Excellent as an aperitif or dessert wine. Hand picked plums skillfully blended by Japanese wine experts. Served on the rocks or up with a twist of lemon.     **3.00**
By the Bottle **13.95**

# Appetizers

**Tempura -** Very delicate and extremely delicious.  Please choose from these varieties.

| | |
|---|---|
| **Scallop** | **4.95** |
| **Shrimp** | **3.95** |
| **Chicken** | **4.50** |
| **Vegetable** | **3.95** |
| **Combo** | **4.95** |

**Teppanyaki Shrimp Flambe**
Served with special seafood sauce.     **3.95**

**Scallops Flambe -** Bay scallops with hint of herbs and lemon.     **3.95**

**Japanese Egg Rolls**     **2.95**

**Mushrooms**
Cooked in traditional teppan style.     **2.50**

# TEMPURA

*During the Eido Age of Japan, some 200 to 300 years ago, the Shogun Tokugawa popularized the frying of different foods in very hot oils which we now refer to as Tempura. Very delicate by nature and extremely delicious. A taste that will surely please everyone.*

**Vegetable Tempura**
An assortment of vegetables lightly batter fried.     **9.50**

**Chicken Tempura**
Light batter fried tender chicken with an assortment of stir-fried vegetables.     **11.50**

**Shrimp Tempura**
Light batter fried shrimp with an assortment of stir-fried vegetables.     **14.50**

**Combination Tempura**
An assortment of Shrimp and Chicken lightly batter fried and garden fresh stir-fried vegetables.     **14.50**

## Domo Arigato

*Thank You Very Much.*
*You are served by both a chef and a waitress . . . who share all gratuities equally. Therefore, if the service is up to your expectations, we recommend a minimum of 15%.*

Arigato usage of the Heart Smart logo insures that all items indicated meet the standards set forth by Heart Smart Restaurants International™ as having 30% or less calories from fat, 10% or less calories from saturated fat, 150 mg or less cholesterol and 1100 mg or less sodium. *Please note that the Heart Smart analysis is performed on the <u>main</u> <u>entrees</u> <u>only</u> and does not apply to Fried Rice, Seafood Sauce, Steak Sauce, Dinner Salad or Shoyu Onion Soup. Nutritional information is available upon request.*

**Exhibit 3-11**
**Japanese restaurant menu**
*(Reprinted with permission from Arigato, Dale DelBello, President & Founder)*

# ARIGATO ENTREES

The unique preparation of Steak, Chicken and Seafood combined with the quality of our ingredients will make your visit to the Arigato an enjoyable experience.

**Teppanyaki Vegetables -** Lightly seasoned mushrooms, zucchini, onions, carrots, broccoli, snow peas and fried rice.   **9.50**

**Chicken Arigato -** Boneless breast of chicken cooked with sesame seeds, mushrooms, lemon and a hint of Japanese herbs.   **12.50**

**Sukiyaki Steak -** Thinly sliced choice sirloin cooked with care to present the natural flavor.   **13.50**

**Shrimp Flambe**
**OR**
**Scallop Flambe**
Seafood cooked with mushrooms and a hint of lemon. Flamed to seal in the delicate flavor.   **14.50**
*You may add filet mignon for $4.00 extra.*

**Hibachi Filet Mignon -** Tender and delicious, the most popular cut. **16.50**

---

### LOBSTER FEAST

**Kobe Lobster**
Lobster, Shrimp, Scallops.   **18.50**

**Mr. Fuji Lobster**
Lobster, Filet, Shrimp.   **19.50**

**Oy-Shee Lobster**
The Prince of the sea cooked with special herbs and a touch of lemon.   **Market Price**

---

*will begin with Shoyu onion soup followed by fresh salad greens with Oriental dressing. They will be served with mushrooms, broccoli, snow peas, carrots, zucchini, onions, and fried rice.*

## Special Celebrations

*Available for your special occasion we have a cake and picture of your party for $5.00.*

## Gift Certificates

*You may purchase our beautiful Gift Certificates in dollar amounts or by specific dinner.*

# THE EMPEROR COMBINATIONS

**OUR MOST POPULAR AND BEST VALUE**

Seasoned with Japanese Herbs and Spices.

**SUKIYAKI STEAK, SHRIMP AND SCALLOPS**   **15.50**

**CHICKEN, SHRIMP AND SCALLOPS**   **15.50**

**SUKIYAKI STEAK, CHICKEN AND SHRIMP**   **15.50**

# ARIGATO COMBINATIONS

**The Banzai**
Shrimp and Chicken. Delicate shrimp and breast of chicken prepared with lemon and sesame seeds.   **14.50**

**The Karate Chop**
Sukiyaki and Chicken. Our two most popular dinner entrees.   **14.50**
*You may substitute filet mignon for $2.00 extra.*

**The Shogun**
Sukiyaki Steak, Chicken and Scallops. Cooked with sesame seeds, a hint of lemon and Japanese herbs.   **16.50**
*You may substitute filet mignon for $2.00 extra.*

**The Ichiban**
Filet Mignon, Shrimp and Chicken. Prepared with delicate herbs and spices.   **17.50**

**The Sumo**
Filet Mignon, Shrimp and Scallops. Seasoned with Japanese herbs and spices.   **17.50**

**The Samurai**
Filet Mignon and Lobster. Traditional partners prepared Arigato style.   **19.50**

### Emperor and Arigato Combinations

*will begin with Shoyu onion soup followed by fresh salad greens with Oriental dressing. They will be served with mushrooms, broccoli, snow peas, carrots, zucchini, onions, and fried rice.*

*Exhibit 3-11, continued*

# 4 Know Your Customers

**Purpose:** To illustrate the many differences in customers' appetites. We stress that you must understand these differences in order to write effective menus.

You really need not ask customers if they are happy with your restaurant. Their reaction to its offerings, principally by either coming back for another meal or saying "goodbye forever," will let you know if there is a "fit" between the restaurant and the customers. The menu, style of cookery, and decor all must be coordinated to fashion the perfect "fit" of restaurant with customer.

In our quest to understand what is necessary to write effective menus, we have reviewed the different types of restaurants, noted their peculiarities, and discussed how the menu should reflect and promote the restaurant. The type of restaurant predetermines what kind of customers it will most likely serve. The different likes and needs of the customers call for various modifications to the menus. Therefore, *know your customers*.

## The Customer as an Individual

A number of characteristics distinguish types of customers. A brief discussion of each will make this clear.

### Age

As people move from youth to old age their approach to most things in life changes. Perhaps "mellowing" is a good word to describe this process—this is certainly true concerning attitudes toward food. Shakespeare, in *As You Like It*, speaks of the "seven ages" of man. To prepare a menu, you will need to be concerned with all seven, because the primary market for a restaurant, as reflected in its theme, will not make up its total clientele. So the menu must have some food items to satisfy this varied patronage. It is common to see menus in signature restaurants that include a "burger corner" for the young and a "senior citizen" section for the elderly. Fast food restaurants have guests of all ages, but the number of elderly guests has increased since the menus have been expanded to include salads, salad bars, chicken breast, and other universally accepted items.

### Sex

Often males and females prefer different foods. This affects banquet menus more than those of restaurants. Different food preferences are particularly noticeable at luncheon banquets. Restaurant menus must include selections for both men and women. Both sexes alter their eating habits as they grow older.

### Income Level

Most people want to consume to the level their incomes will allow, so this becomes a very important factor in designing a restaurant and planning its menu. High-income people are willing to pay a high check for meals, and demand that the restaurant provide good value. This is not to say that persons with lesser incomes are indifferent to good value, but they more often eat at restaurants with lower prices. Food at any price level or in any type of restaurant must be a good value if the restaurant is to succeed.

### Life-style

In previous decades, life-style was directly related to income level. However, in the past few years, a number of other important factors have contributed more than income. Either by necessity or by choice, there are many families in which both parents work; single-parent families are common, with either a mother and child or children or a father and child. The "fun place" restaurant has been an important contributor to the rise of the signature restaurants. A common sight at noon in the fast food restaurants is a young mother and several children eating hamburgers, French fries, and large sodas. It is difficult to say for sure whether the fast food operations fulfilled the market need of those with a hurried life-style or whether they have actually helped to father this life-style.

## Customer Groups

Individuals, as discussed above, have particular "dining-out" desires that influence their choice of food and restaurants. To understand how these wants translate into menu offerings, we need to group these individuals into categories by similar circumstances.

### Family Groups

As we have noted, young couples with children are a common sight in family restaurants. What do they seek in food selections and restaurant atmosphere? First of all, "eating out" is a special treat for many families and they are certainly looking for something different from their fare at home—not necessarily exotic foods, but a change. Shrimp and scallops, for example, are not on the ordinary list of foods eaten regularly in homes. This is also true of many fish entrées. Roast beef in the home is usually a bottom round or a pot roast from the chuck. Prime rib, therefore, is a treat. Examine a home menu for a period of several weeks and compare it with a menu from a family restaurant—the difference in selections will be quite apparent.

A family eating in even a low-priced restaurant will spend a good sum for the total group, so reasonable prices are part of the appeal of the operation. It is important that the prices for full meals are plainly stated; customers should not need to closely study the menu to calculate what dinner will cost.

A dining-out family is obviously interested in restaurants that cater to children. They appreciate a children's menu, which should include items other than hamburgers and French fries. Parents are interested in items on a children's menu that are healthful and filling for their children. Games, coloring books, and cartoons are a great help in occupying children as they await food. For children, waiting ten minutes is unthinkable unless they are somehow occupied. Parents appreciate the help given by incidentals provided by the restaurant. Exhibit 4–1 illustrates a typical children's menu.

Although parents are interested in reasonable prices for the family's meals, they still want to eat their meal in a pleasant place. The dining room, for example, should be warm and carpeted. Large tables to avoid crowding, which often results in spilling, are favored by parents and affect their choice of restaurant. Added together, the good food, comfortable

**Exhibit 4-1**

**The children's menu used in a successful chain of family restaurants**

*From the Bob Evans Restaurants. Reprinted with permission from Bob Evans Barms, Inc., Columbus, Ohio.*

atmosphere, special care of children, and sensible prices equal good value. If you can provide this good value to families, they will be back.

Family business is by no means restricted to family restaurants. In these prosperous times families with children of grade-school age who need little assistance in taking meals patronize the signature restaurants quite frequently. The ethnic restaurants, especially the Italian, Chinese, and Mexican, do a respectable volume in family business. Menu selections and prices often qualify ethnic restaurants as family restaurants also. Hotel restaurants, notably the coffee shops, are equipped to serve the entire traveling family. Fast food operations are crowded with touring families and mothers with small children, especially at luncheon during school vacation time. Given today's life-styles most restaurants are prepared to accommodate small children by having available the minimum requirements of such clients—high chairs and chair lifts.

### Teenagers—Young Adults—College Students

This heading covers a fairly wide range of ages, but similarity in eating habits enables the restaurateur to deal with them as a group. This is by far the easiest group to feed. They prefer light, clean restaurants with cheerful, quick, and simple service. Prices must be reasonable. The food selections most wanted are found in fast food operations and chain/franchise restaurants such as Denny's, Shoney's, or Ponderosa. The inevitable hamburgers top the sales list of favorites by a rather large margin—about two and one-half times the number two favorite—pizza. Hamburgers sell at about four and one-half times the third choice—chicken—in the fast food operations.

Among the older customers in this group, the family restaurants are often chosen as a dining place. Steak, turkey, shrimp, and roast beef sandwiches are favored dishes among college students and young adults. Thus the family restaurant owner, in addition to mak-

ing sure that the restaurant is specially equipped for and has menus geared to the family trade, must think of young adults and college students when planning menus.

Desserts are important in catering to teenagers and young adults. The usual ice cream, pies, and sundaes must be available, but the big, loaded-with-calories, "gobby," and sauce-filled desserts and a variety of shakes must be available too. That the fast food operations have the largest market share of any type of restaurant attests to the importance of this group of customers, because much of the sales in fast food restaurants are to this group.

### Businessmen

This is a group composed of people willing to pay at least a medium price for meals. But to satisfy the good value criteria, it must be noted that the businessman is rather demanding. In a restaurant that he patronizes regularly, he wants recognition—he wants to be called by name by a hostess and waiters who have attended him several times. He often becomes testy if he is kept waiting at the door. He is a bit more tolerant with the server and he enjoys unobtrusive service. The businessman is most apt to choose a restaurant with a quiet, warm atmosphere.

The menu can be simple but it must have a hint of elegance. Some businessmen favor the lo-cal foods, but more prefer beef and plenty of it. A well-stocked bread basket with an ample variety catches his eye and whets his appetite. Accompanying his beef he likes a hefty portion of vegetables, which he prefers over salads. He likes big drinks made with well-known brands of liquor. The beer drinkers among the businessmen want imported beer. Man-sized sandwiches are a favorite at luncheon. Desserts are not important to the businessman.

### Auto Travelers

This category includes some businessmen along with professional people and salesmen.

This group knows the best eating places in and around town. Like all other diners, they prize cleanliness in both the service personnel and the physical surroundings. They are happy with a limited menu, but want quick service. Most are willing to pay high prices. They expect good-sized portions and hefty drinks. With respect to menu selections, they like homemade soups, steaks, roasts, and shrimp. Pot pies are favored at luncheon. Lobster is a frequent choice at dinner, and wines, usually the house variety served in carafes, are ordered regularly. Pastry desserts are popular. These people know of a number of good restaurants, so they are not as loyal to one as is the case with many businessmen. Because they frequent many restaurants, these people do not expect recognition but enjoy such flattery when it occurs.

## Working Women

This is a group with special wants that did not exist or required no special attention by the menu writer until recent times. Consequently, guidelines on how to cater to them are still being developed. Therefore, restaurateurs must be especially alert to anything about working women's patronage that suggests menu changes in order to add attractiveness in the menu for these people. It is never good policy to assume the menu is as good as it can get. Even the finest menus need an injection of new life now and then.

First let us consider what working women look for in the physical surroundings of an eating place. Like other restaurant patrons, they look for cleanliness, but cleanliness or the lack of it stands out prominently in the bright, cheerful room that these customers favor. Restrooms are expected to be a bit fancy as well as spotlessly clean. Formal settings with tablecloths are regarded as a bit ponderous for a luncheon at which reasonably quick service should be given by neat, efficient waitresses. Placemats are a more popular table covering.

Menu selections should include standard entrées but in reduced portion sizes. A listing of lo-cal items should also be part of the menu. Salads that show imagination are appreciated by working women. Salad/relish bars are also well patronized. Homemade desserts are a must. Women, whether working or not, are "turned off" by desserts that look like they come from the supermarket. The big surprise is that big, gobby desserts sell quite well to working women.

## Shoppers

This group is composed mostly of women, but in areas with a large number of retired people, many husbands tag along to enjoy the excitement and air conditioning of the colorful shopping malls. Lunch counters and coffee shops are a favored milieu. Low prices must prevail. The shoppers favor combination meals: soup and salad; soup and sandwich; sandwich and salad. The bagel shops and coffee houses mentioned in Chapter 3 are often found in or near shopping areas and are taking a good share of these customers.

## Budgeters

A group of customers that draws from many other groups is that of people with limited monetary resources. This group is large, even in our so-called affluent society. Cafeterias and buffet restaurants are especially popular because the prices are reasonable and there is a broad selection from which to choose—unlike the fast food operations, which also feature low prices.

The cafeteria is also well adapted to this varied clientele in that it displays a wide selection of foods that meet the desires of young businesspeople, retirees, factory workers, and light-eating customers. The greatest appeal is the good value offered—the best food for the money. Chapter 12 deals more extensively with cafeterias.

## Tourists

Nearly everyone becomes a tourist at times. When this occurs there is not a conscious change in attitudes toward restaurants and their menus, but somehow tourists become different persons when they embark on a journey. What stimulates people into becoming tourists varies, but they usually want to be amused. This demand can be met by seeing new faces and places that offer changes from the ordinary. Persons learning about different cultures that produce different architecture and crafts are of particular interest to the student of food management. Different types of restaurants are particularly attractive for tourists, and this presents a challenge to the restaurateur. Often a tourist visits a restaurant for the first time, and wants something different. He or she often adopts a "show me" attitude: What do you have that I should be here? In such circumstances the menu is an especially crucial merchandising tool. Tourists' eyes search for special food items. They are willing to pay no more than medium prices, but want a full menu from which to choose—a menu that adds to the amusement of the occasion. Flaming dishes are popular, but the server must be adept at this kind of presentation. This rather demanding customer also wants all these happy things to take place in a room with a warm atmosphere and a bit of a flair. The challenge is to make every effort to deliver good value to customers whom you probably will never see again. If tempted to assume an indifferent attitude because of the only slight chance of getting repeat business from tourists, remember that they have friends who will become tourists and potential customers at some point in the future.

## Elderly

Principally through the efforts of the American Association of Retired Persons (AARP) and the late Congressman Claude Pepper, this group has become an organized force politically, and merchants of all kinds have made adaptations to accommodate their particular needs. There is very much written and said about the plight of destitute senior citizens, but they are a small, if perhaps significant, number. The elderly in the United States are an economic as well as a political force. The majority of retired people are situated in the middle to upper-middle income groups, as measured by disposable income.

Fortunately for the food business the elderly's proclivity for restaurant patronage is quite strong. Eating out has become a regular recreation for many, so it behooves the menu writer to provide seniors with menus that readily add to the enjoyment of the occasion. This is of added importance because senior citizens are a loyal group and can be counted on for repeat business if interest can be maintained by innovation in food and service. Innovation need not be focused on food—flowers, small gifts, or even cookies to commemorate occasions, or just saying thanks for their patronage, can suffice. It is important to be the first to offer seasonal items to the elderly; in fact it is an excellent merchandising tool attractive to everyone. Holiday menus built on the theme of the day can be especially entertaining to the elderly.

The above description might seem to characterize the elderly as a particularly demanding group, but this characterization does not apply to their food preferences, which are for simple, plain cooking with simple service at moderate prices. Certainly they appreciate nice surroundings, nothing fancy but clean—especially clean restrooms.

In areas with a large retired community, the "early bird" menu is an excellent customer attraction. Retirees are free to eat at their convenience, which is not ordinarily true of working people. This flexibility is quite favorable for the food operator because it facilitates turnover. The appropriate early bird menu consists of selections from the regular bill of fare at lower prices for smaller portions. Additional specials, however, add interest and exhibit some imagination, which customers welcome.

## Social Groups and Functions

We have not included banquet functions in private rooms in our discussion of customer groups. Writing banquet menus is the subject of Chapter 9.

It seems that people have undergone myriad changes in life-styles over the past few hundred years. But now, much like in the days of yore, when people gather for a celebration of any kind it is accompanied by food and drink. This tradition furnishes a great opportunity for the restaurateur. Small groups of up to about eight persons can usually be served from the regular menu, with individuals making their own choices. Larger groups that can be accommodated in a restaurant are happier with the meal if one item or a choice between two is made for the group. Be sure to enhance sales by offering such groups wine with the meal and champagne with a special dessert. However the meal is arranged, it is good business for the restaurant to do or give something that surprises even the host.

## Athletes

This chapter is devoted to discussing customers as individuals and as groups. Athletes can be considered in either category. For the menu writer it means that the menu must include hearty meals such as 26-ounce T-bone steaks or heavy stews. Alfalfa sprouts, sesame seeds, and the like must be part of the salad bar.

Hotels, particularly in large cities that are homes to professional athletic teams or in college towns, have more contacts in this type of catering than do other eating establishments. Many people other than athletes devour rather large meals at dinner or luncheon; however, if an athletic team is housed in a hotel, the menu planner's greatest concern should be centered on breakfast. Athletes can make a meal from a regular breakfast menu, but it is better policy to do what is necessary and a little extra to satisfy and make a happy customer. Extra-thick French toast, large portions of waffles and pancakes, fruited yogurt, and dinner-sized steaks with eggs will make the traveling athlete look forward to a return engagement with the home team.

# 5 Who Writes Menus?

**Purpose:** To discuss who does write the menu and to explain why the proper choice of "who" is critical to a successful menu and restaurant.

Who should write menus is a question that has been bandied about in the food industry as well as in the academic world. Ask this question in five different places and you might get five different answers. But by analyzing the elements required to produce a successful menu, determining who should be involved in this important task will naturally emerge as a logical conclusion. Our discussion concerns who should write the menus and why.

Different organizations have individual methods of assigning this responsibility, so the persons involved may vary from restaurant to restaurant. The first principle in effective menu writing, however, is the same: No one person writes the menus; it must be a team. When you analyze the information needed to write a menu, you will plainly see that no one person has sufficient knowledge of all the needed facts about an operation. Consequently, a team is necessary to "input the data." We use the term "team" rather than "committee" because a team has a leader, who is in the end responsible for the team's actions. Committees, more often than not, produce a product with features to satisfy each member of the committee. Thus this product might lack focus or be awkward. As C. F. Kettering, the great American industrialist, said of a camel, "It looks like a horse designed by a committee." Writing a good menu requires team work, with one person responsible for the final product.

## Organizational Charts

Exhibit 5-1 is a typical plan of organization for a hotel with a substantial food and beverage volume. The menu-writing team in this setup is composed of the team captain—the person with final responsibility for the finished product—who in this case is the food and beverage manager. His sources of varied information for preparing the menu are the restaurant's chef, the food and beverage controller, the purchasing agent, and the dining room manager. In large operations, the banquet manager and the banquet salesperson are members of the team. Later in this chapter we will discuss the specific contributions of these participants.

Exhibit 5-2 illustrates the organization of a motor inn. In this setup the assistant innkeeper ordinarily is the team leader. The balance of the team is made up of the chef, the food and beverage controller, the purchaser, and the dining room hostess.

Exhibit 5-3 shows the organization of the

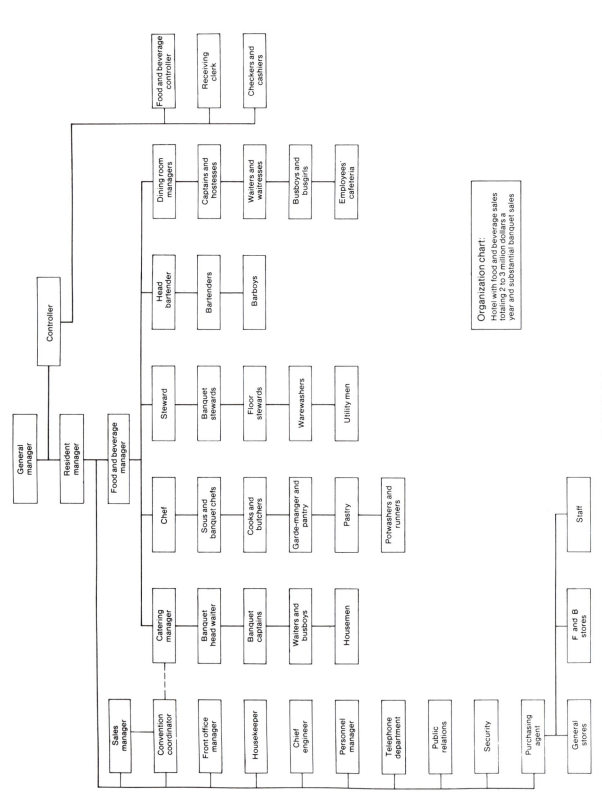

**Exhibit 5-1**

**Chart showing an organization plan for a hotel**

Organization chart:
Hotel with food and beverage sales totaling 2 to 3 million dollars a year and substantial banquet sales

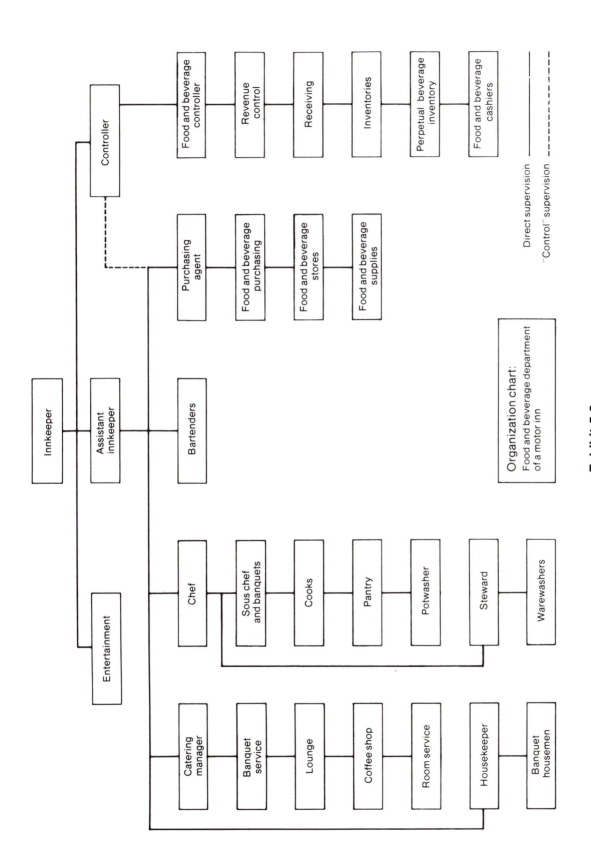

**Exhibit 5-2**

**Chart showing an organization plan for the food and beverage department in a franchised motor inn**

Innkeeper

Assistant innkeeper

Entertainment

Controller

Bartenders

Chef

Catering manager

Purchasing agent

Food and beverage controller

Revenue control

Receiving

Inventories

Perpetual beverage inventory

Food and beverage cashiers

Food and beverage purchasing

Food and beverage stores

Food and beverage supplies

Sous chef and banquets

Cooks

Pantry

Potwasher

Steward

Warewashers

Banquet service

Lounge

Coffee shop

Room service

Housekeeper

Banquet housemen

Organization chart:
Food and beverage department of a motor inn

——————— Direct supervision

----------- "Control" supervision

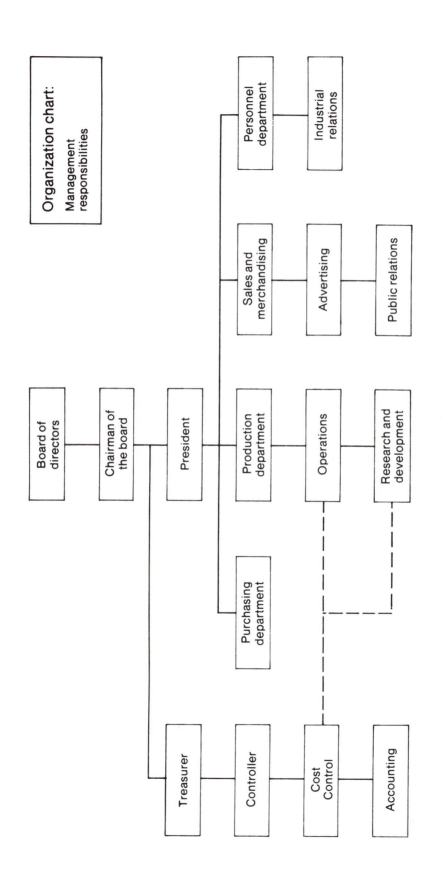

Organization chart:
Management
responsibilities

Board of
directors

Chairman of
the board

President

Treasurer

Controller

Cost
Control

Accounting

Purchasing
department

Production
department

Operations

Research and
development

Sales and
merchandising

Advertising

Public relations

Personnel
department

Industrial
relations

**Exhibit 5-3**

**Chart showing management responsibilities in the general organization plan often used in the food service industry**

corporate headquarters of a restaurant chain/ franchise. This headquarters initiates the standard menus for all outlets. There is a slight variation in the makeup of the menu-writing team, but the same skills are needed. The captain of this team can vary because in one instance, for example, the president may be a food and beverage operator. In another organization the president may hold this position because he or she possesses financial skills. In any case the chief of operations will be the captain of the team. Purchasing and cost control representatives will be included. In this organization the research and development group might be represented, and the sales and merchandising manager or marketing manager will complete the team. It is quite likely that someone from a field operation will also participate.

There is ordinarily no formal organizational chart for the individual, free-standing restaurant. Nevertheless, the equivalent resides in the owner's or manager's mind. Again, the same skills will be represented on the team. In a restaurant operation it is likely that one person will have more than one of the required skills; for example, the manager is very likely also the food purchaser.

Exhibit 5-4 is a diagram of the dietary department of a hospital. To meet patients' needs the chief dietition would have the final responsibility in choosing menu items, but the food purchaser would be an important contributor. Some large hospitals are employing food and beverage directors as business managers because the food volume from sources other than patients' meals is the greater portion of the total food business.

## The Menu-Writing Coordinator

The food and beverage manager, the assistant innkeeper, and the other designated persons who function as captains of the menu-writing teams are the coordinators of the information gathered in the process of

creating or reviewing menus. The following job description of a food and beverage manager of a large hotel enumerates the skills required of one who is to lead the property's menu-writing team.

### Job Description, Food and Beverage Manager

**Basic Responsibilities.** This person is responsible to the general manager of the hotel for the direction and daily supervision of the operation of the entire food and beverage department. This responsibility covers food and beverage purchasing, receiving, storing and issuing, and preparation and service in all food and beverage outlets in keeping with the high standards of quality and service established for this hotel.

This person is responsible for maintaining sanitary conditions in the hotel in accordance with the standards set by the State Department of Health and augmented by hotel policy as set forth in the "Sanitation Manual." The food and beverage manager is also responsible for the coordination of food and beverage activities with other departmental activities throughout the hotel.

### Outline of Responsibilities

1. The food and beverage manager is responsible for the day-to-day operation of the banquet department. He will see that the catering manager prepares banquet menus, arranges for the service of banquet functions, and adheres to cost policies as established. He will further see that the catering manager maintains files following the prescribed system and pursues sales and promotional programs.

2. The food and beverage manager will visit the market with the purchasing agent at least once a month to keep himself well informed on the availability of goods and market prices. He will make sure that the best available quality of goods is purchased for the hotel

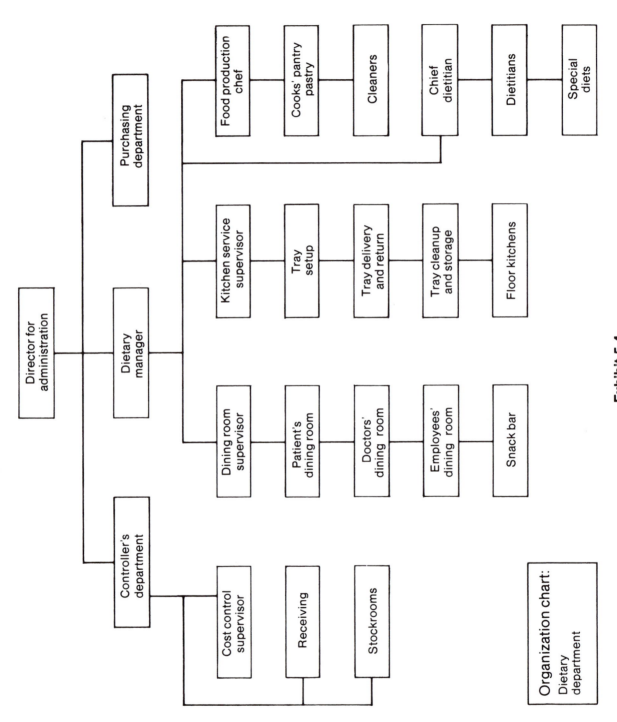

**Exhibit 5-4**

**Chart showing an organization plan for the dietary department in a hospital**

and the prices are according to market conditions.

3. He will supervise the receiving function by spending fifteen to twenty minutes each day checking the quality as well as the quantity of goods received.

4. At least once each week the food and beverage manager will accompany the chef and food purchaser on their daily inspection of the food storeroom, refrigerators, and freezers.

5. Each day he will meet the food and beverage controller and review the sales abstract, bar costs, and daily flash food cost report. Any problems should be discussed with the chef and other department heads, and corrective action should be taken.

6. With the restaurant and coffee shop managers he will review the log books every day and give proper guidance to department heads to improve the service to the customers.

7. The food and beverage manager will be responsible for setting up and maintaining training programs in all departments of the food and beverage operation.

8. With the chef and other staff members the food and beverage manager will review dining room and banquet menus quarterly, looking specifically at cost and merchandising. With the menu writing team he will make necessary adjustments and prepare new menus as needed.

9. The food and beverage manager is responsible for achieving the budgeted cost, payroll, and profit goals.

*Other Duties and Responsibilities*

a. With the sales manager he reviews sales promotion programs, customer complaints, follow-up letters, future bookings, and so forth.

b. With the food and beverage controller and other department heads he reviews weekly, monthly, and fiscal forecasts.

c. He will shop competitive restaurants and bars periodically to keep abreast of the hotel's changing competitive position. A file should be maintained of the shopping reports as well as of the competitive menus and beverage lists.

*Supervision Exercised*

a. Positions directly supervised: food and beverage department heads.

b. Positions indirectly supervised: food and beverage personnel.

*Supervision Received*

a. Reports to general manager

*Responsibility and Authority*

a. Employee relations—Expected to maintain a high degree of employee morale through training, communication, and coordination of employees' efforts.

b. Materials or products—Responsible for maintaining established standards in purchasing, preparation, and service of foods and beverages.

c. Equipment—Responsible for maintaining adequate inventories of china, silver, linen, glass, equipment, and operating supplies.

## Functional Relationships

It is clear from the job description that the food and beverage manager is qualified to be captain of the menu-writing team. The same situation prevails whether the hotel team is writing menus for the restaurants or for room service. A team to write banquet menus may be of slightly different makeup. Chapters 8 and 9 will develop more fully menu writing for all food outlets in a hotel. The teams for free-standing restaurants, institutions, or chain operations must have a similar relationship among the several members and the coordinator or captain.

When the menu-writing team has completed its task, there is considerable work to be done before the menu is ready to be presented to guests. This will be fully discussed in Chapter 13, "Menu Mechanics."

## The Purchasing Agent and the Menu-Writing Team

One of the principal duties of the purchasing department is to research market conditions and prices. For any food operation, this research and the resulting contribution the purchasing agent can make to the menu-writing process are vital. Much of the food operation's cost efficiency will depend on the accuracy of this market research.

A few years ago, when hotels had print shops, the menus for the hotel restaurants were printed daily. Cyclical menus were used with day-to-day changes of certain items to take advantage of the availability of products and favorable prices. Today, except in rare instances, daily printing of menus does not exist. Most restaurants—both free standing and in hotels—use set menus, with daily specials offered by the waiter or waitress. The set menus are adjusted at least quarterly to accommodate seasonal items and to insert new entrées.

Hotels and restaurants with banquet business can use the market information from the purchasing agent to great advantage, since banquet menus are generally priced at the time the customer requests the banquet services. The banquet manager can also help customers make economical choices of foods if he is kept current on the market prices and availability of items. The purchasing agent will advise which foods are in short supply or out of season, of poor quality, or overpriced.

## The Chef and the Menu-Writing Process

The chef, in one sense, needs the final say in what will appear on a menu. His responsibility in the food operation is to produce the food for sale. He knows the capacity of the preparation staff, what they can produce or cannot produce. Equally important, the chef must see to a proper balance in menu selection, especially in large operations in which the cooking chores are divided by stations. The perfect balance would be to have orders flow evenly to all stations. In addition to the chef's knowledge of his kitchen, he needs to know how many covers of the several menu items are expected to be sold.

## The Food Controller and the Menu-Writing Process

The sales histories of menu items are vital to the menu-writing team. These histories are gathered in a variety of ways. In some food operations, this is still accomplished through manual counting by clerks, cashiers, cooks, and dining-room managers. In most operations today, the computer cash register provides this information. Chapter 18 discusses fully the computer service in gathering sales histories. Regardless of the method used, it usually rests with the food and beverage controller to shepherd this information and provide it when needed. In the menu-writing process, this information is necessary to attain the balance of items needed to properly distribute the workload among the cooking stations. The food and beverage controller's primary responsibility and principal contribution is to supply the cost information on individual items being considered for inclusion in the menu. The food purchaser has the raw costs of food stuffs, but it rests with the food and beverage controller to supply the portion costs. In Chapter 7, we will discuss food cost factors and yields from raw materials.

## The Dining Room Manager and Menu Writing

Just as the chef, food purchaser, and food controller make unique contributions, so does the dining room manager, host, or maitre d'hotel (whatever title he or she carries). This person has direct contact with the customers —the all-important group for whom the menu is being created. The feedback from the customer is funnelled through this position. What does the customer say about the menu selections? format? pricing? color? This feedback is crucial, especially at menu-revision sessions.

## The Banquet Manager and Menu Writing

The menu-writing team for banquets must include the banquet manager and possibly a banquet salesman. In large hotels the banquet manager very often is the team captain, the coordinator, when banquet menus are being prepared or revised. In Chapter 9 we will discuss the writing of banquet menus. As we shall indicate there, banquet menus in many instances are developed item by item in a dialogue between the banquet manager and the customer.

## Summary

In every organization employees are evaluated annually, semi-annually, or even quarterly. The performance of the team at a menu-writing session provides an excellent opportunity for the food and beverage manager to evaluate the team members. The success or lack of success of a menu depends on the quality of the members' contributions.

This discussion of the information necessary to an efficient production of a menu and the several sources from whom it comes substantiates that a team is necessary. We could easily find numerous restaurants at which one person writes the menus. And, of course, we could just as easily find an equal number of restaurants that fail.

# 6 How Do You Price and Cost a Menu?

**Purpose:** To assign to the different types of menus the proper pricing methods and to illustrate how such pricings are derived.

Chapter 1 lists eight different commercial food services, ranging from the quick-service restaurants to the white-tablecloth classical restaurants. Naturally, pricing procedures will differ for the several types of operations. The United States has enjoyed a fair amount of prosperity since World War II, interrupted by several recessions. Price was not a major factor in restaurant patronage until the mid 1970's, when the country experienced the worst inflation in several generations. Although inflation has been under control during the past decade, we are kept conscious of its threat by the daily reminders from the media reporting moves by the Federal Reserve Board to change interest rates in order to keep inflation low.

Four situations call for menu pricing. The first is when a new food operation is begun. The price structure anticipated in the feasibility study that prompted the opening of the restaurant and the competition immediately surrounding the new operation are guides for pricing the menu. The second situation is when wholesale prices are rising, or volume is dropping along with profits. Third, menus need new pricing when competitors initiate price changes either upward or downward. If competitors raise prices but the cost situation does not require an increase to preserve profits, the restaurant is wise to hold its price level and gain a price advantage over the competitor. However, if volume is high, prices may be raised to meet the competitor and yield a windfall profit. If competitors lower prices, a restaurant should ascertain if similar action will require a sacrifice of profit. If this is true, an alternate course is to retain the price level and provide some kind of compensation to make the higher prices become a good value to customers. The fourth situation is not influenced by anything but time—a menu's offerings and basic prices should be reviewed quarterly as a matter of management policy.

## Menu Prices and Revenue

Whichever type of restaurant you are writing a menu for, you must observe certain menu-writing fundamentals if the menu is to fulfill its functions of communication and merchandising. Pricing is the most important of these fundamentals. Pricing is a key element in the sales of a restaurant operation, and sales are the only sources of the operator's income.

Materials, labor, and rent, for example, are all sources of cost. When writing and pricing menus you must also consider customers, competitors, and the type of operation.

## Customers

The number one consideration in writing and pricing menus is the customers. In Chapter 4, we presented customers as individuals with many different characteristics that make up their life-styles. The age, sex, and income level of potential customers all indicate to management what food items will most appeal to their tastes and at what prices the selections are considered good value by these customers. Anthropologists write that humans are social beings who gravitate toward one another because they share likes and dislikes and similar pursuits. Consequently, groups must also be considered in writing and pricing menus. In Chapter 4 we outlined the several menu selections and price structures favored by different groups.

The preferences of individuals and groups vary with the seasons and are subject to trends and fads that are affected by influences as varied as economic conditions and advertising programs. This suggests the need for the quarterly review of menu selections and prices as discussed previously.

## Current Market Conditions

The price structure of a menu is a fundamental and critical factor in attaining the budgeted profit. Ultimately, the level of profits or the lack of profits determines whether or not the restaurant will continue operation. We have previously discussed product availability and prices as important current market conditions. The price structure of the competition is also an important market condition. Although their prices certainly must be considered, the prices should not be accepted uncritically as reflecting proper pricing. The customers' perceptions of good value are based on

several criteria, and a restaurant's individuality may allow upward variance from the competitors' prices if other factors compensate for the differences and lead consumers to decide that the restaurant has good value at the prices charged.

## Type of Operation

In Chapter 3, "Know Your Restaurant," we propose concepts basic to assigning prices to menu selections. The classical restaurants found principally in metropolitan cities, often in hotels, must carry low food costs—25 to 30 percent—to cover the high cost of labor, expensive linen and china, and high maintenance costs associated with elaborate service and luxurious ambience. Food cost (also called cost of sales) as a percentage is calculated by dividing material cost (i.e., the cost of food) by the selling price.

Family restaurants, common in middle-class suburban districts throughout the United States, feature simple friendly service and neat but inexpensive decor; these restaurants operate successfully with food costs of 32 to 36 percent. Hotel coffee shops also operate at this level of cost of sales.

Fast food operations and cafeterias require less labor and are easily maintained, so food costs of 38 to 40 percent are consistent with adequate profit. However, in recent years, most fast food operations have lowered food costs considerably by raising prices.

Signature restaurants do not fall into one category. Menu items vary from seafoods to heavy beef entrées, and price structures vary accordingly. Expensive items like steak, lobster, and lamb chops can be sold profitably at food costs of 40 to 42 percent or higher. For example, a steak dinner costing $3.00 and sold at $7.50 yields a 40 percent food cost. The gross profit, which must cover labor, operating expenses, overhead, and profit, is $4.50. A fish dinner that costs only $2.00 and sells for $6.00 results in a 33.3 percent food cost. However, the gross profit is only $4.00. In these restaurants, the lower-cost items must have greater markups if they are to contribute to desired profit. Because of the low costs of most breakfast items, a four times markup is necessary to produce a gross profit adequate to cover labor and other expenses that may be the same or only slightly lower than expenses per cover at luncheon and dinner.

Ethnic restaurants offer different qualities of food and service that can characterize them as a fast food operation (such as Taco Bell) or as a family restaurant (such as Olive Garden Italian restaurants). Or, they may fall into the classical group (such as the Cucina Restaurant, an Italian restaurant whose menu appears on pages 43 and 44.

## Pricing Policy

Although a group of restaurants may be categorized as signature restaurants, classical, and so on, they have individual identities, and pricing policies may vary. Different conditions will cause their managements to adopt different price strategies.

### High Volume, Low Markup

When there is a very large group of potential customers with middle to lower-middle incomes, a policy of low prices can perhaps generate sufficient volume to turn over the restaurant seats three times each evening of operation. Fixed expenses such as rent remain the same at any level of volume, and added turnover means lower labor costs. Thus the high food cost caused by moderate prices is offset by lower labor and fixed expenses, which is compatible with good profit.

### Low Volume, High Markup

Conditions in another situation may be that the physical plant allows for only a minimum number of seats. However, if the restaurant is located in an affluent community, a fancy restaurant with high prices can deliver the revenue needed for a good profit despite the limited number of food covers served.

### Leaders and Specials

The key to good advertising is to have some feature in the ad that immediately attracts attention. The menu is most effective as an advertising device when it stimulates the reader to take immediate notice. This is a function of a "leader." A leader must be a popular item. When featured at a special price, prime rib is a very attractive leader. It is normally an expensive item, so even a high food cost still delivers an adequate gross profit. A "loss leader" is really a contradiction—it is no great accomplishment to sell an item at a loss of profit. A true leader both attracts attention as a good value and yields a profit.

High printing costs make it unprofitable to print daily menus. Consequently, restaurants use specials to add variety to a menu. Specials need not be low-priced features, although this quite often might be the case. In areas with many retired persons who have the option of eating dinner at their convenience, the "early bird" specials have become a fixture in many restaurants. Thus an added turnover can be achieved, resulting in additional profit even with the price concessions. In many operations, the "early bird" specials offer lower prices and smaller portions. This gives the added turnover without sacrificing food cost percentage.

### Customers' Perception of Value

Good value is a subjective concept. How suitable or desirable is this product at this price? Individuals vary in their perceptions of good value; in fact, a person's perception can change in different situations. One of the purposes of advertising is to create an idea of value in a potential customer's mind. The well-planned menu suggests value in a number of ways: attractive coloring, interesting descriptions of the food selections, and readable print (especially in "boxed" items that are specialties of the house). Prices can be higher when the whole menu suggests quality products and generous portions.

There must be a consistency in menu prices, and the prices must stay within the range expected by the clientele for whom the restaurant was established, as suggested by the feasibility studies.

## Prices Must Cover Costs

That prices must cover costs appears to be a simplistic and obvious statement, but restaurant costs do require detailed analyses. In standard hotel accounting, for example, the income and expense statement differs considerably from that of a free-standing restaurant. Exhibit 6-1 shows a food and beverage income and expense statement for a hotel or motor inn. Note that the profit figure is designated "departmental profit." This is the profit from sales after all expenses controlled by the food and beverage operating personnel are charged against sales.

In addition to the operating expenses shown, there are both fixed and variable expenses. None are wholly controlled by the food and beverage employees; most are shared with the rooms department, such as repairs and maintenance expenses handled by personnel that work in all departments. Strict allocation of their time is not economically feasible. Real estate taxes for the building apply to spaces used for all purposes. An allocation by square footage is not accurate because function spaces support the rooms department as well as serve as an operating space for the food and beverage department. Allocations of such expenses to the food and beverage departments vary between 8 and 12 percent of sales. It is, therefore, reasonable to assume that a net profit in food and beverage begins at about a 13 percent departmental profit.

Many hotel operations have separate income and expense statements for the food department and for the beverage department. This requires allocating service labor costs to the appropriate

department, which is often done according to sales volume. However, it is an arbitrary allocation and only coincidentally accurate as is the case in any such method of allocation.

In a free-standing restaurant all costs can be accurately applied and a true net profit calculated. In such an operation an accepted standard of volume is twice the cost of building the restaurant. (This excludes the cost of the construction of a building. Amortization of the construction costs becomes part of the capital expense of the restaurant.) A satisfactory minimum net profit is 12.5 percent of sales.

*Example*:
Building cost: $1,000,000
Annual volume: 2,000,000
Net Profit (12.5%): 250,000

An achievement of this minimum profit yields a return of 25 percent on the investment. This is a good profit, but considering the high risk in the restaurant business it is not an unusual demand by an investor. This profit is before income taxes are paid. In a restaurant operation the cost of sales is the cost that can most readily be manipulated upward or downward, so producing an adequate menu price structure, which when combined with the fixed and relatively fixed costs produces the targeted profit, can be the key to a successful operation.

The following example shows a pro forma income and expense statement listing the several expenses that make up the deductions from income. The statement is for the same restaurant considered above.

|  | Food | Beverage | Total |
|---|---|---|---|
| Sales | $1,200,000 | $ 800,000 | $2,000,000 |
| Cost of sales | 384,000 | 216,000 | 600,000 |
| Gross profit | $ 816,000 | $ 584,000 | $1,400,000 |
| Expenses |  |  |  |
| Labor (includes benefits) |  |  | $ 700,000 |
| Departmental expense |  |  | 200,000 |
| Fixed expense (includes rent) |  |  | 250,000 |
| Total expense |  |  | $1,150,000 |
| Net profit |  |  | $ 250,000 |

The food cost of sales is 32 percent; the beverage cost is 27 percent. These targeted costs

**Exhibit 6-1**
**Food and beverage income and expense statement**

|  | Food | | Beverage | |
|---|---|---|---|---|
| Net revenue | $100,000 | | $ 50,000 | |
| Cost of food consumed | 37,000 | 37.0% | 12,000 | 24.0% |
| Less employees' meals | 3,400 | 3.4 | – | |
| Net cost of sales | $ 33,600 | 33.6% | | |
| Gross profit | $ 66,400 | 66.4% | $ 38,000 | 76.0% |
| **Combined** | | | | |
| Revenue | $150,000 | 100.0% | | |
| Cost of sales | 45,600 | 30.4 | | |
| Gross profit | $104,400 | 69.6% | | |
| *Departmental expenses* | | | | |
| Salaries and wages | $ 46,500 | 31.0% | | |
| Employees' meals | 3,400 | 2.3 | | |
| Payroll taxes and benefits | 10,800 | 7.2 | | |
| Total | $ 60,700 | 40.5% | | |
| Music and entertainment | 3,450 | 2.3 | | |
| Laundry and dry cleaning | 1,350 | .9 | | |
| Kitchen fuel | 450 | .3 | | |
| China, glass, silver, linen | 2,550 | 1.7 | | |
| Contract cleaning | 600 | .4 | | |
| Licenses | 300 | .2 | | |
| Miscellaneous | 6,000 | 4.0 | | |
| Total other expense | $14,700 | 9.8% | | |
| Total expenses | $75,400 | 50.3% | | |
| Departmental profit | $29,000 | 19.3% | | |

were determined after study of the competition and the anticipated cost of operation.

## Typical Food Costs by Meal Period

If our sample restaurant operates on a three-meal-per-day basis, at a 32 percent food cost, the approximate breakdown of costs for each meal would be as follows:

| | Sales | Cost | Cost Percentage | Gross Profit |
|---|---|---|---|---|
| Breakfast | 200,000 | 50,000 | 25.0 | 150,000 |
| Luncheon | 400,000 | 125,000 | 31.3 | 275,000 |
| Dinner | 600,000 | 209,000 | 34.8 | 391,000 |
| Total | 1,200,000 | 384,000 | 32.0 | 816,000 |

The 34.8 cost percentage for dinner sales is typical of a restaurant with heavy volume in sales of steaks, lobster, and prime rib. The gross profit at dinner, however, is greater than that at either breakfast or luncheon, although the food costs at these meals are considerably lower.

## Moving from Cost to Selling Price

A quick way to determine what a selling price should be at a desired cost of sales percentage is to divide the cost of the item by the desired food cost percentage. Use the decimal form of the percentage in making calculations. Some examples follow.

| Cost of Meal | Desired Percentage Cost | | Selling Price | Gross Profit |
|---|---|---|---|---|
| 1.52 | 24.8% | .248 | 6.15 | 4.63 |
| 1.78 | 27.2% | .272 | 6.55 | 4.77 |
| 2.09 | 29.6% | .296 | 7.05 | 4.96 |
| 2.65 | 32.4% | .324 | 8.20 | 5.55 |
| 3.40 | 34.5% | .345 | 9.85 | 6.45 |

Note that as the food cost percentage rises the gross profit (selling price minus cost of meal) increases. This clearly illustrates that expensive items can be sold at higher food cost percentages and still yield desired gross profits.

The above selling prices were based strictly on food costs. In pricing a menu the $7.05 price would probably be changed to $6.95 or $7.25. The $6.15 price might be $5.95 or $6.25. This will be discussed more fully in the section on pricing psychology in this chapter.

## Target Pricing

This is a unique but effective pricing strategy. The objective is to achieve a "satisfactory" profit, which implies that even if a different level of pricing could be used to produce a larger rate of return, management is satisfied with a lower return in view of the level of investment and risk. Such a strategy can be applied only in situations in which costs other than food costs are constant and predictable.

The following example demonstrates this strategy. The restaurant serves dinner only.

Sales: $600,000
Number of covers: 100,000
Costs (excluding food cost: $300,000
Desired profit: $90,000

1. The projected number of covers is 100,000, so $.90 profit per cover will deliver the overall desired profit of $90,000 ($90,000 divided by 100,000 covers).
2. The cost per cover excluding food cost is $3.00 ($300,000 divided by 100,000 covers).

3. A markup of $3.90 (fixed cost of $3.00 plus $.90 profit) over the food cost of each meal is the pricing guide, and will produce the $.90 per cover profit.

Use of this strategy results in an interesting price pattern. On high-cost items, selling prices can be far below the competitions'. On average-cost items, selling prices can still be competitive. Although not many operations can predict costs and unit volume with sufficient accuracy to use this target pricing strategy, it is very effective for those who can.

## The Old Reliables

You can follow general guidelines in setting menu prices that have proven reliable for average hotel and motel restaurants, and freestanding restaurants. Following is an uncomplicated but effective guide to cost setting.

*Restaurant meals* (free standing or in a hotel)

Breakfast—4 times cost of meal
Luncheon—3 to 3.5 times cost of meal
Dinner (steaks, chops, lobster)—2 1/2 times cost of meal
Dinner (other)—3 times cost of meal

*Banquet meals*

Breakfast, luncheon, and dinner—3 1/2 to 4 times cost of meal
Steaks, chops, lobster—3 to 3 1/2 times cost of meal

## *Desired Food Costs*

Accounting firms that specialize in hotel and restaurant audits print studies annually that show the level of food costs, labor costs, other expenses, and profits in a variety of different operations. These are broken down by region, sales, size of property, and type of operation. Information from such studies allows managers to compare their particular hotel or restaurant with others, which helps them to establish a desired food cost.

## Normal Food Costs

The following schedule lists normal food costs for different types of food operations.

| Type of Operation | Normal Food Cost (as a percentage) |
| --- | --- |
| Class hotels | 22–25 |
| City hotels | 26–30 |
| Motels/hotels | 30–35 |
| Class restaurants | 26–30 |
| Average restaurants | 30–36 |
| Fast food operations | 37–40 |
| Cafeterias | 38–42 |

Our discussion of food costs has been limited to cost percentages for total operations and total individual meal periods. These food costs are the average of varying costs for individual items. We want to point out, however, that all selections at a given meal cannot be marked up to achieve the same cost percentage.

## Pricing Psychology

Many studies have been made on the pricing strategies of different successful restaurants. The conclusion is that menu pricing is at best an inexact science and at worst, confusing. In choosing a pricing method, it is wise to follow the few truths that the responsible surveys have found. These are based on an analysis of how restaurant patrons look at menu prices.

You should not use even figures for menu prices, such as $5.00 or $8.00, because they are so definite. The customer knows immediately that the price is $5.00 or $8.00. A price of $5.25 would appear to the customer as the same as the $5.00 meal so long as no $5.00 meal is listed. In fact, customers perceive meals priced from about $4.75 to $5.45 as being about the same price—$5.00. A similar picture is conveyed to the customer at other price levels. A "$2.00 meal" may be priced anywhere from $1.75 to $2.25; a "$3.00 meal," from $2.65 to $3.35; and so on.

## Price Spreads

Another maxim that has proved true in menu pricing is to group prices in a narrow range. Or put negatively, do not have large price spreads on a menu. Customers prefer the items to be priced close to the amount that they wish to pay. A menu with $10.00 to $12.00 items and $5.00 to $6.00 selections tends to draw customers to the lower-priced items, which will result in lower gross profits although the food cost of the lower-priced items may be slightly lower. This reduced food cost can be deceiving, at least until the end of the accounting period when lower profits point to faulty pricing as the possible culprit.

## Raising Prices

If you completely overhaul menu prices at one time, customers will usually balk because it is so obvious to the regular patron. Only a few prices at a time should be changed. If, for instance, four prices are to be raised, it is well to increase two of them within the same dollar range, for example, from $5.25 to $5.75. Such a change will not seem as drastic to the customer as a raise from, say, $5.95 to $6.25.

## One-Price Meals

Perhaps the most effective menu price structure is a list of table d'hôte meals at a single price. In addition to this list, some higher-cost items can be listed as specials or house specialties at a higher price. These higher-priced items should include less, for example, no coffee or soup, and thus the price spread between the table d'hôte meals and the specials need not be so great.

During the period of high inflation in the 1970's and early 1980's, many restaurateurs who were featuring full-course meals—appetizers through dessert—shifted to an a la carte strategy in the belief that the prices would appear not to have increased. However, the added prices for coffee, soup, and dessert raised the check to an obviously higher level.

It was like waving a red flag before the guest. Most guests realize that inflation leads to higher prices, but few people enjoy being "conned." The practice of "nickel and diming" guests wins no friends.

## Split-Prices

A successful pricing strategy in family restaurants is the "split-price." For example, an entrée with potato, salad, and rolls and butter is listed at a given price. Next to this price is the price for a full meal, that is, the same meal with appetizer or soup, coffee, and dessert included. The added price can seem fairly small for the added food. This type of pricing can lead customers to the higher price, unlike the menu with a large price spread that moves customers to the lower prices.

## Appetizers, Soups, and Desserts

How to price these "added" items can be the subject of a protracted debate.

**The Usual Way.** The usual pricing of these items is based on the concept that if customers want an appetizer or soup or dessert, they will order it without considering price. Many restaurants mark up these items three to four times cost. However, the sale of these items at such markups has little or no effect on the overall desired food cost. Many restaurant operators therefore conclude that this method of pricing the items is good.

**The Best Way.** The size of entrée portions in most restaurants makes appetizers, soups, and desserts extra baggage that a person can do without, never mind how tempting a dessert display can be. If these "extras" are offered at low prices, say at two times cost or at a 50 percent food cost, customer resistance is lowered considerably. Pricing these items very economically can build their sales volume, which is like making extra profit on the entrée. These items really require little labor or extra overhead, so the markup becomes virtually 100 percent profit. Not only in pricing these

items but in developing an entire menu's price structure, the proper method of analyzing prices is to consider dollar profits, not percentages.

## Cost Factors

In the previous chapter we stated that the primary job of the food controller in the menu-writing process is to provide portion costs of proposed menu items. This information is necessary for pricing purposes, to check that an item's price is consistent with other proposed menu items, and to compare item prices with competitors' prices. The range of entrée items potentially available for inclusion and the myriad supporting foods render it impossible for the food controller to provide information without help. Portion cost factors can help the food controller price entrée meat, poultry, fish, and shellfish dishes. Over our combined ninety years in food and beverage operations we have compiled lists of portion cost factors. Table 6-1 shows a sample list of these cost factors. A complete list is in Appendix A.

### Explanation of Listing

The first column, "Wholesale Cut," lists the purchased item from which the portion in question is cut. The second column, "IMPS Code Number," shows the IMPS (International Meat Purchasing Specification) code number. IMPS code numbers are available for fresh beef; fresh lamb and mutton; fresh veal and calf; fresh pork; cured and smoked, and fully cooked pork products; cured, dried, and smoked beef products; sausage products; and edible by-products (such as liver, tongue, and heart). Individual pamphlets (with the same titles as the items in the preceding list) can be obtained from the U.S. Government Superintendent of Documents, Washington, D.C. The same information is available from the National Association of Meat Purveyors (at 252 W. Iva Rd., Tucson, AZ 85704) in the form of a book, with color photographs, entitled *The Meat Buyer's Guide to Standardized Meat Cuts.*

**Table 6-1**
**Sample portion cost factors**

| Wholesale Cut | IMPS Code Number | Entrée | Yield Factor (percent) | PORTION FACTORS | | # Average Servings |
|---|---|---|---|---|---|---|
| | | | | Size and State | Cost | |
| **MEATS** | | | | | | |
| *Beef* | | | | | | |
| Rib, primal (regular, 34 to 38 lb.) | 103 | Roast Ribs of Beef | 26 | 15 oz. cooked | 3.60 | 10 |
| | | | | 11 oz. cooked | 2.64 | 14 |
| | | | | $9\frac{1}{2}$ oz. cooked | 2.23 | 16 |
| | | | | $8\frac{1}{2}$ oz. cooked | 2.04 | 18 |
| Bottom Round 25 to 28 lb.) | 170 | Pot Roast | 55 | 8 oz. cooked | .91 | 28 |
| | | Hamburger | 90 | 6 oz. cooked | .68 | 37 |
| | | | | 8 oz. raw | .55 | 47 |
| | | | | 6 oz. raw | .42 | 63 |
| Strip loin (boneless, 12 to 14 lbs.) | 180 | Sirloin Steak (2 inch tail, 1/8 inch fat) | 70 | 16 oz. raw | 1.42 | 10 |
| | | | | 14. oz. raw | 1.24 | 12 |
| | | | | 12 oz. raw | 1.06 | 14 |
| | | | | 10 oz. raw | .89 | 16 |
| | | | | 8 oz. raw | .71 | 20 |
| Tenderloin (full, 7 to 9 lb.) (short, 5 to 6 lb.) | 189 192 | Tenderloin Steak | 50 | 10 oz. raw | 1.25 | 5 to 7 |
| | | | | 8 oz. raw | 1.00 | 7 to 9 |
| | | | | 6 oz. raw | .75 | 9 to 12 |
| | | Roast Tenderloin | 40 | 8 oz. cooked | 1.25 | 5 to 7 |
| *Lamb* | | | | | | |
| Lamb Rack (6 to 8 lb.) | 204 | Lamb Chops | 50 | 8 oz. raw | 2.00 | 6 to 8 |
| | | | | 6 oz. raw | .87 | 8 to 10 |
| | | | | 4 oz. raw | .50 | 12 to 16 |
| *Veal* | | | | | | |
| Veal Leg (single 25 to 28 lbs.) | 334 | Roast Leg | 40 | 8 oz. cooked | 1.25 | 20 to 22 |
| | | | | 6 oz. cooked | .94 | 26 to 28 |
| | | | | 4 oz. cooked | .63 | 40 to 42 |
| | | Veal Cutlets | 47 | 8 oz. raw | 1.06 | 23 to 26 |
| | | | | 6 oz. raw | .80 | 31 to 35 |
| | | | | 4 oz. raw | .64 | 47 to 52 |

Also available is *The Meat Buyer's Guide to Portion Control Meat Cuts.* In many hotels and perhaps most restaurants, the purchasing of portion-ready meat cuts is the rule rather than the exception. Thus we recommend you obtain the two manuals.

The third column in Table 6-1, "Entrée," lists the portion. Column four, "Yield Factor," shows the amount of usable meat available for portions. The sixth column, the "Portion Cost Factor," is the aid to pricing entrée meat, poultry, fish, and shellfish dishes, as men-

tioned above. The size of the portion in either raw or cooked size, whichever is proper for the particular item, is located in column five. The last column lists the average number of portions you can expect from the wholesale cut of meat listed.

### How to Use Cost Factors

To illustrate how to use cost factors to price items, we will work with the common beef item listed as Strip Loin (Boneless) (12 to 14 lbs.). The International Meat Purchasing

Specification Code number for this item is 180. The specification for the item to be cut is a sirloin steak with a 2-inch tail and 1/8-inch fat cover. The steak to be cut will weigh 14 ounces. Note that this is a raw weight. The cost factor for this 14-ounce steak is 1.24. If the price paid for the wholesale cut—Strip loin, No. 180—is $2.50 per pound, by application of the cost factor of 1.24 we find that the 14-ounce steak will cost $3.10 ($2.50 times 1.24).

## House Specifications

A restaurant is not bound to purchase only standard items listed in the *Meat Buyer's Guide*. A restaurant serving bone-in sirloin steaks will find that purchasing a bone-in strip loin with a 9-inch flank trim is better suited to fabricating bone-in sirloin steaks than a strip loin with the standard 10-inch flank trim, which is cut number 175 in the *Meat Buyer's Guide*. Such a deviation from the standard is called a "house specification." This is practical only when a restaurant deals with a purveyor from whom substantial quantities of meat are purchased, and who has proven reliable in delivering properly trimmed meat cuts.

## Source of Cost Factors

To develop cost factors for items listed you must conduct meat-butchering tests with portion sizes of raw meat. For cooked items, such as roast beef, you must conduct cooking tests in addition to the butcher tests. Samples of the forms used in conducting these tests are found in Appendix A with explanations of how to use them.

## Makeup Costs

In addition to the cost of the entrée, the costs of the additional items served with the entrée for the price listed on the menu must also be considered. These might be soups, potatoes, vegetables, salads, beverages, and desserts, or only two or three of these items: Many restaurants include salad bars in the menu prices of the different entrées. The cost of the entrées must also be increased by the costs for the so-called nonproductive items, including spices used in cooking and fat used in deep-fat frying. Appendix B provides the information needed to compute these costs, and includes schedules on fruits and vegetables (fresh, frozen, and canned), dairy products, and staples (e.g., rice, noodles, coffee, bread).

## Summary

Writing menus and pricing menus are two facets of the same function. As shown in Chapter 5, a team is essential for effective menu writing and pricing simply because several skills are needed in the process. Keys to successful menu pricing are the following:

1. Prices must cover costs; consequently, all operating costs must be known and considered. Accurate pricing depends in large part on good cost information.
2. Menu costs must be updated regularly. As operating costs either increase or decrease, menu prices should be adjusted accordingly.
3. There are several effective methods of pricing menus. Choose the one best suited to the restaurant, its customers, and the competition.
4. Follow up on price changes to ascertain the effect of the changes on customers and consumer demand.

In Chapter 18, on the use of the computer in food and beverage operations, we place special emphasis on the evaluation of menus and the establishment of potential costs.

# 7 The Life Cycle of a Restaurant

**Purpose:** To acquaint the student with the different strategies available to begin the operation of a restaurant, the problems that occur during stages of development, and the use of the menu in possible solutions to the problems.

The menu is a vital marketing tool in all the stages of a restaurant's life cycle. Changes in items and prices to meet the changing tastes of the clientele require a lengthy list of menu selections. Appendix D offers 1,001 items as a handy reference for the menu writer.

## Failure: The Cost of Being in a Rut

"*Marketing*: An aggregate of functions involved in moving goods from producer to consumer." This dictionary definition of marketing, applied to a restaurant, includes everything from purchasing to cooking to service. Certainly, these functions all contribute to customer satisfaction and rightly belong in the *broad definition* of marketing. But for purposes of menu planning and merchandising, a specialized definition of marketing is this: "Marketing starts with the customers' needs (real or imaginary) and proceeds to a program of action to help fulfill these needs."

Marketing studies reveal that the restaurant business follows the same type of curve that packaged products do in what is called the life-cycle concept. It is the responsibility of those charged with producing a restaurant's

menu to attempt to recognize the distinct stages of the restaurant's life cycle in the sales history of menu selections. The four life-cycle stages are the introduction stage, the growth stage, the maturity stage, and the decline stage.

## Introduction Stage

As the name of this stage indicates, it is here that the product—the restaurant's menu selections—is first presented to customers. This presentation takes its form as suggested by feasibility studies, general analysis of the market, and surveys of the competition. There are four ways a restaurant can be introduced, and each depends on certain conditions.

### Rapid-Skimming Strategy

This option consists of opening after a period of high promotion, with menu prices at the highest level that you think will be acceptable to the anticipated clientele. This strategy is to be used in an area that has potential customers who are eager for an alternative to the available eating establishments.

A second condition that would lead you to use this strategy is that you know that you will face competition in the near future. Use of this strategy will help you to rapidly build a loyal clientele before the new competition opens.

### Slow-Skimming Strategy

This method consists of beginning operations with little in the way of promotion but with high prices. Unlike rapid skimming, which operates at little or no profit in its early stages because of high promotion costs, slow-skimming recovers as much profit as possible from the outset because of low promotion costs. Use this strategy if there is little threat from competition, the potential market is limited in size, and the potential customers are able and willing to pay a high price.

### Rapid-Penetration Strategy

This strategy consists of low prices and high promotion. Such a strategy is practical when the following conditions exist:

1. Potential customers are price sensitive.
2. The restaurant will draw from a very large market.
3. The competition is strong.
4. The large market and the reasonable prices can be expected to draw sufficient volume to create a good turnover of restaurant seats, thereby reducing labor costs and fixed charges in relation to sales volume.

By using this strategy you can quickly penetrate the market; that is, your volume is large.

### Slow-Penetration Strategy

This fourth alternative entails low prices and a low level of promotion. The aim is to build volume by charging low prices but still retain reasonable profits because of the low promotion costs. Use this strategy if your restaurant has high visibility without promotion because of its location and traffic patterns. Another prerequisite is that a large market exists, but there is some potential competition.

You might also choose to use the slow-penetration strategy if you anticipate that customers will be price conscious.

## Growth Stage

If the introduction stage strategies are successful, you can expect a steady climb in your restaurant's volume. From satisfied early customers repeat business will develop, and new customers will follow because the restaurant's reputation will spread through word-of-mouth advertising. New competition will likely appear, so it is extremely important to introduce new features on a regular basis to keep interest alive.

Unless inflation demands are present, prices should remain constant, although the average check may drop slightly as new customers are added to the clientele. Promotion expenditures should also remain constant. Profit will peak during this growth stage because promotion costs are spread over a larger volume, and labor and fixed costs also are favorably affected by the increased sales.

## Maturity Stage

As much as a restaurateur or purveyors of other products would like to see sales continue to climb, the growth stage will inevitably end. The sales growth slows down as the restaurant enters the stage of maturity. This stage lasts much longer than the two previous stages, and it presents the greatest challenges to the restaurant manager. Proper use of the menu is crucial to maintenance of volume. The maturity stage has three phases.

### Growth Maturity

In this phase growth continues but at a declining rate. The restaurant is operating at or near capacity.

## Stable Maturity

At this point sales become level. Loss of regular customers is replaced by the addition of new customers, which maintains a relatively stable volume.

## Decaying Maturity

Here the food outlet experiences a reasonably steady volume but at a slightly lower level. Additional competition is ordinarily the cause.

As noted above, the maturity stage in the life cycle of a restaurant poses the most formidable challenges to management methods. It is not enough to adopt a strategy of defending the current position. The status quo is seldom maintained—there is either progress or decline. That a good offense is the best defense is certainly a truism and perhaps a bit trite, but it should be basic to the strategies you choose to instill viability into an operation well into the maturity stage. However, change for the sake of change is seldom productive. To stimulate interest at this stage, you must deal with two elements—market and product.

**Market.** It is prudent to begin with the current clientele and search for ways to stimulate increased patronage, particularly through menu incentives. In Chapter 20, "Brainstorming a Sales Program," we will offer suggestions that are geared to this approach to enliven interest among present customers.

A second method of launching an offense is to adjust the menu to attract a new segment of the market; for example, if the menu has been directed to a youthful clientele, perhaps an "early bird" promotion directed to senior citizens, with specials, will add a turnover of seats prior to the regularly timed dinner period. Luncheon menus that have been aimed at businessmen can offer "shoppers' specials" if the restaurant is in a location in which it can profit from such an addition.

**Product.** After moving into the maturity stage following the relatively short stages of introduction and growth, it is very likely time to review the basic structure of the menu to determine if a fairly drastic change in menu selections is needed to maintain the interest of regular customers. You can add new features to expand the menu's versatility and appeal. This is an effective means of building the restaurant's image of progressiveness. In addition to being of enhanced interest to customers, new features can improve morale and enthusiasm in employees. Better attitudes among service personnel are obvious to the customers.

## Decline Stage

This stage in the life cycle is not inevitable and can be avoided if proper conditions are met. Restaurants have continued for several hundred years in different countries in Europe, and some in the United States have experienced an enviable longevity. Such long life is possible if management recognizes which life-cycle stage the operation has reached and acts on that acute recognition. To maintain a long-lasting successful operation you must update menus, keep the decor fresh, and know your customers. In any given area, the people who patronize a restaurant and make it successful gradually move to other interests. Knowing the customers can mean finding out what new customers are to replace the old. The "six g's" explained in Chapter 2 must remain in force.

Nevertheless, sometimes, such as when there is a change in the neighborhood, it is impossible or at least uneconomic to salvage or revitalize an operation. It is a perceptive management that recognizes when it is time to withdraw and invest its resources in more profitable areas.

# 8 Writing Menus for Hotel Food Operations

**Purpose:** To discuss how writing menus for hotel food operations is similar to and different from writing menus for free-standing restaurants.

Hotel operations may be compared to conglomerate corporations composed of several related and unrelated businesses. However, in the hotel business each of the businesses have the same customer at the same time. This suggests that the different businesses, though not necessarily related, must support each other. The hotel manager must decide who gets "pushed" and who gets "shoved" to please the customers.

An examination of how the various segments of a hotel contribute revenue and profits will suggest a background for decision making by the manager.

| Department | Revenue | Profit |
|---|---|---|
| | (Percentage of total) | |
| Rooms | 60 | 70–75 |
| Food and beverage | 35 | 20–25 |
| Minor departments | 5 | 5–10 |

Departmental profit is the profit before undistributed operating expenses, interest, taxes, insurance, and depreciation.

Minor departments are laundry, valet, parking, rentals, and so on. Undistributed expenses include heat, air conditioning, and electricity from one source but used by each segment.

These statistics illustrate which is the primary business and which are the supporting businesses in hotel operations. Two operations in the food department that require particular consideration are the coffee shop and room service.

## Rooms Business and the Coffee Shop

In determining the size of a restaurant, that is, the number of seats the potential business will support, you should plan fewer seats than the number of persons you anticipate will be served at a meal period. This allows for turnover, which facilitates economic use of service personnel. To determine the size of a coffee shop you must consider the number of rooms in the hotel; the number of seats in the coffee shop should be set at the number of guests expected between average and maximum occupancy. This allows for some turnover at average or slightly higher than the average rooms business. At times of lower room occupancy, which includes off-season periods and weekends in many hotels, the coffee shop will seat a slightly better than average house count most of the time. If the architectural plan of the hotel permits, it is wise to design the coffee shop layout in such a manner that sections can be closed in slow periods without creating an inconvenience for the guests. Reduced staffing of service personnel can be accomplished without enlarging any one server station, which detracts from good service even when there are few guests to serve.

### The Coffee Shop Menu

Writing a coffee shop menu must be approached in the same manner as preparing a menu for a free-standing restaurant. You must consider who the guests are and what they are willing to pay. Planning breakfast and, to a certain degree, luncheon menus is similar to planning the menu for a family restaurant. Men, women, and children compose part of the guest list in all hotel properties. In large convention hotels, which cater to sizable groups of businessmen and businesswomen, some consideration must be given to their particular wants (see Chapter 4) on luncheon menus and, particularly, on dinner menus. Other food facilities in the hotel, and outside restaurants that invariably locate near a large hotel, must be considered competitors.

## Room Service

This food business is unique to hotels. With sufficient beverage business it can be a profit center. Food service, on the other hand, is a cost center in many hotels. We want to again emphasize that the manager is running a hotel, not a rooms, food, or beverage business. Consistent with that thought, the food service to the rooms should be operated in a manner that gives the best food and service to the room guest that physical conditions will allow. In pursuit of this ideal some interesting programs have been initiated.

Long before any pizza parlor promised delivery service in a specified time, ambitious hotels (in some cases foolishly ambitious) promised continental breakfasts delivered with breakneck speed, or the food would be complimentary. To achieve this noble ambition a service elevator, or in very large properties more than one service elevator, was used exclusively for this purpose. The elevator was equipped with juice, coffee, and rolls and the appropriate equipment to keep the products hot or cold. This type of service is still used in some properties, but the time guarantees have been removed. Other than at breakfast, there is not a great premium on speed.

Common in many hotels is a service that allows guests to place breakfast orders by telephone the previous night and to specify the time they want the food delivered.

### Room Service Menus

In years past when some hotels thrived on the travel of the wealthy, an excellent food service to rooms was a point of pride for the hotel, as was a very fancy classical restaurant with fine linens and a profusion of silver. Few such hotels exist today. They may be seen in the television show devoted to the antics of the "rich and famous." Today the traveling public include many more businesspeople and vacationing families. Some of the former and most of the latter patronize motor inns that have no room service and no restaurant. The continental breakfast in the lobby is the beginning and end of such hotels' adventuring into the food business. However, there remain many fine hotels in the medium to large cities that still fit the conglomerate category.

Room service menus should be written after the menus for the hotel restaurants have been completed, because room service items that require advanced preparation can be chosen from those other menus without creating any additional work for the kitchen staff and becoming a source of leftovers. The emphasis on not creating extra work for the preparation staff also means that the best possible service can be given to the room service guests.

Hotel suites are often used for serving small banquets of ten to fifteen persons. Banquet rooms are usually built to accommodate twenty-five or more, so a group of ten or fifteen are "lost" in a larger room.

Most hotels offer a between-meals menu that consists of a limited number of a la carte items. In the directory of services, a card offering hot and cold hors d'oeuvres, canapés, and snack items is found.

## Hotel Restaurants

In recent years, without abandoning the idea that the food department is supportive of the primary rooms department, many hotels have been depending more on the food department as a profit center. This has been characterized by the creation of theme restaurants operated, for the most part, independent of the overall hotel operation. Another step toward a profitable food operation in hotels has been the contracting of the business to outside food companies, particularly chain operations.

## The American Plan

This type of operation is normally limited to resort hotels. Guests pay one price, which includes the room rent and the cost of the meals. As part of the accounting procedures, prices are allotted to each meal. The prices assigned to the meals are important to the menu-writing team because the food operation is expected to produce profit on the same basis as do hotels on the so-called European Plan, in which guests are charged separately for rooms and meals. Food selections must therefore be made to yield a budgeted food cost of sales.

The use of "cycle" menus is a practical approach to planning menus for properties using the American Plan. The length of the cycle can be based on the average stay of customers. A seven-day rotation covers the needs of most resort properties. The ability to forecast with great accuracy how much food to prepare yields food costs two to three points lower than the food costs of a city restaurant with the same menu selections and prices. Another contributing factor to low food costs in resort operations is that meals are paid for but sometimes not eaten. The pattern of guests' consumption is that they eat rather heartily during the first two days of their stay. Their food consumption then tapers off considerably, and some guests even skip meals completely.

## Conventions

Resort hotels have become popular places for convention groups. The recreation facilities on premises make it possible to control the time participants spend outside of meetings by scheduling events such as golf tournaments and tennis competitions. This combination of work and play is conducive to successful business sessions.

Convention banquet meals in an American Plan property in which dining room meals are included in the daily room rate are handled by charging only an additional amount per person rather than a regular banquet price. This is arranged in personal negotiations with the people in charge of the convention. Resort properties located near independent restaurant facilities may operate on a modified American Plan. Breakfast and dinner may be part of the overall price, and guests can take luncheon wherever they want. Dinner may be the open meal in some resorts.

## Hotel Banquets

Banquets are an important part of food revenue in many hotels, contributing 50 percent or more of the total sales. Chapter 9 is devoted exclusively to a consideration of banquet menus.

# 9 Writing Banquet Menus

**Purpose:** To review points that must be considered in writing banquet menus.

The Merriam-Webster dictionary defines banquet as "an elaborate and often ceremonious meal for numerous people often in honor of a person." The average person booking a banquet or attending one probably defines a banquet in much the same way as Merriam-Webster. In the interest of good marketing, the banquet manager need merely think of two things: first, present a meal a bit above the ordinary fare of the customer and, second, stage it in surroundings that are in keeping with the special occasion.

## The Banquet Office

The first thing to remember about the banquet office is that it is the customer's initial contact with the business. First impressions are important impressions. The banquet office itself must be a selling instrument. The location should be easy to find and in a pleasant environment. The waiting room can continue this selling process by having comfortable and attractive furniture and floor coverings. If space is ample, a glass cabinet can act as a display case for several pieces of highly polished holloware; such a display accentuates the prospect of elegant service. To continue selling to customers, use wall space to hang pictures of past successful banquets. Fresh flowers add warmth. A tea wagon can be brought into the banquet waiting room, and tea and coffee and small pastries can be served by room service. Consider including a small bar in the waiting room. You may be surprised to find that many elderly ladies enjoy a cocktail in the morning.

The banquet manager's private office, in which the final arrangements are usually made, must also contribute to the selling effort by offering comfortable furniture and an orderly desk that suggests confidence and competence. The customer's ego can be used to great advantage in banquet selling, especially in increasing the size of the banquet check. A large hotel in the northeast had, and perhaps still has, an arrangement of banquet-selling rooms specifically designed to play on the customer's ego. There is a large banquet office waiting room and two smaller rooms. All three rooms have a wall with a one-way mirror. (You can look in and observe customers but customers cannot see you.) A customer is ushered into the central waiting room, and when one of the smaller rooms becomes available is escorted into this auxiliary space. If space is immediately available in a smaller room, the customer is still given a short period to relax in the central room, which is luxuriously furnished and suggests that a beautiful banquet is waiting. On a table in the smaller room is a book of color photographs showing affairs of the type the customer is there to arrange. As the customer looks at this book, he or she is being watched through the one-way mirror. After the guest has had ample time to examine the book of photographs, the salesperson enters and looks at the picture in the opened book, commenting that it depicts the wedding of the daughter of a person known by this potential customer who is, incidentally, there to arrange for her daughter's wedding banquet. She is subtly told that the cost of the pictured banquet was $50.00 per person. The customer unconsciously decides immediately that she must arrange for an affair at $60.00.

This is an illustration of the ultimate method of playing on the customer's ego to raise the banquet check. It has proven to be almost always effective. You decide on the ethics of the system.

## Planning the Banquet Menu

Banquet menus for affairs such as weddings are usually tailored for the occasion; each item is suggested by the salesperson and agreed on by the customer. Most banquet menus sold in average hotels and restaurants are selected from previously written menus, with minor alterations made. These menus are properly coordinated in the selection of an entrée and the supporting items—appetizer through dessert. When an appointment is made, the banquet salesperson ascertains the type of affair to be arranged and chooses appropriate menus to offer as suggestions. Several crucial points must be considered in correctly fitting the customer's affair with a menu.

### How Many Will Be Served?

Food items, whether appetizer, entrée, salad, or dessert, have minimum and maxi-
mum amounts that can be served. You must consider these limitations to create a successful banquet. For example, a dinner of boiled lobster for eight hundred people is beyond the physical capacity of most hotels and restaurants unless special equipment is set up for the occasion. Most customers will accept the fact that very large parties will limit the number of items that can be successfully served.

It is the practice in some hotels that a small banquet committee will be served a sample meal of the one chosen for a large group. It is important not to add frills at this sample meal that cannot be practically supplied for the larger function.

### Who Will Be Served?

Another point to observe in selling a banquet function is the type of group to be served. Are they businessmen, working women, young people, the elderly? Perhaps it is a mixed group of men and women of a wide age range. Do they all share a common ethnic background? Often banquets cater to groups of the same occupation. Most professional groups have annual meetings or conventions that include private luncheons and dinners.

It has been said that to be successful most actions depend 90 percent on preparation and 10 percent on execution. This is certainly true of food and beverage functions. To guests, last-minute decisions usually translate into no preparation. In Chapter 4 we advised people in the food business to know their customers. In selling banquets you may encounter representatives of every group on any given day. It behooves the banquet planner to properly identify them and adjust plans as necessary.

### What Is the Occasion?

By definition, a banquet is "an elaborate and sometimes a ceremonious meal for numerous people often in honor of a person." To make proper arrangements you must know why the customer is requesting a particular banquet. In commercial hotels, business functions are the most common affairs. You must know *who* is to attend, as we outlined above. But more specifically, you must know the purpose of the banquet: Is this a routine business luncheon or dinner or is it commemorating a special occasion? Although sometimes we deplore the fact that congressional elections are held every two years, those involved in the banquet business do not. Political rallies and meetings often include banquets not only at congressional election time but on the occasion of presidential, state, and local elections. These gatherings are often fund-raising events, and tickets are sold at a much greater price than the catering unit's fee. Often the sponsors of such events want to arrange for as cheap a meal as possible in order to increase the amount raised. You should do your best to resist such a request because if persons buy tickets for, say, $50.00 and are served an obviously low-priced meal, they tend to be dissatisfied with the caterer rather than with the sponsor of the banquet. In such cases the caterer is a loser in more than one respect. The profit is low even on this cheap meal, enemies are made, and the prestige of the establishment is lowered.

The inconsistencies of drinking persons are often demonstrated by the fact that the "eye opener" and the "night cap" are poured from the same whiskey bottle. In the same vein, it may seem that banquets are held both as welcoming affairs for persons arriving on the scene and as going away parties for those leaving. In any case banquets serve as occasions for ceremonious get-togethers. In Jewish tradition a young man's bar mitzvah is an occasion for a party. Young Jewish ladies are honored at bas mitzvah ceremonies. Springtime can be identified in many hotels by the profusion of both high school and college proms and later by graduation parties. New businesses are opened by ribbon cuttings, special sales, gifts, and, of course, the banquet. Anniversaries of all kinds offer banquet opportunities to the caterer who pursues all the sources of possible business.

A few years ago, retirement from a business meant an inevitable gold watch properly inscribed and presented with great emotion at a banquet. The tradition of the watch has faded away, but to the delight of the purveyor of food functions, the tradition of the banquet has survived. At the beginning of this section we defined a banquet as often given in honor of a person. We will end discussion of possible occasions for a banquet here, but with a little imagination you can extend the list indefinitely.

## What Do Customers Want?

In Chapter 4 we outlined the preferences of different individuals and groups. Those suggestions have some bearing on banquets but are primarily directed to customers' desires for restaurant dining. In the following outline we list what the banquet manager or salesperson needs to know about what items are popular with different groups. Only two groups need to be considered—men and women. At breakfast both men and women order the same foods, but they have different preferences at luncheon.

### Luncheon—Women
*First Course*
Stock soup
Consommé
Cold soups
Fruit soups
Salad-tizers
Chef's
Avocado
Fruit
Mixed vegetable
Mixed green
Compotes
Fruits
Melons
*Entrées*
Chicken (not fried)
Fresh fish
Creamed, au gratin dishes
Mixed grills
Lamb chops—cutlets
Individual casserole dishes

Salad plates
    Chicken
    Shrimp
    Tuna
    Fruit gelatin molds
    Stuffed tomato (chicken, shrimp, tuna)
*Vegetables*
  Asparagus
  Peas
  Fresh (in season)
*Colorful Garnishes*
*Desserts*
  Fruit ices
  Melon
  Grapefruit
  Cobblers
  Decorated gelatin
  Parfaits
  Flan (custards)
  Ice cream bombs
  Strawberries
  Big "gobby" desserts
  (No pies or cakes)
*Breads*
  Melba toast
  Toasted rolls
*Wines*
  Chablis
  Rose
  Liebfraumilch
*Coffee*—plenty

**Luncheon—Men**
  *First Course*
    "Gutsy" soups
    Big salads—bleu cheese dressing
    Baked grapefruit
    Melons
    Shrimp cocktail
    Fruit cocktail
    Asparagus vinaigrette
(*Note*: A favorite at luncheon for both men and women is the Colonel Huntington Salad made with chicken, avocado, greens, raw cauliflower, tomato, and lo-cal dressing)
  *Entrées*
    Pot roast
    Lamb chop
    Veal cutlet

Small steak
Prime rib
Crab cakes
Broiled fresh fish
Mixed grill
Shish kebab
Fried shrimp
Beef or lamb stew
Curries
*Potatoes*
  Hashed browns
  Baked
  Au gratin
  Oven roasted
  O'Brien
  Scalloped
  French fries
  Potato pancakes
  Rice pilaf
*Vegetables*
  Two fresh
  String beans
  Summer squash
  Peas and mushrooms
  Scalloped tomatoes
  Broccoli
  Asparagus
  Onion rings
  Mashed butternut squash
*Salads as a Main Course*
    Shrimp
    Crabmeat
    Lobster
*Side Salads*
  Mixed green
  Cole slaw
  Spinach
  Lettuce and tomato
*Desserts*
  Apple pie cobbler
  Chocolate cake
  Ice cream sundaes
  Banana split cake
  French pastry tarts
  Baked apple
  Bombs
  Gobs—Gobs—Gobs
*Bread*—hot
*Coffee*—plenty

**Dinner**

Men and women order the same entrées. The different preferences for appetizers and desserts parallel what they want for a luncheon. Women take smaller portions.

## Booking a Banquet

In addition to arranging what food to serve at a banquet, you need considerable additional information in order to execute a successful function. Gather the name, address, telephone number, and the organization involved (if there is one) during the initial contact, which is ordinarily by telephone; at this time also set up a personal appointment. If the date of the function was not set in the telephone conversation, it should be the first thing to establish at the personal meeting. The desired space must be available. You need to know the starting time of the meal and the number to be served in order to establish a schedule for preparing the room, preparing the food, and arranging for service personnel. Banquet business follows an irregular pattern, so waiters and waitresses to service functions, except for a core staff, are not on the regular payroll. In areas in which there are labor unions, the temporary hiring of service personnel is arranged through the union.

Note the table arrangement and linens. Is it a formal affair? Flowers are a usual decoration for all banquets except regularly scheduled business luncheons. If there is to be music, is the booking to be made by the hotel or by the group having the party? Will a stage be necessary? Will there be a show? If so, are special lighting effects needed? Most business banquets and some social affairs have speeches to be made. A lectern will handily facilitate this and any introductions, speeches, or reports that are to be given. A perhaps unfortunate need is provisions for security. Business meetings often require a blackboard or a projector and screen, and a public-address system. Providing cigars and cigarettes was a routine part of social and business functions, but this practice has been diminished or eliminated in most places since the health warnings

from the Department of Health during the past twenty or thirty years. However, cigars are making a strong and well-publicized comeback.

Exhibit 9-1 is a banquet booking sheet. Note that it lists most of the needs of a function. This provides a handy reference as well as a regular space to note requirements. The service of beverages and proper arrangements will be discussed in Chapter 15.

## How Much Will the Customer Spend?

You can successfully set the price of a banquet as part of the sale, or you can cause price to become an abrasive element for the customer. It is best to refrain from quoting a price until all arrangements have been made. At that point, one price should be quoted that includes all the patron's needs. A particularly irritating way to handle price is to present it as a "laundry list": $12.00 for the meal, $5.00 for the lectern, $10.00 for the P.A. system, $6.50 for the checkroom, and so on. These additional charges are really minimal when reduced to a per-meal charge for a banquet serving even a modest number of people, but it is still irritating to the customer who, at the time, is not interested in engaging in arithmetic. Part of the skill of a good salesperson is to be able to judge how much customers are willing to spend. After making this judgment, you should not accept it as a certain maximum but begin by offering products priced somewhat higher. In this way, you provide for a slight error, but an error in your favor. A good salesperson will quickly ascertain if the misjudgment was on the high side and adjust accordingly. Quite often when a hotel books a convention, the person making the arrangements requests sample menus be mailed, sometimes months in advance of the convention. The price the group expects to pay is given. In honoring this request, a letter specifically designed as a selling tool should accompany the material.

**Exhibit 9-1**
**Banquet booking sheet**

Name of organization: _____

Address: _____

Nature of function: _____

Day of week: _____ Date: _____ Time: _____

Room: _____ Rent: _____

Name of engagor: _____

Address: _____

Responsibility of party: _____

Price per person: $_____ Gratuity: _____ Minimum no.: _____

Guarantee: _____ Maximum attendance: _____

| **Food menu** | **Beverage menu** |
|---|---|
| | Cash: _____ Charge: _____ |
| | Corkage: _____ |
| | Room for bar: _____ |
| | Open: _____ Close: _____ |
| | Bartender charge: _____ |
| | Types of beverages: _____ |
| | |
| | **Staff** |

Table arrangements: _____ Head: _____

Flowers: _____ Centerpiece: _____ Checking: _____

Ticket table: _____ Blackboard: _____ P.A.: _____ Stage: _____

Lectern: _____ Screen: _____ Piano: _____ Music: _____

Platform: _____ Dance floor: _____

**Remarks:**                **Comments by party:**

Copies to:                     **Date booked:** _____

Customer: _____ Chef: _____

Catering office: _____ Accounting: _____

Housemen: _____ Maitre d': _____

Bar: _____                                              By: _____

## Who Pays, and Can He or She?

There is an old maxim in business that advises, "The sale isn't completed until payment is received." This suggests that it makes little sense to go ahead with arrangements until the matter of who is going to pay the bill is settled. The widespread use of credit cards makes payment routine, but only when a card is to be used. You simply need to acquire the card number prior to the banquet and check if the credit card is valid. If payment is to be made by check, the banquet manager should not hesitate to get the information necessary to check the customer's ability to pay. A word to the wise: In the case of political parties, get money in advance!

## Writing Banquet Menus

As we mentioned, some banquet menus, especially for very high-priced affairs, are developed item by item through management's suggestion and customer's agreement. However, *most* banquets are arranged by customers' selecting from previously prepared menus. Such menus can be in several different formats. For example, individual menus listing appetizers through desserts present a complete package. There is an advantage to this kind of menu in that they were prepared by professionals who consider the following: the colors of the different food items in order to arrange an attractive plate; a balance of foods with respect to their type—starch, protein, and so forth; and the bulk of foods, for the comfort of the diner in consuming the meal. A common method of preparing banquet menus for the customer to consider is to offer a page that contains an assortment of appetizers, soups, entrées, vegetables, salads, desserts, and beverages. Whatever the customer selects, the price will be the same. This same type of presentation may show separate prices for different entrée items, and additional charges for certain appetizers, soups, and salad dressings. The guest makes the choices among the appetizers, entrées, desserts, and so on under the guidance of the banquet manager, whose counsel is important to avoid choices that can be disappointing when served—for example, a plate containing a cream sauce on the entrée with cauliflower and mashed potatoes. In this case guests are presented a sea of white, which is not an appealing sight.

### The Wording of Banquet Menus

Writing banquet menus with respect to verbally presenting items is the same as writing restaurant menus. You should provide an interesting, appetizing, factual description of each item. Some pizzazz is welcome, but wording should not be too flowery and certainly not dishonest. Some French terms can be used in describing classical items, but the use of foreign terms could seem snobbish. Very simply put, descriptive conversational language is the best. Consider this example:

Cutlet of Plume du veau Veal Sautéed in Fresh
Lemon Juice and Sweet Creamery Butter

The next example gives a quite elegant impression and possibly borders on being flowery. But on close examination it is a series of words familiar to anyone booking a banquet, with a musical flow that whets the appetite.

Fresh California Strawberries Marinated
in Fine Cognac and Served on
Baked Alaska—Paraded Flambé and
Served in Room—Saluté

## Pricing Banquet Menus

The ideal situation for pricing banquet menus is the "tailor-made" method mentioned; that is, when a customer has made all the decisions regarding the food to be served and additional items needed (e.g., lectern, microphone). However, it is a good policy to have guidelines in pricing the meal. Markups on low-cost items need to be more than on high-cost items because labor and surrounding costs are much the same in both instances. Sample banquet menus presented to potential guests need not be complete with prices. Persons arranging banquets should be aware of market conditions and adjust pricing accordingly. This is important not only to be sure prices are increased as the cost of an item moves upward, but also to offer pleasing price incentives to customers that at the same time provide a better profit.

## Banquet Menus

Following are menus that form a packet for the customers' perusal, prepared by the Radisson Suite Resort on Sand Key in Clearwater, Florida. Note there are no prices on any of the menus except some specialty items on the dinner menu for addition to or substitution from the regular items that range from soup through dessert.

Exhibit 9-2, the selection of breakfast menus, includes both buffet and waiter-served meals. Note the buffet requires a minimum of fifty guests. This allow an attractive and generous presentation of the foods. A brunch menu is also included in the exhibit. It is a pleasure just to imagine this variety of items served on a seaside veranda and accompanied by champagne.

## Breakfast Buffet

### LAND LOVER

Selection of Chilled Fruit Juices on Ice
Carved Watermelon Boat with Fresh Fruit
Fluffy Scrambled Eggs        Potatoes O'Brien
Hickory Bacon and Country Link Sausages
Baskets of Muffins, Croissants and Petite Danish with Creamery Butter and Fruit Preserves
Coffee, Selected Teas and Fresh Brewed Decaffeinated Coffee

## Brunch

### THE RADISSON BAYSIDE BRUNCH

Mimosa Sand Key - Fresh Orange Juice with Champagne and a Splash of Triple Sec (One Per Person)
Iced Carafes of Select Chilled Juices
Chef's Selection of Breakfast Bakeries (Croissants, Bagels and Muffins with Preserves and Creamery Butter)
Mirrors of Sliced Fresh Tropical Fruits
Hearty Mueslix and Fruit Yogurt on Ice with Milk, Cream and Honey
Fluffy Scrambled Eggs        Crisp Bacon and Sausage
Cottage Fried Potatoes or Roast Potatoes

*– Select Two Salads –*
Pasta Primavera Salad        Sliced Beefsteak Tomato and Fresh Mozzarella        Fresh Seasonal Greens and Dressings
Marinated Baby Shrimp and Pasta Salad        Cucumber and Dill Salad

*– Select Three Entrees –*
Eggs Benedict        Slices of Smoked Salmon with Mini Bagels and Cream Cheese        Sliced Sirloin of Beef
Grilled Mahi Mahi with Key Lime Butter        Apple Crepes with Fruit Toppings
Stuffed Medallions of Tropical Chicken with Citrus Herb Sauce        Honey Coconut French Toast
Eggs Bona-Vita (Toasted English Muffin topped with Artichoke Bottoms, Poached Eggs and Bearnaise)

Coffee, Selected Teas and Brewed Decaffeinated Coffee

### Exhibit 9-2
### Breakfast banquet and buffet menus
*Reprinted with permission from the Radisson Suite Resort on Sand Key in Clearwater, Florida*

## Breakfast

### THE AMERICAN
Selection of Chilled Juices, Farm Fresh Scrambled
Eggs, Crisp Bacon or Grilled Country Sausages,
Breakfast Potatoes, Basket of Muffins, Croissants
and Petite Danish Pastries, Coffee, Selected Teas
and Brewed Decaffeinated Coffee.

### HARBOR BENEDICT
Fresh Squeezed Orange Juice, Twin Poached Eggs
with Grilled Canadian Bacon on Crisp
English Muffins with Sauce Hollandaise,
Coffee, Selected Teas and
Brewed Decaffeinated Coffee.

### THE CONTINENTAL
Selection of Chilled Juices, Fruit Flavored Yogurt
on Ice, Rainbow of Sliced Fresh Fruits, Warm
Assortment of Breakfast Bakeries, Butter and
Preserves, Coffee, Selected Teas and
Brewed Decaffeinated Coffee.

### HONEY COCONUT TOAST
Selection of Chilled Juices, Lightly Battered Raisin
Bread browned on the Griddle, glazed with
Honey and Toasted Coconut, Crisp Bacon or
Country Sausage, Coffee, Selected Teas
and Brewed Decaffeinated Coffee.

## Breakfast Buffet

### OUTRIGGER
*(Minimum 50 Guests)*

Selection of Chilled Fruit Juices on Ice

Mirrors of Whole and Sliced Fresh Tropical Fruits

Selected Dry Cereals

Fluffy Scrambled Eggs with Shredded Cheddar Cheese

Choice of Pancakes or Apple Crepes with Fruit Toppings

Crisp Bacon and Spicy Link Sausages

Cottage Fried Potatoes

Baskets of Muffins, Croissants and Petite Danish with Creamery Butter and Fruit Preserves

Coffee, Selected Teas and Fresh Brewed Decaffeinated Coffee

*Exhibit 9-2, continued*

Exhibit 9-3 presents a variety of luncheons to satisfy every appetite and occasion. If you would rather have a buffet, see Exhibit 9-4 for four items ranging from simple to deluxe.

Exhibit 9-5 is an offering of banquet dinners. The white, red, and blush (White Zinfandel) wines are suggested to complement the meals.

Exhibit 9-6 is a list of items from which to build reception menus. The wide selection of items can be fashioned in numerous combinations, from very simple to very sumptuous.

What has become an important part of conventions and meetings is the break for coffee or refreshments. Exhibit 9-7 offers items for about any type of break one can dream up. Note that not all breaks need include food and drink.

## Salads & Fruits

*All Luncheon Salads will include Rolls and Butter, Selection of Dessert and Beverage.*

### CHEF SALAD
Julienne of Ham, Turkey, American, Swiss Cheese
on a Bed of Chilled Greens with Tomato and
Hard Boiled Egg, Choice of Dressing.

### SAND KEY DUO
Chicken and Tuna Salad atop Vine-Ripe Tomato,
accompanied with Fresh Fruits in Season.

### GRILLED CHICKEN CAESAR
Marinated Chicken Breast grilled and nestled
atop Crisp Caesar Salad.

### FLORIDA FRESH FRUIT PLATE
Seasonal Fresh Fruit surrounded by Date-Nut
Bread and Cream Cheese Finger Sandwiches
and a Scoop of Cottage Cheese or
Strawberry Honey Yogurt.

### SALAD NICOISE
Grilled Swordfish, New Potatoes, Egg Wedges,
Olives, Tomato Wedges, Green Beans and Sprouts
on a Bed of Bibb Lettuce and Radicchio
with Fresh Oregano Dressing.

## Specialty Items & Hot Sandwiches

*All Luncheon Sandwiches will include Selection of Dessert and Beverage.*

### QUICHE LORRAINE
A Delicate Pie Crust filled with Swiss Cheese and
Ham, baked in a Light Custard, accompanied with
Fruit Garnish, House Salad and Rolls and Butter.

### "YACHT CLUB" CROISSANT
A Light and Flaky Croissant filled with Shaved Ham
and Turkey, Crisp Bacon, Lettuce, Tomato and
Mayonnaise. Accompanied with Potato Chips.

### "PELICAN'S POUCH"
Shaved Lean Ham with Shredded Cheddar Cheese
in a Pita Pocket with Lettuce and Tomato.
Accompanied with a Pasta Salad.

### REUBEN
A Combination of Corned Beef, Sauerkraut and
Swiss Cheese on Marble Rye with Our Special Dressing.
Accompanied with French Fries.

### CHICKEN CASHEW CROISSANT SANDWICH
Tender Chicken Breast rolled in Chopped Cashews
and sauteed with Our Special Dijonnaise.
Accompanied with French Fries.

### TENDERLOIN TIPS SANDWICH
Tender Tips of Filet sauteed with Onions and topped with
Cheddar Cheese, served on a Sourdough Baguette.
Accompanied with French Fries.

## Box Lunches

### DELI SANDWICH
Layered Slices of Ham, Turkey, Genoa Salami,
Swiss Cheese and Provolone Cheese garnished with
Onion and Tomato on a French Roll, Hard Boiled Egg,
Fresh Fruit in Season, Potato Chips and Granola Bar.

### FRIED CHICKEN
Golden Fried Chicken, Hard Boiled Egg, Half Sandwich
of Baked Ham and Swiss Cheese on Rye,
Pasta Salad, Fresh Fruit in Season
and Chocolate Brownie.

*All Box Lunches include Appropriate Condiments and Disposable Ware.*

**Exhibit 9-3**
**Luncheon banquet menus**
*Reprinted with permission from the Radisson Suite Resort on Sand Key in Clearwater, Florida*

# Lunch Entrees

*All Luncheon Entrees will include Our Garden Fresh Salad with Champagne Dressing, Fresh Vegetable Medley, Choice of Potato, Rolls and Butter, Selection of Dessert and Beverage.*

## Beef & Pork Entrees

**SLICED ROAST TOP SIRLOIN of BEEF**
Served with a Mushroom Cabernet Sauce.

**LONDON BROIL**
*(Maximum 50 Guests)*
Sliced Marinated Flank Steak served with Bordelaise Sauce.

**NEW YORK STRIP STEAK**
We Cut Our Strip Steaks from the Center of the Loin for the most Tender Steaks, crowned with Maitre d'Butter.

**ROAST LOIN of PORK**
Cuban Style Roast Pork served with Black Bean Salsa, Yellow Rice and Fried Plantains.

## Seafood Entrees

**GRILLED CARIBBEAN SHRIMP**
Grilled Shrimp in Tropical Fruit Salsa and Passion Fruit Glaze.

**GRILLED SWORDFISH**
Seasoned with Lemon Pepper and served with a Pineapple Papaya Chutney.

**GROUPER FILLET**
Fresh Florida Grouper served Your Way: Broiled, Blackened or Baked.

## Poultry & Veal Entrees

**CHICKEN CASHEW**
Tender Boneless, Skinless Breast of Chicken seasoned with Dijon Mustard and a touch of Dill, sprinkled with Chopped Cashews.

**CHICKEN ORIENTAL**
A Skinless, Boneless Chicken Breast marinated in a Teriyaki Marinade, broiled and served with Oriental Vegetables.

**CHICKEN & SHRIMP STIR-FRY**
Sliced Chicken Breast and Tender Gulf Shrimp, stir-fried with Oriental Vegetables and served with a Light Teriyaki Glaze.

**ISLAND CHICKEN**
Tender, Boneless, Skinless Chicken Breast seasoned with Tropical Spices, grilled and topped with a Zesty Citrus Sauce.

**VEAL MARSALA**
Tender Veal lightly sauteed in Marsala Wine Sauce.

**VEAL PICCATA**
Lightly Sauteed Veal Medallions served with Fresh Lemon and Capers.

**VEAL OSCAR**
Lightly Breaded Sauteed Veal Medallions topped with Asparagus, Crabmeat and Bearnaise.

## Pasta Entrees

**SEAFOOD FETTUCCINI**
Tender Fettuccini Noodles with Shrimp, Crabmeat and Grouper, sauteed and served in a Light Cream Sauce.

**CHICKEN & PASTA PRIMAVERA**
Strips of Chicken Tenderloin sauteed with Fresh Vegetables, tossed with Fettuccini Noodles in a Light Cream Sauce.

**VEGETABLE PASTA**
Tender Fettuccini Noodles sauteed with Tomatoes, Mushrooms, Artichoke Hearts, Black Olives and served in a Light White Wine Parmesan Cheese Sauce.

*Exhibit 9-3, continued*

# Isle Del Sol Buffet
### (Minimum of 50 Guests)

Soup of the Day

Marinated Vegetable and Penne Pasta Salad

Salad of Seasonal Greens with Choice of Dressing

*– Select Two Entrees –*

Scaloppine of Veal with Lemon and Herbs

Roast Top Sirloin of Beef

Broiled Grouper with Lemon Butter Sauce

Chicken and Pasta Primavera

Potato and Seasonal Vegetables

New York Cheesecake with Fresh Strawberries

Islander Key Lime Pie

Beverage

# American Grill Buffet
### (Minimum 50 Guests)

Relish Tray

Potato Salad     Cole Slaw     Macaroni Salad

Hamburgers (Cheese on request) and Hot Dogs Cooked on the Grill

Hamburger and Hot Dog Buns

Baked Beans

Sliced Tomatoes, Onions and Lettuce

Watermelon

Assorted Large Cookies

Beverage

**Exhibit 9-4**
**Luncheon buffet menus**
*Reprinted with permission from the Radisson Suite Resort on Sand Key in Clearwater, Florida*

# Southern Plantation Buffet
*(Minimum of 50 Guests)*

Tropical Fruit Salad

Green Bean, Tomato and Red Potato Salad

Salad of Seasonal Greens with Choice of Dressing

*– Select Two Entrees –*

Baked Breast of Chicken with Herb Stuffing

Maryland Crabcakes with Louisiana Relish

Broiled Red Snapper with Lemon Butter Sauce

Potato and Vegetable in Season

Rolls and Creamery Butter

Plantation Pecan Pie

Praline Cake

Beverage

# Key West Deli Buffet
*(For Parties of 20 or More)*

Cup of Soup du Jour

Relish Tray

Assortment of Salads consisting of Pasta Salad, Potato Salad,
Fresh Seasonal Greens with Champagne Dressing

Sliced Ham, Turkey, Roast Beef and Corned Beef

Swiss and American Cheese

Selection of Specialty Breads

Potato Chips

Double Chocolate Brownies

Beverage

(Add Fresh Fruit and Chicken or Tuna Salad for an additional 2.00 Per Person)

*Exhibit 9-4, continued*

## Dinner

*To Enhance Your Dining Experience, May We Suggest the Following Specialties...*

### Appetizers

**Fresh Fruit Cup**   1.50

**Shrimp Cocktail**   5.75

**Escargot with Boursin in Puff Pastry**   5.75

### Soups

**Baked French Onion Soup**   1.50

**Conch Chowder**   1.95

**Gazpacho**   1.50

### Salads

**Caesar Salad**   1.75       **Spinach Salad**   1.75

**Mixed Wild Greens with Raspberry Vinaigrette and Pine Nuts**   2.50

### Dinner Wine Service

*Continuous Dinner Wine Service with Your Meal*

**Chardonnay, Cabernet Sauvignon and White Zinfandel**   4.50 Per Person

### Dinner Entrees

*All Entrees will include Soup du Jour, Our Garden Fresh Salad with Champagne Dressing, Fresh Vegetable Medley, Potatoes or Rice, Rolls and Butter, Selection of Dessert and Beverage.*

### Beef

**SLICED ROAST TOP SIRLOIN of BEEF**
Served with a Mushroom Cabernet Sauce.

**ROAST PRIME RIB of BEEF**
Served in its Natural Juices with
Creamed Horseradish Sauce.

**TOURNEDOS of BEEF**
With a Caramelized Onion and Ale Sauce.

**FILET MIGNON GRILL**
Crowned with a Mushroom Cap and
accompanied with Bearnaise Sauce.

**NEW YORK STRIP MAITRE d'HOTEL**
We Cut Our Strip Steaks from the Center of the Loin, for the most
Tender Steaks, crowned with Maitre d'Butter.

### Seafood

**SAUTEED GROUPER**
Sauteed and topped with a Key Lime Butter,
laced with Macadamia Nuts.

**GRILLED SWORDFISH**
Seasoned with Lemon Pepper, served with
Pineapple Papaya Chutney.

**GRILLED CARIBBEAN SHRIMP**
With Tropical Fruit Salsa and
Passion Fruit Glaze.

**BROILED RED SNAPPER**
Gulf Red Snapper broiled and accompanied with
a Lemon Dill Sauce.

**REEF and BEEF**
A Grilled Filet Mignon and Baked Lobster Tail or Shrimp, accompanied with
Bearnaise, Fresh Lemon and plenty of Drawn Butter.

**Exhibit 9-5**
**Dinner banquet menus**

*Reprinted with permission from the Radisson Suite Resort on Sand Key in Clearwater, Florida*

## Veal & Poultry

**VEAL OSCAR**
Lightly Breaded Veal Medallions
sauteed and topped with Asparagus,
Crabmeat and Bearnaise.

**VEAL PICCATA**
Tender Medallions of Milk-Fed Veal sauteed and
served with Fresh Lemon and Capers.

**VEAL MARSALA**
Tender Veal lightly sauteed, served in
a Marsala Wine Sauce.

**ISLAND CHICKEN**
Tender, Boneless, Skinless Chicken Breast
seasoned with Tropical Spices, grilled and
topped with a Zesty Citrus Sauce.

**CHICKEN SENA**
Boneless Chicken Breast sauteed with Mushrooms,
Rosemary and topped with Mornay Sauce.

**CHICKEN FORMAGE**
Tender Chicken Breast topped with Four Cheeses,
accompanied with a Roast Red Pepper Sauce.

**CHICKEN CASHEW**
Tender, Boneless, Skinless Breast of Chicken seasoned
with Dijon Mustard and a touch of Dill,
sprinkled with Chopped Cashews.

## Pasta

**SEAFOOD FETTUCCINI**
Tender Fettuccini Noodles with Shrimp, Crabmeat
and Grouper, sauteed and served in
a Light Cream Sauce.

**CHICKEN & PASTA PRIMAVERA**
Strips of Chicken Tenderloin sauteed with Fresh
Vegetables, tossed with Fettuccini Noodles
in a Light Cream Sauce.

**VEGETABLE PASTA**
Tender Fettuccini Noodles sauteed with Tomatoes, Mushrooms,
Artichoke Hearts, Black Olives and served in a Light
White Wine Parmesan Cheese Sauce.

## Desserts
*(Please Select One)*

| | | | |
|---|---|---|---|
| Mississippi Fudge | Moonlight Layer | Apple Pie | Carrot Cake |
| Islander Key Lime Pie | Plantation Pecan Pie | | Assorted Cheesecake |
| Chocolate-Chocolate Torte | | Black-White Espresso | |
| Irish Cream Mousse Cake | | Vienna Table | |
| Linzer Torte | | Raspberry Torte | |

For an additional 2.50 Per Person, we offer the following:

Bananas Foster          Cherries Jubilee          Crepes Suzette          Baked Alaska

*Exhibit 9-5, continued*

## *Specialty Stations*

**WHOLE SUGAR CURED HAM**
Carved by Our Chef, served with a
Honey Mustard Sauce, Rolls and Condiments.
*(Serves 50)*

**STEAMSHIP ROUND of BEEF**
A Standing Steamship Round, Expertly Carved,
served with Rolls and Condiments.
*(Approximately 60 Pounds - Serves 100)*

**SLICED TENDERLOIN**
The Most Tender Cut of Beef, Expertly Carved
and served with Bearnaise Sauce.
*(Serves 20)*

**TOP ROUND of BEEF**
Carved Baron of Beef served with Silver Dollar Rolls,
Horseradish Sauce and Au Jus.
*(Serves 40)*

**SCOTTISH SALMON**
A Side of Scottish Salmon, served with
Appropriate Garnish.
*(Serves Approximately 40)*

**CARVED ROAST TURKEY**
Cooked to a Golden Brown and
accompanied with Silver Dollar Rolls.
*(Serves 50)*

**PASTA STATION**
Marinara and Alfredo Sauces with Fettuccini,
Bowtie and Rainbow Tortellini,
Cooked to Order and
served with Garlic Rolls.
*(Minimum 50 Guests)*

**STIR-FRY STATION**
Crisp Garden Vegetables with a
Selection of Chicken or Pork,
served with Sweet & Sour and
Teriyaki Sauces and White Rice.
*(Shrimp or Scallops, additional 1.50 Per Person)*
*(Minimum 50 Guests)*

**FRUIT & CHOCOLATE FONDUE**
Assorted Tropical Fruit served with a
Rich Dark Chocolate. To complement and add
a Real Tropical Flair, let us Create Our
Unique Pineapple Fruit Tree.

**CONTINENTAL COFFEE**
Fresh Brewed Coffee served with
Whipped Cream, Cinnamon Sticks,
Orange Zest and
Shaved Chocolate.

**TACO BAR**
Mini Corn Taco Shells and Tortillas served with Taco Meat, Shredded Cheddar Cheese,
Sour Cream, Guacamole, Tomatoes, Lettuce, Salsa and Mexican Rice.
*(Minimum 25 Guests)*

## *Ice Carvings*

*Our Executive Chef will be pleased to create a replica of Your Company Logo or a Specialty Design in Ice
for Your Event. Our Selections include, but are not limited to:*

**Shrimp Boat     Eagle     Eiffel Tower     Gondola     Dolphin     Swan**

**Washington Monument     Flower Basket     Ice Bowl**

**Exhibit 9-6**
**Reception menu choices**
*Reprinted with permission from the Radisson Suite Resort on Sand Key in Clearwater, Florida*

## Cold Hors d'Oeuvres

*(Priced Per 50 Pieces)*

**JUMBO SHRIMP in ICE BOWL**

**CONTINENTAL FINGER SANDWICHES**

**SMOKED SALMON with APPROPRIATE GARNISH**

**ASSORTED DELUXE CANAPES**

**DEVILED EGGS with BAY SHRIMP**     **CHILLED CRAB CLAWS**

**FOUR FOOT DELI SUBMARINE SANDWICH** *(Serves 25 People)*

**CRISP GARDEN VEGETABLE TRAY** *(Serves 50 People)*
With Herb Cucumber Dip.

**ASSORTED SEAFOOD BAR** *(Minimum 50 People)*
Chilled Gulf Shrimp and Crab Claws served in a Shrimp Boat Ice Carving.

**FRUIT and CHEESE SELECTION** *(Serves 25 People)*
Elegant Mirror Display Selection which includes: Swiss, Cheddar, Monterey Jack, Brie
and Boursin, accompanied with Fresh Seasonal Fruit and Assorted Crackers.

**GUACAMOLE and TOSTADAS** *(Serves 25 People)*

**SELECTION of MIXED NUTS** *(Per Pound)*

**PRETZELS, CHIPS and DIP** *(Serves 25 People)*

## Hot Hors d'Oeuvres

*(Priced Per 50 Pieces)*

**BAKED BRIE en CROUTE**

**CAJUN SHRIMP**

**CAJUN STEAK TIDBITS**

**CHICKEN DRUMSTICKS**

**CHICKEN HAWAIIAN BROCHETTES**

**CHICKEN RUMAKI**

**CHICKEN SATAY**

**CON QUESO and TOSTADOS** *(Serves 25 People)*

**COCONUT FRIED SHRIMP**

**ESCARGOT in PUFF PASTRY
with BOURSIN CHEESE**

**FRIED WONTONS**

**INDIVIDUAL BEEF KABOBS**

**ITALIAN SAUSAGE STUFFED
MUSHROOM CAPS**

**LAMB CHOPS DIJON**

**MINI REUBEN BALLS**

**MUSHROOM CAPS with CRABMEAT**

**PETITE BBQ SPARERIBS**

**POLYNESIAN EGG ROLL**

**POT STICKERS**

**QUICHE LORRAINE**

**SCALLOPS WRAPPED in BACON**

**SESAME CHICKEN STRIPS**

**SWEET & SOUR MEATBALLS**

**TEMPURA VEGETABLES**

*Exhibit 9-6, continued*

## Theme Breaks

*All Theme Breaks served by Appropriately Dressed Attendants.*

### THE HEALTH FANATIC
Baskets of Granola Bars, Healthy Chilled
Yogurt, Fresh Fruit Tray,
Crisp Garden Vegetables and Dip,
Assorted Natural Juices and
Natural Fruit Bars.

### I WISH EVERYDAY WAS SUNDAE
Especially when you get to Create Your Own
with a Selection of Three Ice Creams,
a Luscious Selection of over 10 Fruits,
Chocolate and Novelty Toppings from which
to choose. Served with Assorted Sodas.

### MUFFIN MANIA
An Assortment of Fruit Muffins served with an
Assortment of Select Toppings from which to
choose, accompanied with Fresh Coffee.

### PLAY IT AGAIN SAM-WICH
Four Feet Long and Cut to Order!
Features Mounds of Thinly Sliced Deli Meats
and Imported Cheeses, topped with
Shredded Lettuce and Our Special Dressing.
Served with Assorted Sodas.

### CHOC-CHOC-CHOCOHOLIC BREAK
For Sinfully Rich Tastes! Chocolate Chip Cookies,
M&M's, Hershey's Kisses, Black & White Espresso
Torte, Chocolate Torte and Fresh Fruit Sections
ready to plunge into Pots of Chocolate Fondue.
Served with Ice Cold Milk.

### SEAFOOD FESTIVAL
A Tempting Sampling of Shrimp and Crab Claws
with plenty of Cocktail and Remoulade Sauces.
Served with Assorted Sodas.

## Group Recreation

*Ask for details on Our Complete listing of Theme Breaks and Events.*

### HEALTH FANATIC
A 10 - 15 minute stretch break is all your
attendees will need to re-energize themselves
and get ready for the meetings ahead.

### TOURNAMENTS
Feeling competitive, or if they'd just like a game between
"friends" the recreation department can organize a
volleyball tournament for you. Just say the word.

### BEACH OLYMPICS
Events are designed to boost energy, build camaraderie and
challenge the ability of your attendees.

**Exhibit 9-7**
**Theme break items and a la carte items**
*Reprinted with permission from the Radisson Suite Resort on Sand Key in Clearwater, Florida*

# A la Carte Items

## PASTRY ITEMS

Fresh Danish     Doughnuts     Coffee Cake     Assorted Muffins

Flaky Croissants     New York Style Bagels and Cream Cheese

Rich Chocolate Brownies     Granola Bars

Fresh Baked Cookies

Miniature European Pastries

## FRUIT & CHEESE SELECTIONS

Fresh Fruit Tray (Serves 25)

Domestic Cheese and Mirror of Tropical Fresh Fruit (Serves 25)

Imported Cheese and Mirror of Tropical Fresh Fruit (Serves 25)

## ICED SPECIALTIES

Assorted Ice Cream Bars

Natural Fruit Juice Bars

Individual Fruit Flavored Yogurt on Ice

## BEVERAGES

Mineral Waters (Regular or Flavored)

Assorted Natural Juices

Assorted Juices (Apple, Pineapple and Cranberry)

Freshly Squeezed Orange and Grapefruit Juice

Lemonade (Quart)     Iced Tea (Gallon)

Assorted Bottled Sodas

Specialty Coffees and Selection of Imported Bigelow Teas

*Exhibit 9-7, continued*

## Summary

Both hotels and restaurants that have function facilities will rely on banquets to produce more revenue during the 1990's, as we indicated in Chapter 1. Food and beverage banquets are currently providing 50 percent of the profits in many operations, and this percentage will increase as the added promotion of this type of food service operation adds volume. At the outset of this chapter we discussed the importance of the physical facilities and the administration of the banquet department. Exhibit 9-8, a banquet check list for hotel operations, outlines these facets of the banquet business.

**Exhibit 9-8**
**Banquet check list for hotel operations**

DATE _____ HOTEL _____

| Sat. | Unsat. | N/A | Item Description | Comments |
|------|--------|-----|------------------|----------|
| | | | *Banquet Sales Office* | |
| | | | Is the entire area of the banquet sales and the hotel sales office clean? | |
| | | | Is it attractive and well decorated? | |
| | | | Is it conducive to sales? | |
| | | | Is the office maintained in an orderly and professional manner? | |
| | | | Does the catering manager have an office large enough to accommodate a committee? | |
| | | | Is his office well decorated and does it provide privacy for clients? | |
| | | | *Are the Following Sales Tools Available?* | |
| | | | Are there photographs of various functions that have taken place in your hotel? | |
| | | | Are there pictures of prominent people displayed? | |
| | | | Are there various albums of leather-bound binders? | |
| | | | Do they show complimentary letters? | |
| | | | Do they show menus and colored photographs of various functions that have taken place? | |
| | | | Is there a display in the banquet manager's office? | |
| | | | Does it consist of various china that is available, as well as glassware, silver, candleabras, fancy fold napkins, colored linen? | |

**Exhibit 9-8**
*continued*

| Sat. | Unsat. | N/A | Item Description | Comments |
|------|--------|-----|-----------------|----------|
| | | | If yours is a large hotel, have you provided your catering manager with an attractive cabinet that might house a refrigerator for dispensing ice cubes, liquors, wines, so that during his discussion with clients, he can offer them a cocktail or drink? | |
| | | | *Does Your Banquet Office Have a Fact Book?* | |
| | | | Does this fact book contain current menus for each meal period and price? | |
| | | | Sample menus for special occasions? | |
| | | | Beverage listing and prices? | |
| | | | Miscellaneous food and beverage items and prices, e.g. whole roast turkey—$65.00? | |
| | | | Listing of public rooms and their capacities for various functions? | |
| | | | *Does it Contain an Information Sheet Regarding Guarantees and Policy of Credit?* | |
| | | | Rental listing for function space? | |
| | | | Listing of ballroom and function engineering facilities and their rentals or labor charges? | |
| | | | Data pertinent for exhibits and special functions? | |
| | | | Policy regarding cash and host bars? | |
| | | | Listing of other services and costs such as checkroom, floral, music, and entertainment? | |
| | | | List and samples of brochures of package plans that are available? | |
| | | | Floor plans of all function space? | |
| | | | Color pictures of recent noteworthy functions and meetings of several different rooms? | |
| | | | Copies of complimentary letters? | |
| | | | List of special features your hotel offers? | |
| | | | List and description of your restaurants and lounges? | |
| | | | List of current department heads and telephone extensions? | |
| | | | Number of guest rooms and suites and current rate structure? | |

**Exhibit 9-8**
*continued*

| Sat. | Unsat. | N/A | Item Description | Comments |
|------|--------|-----|-----------------|----------|
| | | | Is your banquet office equipped with a portable video-master? | |
| | | | Does it feature the best of your facilities and expertise? | |
| | | | Does it sell? | |
| | | | Do your banquet people take this for presentation on outside calls? | |
| | | | *Banquet Administration* | |
| | | | Is a regularly scheduled banquet department meeting held in your hotel? | |
| | | | Is the following agenda used?<br>1. Review of progress report of business booked for past week or month.<br>2. Weekly review of files covered by each banquet salesman.<br>3. Review of high food cost menus.<br>4. Lost business reports.<br>5. Referrals.<br>6. Call reports.<br>7. Review of "tentatives" and "definites."<br>8. Sales goals for each banquet salesman.<br>9. Review of banquets in city.<br>10. Review of open dates on prime space.<br>11. Evaluation of quality food and service.<br>12. Evaluation of effectiveness of guidelines.<br>13. Review of high labor costs.<br>14. Late distribution of menus.<br>15. Guarantees.<br>16. Condition of banquet space.<br>17. Engineering charges.<br>18. Condition of "big four."<br>19. Open discussion, special promotion, general comments, new ideas. | |
| | | | *Function Room Book* | |
| | | | Are "tentatives" and "definites" bookings entered according to correct sales and banquet procedure? | |
| | | | Does it state the name of the function? | |
| | | | Does it indicate the number of people in attendance? | |
| | | | Does it tell whether it is a dinner dance, a meeting, or an exhibit? | |

**Exhibit 9-8**
*continued*

| Sat. | Unsat. | N/A | Item Description | Comments |
|---|---|---|---|---|
| | | | Does it state when the function will commence and when it will terminate? | |
| | | | Does it list the name, address, and telephone number of the engager? | |
| | | | Does it include the file number, and is it initialed by the salesperson as well as the person who has entered the information into the function book? | |
| | | | *Who Controls Function Book?* | |
| | | | Does the general manager personally review the function books periodically? | |
| | | | Who in sales and banquet are responsible for seeing that you are getting optimum results with regards to bookings for your public facilities? | |
| | | | Who monitors to see that three hundred people are not put into a room that can take a thousand? | |
| | | | When are convention programs entered? | |
| | | | Is space released far enough in advance so that these facilities may be sold? | |
| | | | *Rentals* | |
| | | | Have the rentals for the public space been revised recently? | |
| | | | Is there a weekly review with sales and banquet personnel regarding the status of tentative entries in the function book? | |
| | | | *Filing and Tracing Procedures* | |
| | | | Does your banquet department have, to your satisfaction, a workable file and trace system? | |
| | | | Is this system tied in with a cardex that lists annual groups and organizations by number, with pertinent information on the file card? | |
| | | | Does it indicate a permanent trace date? | |
| | | | Does the control card with number indicate the name, the organization, the address, and a contact of a chairman for each file? | |
| | | | Do your files contain historical data of previous and current function arrangements, your | |

**Exhibit 9-8**
*continued*

| Sat. | Unsat. | N/A | Item Description | Comments |
|------|--------|-----|------------------|----------|
| | | | solicitation efforts, the followup and thank-you letters? | |
| | | | Once groups have been booked, are you satisfied with the procedures that your banquet personnel used in rebooking? | |
| | | | Do your banquet people view large banquets taking place in competitive hotels? | |
| | | | Do they call the chairman the next day? | |
| | | | *Evaluation of Solicitation Efforts Performed by Your Banquet Office* | |
| | | | Is a call report made up after every personal or telephone call on groups being solicited by either your banquet manager or assistants or your banquet representative? | |
| | | | Is this compiled into a monthly booking report? | |
| | | | Does your banquet office maintain a readers' file? | |
| | | | *Lost Business Reports* | |
| | | | Are they made by your banquet department? | |
| | | | Do they state the facts? | |
| | | | *Banquet Office Communications* | |
| | | | Are the function stencils delivered to all departments that require this information? | |
| | | | Are the delivered in ample time? | |
| | | | *Banquet Menus* | |
| | | | Are all prepriced banquet menus attractive? | |
| | | | Are they printed on good quality paper? | |
| | | | Do they offer, in a professional manner, items desired by the groups your hotel services? | |
| | | | Do they feature local specialties? | |
| | | | Are the menus well written, with romance and descriptions? | |
| | | | Are your menus precosted? | |
| | | | Is your banquet department capable of suggesting and selling custom menus? | |
| | | | Before they quote prices, do they check with | |

**Exhibit 9-8**
*continued*

| Sat. | Unsat. | N/A | Item Description | Comments |
|------|--------|-----|------------------|----------|
| | | | your food and beverage manager and controller as to the cost of those items on today's market? | |
| | | | Does management approve menu prices that are quoted for groups one year prior to their function date? | |
| | | | Does management build in a percentage increase for inflation? | |
| | | | *Function Facilities* | |
| | | | Are all doors to function rooms kept locked when not in use? | |
| | | | Are lights and air conditioning turned off when not in use? | |
| | | | Do housemen use partial or full lighting when setting up rooms? | |
| | | | Are your function rooms clean and well decorated? | |
| | | | Is your public space a cut above your competitors'? | |
| | | | Are your rostrums, flags, podiums, skirting in good repair? | |
| | | | Are all the light bulbs working? | |
| | | | Are your sound and electrical systems satisfactory? | |
| | | | Do your housemen and banquet service staff have clean and proper uniforms? | |
| | | | Are premeal classes and instructions conducted before major functions? | |
| | | | *Controls* | |
| | | | Do you have an effective guarantee and set-up policy? | |
| | | | Do you receive guarantees forty-eight hours prior to scheduled time of service? | |
| | | | Is it being followed? | |
| | | | Is there a salvage program in effect? | |
| | | | Who checks on reliability of banquet waiters, extra payrolls, extra cover fee, set-up and breakdown wages? | |

**Exhibit 9-8**
*continued*

| Sat. | Unsat. | N/A | Item Description | Comments |
|------|--------|-----|------------------|----------|
| | | | Do you get a profit and loss statement on most banquets?<br><br>Are special-priced banquets preapproved by the general manager?<br><br><br><br><br><br>**Completed by** _____ | |

*Sat.*: Satisfactory
*Unsat.*: Unsatisfactory
*N/A*: Not Applicable

# 10 Holiday Menus and Special Promotions

**Purpose:** To consider ways to use the opportunities provided by the annual holidays to promote restaurant business.

Even a sketchy reading of history reveals that all cultures have been enriched by celebrations to commemorate happy and not-so-happy events. In the United States we have twenty-five holidays that are noted on the calendar. Many of them can be used as occasions for special restaurant promotions. These holidays are distributed rather evenly among the months, except for August. But if you use a little imagination, you can create a special celebration in August for the zodiacal sign Leo, which signifies cheer, pride, and power.

Some holidays, such as Patriots' Day in Boston, have little significance outside the area, but other area-specific events, such as the Boston Marathon, are famous nationwide. Even seemingly silly days have been observed with food functions; for example, "Sadie Hawkins Day" has been the theme of restaurant promotions in Kentucky. In some northern states the first day of winter is observed by "Snow Festivals" and, of course, its accompanying banquet functions. With a little research into local history you can unearth days that are perfectly suited to promotional activities.

Different industries have provided food and beverage operators with additional opportunities to promote business. Certain weeks and months are recognized as National Food Promotion Periods. These include the following:

Egg Month
National Iced Tea Time
Cheese Festival Month
National Restaurant Month
Dairy Month
National Sandwich Month
Aloha Week in Hawaii
Wine Week
Honey Week

Each year local, state, and national politicians name new days and weeks for special observance.

Other promotional opportunities include the following:

Weddings
Homecomings
Engagements
Testimonials
Bon voyage parties
Graduations
Christenings
Retirement parties

## The "Big Four" Holidays

To facilitate service at the heavily attended holiday dinners, the special menus have fewer selections than the regular menus, and most items can be prepared in advance. However, on the sample menus shown, beef, pork, veal, poultry, and fish are featured so that menu selections do not appear limited.

### Easter

Easter is traditionally a Christian holiday with a great deal of religious significance. But today's celebration goes much beyond religious tradition. The many symbols with which we associate Easter, such as eggs, the serving of lamb, and the traditional Easter ham, come from different backgrounds. In the past the Greeks, Persians, Egyptians, and even Romans have used the egg as a symbol of spring. The most elaborate were the jeweled and enameled eggs given by nobility. Ham is often served on Easter, a tradition from the ancient Germanic and Slavic cultures, which smoked ham (in many cultures the pig is a symbol of prosperity) for Easter far back into ancient

---

**Easter Feast Menu**

Frosted Apricot Shrub • Iced Spring Melon with Lemon Wedge
Stuffed Easter Eggs with Fresh Asparagus Vinaigrette
A Cup of Seasonal Fruit with Fresh Mint and Lime Sherbet
Chilled Pink Grapefruit with Sliced Strawberry
Baby Shrimp on Ice, Cocktail Sauce

---

Ripe and Green Olives • Celery Hearts • Carrot Pennies

---

Cream of Chicken Soup with Watercress
Spiced Tomato Bisque

---

Pink Roasted Rack and Leg of Spring Lamb
Flavored with Rosemary
Baked Easter Ham with Glazed Orange Wheels
Roast Top Sirloin of Beef with Natural Pan Gravy
Oven-Broiled Chicken Basted with Lemon Butter
Baked Jumbo Shrimp Stuffed with Crabmeat, Lobster Sauce
Migonnettes of Veal Scallopini Marsala

---

Fresh Asparagus Spears • Buttered Fresh Green Beans
Baby Carrots and Mushrooms in Cream • Oven-Roasted Potatoes
Parslied New Potatoes • Sweet Potato with Marshmallow

---

Waldorf Salad Topped with Walnuts
Hearts of Romaine and Escarole, Bleu Cheese Dressing, with Tomato
Minted Pear and Cottage Cheese Salad on Watercress

---

Hot Cross Buns • Basket of Easter Breads

---

Slice of Fruited Easter Egg • Easter Bonnet Parfait
Lattice Rhubarb Pie • Holiday Layer Cake
Double Rich Ice Creams and Sherbets
Basket of Jelly Beans (for the Children)
Beverages

**Easter Brunch Buffet**
Baskets of Decorated Hard-Cooked Eggs
(for decoration and service)
Iced Pitchers of Fresh Orange Juice
Fresh Strawberries with Powdered Sugar
Chilled V-8 Juice ● Prune Juice ● Baked Rhubarb and Pineapple

---

A Variety of Hot and Cold Cereals
Enriched Milk

---

*Chafing Dishes of:*
Chicken a la King—Toast Points
Scrambled Eggs with Little Pork Sausages
Bunny-Burgers, Potato Chips
Chicken Livers with Mushrooms Sauté
Creamed Eggs on Toast
Seafood Newberg ● Parsley Buttered Rice
Cinnamon French Toast ● Crisp Bacon
Hashed in Cream Potatoes ● Julienne Celery Amandine
Yam Soufflé with Marshmallows

---

Caramel Custard ● Easter Bonnet Cake
Molded Fruit Gelatine, Chantilly ● Key Lime Pie
Coconut Nest of Sherbets ● Peppermint Stick Cream Roll
Basket of Jelly Beans
Milk ● Hot Chocolate ● Tea ● Coffee

---

times. In fact the word "Easter" comes from the prehistoric Germanic name of a pagan spring festival.

Eating lamb on Easter Sunday is a carryover from the Jewish Passover ritual. The Old Testament book of Exodus prescribes in detail that the lamb must be a year-old male, that it must be roasted and eaten with unleavened bread and bitter herbs. Instructions are given on how it is to be eaten: "with your loins girt, sandals on your feet, and your staff in hand. You shall eat like those who are in flight." This memorial feast is still celebrated in Jewish homes throughout the world on the feast of Passover, which occurs about the same time as the Christian feast of Easter.

The tradition of sending Easter cards began when the early Christians conducted their religious services in secret to avoid persecutions by the Romans. Crosses adorned with flowers were painted on the walls of the catacombs. Crosses and flowers are still popular on Easter cards. There is mention of an Easter Bunny and eggs in a German book of 1572. The Easter Bunny comes from pre-Christian fertility lore. The rabbit was the most fertile animal the ancients knew, and it served as a symbol of abundant new life in spring.

For many people, Irving Berlin's popular song was their introduction to the Easter Parade. It is associated with the traditional walk down Fifth Avenue in New York on Easter Sunday. Actually the tradition began as a walk through the fields after Mass on Easter Sunday in many Catholic sections of Europe. There were processions led by groups carrying a crucifix or the Easter candle. The Easter walk lost its religious character in some countries after the Reformation, but was continued as a popular secular custom.

**Easter Family Brunch.** Many families go to sunrise or early services on Easter morn-

---

**Easter Dinner Menu**
A Cup of Minted Fresh Pineapple with Lemon Sherbet
Fresh Seafood with Grapefruit Slices • Frosted Apricot Shrub
Devilled Eggs on Shredded Lettuce with Avocado Slices
Russian Dressing
Carrot Pennies • Celery Hearts • Ripe and Green Olives

---

Old-Fashioned Chicken Soup • Tomato Bisque aux Profiteroles

---

Sugar-Baked Ham with Mustard, Whipped Cream Sauce
Cornish Game Hen Stuffed with Wild Rice, Red Currant Jelly
Pink-Roasted Leg of Baby Lamb with Rosemary
Braised Long Island Duckling in Black Cherry Sauce
Southern Fried Chicken with Cream Gravy, Banana Fritters

---

Fresh Asparagus with Toasted Almonds • Tiny Buttered Carrots
Spinach Timbale, Hollandaise • Green Beans with Mushrooms
Whipped Sweet Potatoes in Orange Cup
New Potato Balls, Chive Butter

---

Popovers • Hot Cross Buns

---

Strawberry Sponge Shortcake • Angel Pecan Pie
Fruit Ambrosia Topped with Sherbet • Fresh Rhubarb Pie
Polk-a-dot Chocolate Pudding • Easter Daffodil Cake a la Mode
Eggnog Ice Cream Tart, Chocolate Flakes

---

Coffee • Milk • Tea • Chocolate Milk

---

ing and then return home for a big breakfast or brunch. In some areas there may well be a very large market on Easter for a family Easter brunch that offers a large buffet table filled with such traditional breakfast items as country sausage, ham, and eggs and with such traditional Easter items as freshly baked breads, hot-cross buns, and spring fruit turnovers. A set price can be advertised for adults, with children at half-price. The buffet can be decorated very attractively, and advertising and promotion can be based solely on the menu and the family concept.

**Easter Dinner Buffet.** A promotion for a large Easter buffet can offer ham, lamb, and many of the traditional fruits and baked items associated with Easter. Guests appreciate see-

ing someone carve the ham and the lamb. This and the many prepared dishes can create a very attractive Easter dinner of good value for the family. Advertising should list the items featured on the buffet. Price is very important to the family and should definitely be mentioned in the advertising, possibly as an added feature.

**Special Old-Fashioned Jelly Bean Guessing Promotion.** A promotion that has proved to be very successful in attracting attention to hotels' and restaurants' Easter dinners is the jelly bean guessing contest. It can be tied into the special menu for a family-style dinner. A large jar filled with multi-colored jelly beans and placed in the center of the hotel lobby or at the entrance of a restaurant can generate a great deal of enthusiasm. Guests of the hotel or restaurant guess how many jelly beans are in the jar, and prizes can be awarded to the five closest guesses. The prize in a hotel might be a free night in the hotel. Restaurants can give vouchers for a number of free dinners. This kind of promotion can be attractively advertised along with the Easter menu. It also has a potential of capturing the interest of the local press, which should be notified of the promotion.

Resort facilities with plenty of lawn and shrubbery might hold an Easter Egg Hunt, giving appropriate prizes for the children and perhaps a prize for the family of the number one hunter. The annual White House Easter Egg Hunt points to the popularity of this game.

**Advertising.** Advertising should begin approximately one and a half to two weeks prior to Easter, and adequate coverage should be given to the special plans and preparations for Easter Day festivities. You can buy advertising but you cannot buy merchandising—you do it. Serving food on the plate is the merchandising key. Consequently, it is important at all times but especially at an Easter celebration to concentrate on food preparation and presentation. Easter is a time for family celebration. The food should be something special. In planning the Easter menu, think spring! Yellows and greens predominate.

## Mother's Day

A day that has shown it has heart and living interest for all classes, races, creeds, native and foreign born, high and low, rich and poor, scoffer and churchman, man, woman, and child—is Mother's day, observed the second Sunday of May. The common possession of a living world is a mother. Everyone has or has had a mother. The marvelous growth of a Mother's day in a few years to a National and an International day can be attributed to the heart and living interest it possesses for almost every home and every person of a mother-loving heart in this and other countries.

This statement is from a leaflet printed in 1911 in ten languages. It is as true today as it was then.

Mother's Day dates from 1907. It was begun by Anna Jarvis, of Philadelphia, who thought sons and daughters should remember their mothers at least once a year. A special Mother's Day service was arranged to be conducted in a church. It was requested that white carnations be worn. By 1911 observance had spread widely, with all states participating. In December 1912 the Mother's Day International Association was incorporated to further greater observance of the day. Finally, Congress in 1914 designated the second Sunday of May as Mother's Day and requested President Wilson to issue a proclamation calling on government officials to display the flag on public buildings.

The custom of holding a festival in honor of motherhood dates back to the ancient Greeks who worshipped Cybele, Mother of the gods. Rites were conducted in her honor in woods and in caves. The custom was introduced into Rome by the Greeks about 250 B.C., and on the Ides of March (the 15th) the festival of *hilaria* (Latin for hilarity) began and continued for three days.

**Promotions.** Like Easter, Mother's Day is a spring holiday, and what better way to decorate a restaurant for the occasion than with a profusion of spring flowers? Pink and white carnations are the traditional flowers of Mother's Day, so they should be highlighted in decorations for the day along with the other flowers.

Some traditional and successful activities for the day in restaurants across the United States are the following:

- A carnation is given to each mother and expectant mother.
- Mother's Day is a family day dinner, so special children's menu prices can be included in any advertising features.
- Young parents welcome and appreciate a baby-sitting service.
- If facilities are available, special parties of

eight or more with mother can be served in a private room. A complimentary cake for such groups adds a warm touch to a festive family gathering.

A number of things can make Mother's Day dinner an event to fondly remember: flowers for mothers, as mentioned above, individual cakes for mothers, strolling musicians, special dessert for mothers at no charge.

Promotions in cooperation with local merchants can be worked out in some areas. Purveyors of candy, flowers, perfume, and beauty shops are particularly involved in Mother's Day activities.

Full advantage should be taken of Mother's Day as a great opportunity for restaurant business. The most successful Mother's Day for a restaurant is bound to be the one that has made the most people happy.

Approximately two to three weeks before Mother's Day, promotion should begin within the restaurant. Preparation can begin immediately for signs and displays to be used in the restaurant and for ads to be ready to run in local newspapers.

Suggested menus for Mother's Day follow.

---

**Mother's Day Menu**
Avocado Boat with Fresh Strawberries, Honey Dressing
Chilled Spring Melon with Iced Lime
Pineapple Boat with Fresh Fruit and Sherbet
Coquille of Jumbo Shrimp on Ice
Pink Grapefruit with Grapes
Chunks of Alaskan King Crab, Remoulade Sauce

---

Spring Onions • Radish Rosettes
Pascal Celery

---

Chicken Broth with Rice • Cream of Fresh Asparagus Soup

---

Twin Filets of Beef Simmered in Burgundy Butter
Stuffed Mushroom Caps
Baked Jumbo Shrimp Stuffed with Crabmeat, Lobster Sauce
Milk-Fed Veal Cutlet Cordon Bleu
Boneless Breast of Chicken on Ham Slice, Sauce Supreme
Roast Prime Ribs of Beef with Natural Gravy
Yorkshire Pudding
Broiled Fresh Salmon Steak, Dilled Cucumbers

---

Fresh Asparagus Polonaise • Green Peas and Mushrooms
Parsley New Potatoes • Maple-Glazed Sweet Potatoes
Spring Greens Tossed In French Dressing
Fresh Grapefruit Sections with Sliced Avocado, Honey Dressing

---

Hot Biscuits • Dinner Rolls

---

Key Lime Pie • Chocolate, Marshmallow Nut Sundae
Angelfood Cake a la Mode, Melba Sauce
Fresh Strawberry Shortcake • Rainbow Parfait
Compote of Fresh Fruit • Ice Cream Pie
Double Rich Ice Creams and Sherbet

---

Beverages

**Mother's Day Menu**
Pickled Pink Eggs and Fresh Asparagus Vinaigrette
Small Tomato Stuffed with Shrimp Salad
Honeydew Melon with Smoked Salmon
Devilled Eggs with Caviar on Shredded Lettuce
A Medley of Chilled Fruits, Fresh Mint

---

Bowls of Relishes on Tables

---

Steaming Onion Soup with Cheese
Essence of Tomatoes Madrilene

---

Baked Fresh Salmon in Cream with Cucumbers
Roast Prime Ribs of Beef, Natural Pan Gravy
Braised Long Island Duckling a l'Orange with Bing Cherries
Grilled Twin Lamb Chops with Glazed Peach, Currant Jelly
Roast Filet of Beef with Rosemary, Burgundy Sauce
Scallopini of Milk-fed Veal, Marsala
Pan Roasted Spring Chicken, Maryland Style, Sauce Supreme

---

Buttered Baby Beets • Fresh Asparagus, Drawn Butter
Creamed New Potatoes and Peas • Pan Browned Potatoes
Julienne Green Beans • Spinach Soufflé

---

Tossed Spring Vegetable Salad, Traditional French Dressing
Jellied Pineapple and Carrot Salad, Honey Mayonnaise

---

Popovers • Hot Buttermilk Biscuits • Clover Rolls

---

Chocolate Pistachio Ice Cream Roll, Fudge Sauce
Spring Tulip Parfait • Cherry Jubilee Meringue
Orange Snow Pudding with Fresh Strawberries, Lace Cookie
Ice Cream or Sherbet with Petit Four
Fresh Apple Pie
Coffee • Tea • Milk
Pastel Mints • Assorted Nuts

## Thanksgiving Day

Thanksgiving, like the other three of the Big Four holidays, is for the restaurant business a "family get-together day." To emphasize this "togetherness" point, hotels can use function rooms for family dinner parties. A traditional New England dinner can be served buffet style in a private room. Many families travel hundreds of miles to be together on this important holiday, and a private dining room is an ideal place for a reunion. Restaurants with private areas can also provide this service. In any food outlet whole turkeys can be carved at the table for six or more guests. A bag for carrying away the leftovers can be provided—this can be a good advertising point.

**Promotions.** Promotions for Thanksgiving dinner should begin several weeks prior to the holiday. Waiters and waitresses can wear large buttons inviting Thanksgiving Day reservations.

The special Thanksgiving Day menu can be prominently displayed near the entrance of a restaurant or in the lobby of a hotel, with appropriate holiday decorations. Miniature menus can be made available to restaurant customers several weeks prior to the holiday.

On Thanksgiving Day, a welcoming banner can be displayed. Thanksgiving corsages for the ladies are much appreciated. Do not forget future customers—children appreciate special ice cream molds of turkeys, holiday cookies, lollipops, and special "cocktails" of sweet cider or cranberry juice. With the children drinking, the adults will not feel the need to forego their cocktails.

Restaurants and private function rooms

---

**Thanksgiving Day Menu**

A Cup of Autumn Fruits Ambrosia • Oysters on Half Shell
Shrimp Mayonnaise with Avocado • Honey-Grilled Grapefruit
Herring Salad, McIntosh Apple Slices
Cape Cod Cocktail, Orange Sherbet
Herbed Tomato Juice, Cheese Sticks

---

Old-Fashioned Chicken Soup • Cream of Corn Soup
New England Clam Chowder

---

Roast Native Turkey with Chestnut Stuffing
Giblet Gravy, Whole Cranberry Sauce
Roast Suckling Pig, Spiced Apple Sauce
Orange-Fried Chicken, Old-Fashioned Cream Gravy
Baked Sugar-Cured Country Ham, Plum and Pineapple Sauce
Roast Prime Ribs of Beef, Natural Pan Gravy
Filet of Sole Stuffed with Crabmeat, Lobster Sauce
Roast Larded Haunch of Venison, Rich Wine Sauce

---

Lemon-Glazed Sweet Potato • Baked Stuffed Onions
Succotash in Cream • Butternut Squash with Pecans
Creamy Mashed Potatoes • Buttered Fresh Brussels Sprouts

---

Harvest Apple, White Grape and Walnut Salad
Jellied Sunset Salad
Hearts of Lettuce, Quartered Tomato, Choice of Dressing

---

Orange Biscuits • Cinnamon Rolls • Cranberry Bread

---

Pumpkin Pie Topped with Whipped Cream
Chocolate Layer Cake • Apple Pie, Cider Raisin Sauce
Fresh Pear Baked in Maple Syrup, Whipped Cream
Indian Pudding with Vanilla Ice Cream • Grape Jello Chantilly
Coffee Ice Cream and Orange Sherbet, Sugar Wafers

---

Coffee • Chilled Cider • Tea • Milk
Malaga Raisins • Fresh Fruit Bowl • Mints and Nuts in Shell
HAVE AN APPLE FROM THE BARREL!

should be decorated in harvest colors with fruits of the field. Ears of colorful Indian corn tied together with a ribbon hanging over the door is a sign of hospitality. To add atmosphere a horn of plenty can be filled with bright red and yellow apples, russet and green pears, tomatoes, and red and white onions with large bunches of parsley. Cornstalks and pumpkins dress up bare corners. Flowers always add a cheerful touch.

---

**Buffet Menu for Thanksgiving Day Bountiful Feast**
A Bowl of Autumn Fruits with Port • Slices of Fall Melon
Clamato Juice Cocktail with Lemon • Chilled Apple Cider
Marinated Herring in Cream

---

Old-Fashioned Chicken Soup with Noodles

---

Roast Stuffed Native Turkey, Cornbread Dressing, Giblet Gravy
Curried Fresh Seafood with Shrimp and Crabmeat
Baked Sugar-Cured Ham, Glazed with Honey
Roast Round of Beef, Natural Pan Gravy

---

New England Baked Beans • New Peas in Butter
Browned Rice with Walnuts • Corn and Bean Succotash
Mashed Hubbard Squash
Candied Sweet Potatoes with Marshmallow and Coconut
Whipped Potatoes

---

Molded Cranberry Apple and Nut Salad, Cottage Cheese Dressing
A Bowl of Tossed Greens, Olive Oil and Wine Vinegar Dressing
Carrot and Cabbage Slaw

---

Hearts of Celery • Green and Ripe Olives • Rose Bud Radishes
Corn and Red Pepper Relish

---

Pumpkin Pie, Whipped Cream • Southern Pecan Pie
Hot Mincemeat Pie
Old Fashioned Apple Dumpling, Raisin and Currant Sauce
Indian Pudding • Chocolate Fudge Cake
Whole Pears Stewed in Honey • Assorted Fresh Fruits

---

Apple Cider • Coffee • Tea • Milk
Mixed Nuts • Cluster Raisins • Mints

**Thanksgiving Day Menu**
Curried Stuffed Eggs, Shredded Lettuce
Baked Coquille of Crabmeat • Shrimp Cocktail
Melon Decorated with Fresh Fruits
Baked Honeyed Grapefruit • Frosted Cranberry Shrub

---

Spiced Tomato Bisque • Old-Fashioned Chicken and Corn Soup

---

Mixed Mustard Pickles • Spiced Sekel Pears
Pascale Celery and Ripe Olives • Green Tomato Relish

---

Roast Native Turkey, Chestnut-Sage Dressing
Giblet Gravy, Whole Cranberry Sauce
Old-Fashioned Yankee Pot Roast with Vegetables
Poached Fresh Salmon, Egg Sauce and Lemon
Baked Sugar-Cured Country Ham with Whole Bing Cherries
Fricassee of Chicken on Buttered Long-Grain Rice
Curry of Fresh Seafood with Lobstermeat and Chutney

---

Boiled Creamed Onions with Chopped Peanuts
String Beans with Mushrooms • Baked Acorn Squash with Nutmeg
Creamy Mashed Potatoes • Candied Sweet Potatoes

---

Waldorf Salad Topped with Walnuts
Asparagus and Tomato Salad, Curried Mayonnaise
Seedless Grape and Apple Salad, Cream Dressing
Heart of Romaine, Blue Cheese Dressing

---

Cold Sweet Apple Cider

---

Traditional Hot Brandied Mince Pie with Cheddar Cheese
Harvest Pumpkin Pie with Whipped Cream and
Crushed Peanut Brittle
Baked Apple Stuffed with Nuts and Raisins
Indian Pudding with Vanilla Ice Cream
Orange Mints • Fresh Fruit and Nut Bowl • Malaga Raisins
Coffee • Tea • Milk

## Christmas

To many Americans, Christmas means carol singing, Santa Claus, presents, holly, and Christmas trees. The customs that have collected around Christmas are various. Many stem from the pagan past. The policy of the early church was to transform pagan festivals, rather than abolish them, by giving ancient practices Christian significance. The Christmas season is the one time of the year when kindliness and generosity have triumphed over materialism and selfishness. The Feast of the Nativity makes it a special festival for children and important to every Christian family, both spiritually and materially.

In the spirit of friendship and regard for peoples of all nations, restaurants can express a desire for peace and cooperation by featuring foods of many lands during the Christmas season. Just as each country has its own customs, so each country has traditional Yuletide foods. In Europe the Christmas feast was usually planned around wild or domestic birds. Some Europeans had goose; others ate duck, turkey, or chicken. In the United States many hotels and restaurants sell roasted turkey or goose to customers to serve in their own homes. Pumpkin and mince pies have also been available for take-out orders.

In the following sections we briefly describe the foods and customs of several countries.

**England.** Favorite Christmas foods in England are goose with sage-onion stuffing, apple sauce, roast beef with Yorkshire pudding, English plum pudding with hard sauce, mince pie with brandy sauce, Christmas trifle (made especially for the children), and marzipan.

**France.** Christmas Day is exclusively for boys and girls. The Yule log and miniature crèche are featured in the celebration. Dinner consists of truffled turkey, black pudding, chestnut consommé, Strasbourg pie, truffles and livers of fattened geese, boar's head jelly, froglegs and snails, dark-brown gingerbread called *pain d'epice*, chocolate chestnut soufflé, Buche Noël.

**Germany.** Almost every family has an Advent wreath with small images and four candles, one of which burns for each of the four Sundays of Advent. Special dinner can include turkey stuffed with chestnuts, raisins, and apples; red wine; meringues; wine jelly; Pfeffernüsse; Springerle; Lubkuchen; almond macaroon cakes; gingerbread men; and lace cookies. Lighting and decorating Christmas trees was started in Germany in the sixteenth century by Martin Luther.

**Italy.** One of the most impressive sights in the country is to see the men come down from the mountains playing melodic music on pipes. In addition to pasta, the Italians feast on eels and chicken with burgundy and walnuts. Magi cakes are exchanged between friends as visiting cards.

**Mexico.** As in many countries, Mexican Christmas fiestas begin on December sixteenth. Each night until Christmas Mexicans re-enact the "miracle plays" of Mary and Joseph's search for shelter in Bethlehem. On the ninth night feasting and breaking the piñata climax the fiesta. The Mexicans traditionally feast on turkey and roast suckling pig, bunelos (thin, sweet pancakes), pork and chicken timbales, and sweet tamales filled with coconut and fruits.

**Arabic.** Dinner includes rice soup, tomato salad, nut-stuffed turkey, baked kobba (finely ground lamb with bulgur, pine nuts, and seasonings), eggplant with olive oil, ghuraybe or ka'hk bi-agwa (butter or date cookies), and coffee. Christmas is a time for special feasting in Arabic homes. Most Arabic families butcher a sacrificial lamb on Christmas morning. Most of the lamb traditionally goes to charity to be used by orphanages or poor families, but some meat is kept for Christmas dinner.

**Finland.** A Finnish Christmas dinner can include meat broth with noodles, boiled codfish snowy-white and fluffy with allspice, boiled potatoes with cream sauce, roast suckling pig or roast fresh ham with Swede pudding, mashed potatoes with peas and red cabbage, puolukka jam, and a variety of breads—Christmas bread of rye flavored with molasses, homemade black bread, and hardtack. Dessert can be prunes with whipped cream, coffee cake and/or toasted coffee cake. The Finns also have a variety of pastries; one of the favorites is Christmas Stars. The children go to bed after dinner and the adults sit up until midnight drinking coffee with neighbors and relatives.

**Denmark.** Here Christmas dinner is traditionally goose stuffed with prune-apple stuffing, bedecked with flags and served with sugar-browned potatoes, red cabbage, and currant jelly. For dessert, apple cake covered with whipped cream and steamed plum pudding are served.

**Bulgaria.** A traditional favorite is goose baked on a bed of sauerkraut.

**Greece.** A traditional Christmas here includes lemon soup, green salad (lettuce, endive, tomato, onion) with feta and anchovies, pita, parsley meat balls, lemon-basted roast chicken, vegetable stuffing, artichokes with peas, olives, and kourabiedes (sugar-coated butter cakes).

**Norway.** Christmas dinner can consist of roast ribs of pork; barbecued young pig or fresh ham and lingonberry relish; Christmas porridge; cookies cut in shapes of people, animals, and hearts; and pastry tarts filled with apples and prunes.

**Sweden.** The Swedes begin with a more elaborate smorgasbord than usual with special kinds of cheese, salad, and bread: lumpa, Swedish rye, pumpernickle, and rye wafers. Also included are herring in sour cream, anchovies, jellies salmon, caviar and cream dip, omelet with creamed crab, Swedish meat balls, calf sylta (pressed veal), and assorted hot and cold sausages.

The dinner course consists of baked ham with glazed apples, prunes, and pears; creamed peas and carrots or buttered broccoli; and pickled beets.

For dessert, the Swedes have cream wafers, morkakor (butter leaves), drommar (dream cookies), mandelformar (almond tarts), nuts in the shell, and a fruit tray of grapes, pears, apples, and tangerines.

**Switzerland.** In Switzerland, Old St. Nicholas has been succeeded in many parts by Christkindli, an angelic figure who travels over the land every Christmas Eve in a beautiful sleigh drawn by reindeer. The sleigh is heavily laden with Christmas trees, fruit, cookies, and toys for children. Every home has a Christmas tree around which the family gathers to sing carols.

The favorite Christmas foods of the Swiss are chicken baked with giblet and rice stuffing, roast beef with browned potato, swiss chocolate pudding with an abundance of whipped cream, and special wines.

**Promotions.** This last holiday of the year gives not just one day for promotion, but an entire season. Business houses create an atmosphere of Christmas even before Thanksgiving Day. In hotels and restaurants with private dining rooms, this seasonal promotion can include programs for banquets as well as the traditional Christmas dinner in restaurants. Here are a dozen ways to promote the food facilities in hotel and restaurants.

1. The restaurant or hotel can show holiday gratitude to groups that have been regular patrons through the year by giving special room decorations, a Christmas tree, special desserts, and, most important, something they do not expect.
2. For larger groups, door prizes can be provided. An example is a restaurant's offering a Christmas dinner for the family.
3. Take-out sales can include the usual service of roasting turkeys and baking mince and pumpkin pies, plus special features such as fruit cake, Christmas cookies, ice cream pie or Christmas breads. Offering an unusual and especially appropriate item for the holiday season can create interest.
4. A good way for a restaurant to promote Christmas dinner is to invite the food editors of the local newspapers to try the special features on the Christmas menu. The items should be special for the holiday season, such as Christmas goose with sage-onion dressing and flaming plum pudding.

5. People in a festive mood welcome specialty flaming desserts. In addition to the flaming plum pudding, the old favorite cherries jubilee is very appropriate at Christmas and offers a touch of glamor to holiday dining. Flaming hot fudge sundaes for the children is a very attractive item.

6. If there is adequate space in a hotel lobby, a live turkey display with a weight-guessing contest for the guests is bound to attract attention for the Christmas dinner. Those who most closely guess the correct weight of the turkey can be given prizes of family dinners or dinners for two.

7. It always creates interest in a food establishment when the chef can be seen on television. It is a common practice for television stations to have a chef demonstrate the proper carving of a turkey before both Thanksgiving Day and Christmas. A restaurant or hotel should make sure its chef has a turn in these demonstrations.

8. When hotels send out bills to their city ledger accounts, they should contain some promotional material for the Christmas menu—perhaps miniature menus.

9. Flyers on restaurant luncheon menus can feature a shoppers' special with items especially attractive to women shoppers. If facilities are available, storage for packages can be provided, which will add incentive for shoppers to patronize the restaurant.

10. Offer a "Family Package Plan for Christmas"—full price for dad and mom (mom gets a special Christmas corsage), half price for children up to three children, and additional children free.

11. Do not forget the children. Each child can be given a Christmas stocking filled with goodies, including a toy.

12. Ethnic dinners with all of the Christmas specialties from the different countries can be a full-sized promotion in itself. But be sure the items are authentic, especially in preparation.

In Atlantic City before the days of the casino, several of the resort hotels had lobby displays of electric trains. Some were quite modest but others were very large, and both delighted children from ages eight to eighty. Several midwestern resorts tried similar displays and were equally successful in pleasing both the hotel's guests and people from the surrounding community.

To purchase such equipment is quite costly, but it is available to rent. In fact, there are decorators who for a fee will furnish the equipment and set up an entire display.

Following are possible Christmas menus.

**Christmas Menu**
Christmas Fruit Cup with Raspberry Sherbet
Devilled Eggs with Red Caviar • Cranberry Shrub
Holiday Shrimp Platter with Stuffed Celery and Red Sauce
(Holly Garnish)
Pink Grapefruit with Pomegranate Seeds

---

Spiced Crabapples • Radish Roses • Cranberry Relish
Midget Gherkins • Chilled Celery Hearts

---

Cream of Tomato Soup Sprinkled with Parsley
Old-Fashioned Chicken Noodle Soup
Spiced Tomato Bisque

---

The Traditional Christmas Goose with Sage-Onion Stuffing and
Apple Sauce
Barron of Beef with Yorkshire Pudding and Horseradish Sauce
Savory Baked Capon with Rice and Sausage Stuffing
Baked Fresh Ham with Prune-Apple Dressing
Roast Tom Turkey with Chestnut Dressing and Cranberry Sauce
Holiday Crown Roast of Lamb with Spiced Crabapples and
Mint Sauce

---

Green Peas with Pimento • Mashed Butternut Squash
Creamed Onions • Candied Yams • Mashed Potatoes
Holiday Fruit Salad with Cottage Cheese Christmas Dressing
Hearts of Lettuce with Rosy Mayonnaise
Molded Cranberry Waldorf Salad with Honey Dressing

---

Flaming Old English Plum Pudding with Hard Sauce
Candy Cane Parfait • Hot Fresh Apple Pie with Cheddar Cheese
Christmas Trifle • Hot Mincemeat Pie with Brandy Sauce
Pumpkin Pie with Minted Whipped Cream
Egg Nog Ice Cream • Red and Green Christmas Jello

---

Christmas Breads • Jams and Jellies

---

Red and Green Mints • Mixed Nuts

---

Coffee • Tea • Milk

### Christmas Day Menu
Fresh Shrimp in Jellied Tomato Ring
Hot Mushroom Caps with Crabmeat a l'Aurore
Hearts of Artichoke with Anchovy Filets Vinaigrette
Minted Grilled Half Grapefruit

---

Pickled Onions • Stuffed Olives • Radish Rosettes
Hearts of Pascale Celery

---

Cream of Chicken Soup • Oyster Bisque • Consomme Madrilene

---

Roast Native Turkey with Prune-Apple Stuffing
Prime Ribs of Beef, Herbed Popovers and Shredded Horseradish
Savory Crown Roast of Pork, Spiced Bing Cherries
Breast of Capon Sautéed in White Wine, Brown Rice and
Stuffed Baked Tomato
Roast Christmas Goose with Sage-Onion Stuffing and Plum Sauce
Crusty Brown Fried Chicken with Pan Gravy and Cranberry Jelly
(for the Children)

---

Rosebud Beets in Butter • Creamed Celery with Pecans
Broccoli Amandine • Green Beans with Water Chestnuts
Garden Peas with Pimientos • Snowflake Potatoes

---

Cranberry Muffins • Della Robbia Sweet Rolls

---

Christmas Cranberry Mold with Cottage Cheese Dressing
Spiced Apple Ring with Avocado on Watercress with French Dressing

---

Traditional English Plum Pudding with Brandy and Hard Sauce
Golden Pumpkin Pie with Whipped Cream
Hot Brandied Mince Pie with Cheddar Cheese
Pistachio Ice Cream with Raspberry Sherbet, Christmas Stars
Hot Fresh Apple Pie with Cider Sauce • Flaming Cherries Jubilee
Buche de Noel (Christmas Log)

---

Beverages

**Christmas Dinner at Mount Vernon, 1792**
An Onion Soup Called the King's Soup • Chicken Rivels Soup*

---

Oysters on the Half Shell • Oyster Pan Roast
Cranberry Shrub • Devilled Eggs and Sea Fare
A Bounce of Winter Fruits**

---

Roast Beef and Yorkshire Pudding • Squab in Compote
Roast Suckling Pig • Roast Turkey with Chestnut Dressing
Cold Roast Leg of Chicken • Cold Baked Virginia Ham

---

Lima Beans • Baked Acorn Squash • Hominy Pudding
Baked Celery and Slivered Almonds
Candied Sweet Potatoes

---

Cantaloupe Pickle • Spiced Peaches in Brandy
Spiced Cranberries

---

Mincemeat Pie • Apple Pie • Cherry Pie • Chess Tarts
Blanc Mange • Plums in Wine Jelly • Indian Pudding
Snowballs • Great Cake • Ice Cream
Plum Pudding

---

Fruits • Nuts • Raisins

---

Port • Madeira
* Chicken Rivels Soup—Chicken-Corn Soup with Egg Drops
** A Bounce of Winter Fruits—A Variety of Fruits Topped with Water Ice

# 11 Hospital Menus

**Purpose:** To acquaint the student with hospital menus.

In recent years, many industries in the United States, including hospitals, have seen numerous mergers. Another change has been the conversion from nonprofit to profit-making hospitals. Hospital Corporation of America and Columbia are two examples of multiple health care units. Often, the volume of meals for the regular diet patients and in the cafeterias for employees and visitors equals that of very large commercial restaurants. Thus, hospital food service requires expert management in order not to be a heavy cost burden on the nonprofit hospital or lead to decreased profits for the commercial operations. Of course, dietitians are still responsible for the special diets for patients.

## Who Writes Hospital Menus?

Exhibit 11-1 shows an organizational chart for the food service department for a large hospital. Like in commercial restaurants, menu writing in hospitals requires a team. In fact, with the dietary considerations, an additional person, the dietitian,

must be involved. In addition to considering special diets, the menu-writing team for a hospital must take into account payroll cost, just as would any hotel or restaurant. The menu-writing team must consider things that could limit its freedom in selecting food items. For example, in addition to the proper diet balance for patients, the items served must be balanced to distribute the workload evenly among the preparation personnel. The capacity of the preparation equipment is another factor. Finally, knowledge of products available on the current market and their prices is as important in a hospital as in restaurants and hotels.

## The Hospital Menu

The menus for hotels and restaurants have multiple functions, but first and foremost they are a selling tool. There are also multiple facets to hospital menus.

1. The menu has the difficult job of performing as a public relations medium with persons who are in the

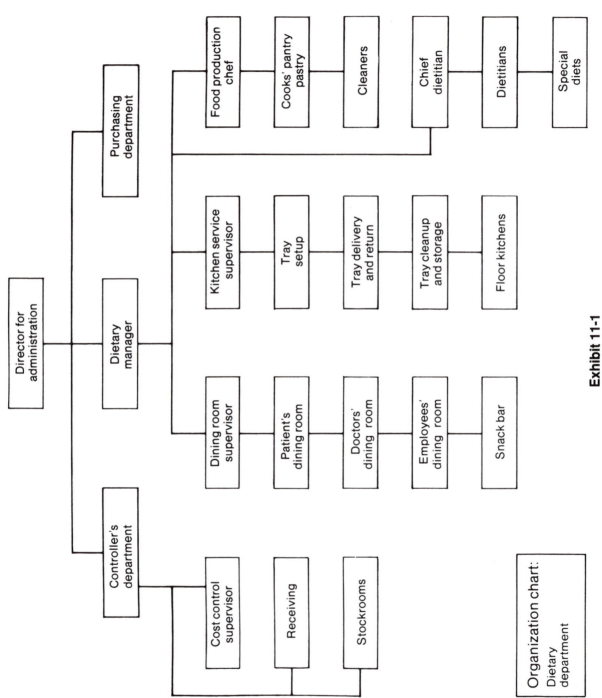

**Exhibit 11-1**

**Chart showing an organizational plan for the dietary department in a hospital**

Organization chart:
Dietary
department

Director for administration

Purchasing department

Dietary manager

Controller's department

Food production chef

Cooks' pantry pastry

Cleaners

Chief dietitian

Dietitians

Special diets

Kitchen service supervisor

Tray setup

Tray delivery and return

Tray cleanup and storage

Floor kitchens

Dining room supervisor

Patient's dining room

Doctors' dining room

Employees' dining room

Snack bar

Cost control supervisor

Receiving

Stockrooms

hospital under compulsion and are not disposed to be enthusiastic about anything related to their stay.

2. The hospital, whether private or public, is a business and operates on a budget; the menu must be economical to operate within the restrictions placed on the food department.

3. The special diets required impose a contradiction, in that the consumer must select among menu items that lack the ingredients that he or she most enjoys.

4. While operating under the restrictions outlined in the first three points, the hospital menu must be functional, that is, it must be possible to put it into use and perform successfully in spite of the limiting circumstances.

In sum, our advice to the hospital menu-planning team is negative: Avoid monotony and an institutional flavor in the meals.

## Hospital Menu Planning

The basic principle to follow in planning menus for patients on a variety of special diets is to regard the special diets as modifications of the normal diet of persons who need not restrict their eating habits. For example, a preoperative diet for an undernourished patient merely requires that a normal diet be altered to give the patient a higher-calorie intake. This simple example is technically correct as a procedure but oversimplifies reality. A few years ago special diets were limited to about four or five general categories; today there are over twenty general categories, some with several subclassifications. As a result, in some instances after a normal diet is modified, little or nothing remains of the normal diet's products in the modified diet.

## Example of a 1990's Hospital Food Service Operation

Since the last edition of this text, the hospitals and menus cited have undergone changes characteristic of these institutions. Tampa General Hospital, the largest hospital in the Tampa Bay area in Florida, has contracted with a catering firm to operate food service. Mease Hospital in Dunedin, Florida, has opened a satellite unit in a nearby town. It has recently merged with two hospitals in neighboring towns—Morton Plant Hospital in Clearwater and North Bay Hospital in New Port Richey. All units are still operated as nonprofit hospitals. Each hospital operates a cafeteria for employees and visitors. However, patients' breakfast, lunch, and dinner meals—both regular diet and special diet—are prepared at the hospital in Dunedin, which is centrally located among the four units, and transported to the three satellite hospitals. The advantages gained are central purchasing and reduced preparation staffs, including just one dietitian for the group. Of course, there is the expense of equipment and personnel to deliver the meals.

This hospital does not share most other hospitals' enthusiasm for using convenience foods. Frozen and canned foods are used, but there is very limited use of convenience entrées.

During a person's stay in the hospital, he or she is given a computer-produced selector menu each day to check food choices for the following day. The marked menus are collected each day and processed by the food control department. Exhibits 11-2 through 11-8 are the menus given Sunday through Saturday for patients' selections. The seven-day rotation is considered sufficient because a patient on a regular diet rarely stays beyond seven days. The menu is perforated between breakfast and lunch selections and between lunch and dinner selections. This separation of the meal periods allows the preparation staff to estimate how much of the different foods need to be produced.

## Special Dietetic Foods

Types of foods typically purchased for dietary use in hospitals are those without added sugar; salt, particularly sodium chloride; spice, particularly pepper; and fat in general or fat from animal sources. Also frequently purchased are diet packs that contain particular combinations of spices or condiments for particular diets. Packs may be free of salt, pepper, or sugar and include salt substitute or nonnutritive sweetener as required by a particular diet. Purchase of commercially prepackaged seasoning helps to eliminate error in selecting the appropriate combination of spices and saves the time in tray assembly that would be required to pick up several items. Particular food items that are typically purchased without salt are butter or margarine, turkey or beef roasts, soup or gravy bases, bread, and canned vegetables. Also available on the market are low-sodium corn flakes. For very restricted diets, sodium-free milk may be purchased.

Sugar-free canned fruits, gelatin, jellies, and sometimes ice cream may be purchased; these may be packed with a nonnutritive sweetener such as saccharine. Low-calorie salad dressings with little or no fat and sugar may be purchased. Also available are margarines high in polyunsaturated fatty acids, low in cholesterol, and with reduced fat. These items may be tasty and useful for low-fat or reduced-calorie diets but may be expensive, and value is related to patient satisfaction.

## Summary

We remind you that this brief overview of planning hospital menus is not intended to be in-depth instruction in the preparation of special diets. However, food management opportunities in hospitals for nondietary specialists are increasing with the growth of the food operations in individual hospitals. We hope this introduction to hospital operations may stimulate you to further investigate this fascinating field.

## Mease Hospital

### ☐ DUNEDIN  ☐ COUNTRYSIDE

## BREAKFAST

### SUNDAY

**JUICES AND FRUITS**
( ) Orange Juice     ( ) Prune Juice
( ) Grapefruit Juice ( ) Chilled Melon Cup

**ENTREES**
( ) Fresh Scrambled Eggs
( ) Belgian Waffle With Syrup

**ON THE SIDE**
( ) Bacon Strips
( ) Sausage Links

**CEREALS**
( ) Oatmeal       ( ) Cream of Wheat
( ) Special K     ( ) Cornflakes
( ) Rice Krispies ( ) Total

**BREAD BASKET**
( ) Soft Roll  ( ) Croissant
( ) Bagel      ( ) Demi Danish

**BEVERAGES AND CONDIMENTS**
( ) Decaf            ( ) Margarine
( ) Coffee           ( ) Butter
( ) Hot Tea          ( ) Cream Cheese
( ) Whole Milk       (X) Salt
(X) Skim Milk        (X) Pepper
( ) Chocolate Milk   (X) Sugar
( ) Hot Chocolate    ( ) Sugar Sub
( ) 1/2 oz Half & Half ( ) Jelly
( ) Lemon            ( ) Honey

---

## Mease Hospital

### ☐ DUNEDIN  ☐ COUNTRYSIDE

## LUNCH

### SUNDAY

**APPETIZERS**
( ) Cranberry Juice
( ) Tomato Soup
( ) Beef Broth

**SALADS**                    **Dressings:**
( ) Tossed Salad              ( ) Ranch
( ) Gelatin Fruit Salad       ( ) Italian
( ) Jello                     ( ) Blue Cheese

**ENTREES**
( ) Oven Fried Chicken Breast
( ) Pepper Steak
    Accompanied with:
    Fluffy White Rice

**VEGETABLES**
( ) Green Peas
( ) Cauliflower

**SWEET ENDINGS**
( ) Carrot Cake  ( ) Chocolate Pudding
( ) Apple        ( ) Vanilla Ice Cream
( ) Banana       ( ) Chocolate Ice Cream
( ) Grapes       ( ) Orange Sherbet
( ) Melon        ( ) Lime Sherbet

**BREADS**
( ) White Dinner Roll
( ) Whole Wheat Dinner Roll
( ) Melba Toast
( ) Saltines

**BEVERAGES AND CONDIMENTS**
( ) Decaf        ( ) Choc Milk
( ) Coffee       ( ) Margarine
( ) Hot Tea      ( ) Butter
( ) Half & Half  (X) Salt
( ) Iced Tea     (X) Pepper
( ) Whole Milk   (X) Sugar
( ) Skim Milk  ( ) Sugar Sub  ( ) Lemon

---

## Mease Hospital

### ☐ DUNEDIN  ☐ COUNTRYSIDE

## DINNER

### SUNDAY

**APPETIZERS**
( ) Apple Juice
( ) Tomato Juice
( ) Tomato Soup

**SALADS**              **Dressings:**
( ) Tossed Salad        ( ) Ranch
( ) Macaroni Salad      ( ) Italian
( ) Jello               ( ) Blue Cheese

**ENTREES**
( ) Lasagna
( ) Turkey Sandwich with Mayonnaise

**VEGETABLES**
( ) Zucchini Summer Squash Blend
( ) Broccoli

**SWEET ENDINGS**
( ) Pecan Pie         ( ) Pear Halves
( ) Apple             ( ) Vanilla Ice Cream
( ) Orange Sections   ( ) Chocolate Ice Cream
( ) Banana            ( ) Orange Sherbet
( ) Grapes            ( ) Lime Sherbet
( ) Melon

**BREADS**
( ) White Dinner Roll
( ) Whole Wheat Dinner Roll
( ) Melba Toast       ( ) Saltines

**BEVERAGES AND CONDIMENTS**
( ) Decaf        ( ) Choc Milk
( ) Coffee       ( ) Margarine
( ) Hot Tea      ( ) Butter
( ) Half & Half  (X) Salt
( ) Iced Tea     (X) Pepper
( ) Whole Milk   (X) Sugar
( ) Skim Milk  ( ) Sugar Sub  ( ) Lemon

---

### Exhibit 11-2
**Sunday menu from a seven-day hospital rotation**
*Reprinted with permission from Morton Plant, Mease Health Care*

## Mease Hospital — BREAKFAST

☐ DUNEDIN  ☐ COUNTRYSIDE

**MONDAY**

### JUICES AND FRUITS
( ) Orange Juice      ( ) Prune Juice
( ) Grapefruit Juice  ( ) Banana

### ENTREES
( ) Fresh Scrambled Eggs
( ) French Toast With Syrup

### ON THE SIDE
( ) Bacon Strips

### CEREALS
( ) Special K   ( ) Cream of Wheat
( ) Cheerios    ( ) Cornflakes
                ( ) Shredded Wheat

### BREAD BASKET
( ) Soft Roll   ( ) Bran Muffin
( ) Bagel       ( ) Crumb Cake

### BEVERAGES AND CONDIMENTS
( ) Decaf            ( ) Margarine
( ) Coffee           ( ) Butter
( ) Hot Tea          ( ) Cream Cheese
(X) Whole Milk       (X) Salt
( ) Skim Milk        (X) Pepper
( ) Chocolate Milk   (X) Sugar
( ) Hot Chocolate    ( ) Sugar Sub
( ) 1/2 oz Half & Half ( ) Jelly
( ) Lemon            ( ) Honey

---

## Mease Hospital — LUNCH

☐ DUNEDIN  ☐ COUNTRYSIDE

**MONDAY**

### APPETIZERS
( ) Cranberry Juice
( ) Hearty Vegetable Soup
( ) Chicken Broth

### SALADS
( ) Tossed Salad     Dressings:
( ) Coleslaw           ( ) Ranch
( ) Jello              ( ) Italian
                       ( ) Blue Cheese
                       ( ) 1000 Isle

### ENTREES
( ) Macaroni & Cheese
( ) Meatloaf with Gravy
Accompanied with:
Whipped Potatoes

### VEGETABLES
( ) Whole Kernel Corn
( ) Spinach

### SWEET ENDINGS
( ) Key Lime Pie    ( ) Fruit Cocktail
( ) Apple           ( ) Vanilla Ice Cream
( ) Banana          ( ) Chocolate Ice Cream
( ) Grapes          ( ) Orange Sherbet
( ) Melon           ( ) Lime Sherbet

### BREADS
( ) White Dinner Roll
( ) Whole Wheat Dinner Roll
( ) Melba Toast     ( ) Saltines

### BEVERAGES AND CONDIMENTS
( ) Decaf          ( ) Choc Milk
( ) Coffee         ( ) Margarine
( ) Hot Tea        ( ) Butter
( ) Half & Half    (X) Salt
( ) Iced Tea       (X) Pepper
( ) Whole Milk     (X) Sugar
( ) Skim Milk   ( ) Sugar Sub   ( ) Lemon

---

## Mease Hospital — DINNER

☐ DUNEDIN  ☐ COUNTRYSIDE

**MONDAY**

### APPETIZERS
( ) Apple Juice
( ) Tomato Juice
( ) Hearty Vegetable Soup

### SALADS
( ) Tossed Salad         Dressings:
( ) Gelatin Fruit Salad    ( ) Ranch
( ) Jello                  ( ) Italian
                           ( ) Blue Cheese
                           ( ) 1000 Isle

### ENTREES
( ) Chicken Chow Mein over Rice
( ) Roast Beef Sandwich with Mayonnaise

### VEGETABLES
( ) Sliced Carrots
( ) Oriental Vegetables

### SWEET ENDINGS
( ) German Choc. Cake  ( ) Tapioca Pudding
( ) Apple              ( ) Vanilla Ice Cream
( ) Orange Sections    ( ) Chocolate Ice Cream
( ) Banana             ( ) Orange Sherbet
( ) Grapes             ( ) Lime Sherbet
( ) Melon

### BREADS
( ) White Dinner Roll
( ) Whole Wheat Dinner Roll
( ) Melba Toast     ( ) Saltines

### BEVERAGES AND CONDIMENTS
( ) Decaf          ( ) Choc Milk
( ) Coffee         ( ) Margarine
( ) Hot Tea        ( ) Butter
( ) Half & Half    (X) Salt
( ) Iced Tea       (X) Pepper
( ) Whole Milk     (X) Sugar
( ) Skim Milk   ( ) Sugar Sub   ( ) Lemon

---

**Exhibit 11-3**

**Monday menu from a seven-day hospital rotation**

*Reprinted with permission from Morton Plant, Mease Health Care*

## Mease Hospital
### BREAKFAST

□ DUNEDIN    □ COUNTRYSIDE

TUESDAY

**JUICES AND FRUITS**
( ) Orange Juice    ( ) Prune Juice
( ) Grapefruit Juice    ( ) Banana

**ENTREES**
( ) Fresh Scrambled Eggs
( ) Belgian Waffle With Syrup

**ON THE SIDE**
( ) Bacon Strips

**CEREALS**
( ) Special K    ( ) Oatmeal
( ) Rice Krispies    ( ) Cornflakes
     ( ) Total

**BREAD BASKET**
( ) Soft Roll    ( ) Croissant
( ) Bagel    ( ) Blueberry Muffin

**BEVERAGES AND CONDIMENTS**
( ) Decaf    ( ) Margarine
( ) Coffee    ( ) Butter
( ) Hot Tea    ( ) Cream Cheese
(X) Whole Milk    (X) Salt
( ) Skim Milk    (X) Pepper
( ) Chocolate Milk    (X) Sugar
( ) Hot Chocolate    ( ) Sugar Sub
( ) 1/2 oz Half & Half    ( ) Jelly
( ) Lemon    ( ) Honey

---

## Mease Hospital
### LUNCH

□ DUNEDIN    □ COUNTRYSIDE

TUESDAY

**APPETIZERS**
( ) Cranberry Juice
( ) Country Potato Soup
( ) Beef Broth

**SALADS**    Dressings:
( ) Tossed Salad    ( ) Ranch
( ) Sliced Marinated Tomatoes    ( ) Italian
( ) Jello    ( ) Blue Cheese
     ( ) 1000 Isle

**ENTREES**
( ) Baked Ziti
( ) Marinated Chicken Breast
     Accompanied with:
     Rice Pilaf

**VEGETABLES**
( ) Lima Beans
( ) Summer Squash Zucchini Blend

**SWEET ENDINGS**
( ) Apple Pie    ( ) Vanilla Pudding
( ) Apple    ( ) Vanilla Ice Cream
( ) Banana    ( ) Chocolate Ice Cream
( ) Grapes    ( ) Orange Sherbet
( ) Melon    ( ) Lime Sherbet

**BREADS**
( ) White Dinner Roll
( ) Whole Wheat Dinner Roll
( ) Melba Toast    ( ) Saltines

**BEVERAGES AND CONDIMENTS**
( ) Decaf    ( ) Choc Milk
( ) Coffee    ( ) Margarine
( ) Hot Tea    ( ) Butter
( ) Half & Half    (X) Salt
( ) Iced Tea    (X) Pepper
( ) Whole Milk    (X) Sugar
( ) Skim Milk    ( ) Sugar Sub    ( ) Lemon

---

## Mease Hospital
### DINNER

□ DUNEDIN    □ COUNTRYSIDE

TUESDAY

**APPETIZERS**
( ) Apple Juice
( ) Tomato Juice
( ) Country Potato Soup

**SALADS**    Dressings:
( ) Tossed Salad    ( ) Ranch
( ) Gelatin Fruit Salad    ( ) Italian
( ) Jello    ( ) Blue Cheese
     ( ) 1000 Isle

**ENTREES**
( ) Beef Stew
( ) Chef's Salad:
Please Choose Salad Dressing from Above List

**VEGETABLES**
( ) Green Beans
( ) Beets

**SWEET ENDINGS**
( ) Orange Cake    ( ) Sliced Peaches
( ) Apple    ( ) Vanilla Ice Cream
( ) Orange Sections    ( ) Chocolate Ice Cream
( ) Banana    ( ) Orange Sherbet
( ) Grapes    ( ) Lime Sherbet
( ) Melon

**BREADS**
( ) White Dinner Roll
( ) Whole Wheat Dinner Roll
( ) Melba Toast    ( ) Saltines

**BEVERAGES AND CONDIMENTS**
( ) Decaf    ( ) Choc Milk
( ) Coffee    ( ) Margarine
( ) Hot Tea    ( ) Butter
( ) Half & Half    (X) Salt
( ) Iced Tea    (X) Pepper
( ) Whole Milk    (X) Sugar
( ) Skim Milk    ( ) Sugar Sub    ( ) Lemon

---

**Exhibit 11-4**
**Tuesday menu from a seven-day hospital rotation**

*Reprinted with permission from Morton Plant, Mease Health Care*

## Mease Hospital

☐ DUNEDIN   ☐ COUNTRYSIDE

### BREAKFAST

**WEDNESDAY**

**JUICES AND FRUITS**
( ) Orange Juice      ( ) Prune Juice
( ) Grapefruit Juice  ( ) Banana

**ENTREES**
( ) Fresh Scrambled Eggs
( ) French Toast With Syrup

**ON THE SIDE**
( ) Bacon Strips

**CEREALS**
( ) Special K      ( ) Cream of Wheat
( ) Cheerios       ( ) Cornflakes
                   ( ) Shredded Wheat

**BREAD BASKET**
( ) Soft Roll      ( ) Corn Muffin
( ) Bagel          ( ) Biscuit

**BEVERAGES AND CONDIMENTS**
( ) Decaf              ( ) Margarine
( ) Coffee            ( ) Butter
( ) Hot Tea           ( ) Cream Cheese
(X) Whole Milk        (X) Salt
( ) Skim Milk         (X) Pepper
( ) Chocolate Milk    (X) Sugar
( ) Hot Chocolate     ( ) Sugar Sub
( ) 1/2 oz Half & Half ( ) Jelly
( ) Lemon             ( ) Honey

---

## Mease Hospital

☐ DUNEDIN   ☐ COUNTRYSIDE

### LUNCH

**WEDNESDAY**

**APPETIZERS**
( ) Cranberry Juice
( ) Turkey Noodle Soup
( ) Chicken Broth

**SALADS**        Dressings:
( ) Tossed Salad       ( ) Ranch
( ) Three Bean Salad   ( ) Italian
( ) Jello              ( ) Blue Cheese
                       ( ) 1000 Isle

**ENTREES**
( ) Creamed Chicken
( ) Baked Fresh Salmon with Tartar Sauce
Accompanied with:
Noodles

**VEGETABLES**
( ) Oriental Vegetables
( ) Sliced Carrots

**SWEET ENDINGS**
( ) Cherry Pie     ( ) Pear Halves
( ) Apple          ( ) Vanilla Ice Cream
( ) Banana         ( ) Chocolate Ice Cream
( ) Grapes         ( ) Orange Sherbet
( ) Melon          ( ) Lime Sherbet

**BREADS**
( ) White Dinner Roll
( ) Whole Wheat Dinner Roll
( ) Melba Toast    ( ) Saltines

**BEVERAGES AND CONDIMENTS**
( ) Decaf          ( ) Choc Milk
( ) Coffee         ( ) Margarine
( ) Hot Tea        ( ) Butter
( ) Half & Half    (X) Salt
( ) Iced Tea       (X) Pepper
( ) Whole Milk     (X) Sugar
( ) Skim Milk  ( ) Sugar Sub  ( ) Lemon

**Exhibit 11-5**
**Wednesday menu from a seven-day hospital rotation**
*Reprinted with permission from Morton Plant, Mease Health Care*

---

## Mease Hospital

☐ DUNEDIN   ☐ COUNTRYSIDE

### DINNER

**WEDNESDAY**

**APPETIZERS**
( ) Apple Juice
( ) Tomato Juice
( ) Turkey Noodle Soup

**SALADS**        Dressings:
( ) Tossed Salad        ( ) Ranch
( ) Gelatin Fruit Salad ( ) Italian
( ) Jello               ( ) Blue Cheese
                        ( ) 1000 Isle

**ENTREES**
( ) Cottage Cheese Fruit Platter
( ) Honey Barbecued Chicken Breast
Accompanied with:
Long Grain & Wild Rice

**VEGETABLES**
( ) Corn        ( ) Zucchini

**SWEET ENDINGS**
( ) Chocolate Cake   ( ) Custard
( ) Apple            ( ) Vanilla Ice Cream
( ) Orange Sections  ( ) Chocolate Ice Cream
( ) Banana           ( ) Orange Sherbet
( ) Grapes           ( ) Lime Sherbet
( ) Melon

**BREADS**
( ) White Dinner Roll
( ) Whole Wheat Dinner Roll
( ) Melba Toast    ( ) Saltines

**BEVERAGES AND CONDIMENTS**
( ) Decaf          ( ) Choc Milk
( ) Coffee         ( ) Margarine
( ) Hot Tea        ( ) Butter
( ) Half & Half    (X) Salt
( ) Iced Tea       (X) Pepper
( ) Whole Milk     (X) Sugar
( ) Skim Milk  ( ) Sugar Sub  ( ) Lemon

## Mease Hospital

☐ DUNEDIN  ☐ COUNTRYSIDE

### BREAKFAST

#### THURSDAY

**JUICES AND FRUITS**
( ) Orange Juice
( ) Apple Juice
( ) Prune Juice
( ) Banana

**ENTREES**
( ) Fresh Scrambled Eggs
( ) Belgian Waffle With Syrup

**ON THE SIDE**
( ) Bacon Strips

**CEREALS**
( ) Special K
( ) Rice Krispies
( ) Oatmeal
( ) Cornflakes
( ) Total

**BREAD BASKET**
( ) Soft Roll
( ) Bagel
( ) Bran Muffin
( ) Crumb Cake

**BEVERAGES AND CONDIMENTS**
( ) Decaf
( ) Coffee
( ) Hot Tea
(X) Whole Milk
( ) Skim Milk
( ) Chocolate Milk
( ) Hot Chocolate
( ) 1/2 oz Half & Half
( ) Lemon
( ) Margarine
( ) Butter
( ) Cream Cheese
(X) Salt
(X) Pepper
(X) Sugar
( ) Sugar Sub
( ) Jelly
( ) Honey

---

## Mease Hospital

☐ DUNEDIN  ☐ COUNTRYSIDE

### LUNCH

#### THURSDAY

**APPETIZERS**
( ) Cranberry Juice
( ) Cream of Broccoli Soup
( ) Beef Broth

**SALADS**          Dressings:
( ) Tossed Salad                    ( ) Ranch
( ) Peach & Cottage Cheese Salad    ( ) Italian
( ) Jello                           ( ) Blue Cheese
                                    ( ) 1000 Isle

**ENTREES**
( ) Vegetable Lasagna
( ) Braised Pork Chop
Accompanied with:
    Yam Patty

**VEGETABLES**
( ) Mixed Vegetables
( ) Green Bean Mushroom Casserole

**SWEET ENDINGS**
( ) Coconut Pie
( ) Apple
( ) Banana
( ) Grapes
( ) Melon
( ) Applesauce
( ) Vanilla Ice Cream
( ) Chocolate Ice Cream
( ) Orange Sherbet
( ) Lime Sherbet

**BREADS**
( ) White Dinner Roll
( ) Whole Wheat Dinner Roll
( ) Melba Toast          ( ) Saltines

**BEVERAGES AND CONDIMENTS**
( ) Decaf
( ) Coffee
( ) Hot Tea
( ) Half & Half
( ) Iced Tea
( ) Whole Milk
( ) Skim Milk    ( ) Sugar Sub
( ) Choc Milk
( ) Margarine
( ) Butter
(X) Salt
(X) Pepper
(X) Sugar
( ) Lemon

---

## Mease Hospital

☐ DUNEDIN  ☐ COUNTRYSIDE

### DINNER

#### THURSDAY

**APPETIZERS**
( ) Apple Juice
( ) Tomato Juice
( ) Cream of Broccoli Soup

**SALADS**          Dressings:
( ) Tossed Salad            ( ) Ranch
( ) Gelatin Fruit Salad     ( ) Italian
( ) Jello                   ( ) Blue Cheese
                            ( ) 1000 Isle

**ENTREES**
( ) Tuna Salad Platter
( ) Beef Tips
Accompanied with:
    Noodles

**VEGETABLES**
( ) Whole Baby Carrots    ( ) Green Peas

**SWEET ENDINGS**
( ) Oatmeal Cookie
( ) Apple
( ) Orange Sections
( ) Banana
( ) Grapes
( ) Melon
( ) Chocolate Pudding
( ) Vanilla Ice Cream
( ) Chocolate Ice Cream
( ) Orange Sherbet
( ) Lime Sherbet

**BREADS**
( ) White Dinner Roll
( ) Whole Wheat Dinner Roll
( ) Melba Toast          ( ) Saltines

**BEVERAGES AND CONDIMENTS**
( ) Decaf
( ) Coffee
( ) Hot Tea
( ) Half & Half
( ) Iced Tea
( ) Whole Milk
( ) Skim Milk    ( ) Sugar Sub
( ) Choc Milk
( ) Margarine
( ) Butter
(X) Salt
(X) Pepper
(X) Sugar
( ) Lemon

---

**Exhibit 11-6**

**Thursday menu from a seven-day hospital rotation**

*Reprinted with permission from Morton Plant, Mease Health Care*

## Mease Hospital

☐ DUNEDIN  ☐ COUNTRYSIDE

### BREAKFAST

#### FRIDAY

**JUICES AND FRUITS**
( ) Orange Juice   ( ) Prune Juice
( ) Apple Juice    ( ) Banana

**ENTREES**
( ) Fresh Scrambled Eggs
( ) French Toast With Syrup

**ON THE SIDE**
( ) Bacon Strips

**CEREALS**
( ) Special K    ( ) Cream of Wheat
( ) Cheerios     ( ) Cornflakes
                 ( ) Shredded Wheat

**BREAD BASKET**
( ) Soft Roll    ( ) Croissant
( ) Bagel        ( ) Demi Danish

**BEVERAGES AND CONDIMENTS**
( ) Decaf            ( ) Margarine
( ) Coffee          ( ) Butter
( ) Hot Tea         ( ) Cream Cheese
(X) Whole Milk      (X) Salt
( ) Skim Milk       (X) Pepper
( ) Chocolate Milk  (X) Sugar
( ) Hot Chocolate   ( ) Sugar Sub
( ) 1/2 oz Half & Half ( ) Jelly
( ) Lemon           ( ) Honey

---

## Mease Hospital

☐ DUNEDIN  ☐ COUNTRYSIDE

### LUNCH

#### FRIDAY

**APPETIZERS**
( ) Cranberry Juice
( ) New England Clam Chowder
( ) Chicken Broth

**SALADS**          Dressings:
( ) Tossed Salad        ( ) Ranch
( ) Gelatin Fruit Salad ( ) Italian
( ) Jello               ( ) Blue Cheese
                        ( ) 1000 Isle

**ENTREES**
( ) Swiss Steak
( ) Fresh Cod
Accompanied with:
Garlic Seasoned Shells

**VEGETABLES**
( ) Green Peas
( ) Cauliflower

**SWEET ENDINGS**
( ) Brownie   ( ) Fruit Cocktail
( ) Apple     ( ) Vanilla Ice Cream
( ) Banana    ( ) Chocolate Ice Cream
( ) Grapes    ( ) Orange Sherbet
( ) Melon     ( ) Lime Sherbet

**BREADS**
( ) White Dinner Roll
( ) Whole Wheat Dinner Roll   ( ) Saltines
( ) Melba Toast

**BEVERAGES AND CONDIMENTS**
( ) Decaf        ( ) Choc Milk
( ) Coffee       ( ) Margarine
( ) Hot Tea      ( ) Butter
( ) Half & Half  (X) Salt
( ) Iced Tea     (X) Pepper
( ) Whole Milk   (X) Sugar
( ) Skim Milk    ( ) Sugar Sub   ( ) Lemon

---

## Mease Hospital

☐ DUNEDIN  ☐ COUNTRYSIDE

### DINNER

#### FRIDAY

**APPETIZERS**
( ) Apple Juice
( ) Tomato Juice
( ) New England Clam Chowder

**SALADS**          Dressings:
( ) Tossed Salad    ( ) Ranch
( ) Pickled Beets   ( ) Italian
( ) Jello           ( ) Blue Cheese
                    ( ) 1000 Isle

**ENTREES**
( ) Egg Salad Sandwich
( ) Roast Turkey
Accompanied with:
Whipped Potatoes, Gravy & Cranberry Sauce

**VEGETABLES**
( ) Broccoli   ( ) Mixed Vegetables

**SWEET ENDINGS**
( ) Pumpkin Pie    ( ) Tapioca Pudding
( ) Apple          ( ) Vanilla Ice Cream
( ) Orange Sections( ) Chocolate Ice Cream
( ) Banana         ( ) Orange Sherbet
( ) Grapes         ( ) Lime Sherbet
( ) Melon

**BREADS**
( ) White Dinner Roll
( ) Whole Wheat Dinner Roll
( ) Melba Toast   ( ) Saltines

**BEVERAGES AND CONDIMENTS**
( ) Decaf        ( ) Choc Milk
( ) Coffee       ( ) Margarine
( ) Hot Tea      ( ) Butter
( ) Half & Half  (X) Salt
( ) Iced Tea     (X) Pepper
( ) Whole Milk   (X) Sugar
( ) Skim Milk    ( ) Sugar Sub   ( ) Lemon

---

**Exhibit 11-7**

**Friday menu from a seven-day hospital rotation**
*Reprinted with permission from Morton Plant, Mease Health Care*

# Mease Hospital

## BREAKFAST

☐ DUNEDIN   ☐ COUNTRYSIDE

### SATURDAY

**JUICES AND FRUITS**
( ) Orange Juice     ( ) Prune Juice
( ) Apple Juice      ( ) Banana

**ENTREES**
( ) Fresh Scrambled Eggs
( ) French Toast With Syrup

**ON THE SIDE**
( ) Bacon Strips

**CEREALS**
( ) Special K        ( ) Oatmeal
( ) Rice Krispies    ( ) Cornflakes
                     ( ) Shredded Wheat

**BREAD BASKET**
( ) Soft Roll        ( ) Corn Muffin
( ) Bagel            ( ) Biscuit

**BEVERAGES AND CONDIMENTS**
( ) Decaf            ( ) Margarine
( ) Coffee           ( ) Butter
( ) Hot Tea          ( ) Cream Cheese
(X) Whole Milk       (X) Salt
( ) Skim Milk        (X) Pepper
( ) Chocolate Milk   (X) Sugar
( ) Hot Chocolate    ( ) Sugar Sub
( ) 1/2 oz Half & Half ( ) Jelly
( ) Lemon            ( ) Honey

---

# Mease Hospital

## LUNCH

☐ DUNEDIN   ☐ COUNTRYSIDE

### SATURDAY

**APPETIZERS**
( ) Cranberry Juice
( ) Vegetable Chicken Soup
( ) Beef Broth

**SALADS**          Dressings:
( ) Tossed Salad     ( ) Ranch
( ) Gelatin Fruit Salad ( ) Italian
( ) Jello            ( ) Blue Cheese
                     ( ) 1000 Isle

**ENTREES**
( ) Ham Hawaiian
( ) Salisbury Steak
Accompanied with:
Long Grain and Wild Rice

**VEGETABLES**
( ) Glazed Carrots
( ) Spinach

**SWEET ENDINGS**
( ) Cheesecake       ( ) Sliced Peaches
( ) Apple            ( ) Vanilla Ice Cream
( ) Banana           ( ) Chocolate Ice Cream
( ) Grapes           ( ) Orange Sherbet
( ) Melon            ( ) Lime Sherbet

**BREADS**
( ) White Dinner Roll
( ) Whole Wheat Dinner Roll
( ) Melba Toast      ( ) Saltines

**BEVERAGES AND CONDIMENTS**
( ) Decaf            ( ) Choc Milk
( ) Coffee           ( ) Margarine
( ) Hot Tea          ( ) Butter
( ) Half & Half      (X) Salt
( ) Iced Tea         (X) Pepper
( ) Whole Milk       (X) Sugar
( ) Skim Milk  ( ) Sugar Sub  ( ) Lemon

**Exhibit 11-8**

**Saturday menu from a seven-day hospital rotation**

*Reprinted with permission from Morton Plant, Mease Health Care*

---

# Mease Hospital

## DINNER

☐ DUNEDIN   ☐ COUNTRYSIDE

### SATURDAY

**APPETIZERS**
( ) Apple Juice
( ) Tomato Juice
( ) Vegetable Chicken Gumbo

**SALADS**          Dressings:
( ) Tossed Salad     ( ) Ranch
( ) Potato Salad     ( ) Italian
( ) Jello            ( ) Blue Cheese
                     ( ) 1000 Isle

**ENTREES**
( ) Chicken Salad Platter
( ) Beef Stroganoff
Accompanied with:
Noodles

**VEGETABLES**
( ) Sliced Beets     ( ) Green Beans

**SWEET ENDINGS**
( ) Choc. Chip Cookie ( ) Vanilla Pudding
( ) Apple            ( ) Vanilla Ice Cream
( ) Orange Sections  ( ) Chocolate Ice Cream
( ) Banana           ( ) Orange Sherbet
( ) Grapes           ( ) Lime Sherbet
( ) Melon

**BREADS**
( ) White Dinner Roll
( ) Whole Wheat Dinner Roll
( ) Melba Toast      ( ) Saltines

**BEVERAGES AND CONDIMENTS**
( ) Decaf            ( ) Choc Milk
( ) Coffee           ( ) Margarine
( ) Hot Tea          ( ) Butter
( ) Half & Half      (X) Salt
( ) Iced Tea         (X) Pepper
( ) Whole Milk       (X) Sugar
( ) Skim Milk  ( ) Sugar Sub  ( ) Lemon

# 12  Cafeteria Menus

**Purpose:** To show that in cafeterias, the order and manner of the presentation of food items as well as the choice of items contribute to merchandising and value.

Cafeteria service sales amount to nearly $5 billion each year, but this represents less than 3 percent of the total commercial food service industry revenue. Cafeteria service growth has lagged behind all except fine dining operations during the past five years. On the other hand, in the industrial segment (nonprofit), cafeterias are the principal mode of service.

As with all other types of food service, menu planning for both commercial and industrial cafeterias requires a consideration of who the potential customers are and what best satisfies their tastes. In cafeterias more consideration must be given to the use of leftovers—What items can be used again in the same form? Which items need to be reworked? For the last customers of the day, the pans must still contain enough food to be presentable.

## Presentation of Food

The printed menus in family restaurants and signature restaurants alike have descriptive copy designed to present the item in the most favorable way possible. Beef often becomes "aged, tender" beef, ham may be "sugar-cured" or "honey-glazed," tomatoes are "vine ripened," beans are "crisp." Such adjectives lead the customer to anticipate an enjoyable meal. In addition to descriptive copy, good menu presentation results from a decorator's expertise in design and color and a printer's ability to set the perfect type to present the message intended by the restaurateur. The cafeteria menu writer can use none of these props to sell the food items. This is not necessarily a disadvantage. An optimist might say that lacking these props eliminates the chance of making numerous mistakes and producing a menu that is more of a liability than a selling tool.

In a cafeteria operation there may be a board listing food items with prices, but there is little opportunity for such a presentation to substitute for a well-written menu. The selling is done by the showmanship exhibited in the layout of the foods, both in the appearance of the items and in the order in which they are offered. The order is influenced by several commonsense considerations; for example, hot foods should be the last or near the last food items offered so that they do not cool too much before the guest is ready to eat. Salads are a popular choice among cafeteria operators to lead off the lineup of foods. They can be made colorful and very appealing so that they are almost automatically taken.

On many restaurant menus salads become one of three items offered; that is, the entrée includes a choice of potato and vegetable or salad. Sometimes it is a choice of potato and soup or salad. Eating a potato plus a vegetable plus a salad is a bit more than many people will want or need. In the cafeteria the salad as the first item for selection does not compete with the vegetable or soup. It stands alone and is usually attractive enough that the customer selects it. In the most often chosen order of foods, salads appear again at the end of the line. These are strictly side salads, while some of the first salad selections were probably entrée salads. Fruit drinks and cups of fruit are usually at the head of the line next to the salads because they are cold foods and high-profit items.

Soup is another food that is not a regular part of a meal as is the entrée or a potato. It is more of a "sometimes" item. One chain of cafeterias features soup only at luncheon and presents it as a soup-and-sandwich special or a soup-and-salad special. So a good spot for soup is at the beginning of the hot foods presentation if it is to appeal to customers. Meat and fish items follow in that or the reverse order, and the vegetables conclude the section of hot foods. The most often used order of food is as follows:

Salads—side and entrée
Fruit cups and fruit drinks
Soup
Meat
Fish
Vegetables
Desserts
Bread
Side salads
Sandwiches

## Combination Plates

Developing combination items, both hot and cold, serves a dual function. They lend themselves to presentation as "specialty" items and also are an excellent way to use up leftover materials. The combinations favored in restaurants and which offer meat and fish can be featured individually or in combination in the cafeteria line.

## Monotony

Monotony is a dreaded concept in the restaurant industry. If customers perceive monotony in presentation, they will eat at another restaurant the next time. This is especially true in cafeteria operations. The order of foods presented above is generally followed, but items can be moved around from front to back and changes in food selections can be made. In the cafeteria line all the different meats are usually featured along with poultry and fish. Certain items, such as roast round of beef and fried quarter chicken, can and should appear every day. Stewing and hash items and special broiled-to-order items can provide variation.

The customers usually more readily perceive monotony in the sameness of breads and desserts than in entrées. This presents an opportunity for the large cafeterias that do their own baking. The same dough for rolls can be shaped in a variety of ways that create interest rather than monotony. Muffins are another item that offers the chance to constantly change presentation. The many varieties include corn, bran, wheat, cheese, apple, coconut, cranberry, pecan, and blueberry, to mention a few.

## Fruit

Fruit can be a colorful group of foods. But canned fruits, while adding color, are uninteresting if they dominate the display. Whole fresh fruits such as bunches of grapes, bananas, and berries can give a horn-of-plenty character to the fruit display.

## Salads

Two reasons for salads to be the first items displayed in a cafeteria line were mentioned above. However, the most important reason may be that salads offer so many possibilities to make their area the most attractive.

Imagination and variety are doubly important in this group, which is the first group seen by the customers day after day. Although many of the same items, such as tomatoes, must appear daily, they need not present a monotonous picture—they can be cut in various ways. Tomatoes can be cut in quarters or thin sections, sliced crosswise, or scooped out and stuffed with tuna fish, egg, crabmeat, and so forth. Raw vegetables can offer variety as well as decoration. Diced celery, cucumbers, green onions, radishes, and grated carrots are popular and especially attractive to persons concentrating on healthful eating. Fresh fruits can be offered in groups, and they give additional variety to salads. Fruits with cheese contribute to the heartiness of a salad. Cheeses in different combinations are attractive salad items, for example, peaches and cottage cheese or balls of cream cheese rolled in chopped nuts.

## Desserts

Desserts offer an opportunity to introduce specialties that customers remember and associate with a particular cafeteria. The opportunity to display desserts is a definite advantage over a dessert menu no matter how well prepared the menu. This is why many fine-dining restaurants and signature restaurants feature dessert carts. There is a great variety in pies, but many look the same and the guests can get the feeling that they are seeing the same pies every day. It is important, therefore, not to have a rigid routine of a fruit pie, a meringue pie, and a custard pie, or some such arrangement, each day. The lattice-top pie, the open-face pie, and the topped pie should each take its place in the rotation. The ideal way to serve cake is to have a whole cake on the counter and serve to order. This has been said to present problems in some cafeterias because it takes the full time of a person to keep the table supplied. But it would seem that the potential for customer satisfaction in such an arrangement would be well worth whatever effort is needed to give the service. We have mentioned several times in other chapters that a restaurant should be famous for one thing. A cafeteria's cake service might very well be that one thing, albeit simple, to set the operation apart from all others.

## Cycle Menus

Rather than attempt to construct a cycle menu for all cafeteria presentations, it is more practical to develop a two-week cycle for only meat and fish items. Fresh fruits can be featured every day in season but in several different ways. For color and character, at least four vegetables must be featured daily. The colors green, white, red, and yellow should be represented daily. Also a starchy, a leafy, and a watery vegetable should be in the group. The preparation methods of buttered, creamed, and mashed should also be represented in the vegetable selections.

## Showmanship

As we have mentioned, by its nature the cafeteria has a unique opportunity to create a display that appeals to customers' senses. Customers' senses of smell, touch, and sight are stimulated as well as is their sense of taste. The sense of smell is important because customers can have negative as well as positive reactions to stimulants. Certain foods, otherwise healthy and attractive (e.g., Brussels sprouts), create overpowering odors that detract from making a positive first impression on customers entering a cafeteria. On the other hand, coffee, especially at breakfast, provides a smell that stimulates the appetite. A restaurateur in a small town in the Midwest left nothing to chance in creating a pleasant odor in his place of business. The person assigned to open the restaurant in the morning had the task of creating the coffee odor. This was not done by brewing an urn of coffee; coffee was brewed in the kitchen and did not permeate the dining area. In the corner of the restaurant was a square of thin steel heated by a candle burning underneath. On the metal was sprinkled a thin covering of dry ground coffee. The resulting smell of roasting coffee created an atmosphere of good spirits for the customers and helped develop a two-turn breakfast volume.

## Convenience Foods

Commercial cafeterias are large-volume operations. The nature of the business calls for considerable advance preparation and ample displays of foods, and a large volume is necessary for survival. Reliance on prepared entrées to relieve a payroll problem have met with little success. The added cost of this type of food is not offset by labor savings. We seldom think of frozen vegetables as convenience foods, but in a general sense they are. Most cafeterias rely heavily on frozen vegetables, because with this product extra cost is more than offset by the savings in the labor needed to transform most fresh vegetables from "scratch" to cooked product. Some canned vegetables, notably peas, are also regularly used. Fresh vegetables (lettuce, carrots, etc.) are used in salads.

## Pricing

In pricing cafeteria menus, the same consideration must be given to clientele, competition, and costs as in pricing any menu. The cafeteria, however, is peculiar in that pricing is done item by item, much as for a strictly a la carte menu. By virtue of this, sales and cost analyses tell a definite story about what is contributing to the actual cost of sales and gross profit. Consequently, corrective actions can be specific and results measured accurately.

Nevertheless there is some disadvantage in this. The customer can also see exactly what contributes to the total of the check. Many people, especially housewives or other persons doing the family shopping, know the approximate cost of a number of items. This should be considered in establishing prices. For example, coffee sells at, say, $3.50 per pound, and people who think about costs know that a cup of black coffee should cost less than $.10 per cup. In a cafeteria that relates costs to individual items, it is wise to keep the price for a cup of coffee low because customers are likely to judge the overall price structure on the basis of this familiar item's price.

## Holding Temperatures

Departments of health in most states have established the following temperatures for holding food:

Hot foods: 140°F or higher
Cold foods: 45°F or lower

Cafeteria operators have found that the following holding temperatures are used to serve hot foods at a temperature that satisfies customers:

Meats, fish, vegetables, pasta: 160°F
Soups: 170°F
Coffee: 185°F

## Service

Both cafeterias and buffet restaurants, especially those commanding higher prices, have bus persons to carry trays to the tables for customers. This is also a service, as needed, in cafeterias that have a large clientele of elderly persons who need help in transferring trays to their tables. One such operation has a signal system operated by the cashier that alerts the bus persons when carry service is needed for a patron.

## Other Cafeteria Operations

Cafeteria volume represents only a small part of commercial food service, but cafeterias are the main form of service in the industrial sector. This apparent discrepancy is understandable in light of the operations that make up the nonprofit group—employee feeding, schools, prisons, the military, and so on.

### In-Plant Feeding

Employee feeding has evolved over the years from a necessary facility that provided meals for employees in the absence of adequate commercial operations in the area of the firm. These were subsidized operations and were part of employees' benefits. Today, employee cafeterias are usually break-even operations, with the firm providing rent and maintenance as the only benefits. Some have become profit centers with in-house operations, and the staff is part of the company's employee group. These and most of the other employee feeding operations must compete with commercial operations located in the area of the plant.

This current status of employee feeding has had a profound effect on menu planning. The potential clientele is the same day after day and the facility often serves only one meal, which can create a serious leftover problem. The response to these problems has been to adopt cycle menus of two weeks plus or minus a day so that the same items do not always

repeat on the same day. Unlike commercial cafeterias, the menu is limited to three or four entrées, two vegetables, two or three salads, two soups, and five or six desserts. With such a restricted menu, the entrées can all be popular items. Another departure from the menu making of commercial cafeterias is the use of convenience food entrées. These are especially adapted to the smaller operations that prepare the food off premises and deliver it in heated and refrigerated carriers.

### Schools

The food served in the public elementary, middle, and high schools currently has an annual sales value of over $17 billion. The United States Department of Agriculture (USDA) has set national nutritional standards for the school feeding program. By the school year 1996–1997, the school lunches and breakfasts have had to comply with the recommendations of the "Dietary Guidelines for Americans," which set forth medical and scientific consensus on proper nutrition as a vital element in disease prevention and long-term health promotion. This rule also establishes specific minimum standards for key nutrients and calories that school meals must meet, and it also incorporates some provisions of the Healthy Meals for Healthy Americans Act of 1994. The effect of this rule will be to provide more healthful and nutritious meals to the nation's schoolchildren.

The federal government supplies the schools with commodities from farm surpluses. In addition to the products from the surplus (referred to as "bonus foods"), the federal government has a buying program that purports to take advantage of volume buying. It also distributes this food to the nation's public schools. The products from the federal government amount to about 15 cents per meal served. There is an additional federal subsidy in the form of reimbursements. Eligibility to receive the reimbursement is based on whether the food served meets the nutritional standards set by the USDA. Some state governments give further small subsidies. Exhibit 12-1 shows the four-week cycle of lunch menus in the Pinellas County (Florida) public schools. Exhibit 12-2 shows the four-week cycle of breakfast menus for this same school system.

### Local Purchasing for Public Schools.
In addition to the food distributed by the federal government, considerable food must be purchased at the local level. Most of this food is bought on a bid basis. If purchases of a particular food amount to $10,000 or more per year, competitive bids must be solicited. Certain foods, such as pizza, have been tested for nutritional value, and qualifying brands can print "CN" (Child Nutrition) on the label.

### Convenience Foods.
Several years ago, nearly 100 percent of the foods served in school cafeterias were convenience foods. Except in areas with acute labor shortages, there

has been considerable movement away from use of these foods. The increased accent on economy in the operations is the principal reason for this change. Many operations discovered that the approximate 25 percent premium paid for these foods was not producing sufficient, if any, offsetting savings in payroll.

### Closed and Open Campuses.
Whether or not children are free to leave the campus during lunch is under the discretion of the individual school districts. If the campus is "open," the school cafeteria must compete with other food operations, if any, in the area. This makes effective production control difficult. It also reduces the number of reimbursable meals. Districts that have a "closed-campus" rule often find the rule difficult to enforce because some students in the course of a day move from one area to another for vocational training. Policing for compliance with the rule is also especially difficult in city schools.

| **WEEK ONE** | **Daily choice of:**<br>One (1) Entree(see below),two (2) Fruits or Vegetables, one (1) Bread, one (1) Milk* and one (1) Dessert<br>**or**<br>One (1)Salad Plate Meal, one (1) Bread or Crackers, one (1) Milk* and one (1) Dessert |
|---|---|
| **Monday** | **Choose 1**       **Choose 2**<br>Chicken Patty on Bun   Side Salad<br>Chicken Nuggets     Green Beans<br>  W/Sweet & Sour Sauce  Fruit Juice<br>Pasta w/Marinara Sauce & Cheese Fresh Fruit<br>Cold Sandwich Selection<br>**Choose 1**   **Choose 1**   **Dessert**<br>Garlic Bread Sticks Milk *   Apple Cobbler |
| **Tuesday** | **Choose 1**       **Choose 2**<br>Potato Turbate     Carrot & Celery Sticks w/Dip<br>Hot Ham & Cheese Sandwich  Seasoned Broccoli<br>Grilled Cheese Sandwich   Chilled Peaches<br>Cold Sandwich Selection   Fresh Fruit<br>**Choose 1**   **Choose 1**   **Dessert**<br>Whole Grain Roll  Milk*   Yellow Cake/Orange Glaze |
| **Wednesday** | **Choose 1**       **Choose 2**<br>Hot Dog on Bun     Oven French Fries<br>Roasted Chicken w/Rice   Cole Slaw<br>Cuban Black Beans w/Rice   Orange/Pineapple Gelatin<br>Cold Sandwich Selection   Fresh Fruit<br>**Choose 1**   **Choose 1**   **Dessert**<br>Whole Grain Roll  Milk*   Chocolate Chip Cookie |
| **Thursday** | **Choose 1**       **Choose 2**<br>Hamburger on Bun    Fresh Steamed Carrots<br>Chicken Noodle Bake    Romaine Salad<br>Tortilla Chips w/Nacho Cheese Sauce Chilled Pears<br>Cold Sandwich Selection   Fresh Fruit<br>**Choose 1**   **Choose 1**   **Dessert**<br>Blueberry Muffin Squares Milk*  Peach Cobbler |
| **Friday** | **Choose 1**       **Choose 2**<br>Cristo's Pizza      Tater Tots<br>Salmon Patty Melt    Tossed Salad<br>Bread Sticks w/ Nacho Cheese Sauce Frozen Juice Bar<br>Cold Sandwich Selection   Fresh Fruit<br>**Choose 1**   **Choose 1**   **Dessert**<br>Whole Grain Roll  Milk*   Chocolate Chip Cookie |
| | *Milk varieties available daily: Whole, Low Fat unflavored, Low Fat Chocolate, Skim |

**Exhibit 12-1**
**Four weeks of lunch menus served in a public school**
*From Pinellas County Schools, Largo, Florida*

| WEEK TWO | **Daily choice of:**<br>One (1) Entree(see below),two (2) Fruits or Vegetables, one (1) Bread, one (1) Milk* and one (1) Dessert<br>or<br>One (1)Salad Plate Meal, one (1) Bread or Crackers, one (1) Milk* and one (1) Dessert |
|---|---|
| **Monday** | **Choose 1**<br>Grilled Cheese Sandwich<br>Rib-B-Q on Bun<br>Turkey & Yellow Rice<br>Cold Sandwich Selection<br>**Choose 1**<br>Whole Grain Roll　　**Choose 1**<br>Milk *　　**Dessert**<br>Cherry Cobbler<br><br>**Choose 2**<br>Mixed Green Salad<br>Vegetable Soup/Crackers<br>Fruit Juice<br>Fresh Fruit |
| **Tuesday** | **Choose 1**<br>Soft Taco's w/Toppings<br>Burrito<br>Taco Salad in Edibowl<br>Cold Sandwich Selection<br>**Choose 1**<br>Corn Bread　　**Choose 1**<br>Milk*　　**Dessert**<br>Chocolate Cake w/Chocolate Glaze<br><br>**Choose 2**<br>Seasoned Corn<br>Strawberry Gelatin w/Peaches<br>Fruit Juice<br>Fresh Fruit |
| **Wednesday** | **Choose 1**<br>Hamburger/Cheeseburger on Bun<br>Chicken Nuggets<br>　　w/Sweet & Sour Sauce<br>Baked Potato w/Cheese<br>Cold Sandwich Selection<br>**Choose 1**<br>Banana Bread Squares　　**Choose 1**<br>Milk*　　**Dessert**<br>Oatmeal Cookie<br><br>**Choose 2**<br>Golden Potato Nuggets<br>Carrot & Celery Sticks w/Dip<br>Broccoli<br>Fresh Fruit |
| **Thursday** | **Choose 1**<br>Beef Stroganoff on Noodles<br>Pork Egg Roll/ Fried Rice<br>Egg Salad w/Tomato Wedges Bowl<br>Cold Sandwich Selection<br>**Choose 1**<br>Whole Grain Roll　　**Choose 1**<br>Milk*　　**Dessert**<br>Apple Cobbler<br><br>**Choose 2**<br>Tossed Salad<br>California Blend Vegetables<br>Pineapple Tidbits<br>Fresh Fruit |
| **Friday** | **Choose 1**<br>Cristo's Pepperoni Pizza<br>Cristo's Cheese Pizza<br>Tuna Salad Sandwich<br>Cold Sandwich Selection<br>**Choose 1**<br>Italian Bread Sticks　　**Choose 1**<br>Milk*　　**Dessert**<br>Oatmeal Cookie<br><br>**Choose 2**<br>Steamed Broccoli<br>Fruit Juice<br>Salad<br>Fresh Fruit |
| *Milk varieties available daily: Whole, Low Fat unflavored, Low Fat Chocolate, Skim | |

*Exhibit 12-1, continued*

| WEEK THREE | Daily choice of:<br>One (1) Entree(see below), two (2) Fruits or Vegetables, one (1) Bread, one (1) Milk* and one (1) Dessert<br>or<br>One (1)Salad Plate Meal, one (1) Bread or Crackers, one (1) Milk* and one (1) Dessert |
|---|---|
| **Monday** | **Choose 1**                                    **Choose 2**<br>Corn Dog                                          Golden Potato Nuggets<br>Bar-B-Que Chicken on Bun                California Blend Vegetables<br>Burrito                                              Baked Beans<br>Cold Sandwich Selection                   Fresh Fruit<br>**Choose 1**                  **Choose 1**                  **Dessert**<br>Oatmeal Muffin Square    Milk *                    Peach Cobbler |
| **Tuesday** | **Choose 1**                                                    **Choose 2**<br>Chicken Nuggets/Sweet & Sour Sauce   Oven Fries<br>Meat Loaf w/Gravy                                     Mixed Vegetables<br>Edibowl w/Bean Dip                                   Carrot, Celery, Broccoli Dippers<br>      & Nacho Cheese Sauce             Fresh Fruit<br>Cold Sandwich Selection<br>**Choose 2**                                  **Choose 1**                  **Dessert**<br>Whole Grain Roll    Steamed Rice    Milk*              Applesauce Cake |
| **Wednesday** | **Choose 1**                              **Choose 2**<br>Rib-B-Q on Bun                         Seasoned Green Beans<br>Spaghetti with Meat Sauce          Tossed Salad<br>Vegetable Lasagna                      Carrot Raisin Salad<br>Cold Sandwich Selection           Fresh Fruit<br>**Choose 1**                  **Choose 1**                  **Dessert**<br>Italian Bread                 Milk*          Peanut Butter Cookie |
| **Thursday** | **Choose 1**                              **Choose 2**<br>Sliced Turkey w/Gravy              Mashed Potatoes<br>Turkey Hoagie                          Broccoli<br>Cheese Quiche                          Spiced Apples<br>Cold Sandwich Selection           Fresh Fruit<br>**Choose 1**                  **Choose 1**                  **Dessert**<br>Whole Grain Roll            Milk*          Brownie |
| **Friday** | **Choose 1**                              **Choose 2**<br>Cristo's Sausage Pizza             Green Salad<br>Cristo's Cheese Pizza               Corn<br>Baked Fish Filet on Bun           Fruit Juice<br>Cold Sandwich Selection           Fresh Fruit<br>**Choose 1**                  **Choose 1**                  **Dessert**<br>Corn Bread                    Milk*          Peanut Butter Cookie |
| *Milk varieties available daily: Whole, Low Fat unflavored, Low Fat Chocolate, Skim | |

*Exhibit 12-1, continued*

| WEEK FOUR | **Daily choice of:**<br>One (1) Entree(see below),two (2) Fruits or Vegetables, one (1) Bread,<br>one (1) Milk* and one (1) Dessert<br>or<br>One (1)Salad Plate Meal, one (1) Bread or Crackers, one (1) Milk* and<br>one (1) Dessert |
|---|---|
| **Monday** | **Choose 1**  **Choose 2**<br>Steak & Cheese Hoagie  Oven Baked Fries<br>Hamburger or Cheeseburger  Seasoned Green Peas<br>Pasta w/Marinara Sauce & Cheese  Tossed Salad<br>Cold Sandwich Selection  Fresh Fruit<br>**Choose 1**  **Choose 1**  **Dessert**<br>Whole Grain Roll  Milk *  Apple Raisin Cobbler |
| **Tuesday** | **Choose 1**  **Choose 2**<br>Chicken Patty on Bun  Steamed Broccoli<br>Turkey Tetrazini  Applesauce<br>Macaroni & Cheese  Fresh Squash/Cherry Tomato Dippers<br>Cold Sandwich Selection  Fresh Fruit<br>**Choose 2**  **Choose 1**  **Dessert**<br>Bread Sticks  Milk*  Whole Wheat Sugar Cookie |
| **Wednesday** | **STUDENT INVOLVEMENT DAY**<br>Rules:1.  Students must be involved in planning the menu.<br>(SAC, Activities Clubs, Classrooms, etc.)<br>2.  Student Group to be given credit on menu, morning<br>announcements, cafeteria bulletin board, etc.<br>3.  Prize awarded at the end of the year to the group which plans<br>the most unusual, innovative menu which best meets  DGA's with<br>all required components using foods & supplies  available on bid. |
| **Thursday** | **Choose 1**  **Choose 2**<br>Baked Chicken  Seasoned Green Beans<br>Bar-B-Que Beef on Bun  Glazed Carrots<br>Arroz con Queso  Mashed Potatoes/Gravy<br>Cold Sandwich Selection  Fresh Fruit<br>**Choose 2**  **Choose 1**  **Dessert**<br>Whole Grain Roll - Spaghetti Side  Milk*  Spice Cake |
| **Friday** | **Choose 1**  **Choose 2**<br>Cristo's Pepperoni Pizza  Tossed Salad<br>Cristo's Spinach Pizza  Golden Potato Nuggets<br>Fish Nuggets  Fruit Juice<br>Cold Sandwich Selection  Fresh Fruit<br>**Choose 1**  **Choose 1**  **Dessert**<br>Corn Bread  Milk*  Whole Grain Sugar Cookie |
| \*Milk varieties available daily:  Whole, Low Fat unflavored, Low Fat Chocolate, Skim | |

*Exhibit 12-1, continued*

|  | MONDAY | TUESDAY | WEDNESDAY | THURSDAY | FRIDAY |
|---|---|---|---|---|---|
| **Week 1** | French Toast Sticks w/Syrup<br><br>Whole Wheat Toast<br><br>*Chilled Fruit<br><br>Milk | Breakfast Pizza or Breakfast Burrito<br><br>Whole Wheat Toast<br><br>*Chilled Banana<br><br>Milk | Cowboy Bread or Cinnamon Bun<br>Oatmeal<br><br>Whole Wheat Toast<br><br>Orange Juice<br><br>Milk | Pancake w/ Syrup & Sausage Pattie<br><br>Whole Wheat Toast<br><br>*Chilled Fruit<br><br>Milk | Dry Cereal or Cheese Toast<br><br>Whole Wheat Toast<br><br>Orange Juice<br><br>Milk |
| **Week 2** | Oatmeal with Raisins<br><br>Whole Wheat Toast<br><br>*Chilled Fruit<br><br>Milk | Breakfast Pizza or Breakfast Burrito<br><br>Whole Wheat Toast<br><br>* Chilled Fruit<br><br>Milk | Cinnamon Bun or Sweet Potato Muffin<br><br>Whole Wheat Toast<br><br>*Fresh Fruit<br><br>Milk | Scrambled Egg & Biscuit Sausage Pattie<br><br>Whole Wheat Toast<br><br>*Orange Juice<br><br>Milk | Dry Cereal or Cheese Toast<br><br>Whole Wheat Toast<br><br>Orange Juice<br><br>Milk |
| **Week 3** | French Toast Sticks w/syrup<br><br>Cinnamon Toast<br><br>Orange Juice<br><br>Milk | Breakfast Pizza or Breakfast Burrito<br><br>Whole Wheat Toast<br><br>*Fresh Fruit<br><br>Milk | Waffle with Syrup & Sausage Pattie<br><br>Whole Wheat Toast<br><br>Orange Juice<br><br>Milk | Egg Handwich<br><br>Whole Wheat Toast<br><br>Chilled Fruit<br><br>Milk | Dry Cereal or Cheese Toast<br><br>Whole Wheat Toast<br><br>Orange Juice<br><br>Milk |
| **Week 4** | Oatmeal with Raisins and Cinnamon<br><br>Whole Wheat Toast<br><br>Peaches<br><br>Milk | Breakfast Pizza or Breakfast Burrito<br><br>Whole Wheat Toast<br><br>Fresh Frozen Blueberries<br><br>Milk | Cinnamon Bun or Blueberry Muffin<br><br>Whole Wheat Toast<br><br>Fresh Fruit<br><br>Milk | Scrambled Eggs/Sausage Pattie<br><br>Whole Wheat Toast<br><br>Orange Juice<br><br>Milk | Dry Cereal or Cheese Toast<br><br>Whole Wheat Toast<br><br>Orange Juice<br><br>Milk |

*Chilled Fruit can be fresh, canned, or frozen. Dry cereal may be offered daily.

NOTE: Offer vs. Serve: Offer 4 components. Student may select 3 or 4 of the items to receive credit for a reimbursable meal. Less than 3 components cannot be counted as a breakfast.

BREAKFAST PATTERN: 1 milk (½ pint), ½ cup fruit/veg. - Elementary * Secondary Schools A GOOD SOURCE OF VITAMIN C IS RECOMMENDED TO BE OFFERED DAILY. 2 Bread, or 2 Meat (2 oz.) or 1 Bread and 1 Meat (1 oz.)

TWO SUGGESTED BAG BREAKFASTS (when needed): 1) Cinnamon Bun or Coffee Cake, Fresh Fruit, Milk or 2) ½ Peanut Butter & Jelly Sandwich, Fresh Fruit & Milk.

**Exhibit 12-2**

**Four-week cycle for a breakfast menu of a public school**

*From Pinellas County Schools, Largo, Florida*

# 13 Menu Mechanics

**Purpose:** To familiarize the student with the "sticks and stones" that make the physical menu interesting and pleasing to the eye and also an overture to an attractive sales presentation.

The menu writer should be familiar with type sizes, menu paper stock, and other elements necessary to produce a menu. However, few people are expert in all these areas, so finding a reliable professional menu printer to provide counsel is normally necessary to properly convey to the customers the image of excellence the restaurant is striving to provide.

During the first third of the twentieth century and before, the menu's principal function was to list the food selections available to customers and to inform them of the prices. It was the waiters' job to sell the items most profitable to the restaurant and balance the load in the kitchen. During the prosperous days immediately following World War I, the restaurant business experienced rapid growth and a resultant deficit of skilled waiters capable of performing the sales function. Enterprising restaurateurs met this crisis by introducing the element of communication into menus, which upgraded them from dull, lifeless lists to interesting and eye-catching sales tools.

But this simple presentation of the evolution of the menu underestimates the difficulties of achieving an effective menu design. Several specialized arts-and-crafts skills are needed to create this important merchandising tool. Knowledge of the culinary arts, an under-

standing of the printer's craft, and a feel for effective advertising are all required.

## The Menu Cover

Guests are first impressed by a restaurant's facade and entrance. As they enter they note the coordination between the type of restaurant and its general appearance, and the appearance of its entrance and exterior. The menu, specifically the menu cover, gives the next visual impression. Not only does the design of the menu cover further identify the type of restaurant, but an attractive cover is evidence of a well-operated restaurant. The menu cover has the function of inviting guests to enjoy the forthcoming meal; however, creating a menu begins not with designing the cover but with determining the contents. The list of what is to be sold, the type size, and the layout determine the size of the menu and the number of pages needed to accommodate the copy. After the dimensions of the menu are settled, the menu cover can be designed.

What should appear on the front cover depends on the type of restaurant. The design must fit with the restaurant's decor and theme. For example, an operation with a nautical theme can build the cover design around a boat or ship. Although this seems rather obvious, the sea and its accompaniments are attractive to most people. An inexpensive source of art for such a cover can come from old prints or engravings, which are usually easy and economical to reproduce.

A menu cover should be basically restful and therefore not too "busy" in its design. Copy describing what credit cards are honored, the schedule of operating hours, and so forth is better placed on the back of the menu. A history of the restaurant or its theme can be used effectively in menus. This copy can appear either on the back of the cover or on the left inside panel of a menu with a limited number of items that can be presented in total on the right inside panel.

Exhibits 13–1 and 13–2 are samples of menu covers effectively tuned to their restaurants' images or themes.

## Menu Size

Many menus are too small to tastefully present the copy, but care should be taken to see that it is not so large as to be unwieldy. To enlarge a menu, adding pages is often more attractive than increasing the menu's dimensions. On the other hand, a specialty restaurant offering a limited number of dishes could choose to print the selections on a large card and in large print well framed with art work appropriate to the restaurant's decor. This large format would overcome any image of sparseness in the choice of items.

## Menu Copy

Menu descriptions must be interesting, appetizing, and accurate and include the primary ingredients and the principal preparation method of each item. Menu copy need not be limited to listing food items and descriptions, however; copy about the restaurant and its history, interesting anecdotes about the

origin of the restaurant's name, and a host of other topics can be included to add interest and create a particular image. Pictures can add interest if they have significance for the restaurant. For example, a restaurant at the Sheraton Centre Hotel in Toronto is named for the old city hall that has become a tourist attraction and local monument. The picture on the menu is especially significant because the old city hall is part of the city square on which the hotel is located.

## Menu Typography

Appealing language in the description of menu items is for naught if the menu type is difficult to read. There are dozens of attractive type faces, but the primary consideration in choosing one for a menu is its readability. Multiple sizes of type on a single page can distract the guest and distort the image that the menu is designed to create. Type that is too small or too closely spaced can create confusion; instead of the ordering process being a pleasurable prelude to a fine meal, it becomes a wearisome job.

Menu type is measured in points. There are 72 points to the inch, and for readability, type smaller than 12 points (one-sixth of an inch) should not be used. Also, experts in the printing business advise that copy set in lower-case type is easier to read than type set with all upper-case letters. This is probably because we are all accustomed to this type, which is used in the books, magazines, and newspapers we read daily. Use of all upper-case type for words should be limited to headings and subheadings. Variation in type by using italics for emphasis is effective if done sparingly. If too much copy is set in italics, it tires the eyes because it is hard to read.

Varieties of Roman typeface are the most commonly used because of their readability; however, in ethnic or "Early American" restaurants or those with some other theme, the appropriate type should be used. Care should

KEY WEST® GRILL

OUR GOAL.... To serve you the best you've ever had.

KEY WEST® GRILL uses only <u>fresh</u> fish and stone crabs, flown in daily. We serve top quality "baby-back" ribs and burgers hand-formed from fresh ground chuck. For flavor, our cooks grill over mesquite wood and custom smoke all our ribs. You'll always be served hot, fresh vegetables prepared to order. The island breads are baked in house and our variety of soups and butter sauces are all scratch-made from unique recipes. And the Key Lime Pie is authentic — we think it to be the world's finest.

**Exhibit 13-1**
**The cover of the Key West Grill menu**
*Reprinted with permission of Key West Grill, Clearwater, Florida*

**Exhibit 13-2**
**The cover of Applebee's Neighborhood Grill and Bar menu**
*Reprinted with permission of Applebee's International*

be taken to ensure that the color of the paper and type enhance readability. Black type on white paper is the most easily read. If you choose to use colors, make sure that the contrast is as close as possible to black on white. Exhibit 13–3 illustrates some type varieties.

This sample shows 11 point Helvetica Regular:
Charcoal Broiled
Sautéed in Butter
Simmered in Red Wine

**This sample shows 11 point Cooper Black Italic:**
**Charcoal Broiled**
**Sautéed in Butter**
**Simmered in Red Wine**

This sample shows 11 pt. Serif Gothic:
Charcoal Broiled
Sautéed in Butter
Simmered in Red Wine

*This sample shows 11 pt. Commercial Script:*
*Charcoal Broiled*
*Sautéed in Butter*
*Simmered in Red Wine*

**Exhibit 13-3**
**Some different print types**

## Focal Point of the Menu

Where to place copy in a menu can be the most important part of menu mechanics. Assistance from a menu-design expert is usually necessary to properly establish the reader's focal point. The items that the restaurant wants to feature should normally occupy the menu's most prominent place (see below for a variation of this rule). On a single-card menu the focal point is immediately above the center of the menu as measured from top to bottom and centered on the horizontal dimension. On a single-fold menu, the prime position is above the middle line of the menu on the right panel.

In restaurants that specialize in a certain item, most of the customers will buy the item regardless of its position on the menu. A good example is a lobster house on the coast of Maine. Featuring the lobster in the number-one position on the menu is wasting the focal point's potential to influence customers. In such a case the premier place on the menu can be used to merchandise another high-profit item, or even appetizers, which are so often skipped in favor of an "appetizer" salad. Our consideration of the focal point illustrates why menu planning, which is fraught with other important complexities, should never be regarded as a sideline effort to "whip up" a menu in a hurry.

The order of items also influences the customers' choices. We read from left to right and from top to bottom, so we initially focus on the first item listed in each category. It is likely that the guest will believe that the item listed first is really "number one" in the restaurateur's opinion, so why "fight the odds"?

Exhibit 13-4, showing a three-panel menu, illustrates a number of the points covered above. It is a seafood restaurant, so the focal point, the center panel, features the items most favored by patrons choosing a seafood house. The menu writers listed the several items with specialty preparation in the order most likely favored by their guests. The combination "script/print" printing is large, quite legible, and entertaining.

The two side panels of Exhibit 13-4, although secondary to the center panel, present items in the same amusing manner.

Exhibit 13-5, the back cover of the menu, presents a romantic literary exposition of Key West, which is especially interesting reading for the tourists who visit Florida every year.

## Menu Cover Materials and Paper

Because of the cost of printing, daily changes in menus are seldom made. So the choice of paper for the menu should be based

## Tropical Drinks

| | |
|---|---|
| Chocolate Gorilla | Strawberry Daiquiri |
| Pina Colada | Mai Tai |
| Goombay Smash | Zombie |
| Bahama Mama | Yellowbird |

"Barefoot" Margarita .... the house specialty

## Appetizers

Key West Conch Fritters (pronounced "konk") . . . . . . . . . 3.95

Stuffed Bermuda Shorts (onion wedges stuffed with bacon and cheese) . . 4.75

Beer-Boiled Shrimp (¼ lb peel-and-eat shrimp) . . . . 4.95

Chicken Calypso (spicy chicken quesadilla) . . . . . 3.75

Shrimp & Pineapple Quesadilla . . . . . . . . . 4.95

Bacon-Cheese Nacho Fries (with or without jalapenos) . . . . 4.50

Sanibel Blackened Scallops (topped with a pineapple ginger sauce) . . . . 4.50

Hemingway's BBQ Rib Sampler . . . . . . . . . 4.95

Fresh Stone Crab Claws (seasonal) . . . . . . . . . market

Jamaican Jerk Chicken Tenders (marinated chicken) . . . 4.25

Caribbean Smoked Fish Dip (made with cream cheese and smoked fish) . . . . . 4.75

## Soups of the Day

Your server will inform you of today's offering of unique soups.

CUP . . . . . 2.75    BOWL . . . . . . . 3.50

## Salads of the Tropics

St. Croix (chunks of blackened, grilled, or fried chicken on lettuce w/cheese, tomato & green onion) . . . . . . . 5.95

Fresh Seasonal Fruit Salad . . . . . 5.95

The West Indies (a vegetarian salad with artichoke hearts, avocado, eggs, black olives, cheese, tomatoes & lots of greens) . 5.95

Salad of the Day (ask your server) . . . . . . . . . market

HOUSE SPECIALTY → Paradise Dinner Salad (with our coconut-mango dressing) . . 2.25

**Exhibit 13-4**
**Inside panels of the Key West Grill menu**
*Reprinted with permission of Key West Grill, Clearwater, Florida*

# The Fishery

An excellent variety of fresh fish shipped in daily and offered at <u>market price</u>. The following preparations are available for each of our fish. Includes vegetables, orzo pasta, and our Paradise dinner salad.

**MESQUITE GRILLED**
Choice of grilled fish, available with key Lime, coconut, or garlic herb butter sauce.

**"ISLAND"- BLACKENED**
Any fish blackened, topped with a pineapple ginger sauce.

**THE MIXED GRILL**
A grilled or blackened fish combination.

**"MAUI"-STYLE**
A teriyaki-marinated fish of the day.

**THE NATIVE'S SPECIAL**
Choice of fish topped with coconut butter sauce and toasted almonds.

# Mallory Wharf Shellfish

Includes our Paradise dinner salad

**BLACKENED SHRIMP or CHICKEN FAJITAS**
with red beans & rice . . . 10.45

**TERIYAKI-SPICED SHRIMP** . . . 9.25
mesquite grilled, with orzo pasta & vegetables

**GRILLED COCONUT SHRIMP** . . . 9.50
with orzo pasta & vegetables

**FRIED SHRIMP** . . . . . . 9.25
with fries & coleslaw

**SANIBEL BLACKENED SHRIMP & SCALLOPS** with orzo pasta & vegetables . . . . . . . . 10.25

**GRILLED LOBSTER TAIL**
with orzo pasta & vegetables . market

**STEAMED SNOW CRAB** . . . market
with orzo pasta & vegetables

**FRESH STONE CRAB CLAWS** *A Rare Treat*
served cold (seasonal) . . . . . market

## PASTAS
includes our Paradise dinner salad

**SEAFARER'S** (sauteed shrimp & scallops in an alfredo sauce) . . 9.25
**KINGSTON FETTUCCINE** (jerk chicken & veggies) . . . . . 9.25
**PASTA OF THE DAY** (ask your server) . . . . . market

# Sun Coast Combinations

Served with orzo pasta, vegetables and our Paradise dinner salad

**RIBS & CHICKEN PLATTER** (served with fries & slaw) . . . 11.50
**CHICKEN & SHRIMP** (teriyaki-spiced) . . . . . 10.75
**STEAK & FISH** (your choice) . . . . . . . 15.95
**STEAK & SHRIMP** (teriyaki-spiced) . . . . 14.95

*Exhibit 13-4, continued*

## The Wood Grill and Smoker

Served with fries and coleslaw or red beans and rice.
Includes our Paradise dinner salad.

HEMINGWAY'S BABY BACK RIBS . . . . . . . . . . . . . 10.95
CHICKEN BREASTS (mesquite grilled w/BBQ or blackened) . . . . . . 9.50
PORTERHOUSE STEAK (16 oz. choice) . . . . . . . . . 14.95
CASTAWAY STEAK (8 oz. Top Sirloin) . . . . . . . . . 11.45

## Bimini Bread Sandwiches

All sandwiches served with fries and coleslaw or red beans and rice

THE ORIGINAL "CHEESEBURGER OF PARADISE" (½ lb. with mushrooms) . 6.25
BIMINI BACON-SWISS BURGER (½ lb.) . . . . . . . . . . 5.95
FISH SANDWICH (blackened, grilled or fried) . . . . . . . 6.25
CLARKSTOWN CLUB (mesquite grilled, seasoned, chicken breast topped with pineapple, provolone, and bacon) . 5.95
CHICKEN BREAST (blackened or grilled w/BBQ & swiss) . . . . . 5.95
JERK CHICKEN SANDWICH (spiced chicken tenders & topped with provolone) . . . . . . 5.95

## Side Dishes

CREAMY COLESLAW . . . . . . . . . . . 1.00
GLAZED VEGETABLES . . . . . . . . . . 1.35
DUVAL ST. FRIES . . . . . . . . . . . 1.35
ORZO PASTA . . . . . . . . . . . . 1.00
RED BEANS & RICE . . . . . . . . . . 1.35

## Dessert Specialties

MACADAMIA NUT ICE CREAM PIE . . . . . . . 3.95
KILLER HOT FUDGE BROWNIE (go for it!!) . . . 3.25
PINA COLADA CHEESE CAKE . . . . . . . . 3.50
BANANAS FOSTER . . . . . . . . . . . 2.95
ISLAND BREADS (per doz.) . . . . . . . . 1.95

HOUSE SPECIALTY: OUR OWN

KEY LIME PIE . . . 2.95

*Exhibit 13-4, continued*

# THE TASTE OF PARADISE

KEY WEST... the end of the line, the last resort, a smuggler's den, a special place that many call paradise. An outpost of civilization on the edge of antiquity, once the Gibraltar of America. Hemingway called it, "an island in the sun."

KEY WEST is a polyglot-part conch, part Cuban, part Latino, a dash of Hawaii and more than a touch of the Bahamas. It's an attitude, a point of view, a frame of mind, a microcosm. Filled with conchs and rednecks, natives and tourists, famous writers and struggling painters, fishermen and shrimpers, the Navy and would-be developers, windsurfers and sun-worshippers, recluses and gadabouts.

KEY WEST is also a walker's or bicyclist's dream, where cars are scorned and two wheelers are preferred. They come in all shapes and sizes—ten speeds, no speeds, fat tires, thin speeders, three wheelers, rusty old crates, tandems and conch cruisers dressed either up or down. High rise handle bars and a basket big enough to carry a sack of groceries will get you everywhere you want to go. This is indeed a city where you don't need a car.

It is a very special place here. Especially at night – in the cool quiet, with jasmine-perfumed air and charming restaurants that beckon you to come enjoy KEY WEST is an epicurean haven where you'll find an ambrosia of savory delights. It's the place for conch chowder and conch fritters, stone crabs and key lime pie, fried shrimp and beer boiled shrimp. It's the freshest seafood and the tallest, coolest drinks served with spectacular sunsets, swaying palms and gentle breezes.

KEY WESTERS see themselves as hardly a part of the Real World. It's a laid-back world of its own that invites you to really see what surrounds you. The peaceful island that charmed and inspired Ernest Hemingway. A casual, carefree lifestyle– ethereal and alluring– KEY WEST is like no other place, the taste of Paradise. — Sharon Wells.

**Exhibit 13-5**
**Back cover of the Key West Grill menu**
*Reprinted with permission of Key West Grill, Clearwater, Florida*

on its durability and ability to retain an attractive appearance after many uses. In evaluating the cost of menu paper, its length of service and cost per seating should be factored into the calculations. A "water-resistant" paper that can be wiped clean with a damp cloth is a feature that adds to menu life. Lamination is expensive and in the opinion of many "experts" detracts from a menu's attractiveness, although it does have a place in menu mechanics. Many family restaurants use laminated menus, which are cost effective in this type of restaurant because of the high incidence of menu soiling through mishandling by children. Laminated menus are usually supplemented by "clip-ons" to reduce the frequency of menu revision. By using menu covers and inserts, the expense of revision is greatly reduced because paper suitable for inserts can be had at a fraction of the cost of more durable paper.

Materials other than paper are being used effectively in many food operations. Vinyl has become a popular fabric for menu covers because designs and colors can be readily applied to this material, and this can facilitate the projection of a theme or carry out a feature of the decor. In our experience the most radical departure from paper is the stainless steel menu cover of the Bern's Steak House in Tampa, Florida. Although quite expensive to produce, it has achieved its purpose of drawing attention to the restaurant by being the subject of many articles in food and beverage trade publications circulated nationally and in nonfood-related magazines. However, if it were not an excellent restaurant, it is unlikely that a menu cover of gold would have elicited such attention.

## Menu Shapes

In creating a menu, an unusual shape may be effective in projecting a particular image. Paper can be cut into shapes different from the usual rectangular form most commonly seen.

In a family restaurant, for example, breakfast, luncheon, and dinner are sometimes included on one menu. The usual division is by panel, but a division that involves a change in menu shape adds interest. For example, the breakfast menu in the shape of a coffee cup, the luncheon menu shaped like a salad bowl, and the dinner menu as an oval steak platter. Each says something pertinent to the meal listing offered. The three special-shaped menus can be pages inside a standard, rectangular menu cover.

Hotel room service is one particular food service operation that can benefit from the interest unusual menu shapes can generate. Considering that the room service menu is usually read by the guest without a waiter to supply information, and the guest is not in a restaurant where tempting food odors from nearby tables can be smelled, the room service menu has the most difficult selling job of all the menus. It is expected to sell breakfast, luncheon, dinner, wines, cocktails, and hors d'oeuvres. In addition, it is sometimes placed in a folder with other materials selling laundry and valet services, car rentals, and the like. Designers of this kind of menu should consider anything that attracts attention to the menu. An appropriately shaped menu for room service breakfast is the key form, as shown in Exhibit 13-6. Space is provided on the menu so that guests can write in orders and indicate the desired time for service. This sells food and facilitates its preparation by the kitchen staff.

## Menu Printing

The many processes involved in printing a menu can make this stage seem a harder job than menu planning. After all concerned have agreed on what items are to be included on the menu, the process of getting the menu ready for service in the restaurant begins. In opening a new restaurant, the first consideration is time: When will it open? Menu printing is a time-consuming process, and you must allocate enough time to production if the menu is to be ready when the restaurant opens. In the following pages we outline the steps that occur between choosing the menu items and having a finished menu.

## Design

In a new restaurant that has been decorated by a professional, the menu's cover design and colors can be chosen by the decorator. Take care, however, to limit this person's contribution to his or her area of expertise. The size of the menu should be determined at this time so that a layout can be worked on while a sample of the cover is being prepared. Adequate dimensions or enough pages is important to eliminate the common error of a menu too small to accommodate the copy. It is better to overestimate the size needed. Artwork in the menu will probably add attractiveness to the menu while filling unused space.

## Layout

Positioning the copy on the menu is the responsibility of the menu writer. It is wise to take the advice of the printer as to what locations on the menu are best for selling, but choosing the items to most prominently display is the prerogative and the duty of the restaurateur. After the layout is designed it is presented to the printer for typesetting and preparation of proofs.

## Proofreading and Corrections

At this point time has elapsed while choosing the design of the menu, determining the size, preparing the layout, presenting it to the printer, typesetting, and printing proofs, and the deadline for having a finished menu might be quickly approaching. Nonetheless, you should take the time to carefully review the proof of the menu because it is at this point that you can correct any errors or make any changes. The proofs may present a picture of

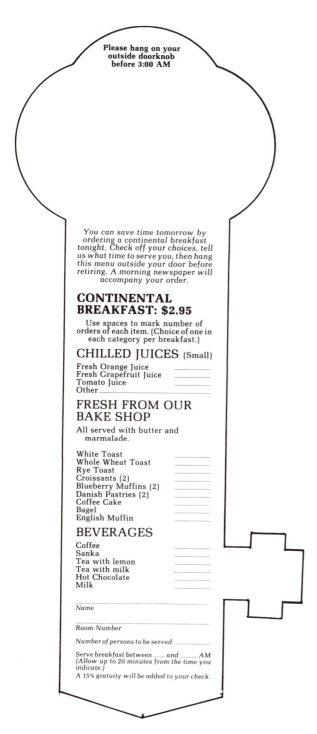

**Please hang on your
outside doorknob
before 3:00 AM**

*You can save time tomorrow by ordering a continental breakfast tonight. Check off your choices, tell us what time to serve you, then hang this menu outside your door before retiring. A morning newspaper will accompany your order.*

### CONTINENTAL BREAKFAST: $2.95

Use spaces to mark number of orders of each item. (Choice of one in each category per breakfast.)

### CHILLED JUICES (Small)

Fresh Orange Juice _____
Fresh Grapefruit Juice _____
Tomato Juice _____
Other _____

### FRESH FROM OUR BAKE SHOP

All served with butter and marmalade.

White Toast _____
Whole Wheat Toast _____
Rye Toast _____
Croissants (2) _____
Blueberry Muffins (2) _____
Danish Pastries (2) _____
Coffee Cake _____
Bagel _____
English Muffin _____

### BEVERAGES

Coffee _____
Sanka _____
Tea with lemon _____
Tea with milk _____
Hot Chocolate _____
Milk _____

*Name* _____

*Room Number* _____

*Number of persons to be served* _____

*Serve breakfast between ____ and ____ AM (Allow up to 20 minutes from the time you indicate.)*
*A 15% gratuity will be added to your check.*

**Exhibit 13-6
Illustrates a room service menu in the shape of a key, which is an interesting way to attract attention to the menu and promote its use**

*From the Colony Square Hotel, which was in Atlanta, Georgia.*

exactly what you expected, but this is not usually the case. A new perspective is gained by studying the menu copy in the context of the overall design, and thus changes are often made at this time. Spelling, punctuation, spacing, and the like must also be reviewed carefully, and changes should be marked on the proof, which is then sent back to the printer.

**Second Reading and Approval.** After reviewing proofs and possibly making minor corrections, you can approve the menu for final printing. This is not routine, however, because an additional reading is sometimes necessary. Two readings of proofs are expected by the printer, but additional proofs and further delay will probably result in an additional charge. You should clarify this with the printer before any work begins.

## How Many Covers and Inserts to Print

If inserts are used, you can determine the number of covers to order by what is the most economical number to order. This amount should be tempered by investment and storage considerations. The number of inserts to order is also influenced by the number of seats in the restaurant and the estimated discard rate. Two important factors that are often overlooked are (1) Is the restaurant clientele made up of a high percentage of repeat business? and (2) Are the items featured volatile in prices? Yes to either or both of these questions indicates that fewer menus or inserts should be printed than in, say, a resort property with relatively little repeat business or in a restaurant whose menu features items with steady price patterns. Menus should be reviewed and very likely revised four times a year; thus a ninety-day supply of inserts is a basic figure with which to begin calculations.

If copy is printed directly on the menu cover, use the same reasoning to determine the number of covers to order. This number would be modified by the same considerations that we listed for inserts, but the rate of discard between inserts and imprinted menu covers can vary quite widely. The use of clip-ons and partial inserts provides a flexibility in the menu, which allows a larger and presumably more economical number of menus to be printed. The menu design should include a place for inserts and clip-ons so that they do not cover a part of the regular menu.

All restaurants need copies of the menu for the cooks, cashiers, and people working in control and other supporting jobs. A number of copies of the menu should be printed on inexpensive paper for these uses.

## Printing and Delivery

At this point everything that needs to be done has been done. It will still be another week or more before menus will be in the restaurant ready for use. Getting a menu printed is not merely a time-consuming, necessary evil that must be done—it is an important contributor to a successful menu. For an experienced restaurateur who has a clear picture of what foods will be attractive to the potential clientele, developing the items to be featured can be a rather simple task. But presenting these foods in a menu that will sell is never a simple task. At the outset of this chapter we stated that several arts-and-crafts skills are needed to put menu mechanics in motion. Some of these specialties are beyond the experience and competence of the food operator, so the final product will depend on good managerial judgment that reflects back to the "six g's"—the crux of what makes a successful restaurant.

# 14  Know Your Menus

**Purpose:** To discuss the significance of the menu's relationship to the internal working of a food operation and to the customers.

The Merriam-Webster dictionary defines a menu as "a: a list of dishes that may be ordered (as in a restaurant); b: a list of the dishes available for or served at a meal; also: the meal itself." Thank you, Merriam-Webster, but a restaurateur or food service manager would say that the menu describes in detail, perhaps covertly to the layman, his opinions about the several functions that are vital to the restaurant's operation, and is the restaurant's primary merchandising marketing tool.

## Know Your Market

Chapter 4 of this text, "Know Your Customers," explored the likes and dislikes of the different potential customers who may patronize a particular restaurant. We also thoroughly investigated the prices such customers might be willing to pay and what represents good value to them. The practical application of that information is to develop a menu to fit the food and beverage preferences of a restaurant's potential clientele and place the items within the appropriate price range. The sequel to knowing your customers is knowing that your menu reflects their wants.

## Know Your Competition

One of the mainstays of the free-enterprise system is that the competitive market regulates the supply of a product and its price. When developing a menu you must have a thorough knowledge of what the competition offers in menu selections and prices if your restaurant is to gain a sufficient market share to become viable. The conditions under which the competitor presents his products is equally important, and thus the key to understanding the competition is frequent and thorough shopping. A planned, studied routine to avoid overlooking important information is critical to your successful shopping. We offer a sample "Shopping Report," illustrated in Exhibit 14-1, as an aid in acquiring this information.

Note that the shopping begins immediately on your entering the restaurant. Remember the remark of Benjamin Franklin quoted in Chapter 2, "The taste of the roast is often determined by the handshake of the host." That is more than a clever saying. The greeting at the door can set the stage for an enjoyable or dismal restaurant experience. A warm greeting will stimulate the guest to look for the attractive features in the restaurant's general atmosphere and decor and to anticipate a

Name of Restaurant _____ Date _____
Type _____ Time In _____
Seating Capacity – Bar _____ D. R. _____ Time Out _____

| | Price | Good | Fair | Poor | Comments |
|---|---|---|---|---|---|
| Environment | | | | | |
| Reception | | | | | |
| Quality of Food and Beverages | | | | | |
| *Items Ordered* | | | | | |
| Bar | | | | | |
| Appetizer | | | | | |
| Entrée | | | | | |
| Vegetable | | | | | |
| Vegetable | | | | | |
| Salad | | | | | |
| Dessert | | | | | |
| Coffee | | | | | |
| B and B | | | | | |
| *Service* | | | | | |
| Food | | | | | |
| Beverage | | | | | |
| *Sales effort* | | | | | |
| Cocktail offered | | | | | |
| Wine offered | | | | | |
| Specials suggested | | | | | |
| Appearance of staff | | | | | |
| *Menu* | | | | | |
| Adequate | | | | | |
| Number of entrées | | | | | |
| Special interests | | | | | |

**Exhibit 14-1**
**Food service shopping report**

| | Good | Fair | Poor | Comments |
|---|---|---|---|---|
| Environment | | | | |
| Reception | | | | |
| Quality of Food and Beverages<br>*Items Ordered*          *Price* | | | | |
| *Prices*<br>High | | | | |
| Fair | | | | |
| Value | | | | |
| *Physical Condition and*<br>*General Sanitation*<br>Rest rooms | | | | |
| Dining areas | | | | |
| Bar | | | | |
| Outside | | | | |
| Parking | | | | |

Outstanding Items, Foods, or Ideas _____

_____

_____

_____

_____
Name of Shopper

*Exhibit 14-1, continued*

satisfying meal. On the other hand, a lackadaisical greeting or none at all will set the guest to looking for the next unpleasantness that must surely follow if even the host is not enthusiastic about the place. Generally speaking, the things to look for in shopping the competition are the things positively stressed in a successful restaurant, as we enumerated and explained in our discussion of the "six g's":

- Good Environment
- Good Friendly Service
- Good Food and Beverages
- Good Value
- Good Sales Program
- Good Management

## Restaurant Critics

Not only in the large cities but even in small communities that are serviced by several restaurants, the local newspapers have restaurant critics. These people are very likely the best informed about competitive restaurants. Carefully reading their newspaper reports can greatly assist a restaurant operator in understanding the competition and the local market; it is a logical supplement to personal shopping. Restaurant critics have made a profession of shopping restaurants and reporting on what they find, and you can ordinarily count on them to give an objective account. When a restaurant is the object of a critic's examination, the manager or owner of the establishment should contact him or her to impart some specific information about what has been discovered to be the favorite foods in the region, how the guests prefer the food to be prepared, and the prices customers accept as part of good value. Such information can be a sounding board against which restaurant managers can measure their findings from their own personal shopping expeditions.

## Log Books

Discovering what menu items customers want is very simple—ask them. A very valuable asset to the operation of any restaurant is the Log Book. Like a ship's log, it is a day-to-day record of the important happenings on the voyage—in this instance it is the trip though the meals of the day. Guests' comments are the most important items recorded in the log. The Log Book should also contain information to explain the large or small number of covers served at a particular meal. For example, "The snow storm caused the cancellation of fifteen reservations," or, "The opening of the new play at the Shubert's Theater brought in an unusually large after-theater business." You can gain valuable information by talking with guests. Most guests, if put at ease at the outset of a conversation, will express honest feelings about menu selections, decor, or anything in the restaurant toward which the conversation leads.

Well-run hotels and restaurants hold weekly meetings to discuss current operations and plan for the immediate future. Thursday is the most popular day to do this because it allows ample time to make changes for the upcoming week. Whoever presides at the meeting can find in the Log Book plenty of "meat" for a lively agenda. It is also an indispensable tool at menu-writing sessions.

The Log Book can be used as a record of suggestions by employees as well as by guests. In fact, contests among employees for the best suggestions as determined by management (with appropriate prizes, of course) will reap a harvest of good management and menu ideas and contribute to a healthy cohesiveness among employees and management. Such contests need not be limited to employees. Guests can be solicited for ideas through table tents. Unfortunately, too often there is no feedback to the guests on what happens to suggestions. Prizes of dinners for two or four can be awarded to the most interesting suggestions each month. It is a more successful public relations tool if you subtly convey the information about awarding prizes for suggestions. Rather than imparting this information on a card with copy that reads like a television commercial (e.g. "Make A Suggestion—Win A Prize"), have the waiters and waitresses encourage the guests to use the card provided for evaluation and suggestions and make a low key announcement that management takes their suggestions quite seriously, and in fact thanks guests with complimentary meals for usable ideas.

## Trade Shows

The National Restaurant Association has sponsored an annual trade show since shortly after the turn of the century. The show currently is a joint effort with the National Hotel Association. In addition to this national show, there are state and local shows plus those sponsored by organizations such as the Club Managers Association. All of these shows are replete with information that can help restaurant operators keep abreast of the market and competition. There is a considerable social draw to these events and one can easily be overcome by this attraction. To gain maximum profit from attending these events, you should establish objectives and pinpoint specific items to investigate. At the same time stay open to unanticipated suggestions that you may encounter. The national and state shows usually feature a culinary arts salon, which can provide new menu ideas and innovative styles of presentation.

Some food purveyors and industry associations sponsor annual shows to display their products, especially new products. These events are particularly important for discovering trends in food products. Certain convenience foods that have entered the market in the past few years are of high quality and are not out of place in the most sophisticated restaurants. Patronage of food shows affords the restaurateur the opportunity to see these products in use rather than as part of a test and taste panel, and thus restaurant operators can decide whether they are appropriate for using in a menu.

## What Your Menu Can Do for You

An examination of what is involved in running a food operation will produce quite a lengthy list of items. About 50 percent of the entire operation depends in some way on the menu. In a hotel, for example, since the menu reflects a certain type of food operation (such as a signature restaurant), it indirectly determines the class of the hotel and consequently establishes the room rates.

The menu, its selections, and its prices dictate the environment needed. The color, lighting, decor—the general atmosphere—is built to menu specifications and the class of clientele the restaurant draws. The acceptance of a restaurant in a community depends on its "fit" with the restaurant's customers and the neighborhood in which it is located.

### Purchasing

There is a reciprocal relationship between the menu and food purchasing. In our discussion on who writes menus (Chapter 5) we said that the food purchaser is an important part of the menu-writing team. On the other hand, the menu determines what and how much food the food purchaser must buy. It also defines the quality of product needed. The amount of space needed to store products, refrigerated or other, follows from the extent and type of the menu.

### Payroll Costs

This statement is dramatic but true: Menu writing may be dangerous to the survival of a restaurant. Today labor costs are more critical than food costs. The food preparation staff is hired for the specific purpose of producing the menu items in the amounts needed to meet the customers' needs. Thus the menu is basically responsible for the staff. However, a high kitchen staff payroll can result from a kitchen too big for the menu needs, or too small, or poorly laid out, or with inefficient equipment. All these deficiencies are affected by and in turn affect the menu items to be produced. In addition to these physical deficiencies, excessive staffing can result from poor supervision and training, poor scheduling, inadequate control records, poor working assignments, uncontrolled overtime, low productivity, and restrictive union rules. This last item results from negotiations between management and the labor union representatives, so it is partially, if not wholly, the fault of a short-visioned management that agreed to such rules. Similar deficiencies can produce excessive staffing of service personnel. Again, either directly or indirectly, the shortcomings are produced by an ill-conceived menu.

**Convenience Foods and Payroll Costs.** Convenience foods are often of very high quality. Nevertheless, they are still scorned by some food operators who attempt to produce everything from "scratch." Preparing all recipes from basic ingredients can be devastating to payroll costs in moderately priced restaurants especially, but not exclusively. Very expensive restaurants can only in rare instances absorb costs related to such complete preparation.

The key to practical menu writing is the judicious use of convenience foods. In addition to control of kitchen labor, convenience foods permit an expanded menu without an increase in personnel. Schools, hospitals, and other institutional food services use convenience foods almost exclusively. Hotels, restaurants, and industrial feeding units use a mixture of convenience foods and primary items. Some of the convenience products widely used by this latter group are bases for stocks used for both soup and sauces; canned and dehydrated soups; instant mashed potatoes; frozen vegetables, French fries, and hashed brown potatoes. Such items as canned tomatoes and mayonnaise have been in regular use for so long they are often overlooked in discussions of convenience foods. Portion-control jams and jellies and wrapped crackers and other wafers are used for their convenience and cost but also to meet health department requirements in some areas. Good-quality Danish pastries and croissants can be purchased frozen. Also, Danish and French pastry doughs can be purchased, which makes it possible for some restaurants to fabricate fresh finished items from these convenience basic products.

## Some Available Convenience Foods

*Salad dressings*—Ready to use and dehydrated
*Breads*—Brown and serve
*Beverages*—Instant coffee and tea bags
*Desserts*—Pies
    Strudel
    Jello
    Cakes
    Puddings
    French pastry
*Fresh produce*—Cut lettuce
    Fruit sections
    Potato salad
    Peeled squash
    Cauliflower
    Mixed greens
    Cole slaw
    Macaroni salad
    Broccoli
    Brussels sprouts
*Canned*—Vegetables
    Chili
    Cooked meats
    Tuna
    Beans
    Stews
    Chicken
    Spaghetti
*Portioned foods* (raw and frozen)—
    Steaks
    Cutlets
    Kiev
    Hamburger
    Chops
    Cornish hens
    Cordon bleu
    Fish and shrimp
*Entrées*—Stews
    Casseroles
    TV dinners (about 4,000 on the market)
    Roasts
    Tray packet complete meals

## Cautions

1. Convenience foods normally cost about 25 percent more per portion than foods prepared from "scratch."
2. Will you really save payroll or just increase the loafing time of kitchen personnel?
3. Remember, up to 40 percent of all time spent by preparation personnel is nonproductive.
   a. Schedule work to spread over time.
   b. Vary starting times of kitchen employees. Bar charts provide a graphic picture of work schedules. Exhibit 14-2 illustrates a bar chart for cooks.
4. Most convenience foods can be improved by "doctoring."
5. If food and beverage costs of sales and labor costs (including benefits) exceed

**Hours**

| | 6 | 7 | 8 | 9 | 10 | 11 | 12 | 1 | 2 | 3 | 4 | 5 | 6 | 7 | 8 | 9 | 10 | 11 |
|---|---|---|---|---|---|---|---|---|---|---|---|---|---|---|---|---|---|---|
| Sauce Cook | | | | | | | | | | | | | | | | | | |
| Breakfast–Fry Cook | | | | | | | | | | | | | | | | | | |
| Breakfast–Fry Cook | | | | | | | | | | | | | | | | | | |
| Broiler–Roast Cook | | | | | | | | | | | | | | | | | | |
| Broiler–Roast Cook | | | | | | | | | | | | | | | | | | |
| Sauce Cook | | | | | | | | | | | | | | | | | | |
| Night Chef | | | | | | | | | | | | | | | | | | |
| Cold Meat–Day | | | | | | | | | | | | | | | | | | |
| Cold Meat–Night | | | | | | | | | | | | | | | | | | |

**Exhibit 14-2**
**Bar chart for cooks' work schedules**

75 percent of sales, profit vanishes.

6. The following sample profit-and-loss statement shows a restaurant with $150,000 in food and beverage sales per month, with costs and sales in dollars and percentages broken down to illustrate the minimal profit resulting from 75 percent of the revenue being expended for cost of sales and payroll.

*Sample Profit-and-Loss Statement*

| | | |
|---|---|---|
| Food sales | 62% | $93,000 |
| Beverage sales | 38 | 57,000 |
| Total | | $150,000 |
| | | |
| Cost of sales—food | 35% | $32,550 |
| —beverage | 22 | 12,500 |
| Combined | 30% | $45,000 |
| | | |
| Salaries and wages | 35%* | $52,500 |
| Benefits | 10 | 15,000 |
| Combined | 45% | $67,500 |
| | | |
| Cost of sales and labor | 75% | $112,500 |
| Other expense | 10 | 15,000 |
| Total department costs | 85% | $127,500 |
| | | |
| Departmental profit | 15% | $22,500 |
| Occupation costs | 10 | 15,000 |
| Net profit | 5% | $7,500 |

* 20% Kitchen costs; 15% Service and support costs

## Production Considerations

With the multitude of excellent food items available for service in a restaurant, a keen discrimination is necessary in making choices. The capabilities of the staff and the kitchen equipment capacities must be understood to bring the menu and the production elements into balance.

### Staff and Equipment Capacities

The potential sales volume of a restaurant immediately establishes a maximum dollar amount that can be expended for staff in the kitchen and service areas. Together with the limitations of volume potential, the menu selections determine the types of food preparation to be done. Preparation requires a certain variety of skills among personnel and various types of preparation equipment. The next step, which concerns menu writing, is to select a balance of items that will distribute the food preparation among the work stations so that both staff and equipment work efficiently and to their fullest potential.

## Variety and Balance of Menu Selections for Customers

As we just mentioned, a proper balance of items is necessary to equalize the workload in the kitchen among the several preparation personnel. Simply selecting items to be produced at the sauce station or broiler station or other work stations is a beginning step, but customer preference must also be known, or in spite of variety all the work may end at one station. Sales histories of guests' choices provide this information. In a new operation a guide to what is likely to be customers' selections must come from the experience of personnel, an analysis of the competition's menus, and knowledge of the expectations of the targeted market.

### Description of Menu Items

You should follow a few simple rules when writing descriptions of menu items.

1. Menu descriptions must be interesting, appetizing, accurate, and include the primary ingredients and the principal method of preparation for each item.
2. Do not use French words unless necessary, such as in a menu for a classical restaurant.
3. Avoid flowery language.
4. Descriptive conversational language is best.

### Examples

- Cutlet of Plume du Veau, Veal Sautéed in Fresh Lemon Juice and Sweet Creamery Butter
- Fresh California Strawberries Marinated in Fine Cognac and Served on Baked Alaska—Paraded Flambé and Served in Room—Saluté

### Menu Outline

The following outline is a guide to types of items to include on a menu and how many of a certain item you should offer.

*Breakfast*
Basically Club breakfasts or packaged meals
Fruits, juices, and melons
Egg dishes plus bacon, ham, and sausage
Pancakes and waffles plus bacon, ham, and sausage

Specialty items: Steak and eggs
                 Calves' livers
                 Fish cakes
                 Eggs benedict
                 Pancake sandwich
                 French toast
                 Local favorites
Jams, jellies, toast, Danish pastry, brioche, croissant

*Luncheon*
Appetizers: hot 2–3; cold 4–6
Soups: hot—clear 1; cream 1
       cold—1
Sandwiches: Hot open 1
            Cold open 2–3
            Giant-sized 1
            Grilled 1
Selection of usual sandwiches: ham, cheese, seafood, chicken, BLT, club
            Salad sandwiches 2
Salads: Entrée—Chefs, Seafood, Cold meats,
               Fruit, Chicken salad plate
        Side 2–3
Entrées 6–8: Special of the day
             Poultry
             Fish
             Meat item—solid
             Meat item—stew
             Egg dish
             Lo-cal
             Meat substitute
Desserts: Fresh fruit pie
          Fruit melon
          Pudding
          Ice creams
          Cooked pie
          Lo-cal dessert

Jello

Sundaes

Beverages: Coffee, tea, milk, iced tea,
　　　　　Perrier, soft drinks

*Dinner*

Appetizers: Hot 3–4
　　　　　Cold 6–8

Soups: Hot—1 clear; 1 cream
　　　Cold—1
　　　Specialty soup (e.g., black bean,
　　　snapper, she-crab)

Sandwiches: Steak
　　　　　　Hot meat or chicken

Salads: Family or signature restaurant—
　　　salad bar
　　　classical restaurant—Caesar's and
　　　two added salads for tableside
　　　preparation

Entrées: Steaks and chops 4–6
　　　　Seafood section 4–6
　　　　Entrées on cycle 6–8
　　　　Poultry 2

Fish (fresh of day) 1

Meat 3

Combination dish 1

Pasta 1

Desserts: Same as luncheon plus a flaming
　　　　dessert

Beverages: Same as luncheon plus a
　　　　specialty item (e.g., Irish coffee,
　　　　café Brulot)

## Menu Revisions

Once a restaurant is in operation, the customer, not the chef, manager, or head waiter, determines the menu selections. A daily study of sales will both tell what items should be added, changed, and deleted and point to necessary price changes. Menus should be evaluated every three months, and changes in menu format should be considered yearly.

# 15　Beverage Menus

**Purpose:** To address the importance of beverages to the financial security of most restaurants and to discuss how to sell beverages.

In this chapter we will discuss the few (but crucial) points to consider in the merchandising of beverages in restaurant and banquet operations. Beverages are important to the success of most restaurants. Wine service, for example, can transform a meal that might be mere sustenance into an event of joy. In full-service restaurants about 78 percent of the sales are food and 22 percent alcoholic beverages. This category includes many family restaurants that do not serve alcoholic beverages. In restaurant operations in lodging establishments the breakdown is about 70 percent food and 30 percent alcoholic beverages. Because profit from beverage sales is two to three times that of profit from food sales, the importance of beverages to successful restaurant and banquet operations is obvious.

## Beverages on the Food Menu

Because beverage sales are so important, menu writers should consider some kind of listing of beverages on all menus (excluding breakfast) as necessary for marketing the product. The extent of the listing varies from luncheon menu to dinner menu and from coffee shop to classical and signature restaurants.

Beverage lists range from the minimum suggestion by servers that cocktails, beers, and wines are available to a fairly complete cocktail and wine list. Special holiday menus, for example, could devote one side of a single-fold menu to a wine list that includes several each of white wines, red wines, rosé wines, and champagnes; carafes of house wines; and after-dinner drinks.

## Cardinal Principles

A mere list of beverages, even if very attractively done, is only the first step in selling beverages. Competent waiters and waitresses hardly need to be told to suggest drinks before a meal—they know that increasing the check is in their interest as well as in the interest of the restaurant. To ensure repeat sales give the customers something different; something they do not expect; something they do not get routinely. Cocktails and high balls must be generous (one and a half ounces of liquor in high balls and two ounces in cocktails are proven successful sizes) and served in the fashion of a cocktail lounge rather than barroom style. Big drinks are always welcome.

After prohibition was repealed, a 1-ounce

drink was unofficially established as the norm in New York City. A bar in a popular hotel had what seemed to be all the necessary qualifications for success but was doing less than half of what seemed its potential. One of the authors of this book was with a food and beverage consulting firm in New York at the time, and this particular hotel was a client. He recommended they use 1½ ounces of liquor in high balls and 2 ounces of liquor in cocktails and advertise that the bar served the biggest drinks in town. In a very short time the bar became so popular with late-afternoon commuters that city police were needed to keep order in the lines of customers waiting to get into the bar. Of course, it was not too long before every bar in the city was serving bigger drinks, but the innovator continued to do capacity business.

In the world of marketing it seems packaging a product is as important as the product itself. This follows with drinks, too. The packaging medium is glassware. In a classical restaurant hand-blown glassware should be used. Today, any operation can afford to use "crystal" glassware. Good-quality machine-made glassware is almost indistinguishable from hand blown.

For the customer to consider an establishment's drinks a good value, only first-label brands of liquors and wines should be served. Big drinks might cost a nickel more, so add a dime to the selling price and get an extra nickel of profit on every drink. In an active operation this will add up to a million dollars of additional sales in several years.

## The Big Four

In any selling venture it is good salesmanship to make a suggestion rather than ask customers what they want. Do not expect them to search a list of drinks and make a selection. Instead, give them a list on which several cocktails that are specialties of the house are given special names or brief descriptions. A group of signature restaurants in a hotel chain served what they called the "big four." They were big drinks of four types: martini, manhattan, daiquiri, and whiskey sour. These four drinks are, in fact, the leading four cocktails in many restaurants. This hotel made them special because each contained 2½ ounces of liquor and were served in large, beautiful glassware and colorfully garnished. The olive in the martini was a size 60 on a "gold" spear, the manhattan had two cherries with stems on its "gold" spear. Only imported, first-label vermouths were used in these drinks. The daiquiri and whiskey sour contained fresh-squeezed citrus. Thus the guests were introduced to first-class fare with their first order. These four common cocktails served in an uncommon manner made the difference.

The preparation of drinks varies in different parts of the United States. For example, in the east and the far west, the Manhattan is made with blended whiskey and sweet vermouth; in Wisconsin it is made with brandy and sweet vermouth if no other liquor is requested. The addition of bitters to the Manhattan has been discontinued in most beverage outlets in the United States, although it still appears in some drink recipe books.

## Beers and Ales

According to the Anheuser-Busch Companies *Fact Book*, the origins of beer are older than recorded history, extending into the mythology of ancient civilizations. Beer, the oldest alcoholic beverage, was discovered independently by the most ancient cultures—the Babylonians, Assyrians, Egyptians, Hebrews, Africans, Chinese, Incas, Teutons, Saxons, and various wandering tribes of Eurasia. These ancient peoples left records that indicate they not only enjoyed their beer, but considered brewing to be a serious and important job.

Babylonian clay tablets more than 6,000 years old depict the brewing of beer and give detailed recipes. An extract from an ancient Chinese manuscript states that beer, or "kiu" as it was called, was known to the Chinese as early as the twenty-third century B.C.

Beer was enjoyed by ancient peoples at all levels of society. Of course, some drank with more style than others. For example, the University of Pennsylvania Museum displays a golden straw used by Queen Shubad of Mesopotamia for sipping beer.

With the rise of commerce and the growth of cities during the Middle Ages, brewing became more than a household activity. Municipal brew houses were established, which eventually led to the formation of brewing guilds. Commercial brewing on a significantly larger scale began around the twelfth century in Germany.

Although native Americans had developed a form of beer, Europeans brought their own version with them to the New World. Beer enjoys the distinction of having come over on the Mayflower and, in fact, seems to have played a part in the Pilgrims' decision to land at Plymouth Rock instead of farther south, as intended. An entry dated 1620 in a journal kept by one of the passengers states that the Mayflower landed at Plymouth because "we could not now take time for further search or consideration, our victuals being spent, especially our beere. . . ."

The first commercial brewery in America was founded in New Amsterdam (New York) in 1623. Many patriots owned their own breweries (confer today's microbreweries, described below), among them Samuel Adams and William Penn. Thomas Jefferson was also interested in brewing and made beer at Monticello. George Washington even had his own brew house on the grounds of Mount Vernon, and his handwritten recipe for beer is dated 1757 and preserved in his diary.

## Some Definitions of Beer Products

Beer is a food product made from barley malt, hops, grain adjuncts, yeast, and water. The alcohol in beer results from the fermentation by yeast of an extract from barley malt and other cereal grains. In addition to alcohol, beer commonly contains carbohydrates, proteins, amino acids, vitamins (such as riboflavin and niacin) and minerals (such as calcium and potassium) derived from the original food materials. Ale is made much as beer is, but is heavier in consistency, is more aromatic, contains more hops, is fermented at higher temperatures, and is produced with a different type of yeast.

*Stout* is a very dark ale made with a malt flavor, and is somewhat sweeter than ale.

*Porter* is a variation of ale, with a rich creamy foam. It is made with a very dark malt and is very hoppy and sweet. Porter is not as hoppy, sweet, or strong as stout.

*Bock beer* is a special, heavy brewed beer that is prepared during the winter for spring distribution and sales. The German word *bock* means male goat or buck, and has a connotation of giving the drinker vigor and energy (more imagination than fact).

*Lager beer* is a bright, clear, light-bodied, and effervescent beer, made more sparkling by returning into the beer some of the carbon dioxide that escapes during fermentation. Some call it the ginger ale of beer. Most American beers are of the lager type.

## Alcohol Content

Through custom, the general public has come to refer to the alcohol content of American beers as either "3.2 percent" or "5 percent." The 3.2 percent designation refers to percentage of alcohol by volume. To clarify the real difference in percentage designation, 3.2 percent (an alcohol by weight designation) is equivalent to 4 percent by volume, and 4 percent by weight is equivalent to 5 percent by volume. In comparing the "by volume" numbers, it is clear that there is really only a 1 percent difference in alcohol by volume between so-called 3.2 percent and 5 percent beers.

## Quality Factors for Beers and Ale

The key words in the beer industry are *consistent* and *quality*. There are no secrets within the industry, just care and direction and the willingness to accept a little less profit than average.

Quality assurance begins with the testing of ingredients before brewing ever begins. Perfection can be achieved only through close scrutiny extending down to the smallest detail of the packaging operation, including bottle crowns and can lids. Pure water is also a key ingredient in brewing great beer. Water must be checked as rigidly as other ingredients. When necessary, the water must be treated to ensure conformity to exacting standards.

No scientific test, however, can replace tasting as the final judgment of quality. In a fine brewery, flavor panels meet daily to judge the aroma, appearance, and taste of packaged, filtered, and unfiltered beer.

Control of quality does not cease at the brewery. Wholesalers play a key role in seeing that the quality that begins with the ingredients and continues through the brewing and packaging processes is preserved until the beer reaches consumers. Such care by wholesalers requires controlled-environment warehouse systems that maintain beer freshness during storage.

## Packaging

Beers are packaged for sale in kegs, bottles, and cans. Wooden kegs must be lined with a nontasting plastic, and if a metal keg is used, it too must be lined. Aluminum kegs can be used without a lining. A barrel of beer contains 31 gallons, or the equivalent of 13.8 cases of 12-ounce cans or bottles (24 cans or bottles in each case).

The 12-ounce brown bottle is the most popular for beer, and the 12-ounce green bottle is used primarily for ale. The colored glass filters out light, which affects the quality of beer and ale very rapidly. Some 7-ounce bottles are in use throughout the country, but they have not proven very popular.

Beers and ales, regardless of how packaged, should be stored in a clean, dry, dark storeroom with a temperature tightly controlled between 40 and 50 degrees.

Experience shows that a bar operator can take care of all the basic necessities to draw a good glass of beer at the tap, but if the glasses into which the beer is drawn are not "beer clean," his or her business will disappear. The dishwashing machine and techniques of delivering beer-clean glasses to the bar are vital.

## Nonalcoholic Brew

Prior to the introduction of Sharp's nonalcoholic brew by the Miller Brewing Company in 1989 and O'Doul's by Anheuser-Busch shortly thereafter, the market for nonalcoholic brew was dominated by imports. Moussy from Switzerland led the parade in the 1970's followed by brands like Kaliber from Ireland and Clausthaler from Germany. Since 1990, the local brands—particularly O'Doul's, Sharp's, OMNA (Old Milwaukee Non-Alcoholic) by Stroh's, and Coors' Cutter—have dominated the market, with Heileman's Kingsbury running far behind in fifth place. Currently, five of the top twenty nonalcoholic brews on the market are imported, but together they account for only 4 percent of total sales.

A number of factors have contributed to the appeal and marketability of nonalcoholic brews. First, the continuing trend toward moderation and fitness has many people freely choosing to drink fewer alcoholic beverages or none at all. This is consistent with the demand for lower alcoholic content in whiskies, gin, vodka, and the light beer featured in most American breweries.

Also helping the market for nonalcoholics are ongoing efforts to stiffen drunk-driving penalties.

### Microbreweries

Dating back to Colonial times, microbreweries have had their place in the American culture. However, in modern times they were not a very important part of the brewing picture except during the years of Prohibition in the United States, when "home brew" was produced by many families for home consumption. But during the past several years the microbreweries have made a strong comeback and can be found in every part of the country. In fact, there is competition to determine the most skillful producers of the age-old drink.

Most of the products of the microbreweries are sold in full-service restaurants. Exhibit 15-1 is the beer menu from Hops Grill & Bar, in Palm Harbor, Florida. Hops Grill & Bar is a small chain of restaurants featuring a display kitchen and a microbrewery. Note the variety of beers and ales produced.

Exhibit 15-2, the reverse side of the beer menu, introduces customers to the art of brewing with an explanatory narrative that gives a "tour" through their brewery. Note that they mention that their locally brewed beer is served fresh and frothy in a frozen mug. The idea of "freshness in a beer has become a regular part of the advertising of some national breweries.

## *Liquor Lists*

Except for special promotions of cocktails or exotic drinks, lists consisting of the various cocktails available and the different Scotches, bourbons, ryes, blended whiskies, and so forth are unnecessary in day-to-day restaurant business. The food menu, in addition to mentioning several cocktails and beers, should include after-dinner drinks. After-dinner drinks should be part of a dessert menu, if one is used. The few liquors (cocktails and liqueurs) plus a short wine list and the food fare together present a dining package.

Ethnic restaurants usually promote beverage sales not only by listing drinks but also by tastefully carrying out the theme. The margarita, a traditional tequila drink, has achieved a special prominence with the rise in popularity of Mexican restaurants. Many of these operations have expanded the margarita into three drinks: the regular, the frozen, and the house special (read king-sized).

The Polynesian restaurants have created a unique identity more through their exotic drinks and decor than through their food, which varies little from Chinese. The drink menus in the popular Polynesian restaurants are very expensive but have proved to be an excellent investment. Beverage sales are only slightly less than food sales in most of these operations, and are greater than food sales in some.

A cocktail lounge located in a hotel can use a beverage list as a promotional tool for the hotel restaurant. A small tastefully designed menu with colorful artwork can list cocktails, high-ball whiskies, beers, and wines by the glass and should also suggest that dinner be taken in the restaurant. If reservations are needed, the menu can note that the cocktail waitress will be happy to make such reservations.

## *Pricing*

The large cocktails listed on the food menu should be priced at three and a half to four times cost. Other liquor drinks can be marked up four to five times; and beer at two and a half to three times cost. Wines by the glass can be priced at three to four times cost and carafe wines at two and a half to three times. After-dinner drinks, like desserts, should be moderately priced at two to two and a half times cost, because after a hearty meal high-priced

# We Proudly Serve All Of Our Locally Brewed Beer Fresh & Frothy In A Frozen Mug

### 1 CLEARWATER LIGHT SM

Our reduced carbohydrate, low calorie lager style beer, pale in color, light in body and smooth in character. Remarkably "Clear" and fresh. Approx. 125 calories.

### 3 HAMMERHEAD RED SM

Our rich, full bodied all malt amber ale. Handcrafted using a combination of pale and dextrin malts. This flavorful & aromatic beer is brewed with caramel and chocolate malts to balance hops bitterness with a hint of malt sweetness. A Hops classic & brewmaster's choice.

### 4 SPECIALTY BEERS

Our variety of specialty beers and ales are formulated and brewed by our brewmaster using only natural grains, hops, water and yeast. These quality beers and ales, of a more distinct flavor, are tailored to compliment our signature lagers and ales as well as our complete line of high quality foods. New, exciting & always a Hops original.

### 2 LIGHTNING BOLD GOLD SM

A classic American Lager style beer, beautifully golden hued, slightly dry with a flowery hop aroma. Finished with imported Saaz hops. Very smooth, medium body.

**Exhibit 15-1**
**The beer menu from Hops Grill & Bar Microbrewery**
*Reprinted with permission of Hops Grill & Bar Microbrewery, Palm Harbor, Florida*

# HOPS MICROBREWERY
## "From Grain to Glass"

Hops Microbrewery is dedicated to the traditional Brewer's art. All our beers are handmade the old fashioned, 100% natural way, using "Only The Best" grains, imported hops, yeast & pure water without additives, preservatives or fillers of any kind. Each beer is brewed & aged until it has reached its peak of full bodied flavor and freshness. Hops proudly displays its copper kettled microbrewery and invites you to observe & inspect our brewing process or talk with our Brewmaster as he supervises each phase. Our microbrewery produces different ales & lager style beers, all made with our own original recipes, adapted to contemporary tastes and designed specifically for your drinking pleasure. So sit back and enjoy the best of an old & new tradition. Locally brewed beer served fresh & frothy in a frozen mug.

**MILLED GRAIN**
1. Milling allows the brewer to control milling of the malted wheat and barley in order to maximize extraction.

**MASH LAUTER**
2. Mash Lauter: Hot water is run through a grain bed where sugars are extracted and sent to the brew kettle for cooking.

**HOT LIQUOR**
2A. Hot Liquor is a Brewer's term for Hot Water heated to run through a grain bed to extract sugars used to make beer.

**STEAM GENERATOR**
3. Supplies steam used to heat water in hot liquor and wort in Brew Kettle.

**BREW KETTLE**
4. The Brew Kettle is where the beer is cooked. Fragrance Hops and Bitter Hops are added to make HOPS MICROBREWERY'S Special Recipes complete.

**PLATE FRAME HEAT EXCHANGER**
5. The Plate Frame Heat Exchanger efficiently reduces the temperature of the Hot Beer to Fermentation Temperature.

**FERMENTERS**
6. Fermenters are where Beer is Aged and Carbonated for approximately 14 days, then filtered.

**FILTER**
7. Beer is filtered through All Natural Pads removing any remaining Grains or Yeast.

**FINISHED BEER**
8. Our Filtered Crisp Clear Beer is then held in pressurized serving vessels in our cold room. There it is chilled and pumped directly to our taps.

Outside Viewing

14 BARRELS - 434 GAL. (each) 1 BARREL - 31 GAL.

## BREWERY TOURS AVAILABLE UPON REQUEST.

**Exhibit 15-2**

The back of the Hops Grill & Bar Microbrewery menu

*Reprinted with permission of Hops Grill & Bar Microbrewery, Palm Harbor, Florida*

after-dinner drinks and desserts can lose their appeal; the same pricing policy applies to spirit coffees.

Hotels that have a restaurant (other than a coffee shop) and a separate cocktail lounge should price beverages the same in both areas unless the lounge has entertainment or dancing, in which case drinks can be priced at a higher level. It is not a good policy to have the same prices in both areas and serve smaller drinks in the entertainment lounge. As we indicated, it is profitable to feature something special about drinks. Be consistent—all outlets should present the same image of offering generous drinks, well packaged in attractive glassware, and promptly and pleasantly served.

## Banquets and Other Functions

In the chapter "Writing Banquet Menus" we warned, "Don't nickel and dime customers." This is good advice in selling beverages either in conjunction with a luncheon or dinner banquet or as a beverage-only function.

Wines and liqueurs are the usual alcoholic beverages consumed with banquet meals. There are two ways to sell "food" wines: at a price per bottle or at a price per person served. Each way has its advantages and disadvantages. Which way is used depends on the type of customers making the arrangements. The first method creates an uncertainty in the mind of the purchasers. They pay a definite price per bottle, but are unsure how many bottles will be consumed. At best they have the seller's estimate. They can put a limit on how many bottles are poured, but that would be inconsistent with the image of a genial host. In addition, they depend on the seller to name how many bottles were sold.

If the purchasers choose the second way, they have the security of a definite price per person. This way can also be an advantage to the caterer. In most groups, especially mixed groups, a bottle of wine can serve three persons. If a nominal charge of $3.00 per person is charged for the wine, each bottle is being sold

for $9.00. A bottle very likely costs about $3.75 to $4.25. And because practically no labor is involved in serving the wine, the added revenue is all profit. If the meal is to be sold at $21.00 per person, moving up to $24.00 is not a very great increase. Ideally, the caterer never quotes a price until all details are settled, so the amount paid for the wine is merely part of the total package. However, this pricing psychology is not so effective with low-priced meals; for example, an increase from $10.00 to $13.00 is an obvious 30 percent more.

An important thought for banquet salespersons is this: Wine service on banquets takes an ordinary meal out of the ordinary at very little additional cost.

### Open Bars

You can apply the pricing methods we just discussed to selling open bars at a cocktail party preceding a dinner or as a post-prandial event of some sort, such as a dance. But an additional consideration in selling such events is the expense of the bartender(s). Because of the current labor situation in most cities, it may very well cost a full day's wage to employ a bartender. Consequently, if sales are below a certain level, a charge must be made for the bartender(s) or profit will suffer or disappear. Selling a package deal that includes liquor, service, and snacks can be presented as a more favorable deal than a per bottle, plus snacks, plus service arrangement. We do not present these two methods of selling as definitive—the number of ways a deal can be presented is limited only by the imagination of the sales or catering manager.

### Cash Bars

The arrangement of having a bar at which people personally pay for what they drink is very popular at the functions of social organizations. Such affairs usually do not have a host entertaining, and so the bar can be operated the same as a free-standing cocktail lounge. If the event is held in a hotel, drink prices can be the same as those charged in the dining room or lounge. More often a price or several prices are established through negotiation. For example, four prices can be charged: one for cocktails, one for high balls, one for wine by the glass, and one for beers. A very simple arrangement is one price for all drinks or, perhaps, a separate price for beer. An excellent arrangement from the standpoint of both guests and caterer is the presence of a cashier who sells tickets for drinks at one, two, three, or four prices. The tickets can be different colors to designate the type of drink purchased. The advantage for the caterer is that the bartenders do not handle cash. This allows them to spend all their time exercising their specialty—preparing drinks. Bartenders cost more than cashiers. This method also includes a security advantage. With numbered tickets it takes only a couple of simple calculations to know how much money should be on hand.

### Free Merchandise

As in many other businesses, there are in the hotel business some operators who are willing to use shady or even outright illegal means to gain extra profit. We relate some of these next for your information, not as a recommendation to use one of these illegal procedures!

When a bar is sold to customers by the bottle, they are told that they must pay in full for any bottles that have been partially used. Sometimes they are told that since the liquor has been paid for, they are free to take the partial bottles with them. But in most states, perhaps all states, the license to sell liquor by the bottle includes the stipulation that all opened bottles must be consumed on the premises. Consequently, the above offer is illegal. It is usually not a problem, since few people exercise the option. Therein lies the advantage to the hotel. The next cash bar can use "free merchandise" (that is, it has been paid for by a previous customer). However, it is not legal to issue opened liquor bottles to a bar or

cocktail lounge in the hotel. An allegedly well-documented story holds that a large hotel in the Midwest operated a very busy small street bar near a rail commuter station at a zero beverage cost of sales.

## Wine Lists

Wine lists may be a brief listing on a food menu, a separate simple card, or an elaborate book with scores of different wines. A complete wine list will include the four basic wines: appetizer wines; table wines—red, white, and rosé; dessert wines; and sparkling wines. In some restaurants, only appetizer wines are listed on the food menu. After the food order has been placed, the waiter presents the host a list that includes the table and sparkling wines. Dessert wines are listed on the dessert menu. There are many ways to present wines to customers. What method of presentation is best for selling wines in a particular restaurant is the deciding factor in making the choice.

### The Value of Wine Sales

Wine sales are valuable to an establishment for many reasons, some of which follow.

1. The basic reason for being in business is to make a profit. Wine is a good profit item, especially when sold in conjunction with a meal because there are no added labor costs to make and service the sale.
2. People who enjoy wine with their meals are excellent customers for a restaurant. They can be counted on for repeat business.
3. Wine drinkers (not winos) generally know quality food, so a regular clientele of such customers confirms that a restaurant is on the right track. Loss of such customers is a "red flag" to check the menu, food preparation,

and service for deviations from standards of quality.

4. The service of good-quality wines draws "quality customers" that establish a sound foundation upon which to build a profitable establishment.

5. Wine "makes a meal a feast." Incidentally, heading this statement on a food menu's wine list is a good merchandising strategy.

6. Wine is an impressive and low-cost "giveaway" in promotional programs, whether it be a glass of table wine with a meal or a half bottle for a table of two.

7. Because wine is a relatively low-cost item, it can be priced moderately and does not run up the check to a prohibitive figure, thereby distorting the price structure for the targeted market.

8. Wine sales are a morale builder among service personnel. Because they increase the tips, they help to keep good employees and save the expenses involved in personnel turnover.

9. Good wine service upgrades a restaurant. In a hotel restaurant it tends to upgrade the hotel operation as well as the restaurant.

10. As indicated in the previous section on banquets and other functions, wine service at banquets takes an ordinary meal out of the ordinary at very little additional cost.

### Why Aren't More Wines Sold?

In view of these ten good reasons for selling wine, it seems odd that we can ask this question. It is a valid question because wine sales are far below their potential in most restaurants, which are otherwise good restaurants. The following dialogue illustrates one possible reason for low wine sales.

Scene: A young (maybe twenty-four years old) management trainee in financial services enters a swanky restaurant with a very fetching date on his arm, who hopes to impress him with her "knowledge" of wines.
Date: "What types of carafe wines are you serving?"
Waiter: "You mean jug wines?" (He growls.)
Date: "I suppose so," she hesitatingly offers.
Waiter: "We got red and white." (Bluntly coughed out.)
Date: To embarrassed escort, "Skip the wine."

This poor attitude on the part of the server takes place daily in restaurants. It seems there is a great deal of talk about selling wine; but beyond putting a few cases in the beverage inventory, very little is really done.

## Wine Selling Program

What must be done to make wine an important part of the sales of a restaurant or banquet operation? The merchandising of wines calls for

1. A training program for the staff.
2. Suggestions by the server.
3. Sensible pricing.
4. A balanced wine list of quality wines.
5. Displays (visual suggestions).

### Training Program

A program can be conducted by an employee who has a basic knowledge of wines, or help can be gotten at no cost from organizations set up to aid in the selling of wines. Information about such programs can be obtained from a wine dealer or broker.

**Basic Wine Knowledge.** In most instances, only a very basic knowledge should be part of the training. The study of wines (*enology or oenology*) is a broad and deep subject. The information can very quickly become a mass of confusion in a student's mind, especially that conveyed in so-called crash courses. For example, white wines are made from over forty different types of grapes. Over twenty different grapes are used in producing red wines. Servers do not need to memorize them all. Basic knowledge should, however, include the classes of wines. There are thousands of names of wines, but all are grouped into only four classes: appetizer, table (red, white, and rosé), dessert, and sparkling. Servers should know the following five basics.

1. *To which class each of the wines on the restaurant's wine list belongs.* Most wine lists identify the categories of wines by headings. Servers can learn from such lists. However, the wine list should be reviewed by the servers as a group, with a knowledgeable person leading the discussion. This type of review also tends to stimulate each server to seek further knowledge.

2. *Which wines are most appropriate to serve with the different foods on the menu.* The first thing said at most wine classes is that there are no laws or rules about which wine should be drunk with this, that, or the other food. Nevertheless, oenologists have found that certain wines are compatible with certain foods. If you ignore this knowledge, you are not using common sense.

*Appetizers*

In the United States it is a widespread custom to drink cocktails before a meal. In recent years, with the accent on "light" food and drink, many people have opted for a glass of white wine instead of the cocktail. This is a move in the direction of the traditional aperitifs of sparkling wines and sherry. Following are some suggestions for wines to drink with appetizers. These foods are usually fruit, soup, smoked fish, shellfish, and pâté.

*Fruit*—Wine is often not taken with a fruit appetizer. If desired, the traditional dessert wines, port and Madeira, are the choices.

*Consommé*—A medium-dry sherry is the usual choice, but occasionally Madeira or Marsala are suggested.

*Chowders*—Dry Sauternes and Rhônes are welcome with these heavy soups.

*Smoked fish*—A dry white wine, such as Alsace Gewürztraminer, or vintage champagne complement this classic appetizer.

*Shellfish*—Chablis and white Graves are common suggestions, although some "experts" insist on a nonvintage champagne.

*Pâté*—This appetizer is very friendly to wines. A red Bordeaux like Pomerol, a dry white wine, or even a sherry all complement pâté.

*Main course*

*Fish*—The experts recommend one or another white wine with just about all fish except tuna and eel. A red or rosé are alternates to the white with tuna. With eel, a cup of tea is perhaps the most satisfying drink.

*Beef (roast)*—Red wine of any kind.

*Beef (other)*—Specific red wines, and there are many kinds, are recommended with different beef dishes. A Macon-Villages white wine is an option with boiled beef.

*Veal (roast)*—A Spanish red wine such as Rioja or a German white wine are both considered complementary to this fine food.

*Wiener Schnitzel*—A dichotomy of choice is also true for this interesting dish. An Austrian Riesling is appropriate, but a light red from the Italian Tyrol also satisfies.

*Lamb (roast or chops)*—Red Bordeaux or an American cabernet go well with any lamb selection.

*Chicken and turkey*—The neutrality of these fowl meats when roasted makes any wine, white or red or rosé, a perfect companion. Coq au vin, however, is best with a red Burgundy.

*Desserts*

Sweet with the sweet—white or red from the table wines with a touch of sweetness. Ports, cream sherry, Madeira, and Marsala are most common with desserts. For a special treat try strawberries with a red Bordeaux poured over them.

3. *The difference between varietal and generic wine.* This is ordinarily sufficient knowledge about grapes and their geographical origins. (See glossary of terms at the end of this chapter.)

4. *How to read a wine label.* We next show the information that appears on different labels and explain the wording.

a. *A grower's label for a Burgundy wine.*

> Mis en Bouteilles
> au Domaine
>
> *Volnay*
> les Caillerets
>
> Appellation Controlée
> Domaine de la Pousse D'or
> a Volnay, Côte D'or

"Domaine" in the Burgundy area is the equivalent of "Château" for Bordeaux wines. "Mise en Bouteilles au Domaine" means that the wine was bottled by the grower. "Volnay les Caillerets" identifies the individual vineyard in Volnay. "Appellation Controlée" guarantees that the wine was produced as shown on the label of the grape varieties of the region. It is not a guarantee of quality. "Domaine de la Pousse . . . is the name and address of the grower/producer/bottler of the wine.

b. *A merchant's label for a Burgundy wine.*

> Gevrey-Chambertin
> Clos St. Jacques
> Appellation Controlée
> Remoissenet Pere et Fils
> Negociants a Beaune

The first line names the village; the second line identifies the vineyard. For "Appellation Controlée," see above. The last two lines identify the father and son Remoissenet as a merchant that bought the wine from the grower and then aged and bottled the wine.

c. *A Bordeaux label.*

> Château
> Langoa-Barton
> Grands Cru Classe
> Appellation St. Julien
> Controlée
> Mis en Bouteilles au
> Château

The first two lines name the estate on which the vineyard is located. The next line, "Grands Cru Classe," is a reference to the local classification of this wine. The appellation controllée that guarantees this wine is in the township of St. Julien, which is just east of the Château Langoa-Barton. The last two lines state that the wine was bottled at the estate.

d. *A traditional German wine label.*

> Mosel-Saar-Ruwer
> Bernkasteler
> Schlossberg
> Riesling Auslese
> 1987
> Qualitatswein mit Pradikat
> A.P. NR. 12345678
> Erzeugerabfullund
> Mozarthof Trier

The first line, "Mosel-Saar-Ruwer," is the wine region. The second line is the town, or it could be the parish. The third line is the vineyard. The fourth line is the type of grape from which the wine is made. The fifth line, "1987," is the vintage or year in which the grape was harvested. The next line, "Qualitat-swein mit Pradikat" (sometimes shown as QMP), means that the grape reached a ripeness so that no sugar was needed for fermentation. "A.P. NR. 12345678" identifies the official test number of a quality wine. The final two lines mean that the wine was bottled by the producer at the town of Trier.

e. *An Italian wine label.*

Unlike the German and French wines, Italian wines usually have a single name.

Soave<br>
Classico<br>
Vino a Denominazione di<br>
Origine Controllata<br>
Imbottigliato dal<br>
Produttore all 'Origine<br>
Cantina Sociale di Soave

"Soave" is the name of the wine and the growing region. "Classico" means that the grapes used in making the wine are from the central (usually the best) part of the growing region. "Vino a Demoninazione..." is the Italian equivalent of the French appellation controlée. "Imbottigliato dal Produt-tore all 'Origine" means that the wine was bottled by the producer. The final line of the label identifies the growers' cooperative of Soave.

5. *Proper pronunciation of the listed wines is important.* As wine sales grow, good wine servers will become anxious to broaden their knowledge of wines. At that point further knowledge and in-formation can be given. Volumes of reading material available from wine organizations can be distributed for self-study. We offer a brief glossary of terms pertinent to wine knowledge at the end of this chapter.

## How to Suggest Wines

A sale is seldom made unless the salesperson asks the customer to buy! A restaurant serious about building wine sales will create a wine environment and will make the most of using merchandising techniques to suggest sales. A well-trained staff is the first requisite, as we just discussed. Also helpful to sales are attractive displays placed near the entrance of the dining room or in other highly visible locations. When guests are surrounded by "wine reminders" they are likely to positively respond to a server's simply asking if they care for a glass of wine before dinner or for a bottle at the appropriate time in the order taking. Part of a complete wine environment is to have good-quality house wines. It should be a restaurateur's maxim to never select cheap wines as house wines in order to make a greater profit. Quality wines draw quality customers.

Customer satisfaction should be the goal in all selling. A financial services organization had a television commercial that ended with a comment that can be a proper motto for a restaurant: "We measure our success one customer at a time."

Consider providing tastefully done table tents that suggest "Wines make a meal a feast." These might also include an invitation to try the house wines. The waiter or waitress should call attention to the wine list (if there is one) on the menu when it is presented to a guest. Otherwise the server should present the wine card or wine list with the food menu.

To provide a wine environment a restaurant should have clean, attractive wine glasses in the tablesetting. This is part of anticipating the customers' needs. Wine servers should likewise anticipate guests' needs, while at the same time remaining on the polite side of the fine line between helping guests and being offensively aggressive. Attention to this should be part of the training program.

In helping guests make wine selections, the price category of the wine should be consistent with the price category of the food ordered. Surveys reveal that guests are more likely to order a bottle of wine with the meal after having a wine as an aperitif than after drinking a liquor cocktail. It seems that a wine as an aperitif sets the tone for a further wine order with the meal. Although they are seldom listed as such, sparkling wines, white wines, and rosés make excellent aperitifs along with light, dry sherries. Champagne makes any dinner a special occasion.

The first two points we presented in the outline of a training progam were (1) a basic knowledge of the wines on the wine list and (2) the foods they are usually considered to complement. These enable the wine server to assist the customer in making a selection. However, guests should not be rushed. Give them the chance to state a preference. Some wine enthusiasts enjoy exhibiting their knowledge about wines, and their satisfaction with the dining experience will de diminished if they are deprived of an opportunity to do so. When a guest displays confusion or hesitancy in ordering a wine he or she should be rescued by the wine server with the suggestion of a wine appropriate to accompany the food order.

A complete meal is composed of appetizer through dessert, and there are wines to go with each course. Ports and cream sherries are popular dessert wines. An after-dinner brandy is not breaking the wine series, because a true brandy is by law a pure distillate of grape wine. Fruit brandies such as "apricot brandy" and "peach brandy" are not true brandies. If a guest orders one, however, it is a perfectly satisfactory after-dinner drink.

## How to Serve Wines

The proper presentation and service of wines is important to guest satisfaction, and through the years a "wine ritual" has developed. It begins before the guest arrives, with having wines at the proper serving temperature. The temperature at which wines should be served determines how they are to be stored.

The rule for red table wines is that they be served at room temperature—actually at a cool room temperature of 65 to 70°F. Chilling a red wine at lower temperatures will produce a tartness beyond that of the same wine at the proper temperature. White table wines should be served at about 55°F. This is accomplished by about one hour's refrigeration in a cooler at regular food temperature (about 40°F) or in a special wine refrigerator. The chilling diminishes any sweetness and accents the tartness, which is desirable in many white wines.

The standard refrigeration temperature range for foods is 40 to 45°F, which will retard bacteria growth. This is also a desirable temperature range for sparkling wines, but for a different reason. Chilling slows the release of the carbonation bubbles and keeps the wine in a lively state for a longer period. The aroma and bouquet are also prolonged.

Appetizer wines need some chilling and are best enjoyed at about 55°F, the same as for white table wines. The dessert wines, which have a measure of sweetness, exhibit their finest qualities at the same temperature as the red table wines.

With brandy there is an option. If the guest prefers service in a snifter, brandy should be served at room temperature. Many, however, prefer their brandy over ice. Served either way, brandy makes a delightful postprandial drink.

The next step in the "wine ritual" is the placing of wine glasses in a tablesetting. If the tablesetting includes a selection of wine glasses, they should be placed from right to left in the order in which the wines are to be served. The first glass (to the right and slightly above the base plate) is for the appetizer wine, which may be sherry or champagne, and the appropriate glass is so placed. The appetizer glass is followed by the white wine glass, the red wine glass, and the dessert wine glass. The dessert wine glass may be a port or champagne glass, depending on the wine planned in the service.

The method by which the wine is presented is also part of the ritual. The bottle should be presented to the host with the label visible so that he or she can verify that the wine is the one which was ordered.

The bottle is then opened and a small amount of wine, perhaps one ounce, is poured in the host's glass for approval. After approval the wine is poured for the other guests. Glasses should be filled only one-half to allow for air space above the wine, which enhances the wine's aroma and bouquet. With white wines the partially filled bottle should then be placed in an ice bucket (if a bucket is used), and a red wine should be placed at the right of the host in a wine basket.

Glasses at the table should not be allowed to remain empty except at the request of the host. When the last drinks are poured from the bottle, the server can suggest that another bottle be ordered. This will allow time for a bottle to chill. In the case of a red wine, the new bottle can be opened and allowed to "breathe."

A training program should include demonstrations and actual practice in the opening and pouring of wine. For a server to become adept at properly using corkscrews, especially the spring cork puller, he or she must practice considerably. The "captain's knife" variety of corkscrew is easier for an inexperienced person to use but still requires practice to achieve proficiency.

The opening and serving of sparkling wines requires a different technique because of how these potentially "explosive" wines are capped. Servers must practice pouring to prevent excessive foaming and loss of gas. Again, demonstrations and practice are integral parts of adequate training.

## Sensible Pricing of Wines

Possibly the principal reason why more wines are not sold in many restaurants is the prices asked. The cost of sales of bottled goods cannot approach the low levels of liquor drink sales. This is especially true of bottled wine for sale with a meal.

A 50 to 55 percent cost of sales for wine is quite tolerable because to sell and serve wine in a restaurant involves no labor costs beyond what is needed for food sales. A 50 percent cost yields a 50 percent gross profit. A general policy calls for the following markups:

Carafe wines—3 times cost
Domestic wines—2½ times bottle cost
Imported wines—2 times bottle cost

The following is a guide to fixed mark-ons over cost.

| Bottle cost | Mark-on* |
|---|---|
| $2.00—$2.50 | $2.00 |
| $2.50—$3.00 | $2.50 |
| $3.00—$3.50 | $3.00 |
| $3.50—$4.00 | $3.50 |
| $4.00—$5.00 | $4.00 |
| $5.00—$7.50 | $4.50 |
| $7.50—$10.00 | $5.00 |
| $10.50—$15.00 | $7.50 |
| $15.00—$25.00 | $10.00 |

Domestic champagne—bottle cost plus $5.00
Imported champagne, nonvintage—cost plus $7.50
Imported champagne, vintage—cost plus $10.00
Premium labels—cost plus $12.50
* Amount added to cost to get the selling price.

## Format of Wine Lists

Most restaurants, even classical restaurants, do not need an elaborate wine list. Many first-class hotels with signature restaurants have a wine list for banquets only. Large wine sales can be achieved with a simple listing on the food menu or on a wine card. Some fancy hotels and restaurants have vintage wines dating back twenty years, and to avoid spoilage they offer many of the wines in specials. Upon a change in management a certain large hotel in New York City had a wine specialist check the extensive wine cellar, which boasted several hundred bottles. The wines dated back many years. The specialist found over 30 percent unfit to drink and recommended that another 15 percent should be sold as quickly as possible because they soon would be undrinkable. Sometimes 30 to 50 percent of the wines on extensive wine listings are not available.

For banquets or in a classical restaurant it is best to use a loose-leaf binder book with a page for each wine. This will help you to keep the book current by adding and deleting wines. A common practice is to display the label of each table wine and sparkling wine. A listing of appetizer and dessert wines is sufficient without displaying their labels. There are two basic arrangements for wine books. One lists domestic and imported table wines in separate sections. The other lists both domestic and imported white table wines separately but in the same section and uses the same arrangement for the red table wines.

The sections of the wine book should be arranged to follow the order in which wines are taken at a meal, that is, aperitifs, table wines, and dessert wines. The sparkling wines can either precede or follow the table wine listings. Since champagne is often drunk before the meal as well as after the meal, the choices are best listed immediately following the section on aperitifs.

**Number of Wines to List.** The wine book for a classical restaurant should list fifty to sixty wines to represent the popular wines familiar to customers who have even a minimum of sophistication in selecting wines.

The following outline suggests how many of each kind of wine might be listed.

Aperitifs—6
White table wines—20
Red table wines—12
Rosé—6
Sparkling wines—10
Dessert wines—4

Total—58

A wine card that is sufficient to cover the needs of most restaurants can list as little as ten table wines—four white, four red, and two rosé—and a short collection such as this can be listed on the food menu. Appetizer and dessert wines are also appropriately listed on the food menu.

A good selection of wines, like a good selection of foods, is not synonymous with great length. Quality is the aim. Remember, good value satisfies customers. Nevertheless, in cosmopolitan cities like Paris, Rome, San Francisco, and New York, a fine restaurant should offer a range of wines that will represent the many subtleties of taste to a discriminating clientele, and therefore it must have an extensive wine cellar and a substantial wine list to properly offer its valuable wares.

Exhibit 15-4 is an elaborate wine list featured in a classical Italian restaurant. Note there are over two hundred wines listed from France, Italy, and the United States. It contains items for every taste and nearly every pocketbook.

## Brief Glossary of Wine Terms

*Acidity.* Indicates the quality of tartness, sourness, or sharpness to the taste that is due to the presence of agreeable fruit acids.

*Aftertaste.* The taste remaining in the mouth for a period of time immediately after swallowing a wine.

*Aperitif.* A French word meaning appetizer. Refers to a wine taken before a meal to stimulate appetite.

*Appearance.* Refers to clarity, not color. When evaluated in a glass, the wine should be free of cloudiness and suspended particles.

*Aroma.*  A part of the wine's odor; originates in yeast fermentation and from the grape variety itself.

*Balance.*  Denotes harmony among the principal constituents of a wine.

*Body.*  The feeling of weight or fullness on the palate. Light-bodied wines tend to be low in alcohol, tannin, and extract. Heavy-bodied wines are higher in alcoholic content and tannin and tend toward sweetness.

*Bouquet.*  The part of the wine's odor that develops after it is bottled.

*Color.*  Each type of wine has a "right" color. Experts in judging wines rate the color of a wine against that standard. For example, white wines can be yellow, gold, or straw color, but neither too dark nor too close to the appearance of water. Young red wines can have violet tints. Older reds have amber tints. A wine with too little red or with a brownish color is rated as having a flawed color.

*Decanting.*  Pouring wine slowly and carefully from the bottle to another container to leave sediment behind before serving.

*Dry.*  In the taste sensation of wine, dry denotes the absence of sweetness. Wine tasters begin to perceive the presence of sugar in wine at levels between 0.5 percent and 1.0 percent sugar.

*Fermentation.*  The process of converting natural grape sugar into alcohol and carbon dioxide by yeast growth.

*Generic wine.*  Wine types with names such as burgundy, champagne, and rhine. When European wines carry these names, they refer to wines that are produced from strictly regulated areas of the wine country. In the United States such names denote a wine best described by a general type rather than by the major grape variety used in its production.

*Jug wine.*  Wine generally sold in containers larger than the standard fifth. Historically jug wines have been cheap wines. Some American varietals can now be purchased in large containers.

*Light.*  Denotes low-alcohol and low-sugar table wines. As a consequence, they are low in calories.

*Nose.*  The perceived odor of a wine composed of aroma, bouquet, and other fermentation volatiles.

*Odor.*  The "nose" of a wine.

*Residual sugar.*  The natural sugar remaining unfermented after the fermentation process is complete. The following percentages of residual sugar are used as a guideline:

0.5% or less—dry
0.6% to 1.5%—lightly sweet
1.6% to 3.0%—medium sweet
3.1% to 5.0%—sweet
More than 5.0%—very sweet

*Spritz.*  A wine that contains a small but noticeable amount of carbonation.

*Tannin.*  The naturally occurring astringent, "puckery," and sometimes bitter components of wine. They are collectively known as *tannin.*

*Varietal character.*  The combination of odor and taste that is attributable to the source grape.

*Varietal wine.*  A wine named for the predominant grape variety in its composition. Most of the finest wines of Europe are blends.

*Vintage.*  The calendar year during which the grapes were harvested.

*Vintage wine.*  Wine made from grapes harvested in one given year. Actually, the regulations state that only 95 percent of a wine's volume must be from grapes of the year specified on the label.

*Viticultural area.*  A geographical area within which vineyards may use the name of the area to describe the wine.

# CHAMPAGNES
## FRANCE

| BIN | | BOTTLE |
|---|---|---|
| 1 | MOET & CHANDON, CUVEE DOM PERIGNON, BRUT-MAGNUM | 260.00 |
| 2 | MOET & CHANDON, CUVEE DOM PERIGNON, ROSE | 300.00 |
| 3 | LAURENT ~ PERRIER, CUVEE GRANDE ~ SIECLE, BRUT | 140.00 |
| 4 | KRUG, GRAND CUVEE, BRUT | 135.00 |
| 5 | MOET & CHANDON, CUVEE DOM PERIGNON, BRUT | 130.00 |
| 6 | CHAMPAGNE VEUVE CLIQUOT, LA GRANDE DAME | 120.00 |
| 7 | PERRIER & JOUET, FLEUR DE CHAMPAGNE | 100.00 |
| 8 | CHARBAUT ET FILS, BRUT | 95.00 |
| 9 | VEUVE CLIQUOT PONSARDIN, YELLOW LABEL, BRUT | 65.00 |
| 10 | TAITTINGER, "LA FRANCAISE", BRUT | 55.00 |
| 11 | MOET & CHANDON, "WHITE STAR", EXTRA DRY | 55.00 |
| 12 | MUMM, "CORDON ROUGE", ROSE | 55.00 |
| 13 | MUMM, "CORDON ROUGE", BRUT | 55.00 |

**Exhibit 15-3**
**The wine list of the Toscana Italian Restaurant**
*Reprinted with permission of the Innisbrook Hilton Resort, Tarpon Springs, Florida*

# SPARKLING WINES
## CALIFORNIA

| BIN | | BOTTLE |
|-----|-----|-------|
| 14 | PIPER-SONOMA, TETE DE CUVEE, BRUT | 45.00 |
| 15 | "J" BY JORDAN, BRUT | 50.00 |
| 16 | SCHRAMSBERG | 45.00 |
| 17 | "ETOILE", CHANDON, BRUT | 40.00 |
| 18 | CHANDON, BLANC DE NOIR | 35.00 |
| 19 | CHANDON, BRUT | 35.00 |
| 20 | KORBEL, BRUT | 25.00 |

## ITALY

| | | |
|-----|-----|-------|
| 21 | GIACOMO BOLOGNA, BRACHETTO D'ACQUI | 26.00 |
| 22 | BANFI, BRUT | 30.00 |
| 23 | MARTINI & ROSSI, SPUMANTE | 26.00 |

*Exhibit 15-3, continued*

# RED WINES
## ITALY
*THESE WINES ARE LISTED BY THE GEOGRAPHIC*
*REGIONS IN WHICH THEY ARE PRODUCED*

| BIN | | BOTTLE |
|---|---|---|
| | **TOSCANA** | |
| 24 | CARMIGNANO RISERVA, VILLA DI CAPPEZANA | 40.00 |
| 25 | CHIANTI CLASSICO RISERVA, FELSINA | 38.00 |
| 26 | CHIANTI CLASSICO RISERVA, "PEPPOLI" ANTINORI | 36.00 |
| 27 | CHIANTI CLASSICO RISERVA, CASTELLO DI GABBIANO, GOLD LABEL | 38.00 |
| 28 | CHIANTI CLASSICO RISERVA DUCALE, RUFFINO | 30.00 |
| 29 | CHIANTI CLASSICO RISERVA, CASTELLO DI NIPOZZANO | 30.00 |
| 30 | CHIANTI CLASSICO, RISERVA, MONSANTO | 29.00 |
| 31 | CHIANTI CLASSICO RISERVA, BANFI | 25.00 |
| 32 | CHIANTI CLASSICO, BADIA A PASSIGNANO, ANTINORI | 24.00 |
| 33 | CHIANTI CLASSICO RISERVA, CASTELLO D' ALBOLA | 22.00 |
| 34 | CHIANTI RUFINA, FRESCOBALDI "REMOLE" | 22.00 |
| 35 | SANTA CRISTINA, SANGIOVESE TOSCANO, ANTINORI | 20.00 |
| 36 | SANGIOVESE, "TORGAIO", RUFFINO | 20.00 |
| 37 | CABREO IL BORGO, CAPITOLARE DI BITURICA, RUFFINO | 45.00 |
| 38 | VINO NOBILE DI MONTEPULCIANO, POLIZIANO | 38.00 |
| 39 | COL-DI-SASSO, BANFI | 21.00 |
| 40 | ROSSO DI MONTALCINO, LISINI | 32.00 |
| 41 | BRUNELLO DI MONTALCINO, CASTELLO BANFI | 55.00 |
| 42 | BRUNELLO DI MONTALCINO, IL POGGIONE | 65.00 |
| 43 | ORNELLAIA, MARCHESE LODOVICO ANTINORI | 70.00 |
| 44 | TIGNANELLO, ANTINORI | 75.00 |
| 45 | SASSICAIA, MARCHESI INCISA DELLA ROCCHETTA | 85.00 |
| 46 | SOLAIA, ANTINORI | 90.00 |

*Exhibit 15-3, continued*

# RED WINES
## ITALY

| BIN | | BOTTLE |
|---|---|---|
| | **PIEMONTE** | |
| 47 | BAROLO "SPERSS", ANGELO GAJA | 95.00 |
| 48 | BAROLO RISERVA, "VIGNA RIONDA DI SERRALUNGA", MICHELE CHIARLO | 70.00 |
| 51 | BAROLO, "ZONCHERA" CERETTO | 40.00 |
| 52 | BARBARESCO, ANGELO GAJA | 85.00 |
| 53 | BARBARESCO "ASIJ", CERETTO | 40.00 |
| 54 | NEBBIOLO D'ALBA, PIO CESARE | 35.00 |
| 55 | DOLCETTO D'ALBA, RENATTI RATTI | 25.00 |
| 57 | BARBERA D'ASTI, MICHELE CHIARLO | 24.00 |
| | **VENETO** | |
| 58 | AMARONE CLASSICO SUPERIORE, SANTA SOFIA | 55.00 |
| 59 | AMARONE CLASSICO "CAPITEL DE ROARI" LUIGI RIGHETTI | 35.00 |
| 60 | MERLOT, SANTA MARGHERITA | 27.00 |
| 62 | VALPOLICELLA CLASSICO SUPERIORE, MASI | 24.00 |
| | **TRENTINO-ALTO ADIGE** | |
| 63 | PINOT NERO RISERVA, J. HOFSTATTER | 50.00 |
| | **FRIULI** | |
| 64 | CABERNET SAUVIGNON, BOLLINI | 21.00 |
| | **UMBRIA** | |
| 65 | RUBESCO, LUNGAROTTI | 22.00 |
| 66 | SANGIOVESE, LUNGAROTTI | 23.00 |
| | **CAMPANIA** | |
| 67 | TAURASI, MASTROBERADINO | 37.00 |
| 68 | LACRIMAROSA DRY ROSE, MASTROBERADINO | 27.00 |

*Exhibit 15-3, continued*

# RED WINES
## CAL - ITAL

"THESE WINES ARE EXCELLENT EXAMPLES OF THE RECENT TREND OF CALIFORNIA WINERIES
MAKING ITALIAN STYLE RED WINES USING THE SANGIOVESE GRAPE. THESE WINES ARE
COMPLEX, HIGHLY CONCENTRATED WITH LOTS OF FLAVOR AND FINESSE
AND THEY COMPLEMENT OUR TUSCAN CUISINE VERY WELL"

| BIN | | BOTTLE |
|---|---|---|
| | **SANGIOVESE ~ CALIFORNIA** | |
| 70 | SEGHESIO | 25.00 |
| 71 | SWANSON | 32.00 |
| 72 | FLORA SPRINGS | 27.00 |
| 73 | ATLAS PEAK | 28.00 |
| 74 | ROBERT PEPI, "COLLINE DI SASSI" | 33.00 |

*Exhibit 15-3, continued*

# WHITE WINES
## ITALY

| BIN | | BOTTLE |
|---|---|---|
| | **PIEMONTE** | |
| 75 | GAVI, PRINCIPESSA | 26.00 |
| 76 | GAVI DI GAVI, FIGINI | 28.00 |
| | **FRIULI** | |
| 77 | PINOT GRIGIO, "COLLIO" BORGO CONVENTI | 35.00 |
| | **TRENTINO-ALTO ADIGE** | |
| 78 | PINOT GRIGIO, SANTA MARGHERITA | 34.00 |
| | **VENETO** | |
| 79 | BIANCO DI CUSTOZA, LAMBERTI | 21.00 |
| 80 | SOAVE CLASSICO SUPERIORE, MASI | 24.00 |
| 81 | BREGANZE DI BREGANZE, FAUSTO MACULAN | 24.00 |
| | **UMBRIA** | |
| 82 | PINOT GRIGIO, LUNGAROTTI | 27.00 |
| 83 | CERVARO DELLA SALA, ANTINORI | 45.00 |
| 84 | ORVIETO CLASSICO SECCO, ANTINORI | 22.00 |
| 85 | CHARDONNAY, LUNGAROTTI | 25.00 |
| 86 | TORRE DI GIANO, RISERVA, LUNGAROTTI | 25.00 |
| | **MARCHE** | |
| 87 | VERDICCHIO, FAZI BATTAGLIA | 25.00 |
| | **LAZIO** | |
| 88 | FRASCATI, FONTANA CANDIDA | 20.00 |
| | **TOSCANA** | |
| 89 | VERNACCI DI SAN GIMIGNANO, CECCHI | 20.00 |
| 90 | TERRE DI TUFI, TERUZZI & PUTHOD | 38.00 |
| 91 | CHARDONNAY, "LIBAO", RUFFINO | 22.00 |
| 92 | VILLA BIANCO, ANTINORI | 20.00 |
| | **CAMPANIA** | |
| 93 | LACRYMA CHRISTI DEL VESUVIO, MASTROBERADINO | 31.00 |
| 94 | GRECO DI TUFO, MASTROBERADINO | 34.00 |
| | **SICILY** | |
| 95 | CORVO | 21.00 |

*Exhibit 15-3, continued*

# RED WINES
## CALIFORNIA
# LIBRARY VERTICAL SELECTIONS
### (LIMITED SUPPLY AVAILABLE)

| BIN | | BOTTLE |
|---|---|---|
| | **CABERNET SAUVIGNON - ROBERT MONDAVI WINERY** | |
| 100 | 1977 ROBERT MONDAVI RESERVE | 90.00 |
| 101 | 1979 ROBERT MONDAVI RESERVE | 80.00 |
| 102 | 1980 ROBERT MONDAVI RESERVE | 75.00 |
| 103 | 1982 ROBERT MONDAVI RESERVE | 65.00 |
| 104 | 1989 ROBERT MONDAVI RESERVE | 65.00 |
| 105 | 1991 ROBERT MONDAVI RESERVE | 70.00 |
| | **CABERNET SAUVIGNON - BEAULIEU VINEYARDS** | |
| 106 | 1972 GEORGES DE LATOUR, PRIVATE RESERVE | 120.00 |
| 107 | 1975 GEORGES DE LATOUR, PRIVATE RESERVE | 100.00 |
| 108 | 1976 GEORGES DE LATOUR, PRIVATE RESERVE | 90.00 |
| 111 | 1983 GEORGES DE LATOUR, PRIVATE RESERVE | 65.00 |
| | **CABERNET SAUVIGNON - INGLENOOK VINEYARDS** | |
| 112 | 1976 LIMITED CASK RESERVE | 65.00 |
| 113 | 1980 LIMITED CASK RESERVE | 50.00 |
| 114 | 1981 LIMITED CASK RESERVE | 50.00 |
| 116 | 1983 LIMITED CASK RESERVE | 45.00 |
| 117 | 1985 LIMITED CASK RESERVE | 50.00 |

*Exhibit 15-3, continued*

# RED WINES
## CALIFORNIA

| BIN | | BOTTLE |
|---|---|---|
| | **CABERNET SAUVIGNON** | |
| 118 | 1990 OPUS ONE, ROBERT MONDAVI, BARON PHILIPPE DE ROTHSCHILD | 90.00 |
| 119 | 1991 OPUS ONE, ROBERT MONDAVI, BARON PHILIPPE DE ROTHSCHILD | 95.00 |
| 120 | 1992 OPUS ONE, ROBERT MONDAVI, BARON PHILIPPE DE ROTHSCHILD | 100.00 |
| 122 | 1991 CARDINALE | 75.00 |
| 123 | 1991 JOSEPH PHELPS, "INSIGNIA" | 65.00 |
| 124 | SILVER OAK, "ALEXANDER VALLEY" | 60.00 |
| 125 | FAR NIENTE | 70.00 |
| 126 | CHATEAU MONTELENA | 60.00 |
| 127 | GUENOC RESERVE, "BECKSTOFFER VINEYARD" | 60.00 |
| 128 | GRGICH HILLS | 55.00 |
| 130 | JORDAN, "ALEXANDER VALEY" | 50.00 |
| 131 | CAKEBREAD CELLARS | 48.00 |
| 132 | CAYMUS VINEYARDS | 45.00 |
| 133 | ROBERT MONDAVI, NAPA | 40.00 |
| 134 | GUENOC, "ESTATE BOTTLED" | 34.00 |
| 135 | SILVERADO | 34.00 |
| 136 | STONESTREET | 32.00 |
| 137 | FREEMARK ABBEY | 32.00 |
| 138 | JOSEPH PHELPS | 36.00 |
| 139 | ROBERT MONDAVI, "WOODBRIDGE" | 23.00 |

*Exhibit 15-3, continued*

# RED WINES
## CALIFORNIA

| BIN | | BOTTLE |
|-----|-----|--------|
| | **CABERNET SAUVIGNON** | |
| 140 | SWANSON | 35.00 |
| 141 | MERRYVALE | 30.00 |
| 142 | SIMI, "ALEXANDER VALLEY" | 30.00 |
| 143 | KENWOOD, "SONOMA VALLEY" | 30.00 |
| 144 | VICHON | 28.00 |
| 145 | BERINGER, "KNIGHTS VALLEY" | 28.00 |
| 146 | BEAULIEU VINEYARDS, "RUTHERFORD" | 26.00 |
| 147 | ROBERT MONDAVI, "COASTAL" | 26.00 |
| 148 | FETZER, "BARREL SELECT" | 27.00 |
| 149 | DE LOACH "SONOMA CUVEE" | 22.00 |
| 150 | CAMELOT | 20.00 |
| 151 | STONE PINE | 20.00 |
| | **MERLOT** | |
| 152 | CLOS DU BOIS | 30.00 |
| 153 | CUVAISON | 45.00 |
| 154 | ST. FRANCIS | 36.00 |
| 155 | SWANSON | 35.00 |
| 156 | STERLING | 32.00 |
| 157 | KENDALL - JACKSON | 32.00 |
| 158 | LOLONIS, "PRIVATE RESERVE" | 30.00 |
| 159 | FETZER, "EAGLE PEAK" | 27.00 |

*Exhibit 15-3, continued*

# RED WINES
## CALIFORNIA

| BIN | | BOTTLE |
|-----|-----|-----|
| | **ZINFANDEL** | |
| 160 | MONTEVINA | 20.00 |
| 161 | LYTTON SPRINGS | 33.00 |
| 162 | STEELE, CATFISH VINYARD | 32.00 |
| 163 | SEGHESIO, "OLD VINES" | 27.00 |
| 164 | RAVENSWOOD | 24.00 |
| | **PINOT NOIR** | |
| 165 | ACACIA, RESERVE | 42.00 |
| 166 | ROBERT MONDAVI, NAPA | 32.00 |
| 167 | STEELE, "CARNEROS" | 34.00 |
| 168 | SAINTSBURY, CARNEROS | 32.00 |
| 169 | FETZER, "BARREL SELECT" | 24.00 |

*Exhibit 15-3, continued*

# WHITE WINES
## CALIFORNIA

| BIN | | BOTTLE |
|-----|--|--------|
| | **CHARDONNAY** | |
| 170 | FETZER, "SUNDIAL" | 20.00 |
| 171 | HESS SELECT | 22.00 |
| 172 | BERINGER, "PROPRIETOR GROWN" | 26.00 |
| 173 | WILLIAM HILL RESERVE | 37.00 |
| 174 | GRGICH HILLS | 52.00 |
| 175 | FAR NIENTE | 52.00 |
| 176 | ROBERT MONDAVI RESERVE | 48.00 |
| 177 | CHATEAU MONTELENA | 48.00 |
| 178 | STERLING | 35.00 |
| 179 | CAKEBREAD CELLARS | 40.00 |
| 180 | CUVAISON | 36.00 |
| 181 | ROBERT MONDAVI | 36.00 |
| 182 | SWANSON | 36.00 |
| 183 | ACACIA, "CARNEROS" | 32.00 |
| 184 | SILVERADO | 29.00 |
| 185 | MERRYVALE, "STARMONT" | 30.00 |
| 186 | BEAULIEU VINEYARDS, "CARNEROS" | 26.00 |
| 187 | KENDALL~JACKSON, GRAND RESERVE | 38.00 |
| 188 | STEELE | 36.00 |
| 189 | GUENOC, "ESTATE BOTTLEO" | 35.00 |

*Exhibit 15-3, continued*

# WHITE WINES
## CALIFORNIA

| BIN | | BOTTLE |
|---|---|---|
| | **CHARDONNAY** | |
| 190 | GUENOC RESERVE, "GENEVIEVE MAGOON" VINEYARD | 40.00 |
| 191 | JORDAN | 40.00 |
| 192 | FERRARI - CARANO | 36.00 |
| 193 | SIMI | 31.00 |
| 194 | FETZER, "BONTERRA" | 24.00 |
| 195 | ROBERT MONDAVI, COASTAL | 25.00 |
| 196 | ROBERT MONDAVI, "WOODBRIDGE" | 22.00 |
| 197 | KENDALL - JACKSON, "VINTNER'S RESERVE" | 27.00 |
| 198 | DE LOACH, "SONOMA CUVEE" | 22.00 |
| 199 | CAMELOT | 20.00 |
| 200 | STONE PINE | 20.00 |
| | **SAUVIGNON BLANC** | |
| 201 | CAKEBREAD CELLARS | 29.00 |
| 202 | JOSEPH PHELPS | 25.00 |
| 203 | STERLING | 24.00 |
| 204 | SILVERADO | 22.00 |
| 205 | BEAULIEU VINEYARDS | 26.00 |
| 206 | CAYMUS VINEYARDS | 25.00 |
| 207 | FETZER, "BARREL SELECT" | 24.00 |

*Exhibit 15-3, continued*

# WHITE WINES
## CALIFORNIA

| BIN | | BOTTLE |
|---|---|---|
| | **FUME BLANC** | |
| 208 | ROBERT MONDAVI | 24.00 |
| 209 | FERRARI - CARANO | 24.00 |
| 210 | BENZIGER | 20.00 |
| | **CHENIN BLANC** | |
| 211 | ROBERT MONDAVI | 20.00 |
| | **JOHANNISBERG RIESLING** | |
| 212 | ROBERT MONDAVI | 22.00 |
| | **GEWURZTRAMINER** | |
| 213 | RUTHERFORD HILL | 20.00 |
| 214 | GRAND CRU VINEYARDS | 20.00 |
| | **WHITE ZINFANDEL** | |
| 215 | SUTTER HOME | 20.00 |
| 216 | STONE PINE | 20.00 |
| 217 | ROBERT MONDAVI, "WOODBRIDGE" | 20.00 |
| 218 | BERINGER | 22.00 |

## GERMANY

| BIN | | BOTTLE |
|---|---|---|
| | **MOSEL** | |
| 219 | PIESPORTER GOLDTROPFCHEN, QBA, KABINETT | 25.00 |
| | **RHINE** | |
| 220 | BEREICH JOHANNISBERG, RIESLING, QBA, SICHEL | 20.00 |

*Exhibit 15-3, continued*

# RED WINES
## FRANCE

| BIN | | BOTTLE |
|---|---|---|
| | **BORDEAUX** | |
| 221 | CHATEAU LAFITE - ROTHSCHILD, 1966 | 175.00 |
| 222 | CHATEAU LAFITE - ROTHSCHILD, 1970 | 260.00 |
| 223 | CHATEAU LAFITE - ROTHSCHILD, 1987 | 120.00 |
| 224 | CHATEAU PETRUS, 1981 | 250.00 |
| 225 | CHATEAU PETRUS, 1984 | 175.00 |
| 226 | CHATEAU PETRUS, 1985 | 225.00 |
| 227 | CHATEAU GLORIA | 60.00 |
| 228 | CHATEAU MARGAUX, PAVILLON ROUGE | 50.00 |
| 229 | POMEROL, BARON PHILIPPE DE ROTHSCHILD | 38.00 |
| 230 | CHATEAU COUFRAN | 38.00 |
| | **BEAUJOLAIS** | |
| 231 | BEAUJOLAIS - VILLAGES,  GEORGES DUBOEUF | 25.00 |
| 232 | BEAUJOLAIS - VILLAGES, LOUIS JADOT | 24.00 |
| 233 | MOULIN-A-VENT, GEORGES DUBOEUF | 29.00 |
| | **RHONE** | |
| 234 | CHATEAUNEUF - DU-PAPE, CHATEAU MONT-REDON | 38.00 |
| 235 | CHATEAUNEUF - DU-PAPE, CHATEAU DE BEAUCASTEL | 50.00 |
| | **BURGUNDY** | |
| 236 | ROMANEE ~ CONTI, 1984 | 220.00 |
| 237 | ROMANEE ~ CONTI, 1986 | 250.00 |
| 238 | LA TACHE, 1984 | 175.00 |
| 239 | LA TACHE, 1986 | 200.00 |
| 240 | RICHEBOURG, 1986 | 175.00 |
| 241 | ROMANEE-ST.VIVANT, 1986 | 140.00 |
| 242 | BEAUNE - CLOS DES MOUCHES, JOSEPH DROUHIN | 60.00 |
| 243 | NUITS-SAINT-GEORGES, BOUCHARD PERES & FILS | 50.00 |
| 244 | LAFORET, JOSEPH DROUHIN | 30.00 |

*Exhibit 15-3, continued*

# WHITE WINES
## FRANCE

| BIN | | BOTTLE |
|---|---|---|
| | **BORDEAUX** | |
| 245 | CHATEAU MARGAUX, PAVILLON BLANC | 60.00 |
| 246 | CHATEAU CARBONNIEUX | 48.00 |
| | **BURGUNDY** | |
| 247 | BEAUNE-CLOS DES MOUCHES, JOSEPH DROUHIN | 80.00 |
| 248 | PULIGNY-MONTRACHET, LOUIS JADOT | 60.00 |
| 249 | CHABLIS, MOREAU | 27.00 |
| 250 | POUILLY-FUISSE, GEORGES DUBOEUF | 38.00 |
| 251 | POUILLY-FUISSE, LOUIS JADOT | 40.00 |
| 252 | POUILLY-FUISSE, JOSEPH DROUHIN | 35.00 |
| 253 | MACON-VILLAGES, LE CHAMVILLE | 25.00 |
| 254 | MACON-LUGNY, LES CHARMES | 22.00 |
| | **LOIRE** | |
| 255 | POUILLY-FUME, DE LADOUCETTE | 40.00 |
| | **ALSACE** | |
| 256 | RIESLING, HUGEL | 24.00 |
| 257 | GEWURZTRAMINER, DOPF, "AU MOULIN" | 22.00 |

*Exhibit 15-3, continued*

# DESSERT WINES
## FRENCH

| BIN | | BOTTLE |
|-----|---|--------|
| 260 | CHATEAU D' YQUEM, 1988 | 300.00 |
| 261 | CHATEAU SUDUIRAUT, 1982 | 45.00 |

## CALIFORNIA

| | | |
|-----|---|--------|
| 264 | INGLENOOK LATE HARVEST GEWURZTRAMINER, HALF BOTTLE | 25.00 |
| 265 | ROBERT MONDAVI, MOSCATO D' ORO, HALF BOTTLE | 10.00 |
| 266 | CHATEAU ST. JEAN, JOHANNISBERG RIESLING BELLE TERRE VINEYARDS, SPECIAL SELECT LATE HARVEST - HALF BOTTLE | 35.00 |

## ITALY

| | | |
|-----|---|--------|
| 21 | BRACHETTO D' ACQUI BRAIDA DI GIACOMO BOLOGNA BLUSH SPARKLING WINE | 26.00 |
| 267 | VINO SANTO, LUNGAROTTI HALF BOTTLE | 16.00 |
| 268 | ICARDI, MOSCATO D' ASTI, HALF BOTTLE | 15.00 |

## NON-ALCOHOLIC WINES

| | | |
|-----|---|--------|
| 271 | WHITE ZINFANDEL SUTTER HOME, FRE | 20.00 |
| 272 | SUTTER HOME CHARDONAY, FRE | 20.00 |
| 273 | SUTTER HOME CHAMPAGNE, FRE | 20.00 |
| 274 | ARIEL, BLANC | 16.00 |
| 275 | ARIEL, RED | 20.00 |

*Exhibit 15-3, continued*

# 16 Beverage Promotions

**Purpose:** To outline the methods that will ensure success in selling beverages.

The amount of wine consumed in American restaurants has been rising steadily in recent years. This is due in part to consumers' growing knowledge about wines. But it is also due to restaurant operators' taking advantage of consumers' knowledge by means of various beverage promotional efforts. Successful promotions of wines are twice blessed: They are a great source of added profit and lead to greater satisfaction on the part of the dining public. During this period of rising wine sales, the taste of the American consumer for liquor has moved toward lighter drinks. Many gins, Scotches, bourbons, and blended whiskies have lowered the proof content to 80 from 90 and 86. Vodka has moved to the top of the liquor preference list. Most breweries make and promote light beers along with the regular product. Such changes are reflected in the beverage promotions of alert restaurateurs and lounge operators.

## Environment

Any kind of sales or promotional effort requires a setting that will put the customer in a mood to be open to a suggestion to buy. In restaurants and lounges two essential elements create guest receptivity—friendliness and cleanliness. The friendliness must be all about. Guests note not only the attitudes of the persons at the door and the particular waiter or waitress handling their orders but the other service personnel in the room. Altogether they create the necessary friendliness.

A few years ago a national rating company made a survey to determine just what features the public looks for as a basis for eating at a restaurant. Surprisingly, most people rate the cleanliness of the restrooms as the most important feature affecting their judgment of a restaurant. Clean restrooms were rated more important than pricing, quality of food, and even friendliness of service. This cleanliness must extend to all guest areas. It can result from only well-planned and efficiently executed maintenance programs.

## Atmosphere

A restaurant's good environment (one of the "six g's") is created by its staff's general friendliness and by its cleanliness. The environment must be supplemented by an atmosphere that can be created only by people. The bartenders must be friendly and entertaining as they perform their job.

Cocktail waitresses too should be friendly.

Their uniforms should be attractive and in keeping with the atmosphere of good cheer.

## Action

To build business, a cocktail lounge must have something "going on." This should be entertainment but not necessarily entertainers. Some suggestions follow.

1. A large-screen television for football and baseball games.
2. Old-time movies are especially entertaining for young people. They are entertained because the shows are good and the differences from current films create a curious interest.
3. Video discs are available for rental or purchase on about every subject.
4. Piano bars have been around for a long time, but with the right person at the keyboard they are still popular. A sing-a-long in some bars and lounges has become a tradition. "At ten o'clock the singing begins ready or not" was the invitation (or warning) in a well-patronized "watering hole" in Chicago.
5. Soft rock groups can entertain without doing permanent ear damage. As for the "heavy metal"—best leave it to "hard rock" clubs or the concert hall.
6. Dancing has been an enjoyment for people since biblical times. The music must be targeted to the clientele's taste. Guy Lombardo doesn't do much for most twenty-one year olds, nor do senior citizens "dig" rock.
7. Refer to the discussion on signature restaurants in Chapter 3 for an explanation of the ultimate in unusual entertainment—The Cow and I restaurant.

Most bar or lounge managers are not show business managers, so it is prudent to seek help from professional booking agents to obtain entertainment persons or groups.

## Quality Drinks

A friendly atmosphere in a good environment with entertainment will not compensate for poor drinks. Generous drinks (1½ ounces of liquor in high balls and 2 ounces in cocktails) of first-brand liquors and wines are necessary to complete an attractive package in a cocktail lounge, bar, or restaurant.

## Fair Pricing

To give good value the product and the price must agree. Cheap prices do not make good value. If you serve generous drinks of good-brand liquor and fresh juices (when used), customers will be happy to pay a little extra because they expect good value at that price.

## Unusual Glassware

Many resort areas use unusual glassware as a promotional tool. They serve a special-recipe drink in an unusual glass, and the price of the drink includes the glass. The guest can then take the glass for a souvenir. This is a good marketing tool for a lounge that does not expect much repeat business. However, both cocktail lounges in restaurants or hotels and free-standing lounges must direct their promotional efforts to building loyal clienteles. Their approach should be to use glassware a bit different from what a guest might expect, different from what is found in most other places. Large glasses are immediately noticed. A 12-ounce rocks glass, tall high-ball glasses, and 8- to 10-ounce sours glasses are perfect to accommodate the generous drink that guests will remember. Three-ounce sherry glasses and 12- to 14-ounce table wine glasses carry out this theme.

All-purpose wine glasses have become popular. They were very likely invented by someone whose goal was to save money rather than satisfy guests. Such glasses lead to monotony, which will not build business.

## Serve Some Outstanding Food

A lounge in a restaurant complex has the necessary food preparation facilities to make creative foods to accompany drinks. A good example are the Polynesian restaurants, which have set the standard in this area. Service of appetizers in the lounge as the first course for dinner will stimulate the dinner business. In American service restaurants the cocktail waitresses can present the food menus and take the food orders.

Appetizers served in the cocktail lounge need a different "flavor" from those served at the dinner table. Instead of the fruit cups, glazed grapefruit, or melon commonly served in the dining room, barbecued back ribs, pu-pu's, cabbage balls, and corned beef are usually offered in a cocktail lounge setting. Also consider smoked salmon with chopped hard-cooked eggs and cream cheese balls with capers, as well as chopped chicken livers with onions, hard-cooked eggs, pimiento, and stuffed celery. Meat balls with water chestnuts and broiled cape scallops in butter are two more popular appetizers in lounges.

Use your imagination to add to these ideas.

### Snacks—"Gratis" Foods

Many people entering a cocktail lounge have given no thought at all to whether or not they will have more than one drink. Smart lounge operators provide snacks with drinks as a subtle invitation to have a second drink. We offer this maxim: Never serve a drink without a snack. Vary snacks from day to day, and offer more than one every day. Peanuts are good, but not every day. A few common but welcome snacks follow.

Peanuts
Popcorn
Pretzels
Triscuits

Potato chips
Fritos
Cheese chunks
Cheese puffs

Cheese spreads can be served with

Triangle thins
Sesame thins
Celery thins
Chippers
Wheat thins
Vegetable thins
Thin wheat toasted wafers

Some cheeses and cheese spreads are

Wispride (sharp cheddar spread)
Old Sport (aged sharp New York State cheddar)
Danish Smearcase
Cheddar with beer
Top-secret spread

## Happy Hours

Many people consider "happy hours" a late-afternoon ritual. Many lounges restrict these promotions to weekdays, Monday through Friday. But why eliminate them on weekends? Many people who seldom visit cocktail lounges and restaurants during the week are regular "weekenders." They will be eager customers at Saturday and Sunday happy hours. This type of promotion is today's counterpart to the "free lunch" of preprohibition days.

Many lounges offer hot appetizers as part of happy hour. A dozen hot chafing dish suggestions follow.

1. Codfish cakes
2. Deep-fried bite-sized pieces of haddock
3. Cocktail sausages
4. Tidbits in blankets: cooked shrimp,

oysters, stuffed olives, pickled onions, sautéed chicken livers, or pineapple chunks wrapped in thin strips of bacon secured with toothpicks and baked on a rack in a moderate oven until the bacon is crisp.

5. Swedish meat balls
6. Rumaki Polynesian (chicken liver and water chestnuts wrapped in bacon)
7. Meat balls with water chestnuts
8. Tempura
9. Canapés, hors d'oeurves
10. Chicken wings—"drums of heaven"
11. Kabobs—Japanese steak-house style
12. Fondue

A popular happy hour practice is to feature the "Two For." Two drinks for the price of one skirts the law that forbids the offering of free drinks.

## Inclusives—Where Permitted

Beverages can be promoted as part of a package with food, for example, a cocktail before dinner, an after-dinner drink, or a glass of wine with dinner. Another package deal is the "Theater Dinner"—one price includes drinks, food, and theater tickets. Sport contests shown only on closed-circuit television offer another opportunity to promote a package deal—drinks, snacks, and the T.V. show. Some state laws demand separate billing for food and beverage, which eliminates the use of such promotions.

## Special Drinks

Interest in the "science" of astrology seems to come in cycles, with periods of considerable popularity followed by periods of diminished attention. Julius Wile, a wine-and-spirits expert, worked with some mixicologists to develop drinks to represent each of the twelve signs of the zodiac. Each should

be featured during its period of the year, or served at "horoscopic" birthday parties. The drinks can also be featured as a group to appeal to persons born under a particular sign or having or wishing to have the characteristics of persons born under the sign. Following are "zodiac" drink recipes and their corresponding signs.

- *Aries, the Ram* (March 21 to April 19). Persons born under this sign want a "rambunctious" drink.

*Aries Aperitif*
Pour a jigger of apricot-flavored brandy over cracked ice in an old-fashioned glass. Add juice of a half lemon and a half lime and a splash of grenadine. Stir and add soda.

- *Taurus, the Bull* (April 20 to May 21). For hearty food-loving gourmets.

*Bully Bullshot*
In a double old-fashioned glass pour six ounces of beef bouillon; stir in a jigger of vodka; season with Worstershire, salt, and pepper; and top with a lemon twist. Serve either hot in a mug or cold over ice.

- *Gemini, the Twins* (May 21 to June 20). Pleasing to the changeable guest who cannot decide what to drink.

*B & B*
Serve B & B liqueur in a cordial glass or snifter; or shaken with ice, add a little lemon juice, a teaspoon of Curacao, and pour in a cocktail glass.

- *Cancer, the Crab* (June 22 to July 22). A romantic drink for the Moon child.

*Moontail*
Combine half a jigger each of Benedictine and apple-flavored brandy; add juice of half a lemon and a teaspoon of Curacao; shake with ice and strain into a glass.

- *Leo, the Lion* (July 23 to August 22). For a feeling of royalty.

*Leo Tamer*
Stir two ounces of blackberry-flavored brandy with ice, pour into a cocktail glass, and sprinkle nutmeg on top.

- *Virgo, the Virgin* (August 23 to September 22). The connoisseur drink.

*Virgo Victory*
Pour Pernod over ice, add a little water or orange juice.

- *Libra, the Balance* (September 23 to October 23). For the fun-loving person.

*Libra's Libation*
Mix half and half Benedictine and gin with a dash of angostura bitters. Pour over ice and stir.

- *Scorpio, the Scorpion* (October 24 to November 21). For the sensual, moody party-goer.

*Scorpio Stinger*
Mix three parts B & B and one part white crème de menthe. Shake with ice and serve over ice in a cocktail glass.

- *Sagittarius, the Archer* (November 22 to December 21). For the person newly arrived.

*Sagittarius Sevilla*
Pour half rum and half vermouth over ice, stir, and serve.

- *Capricorn, the Goat* (December 22 to January 19). To stimulate the imaginative guest.

*Capricorn Caper*
Combine two jiggers of gin; juice of half an orange, half a lime, and half a lemon; ¾ jigger of cream; and white of an egg. Shake well or blend, pour into a tall glass, and add soda.

- *Aquarius, the Water Bearer* (January 20 to February 18). To feed the meal-forgetting Aquarian.

*Aquariflip*
Pour two jiggers of Dry Sack sherry, one egg, and a teaspoon of powdered sugar over cracked ice. Shake well into a glass and sprinkle with nutmeg.

- *Pisces, the Fishes* (February 19 to March 20). An artistic drink for the person of impeccable taste.

*Pisces and Chips*
Mix a jigger of cognac, three jiggers of unsweetened pineapple juice, and champagne. Pour into a tall glass of chipped ice topped with fruit chunks on picks.

These examples demonstrate that with imagination, promotions can be based on events and things from the common to the bizarre.

## Wine Promotions

Following are some suggestions to promote the sale of wines:

1. Set up a wine display near the dining room entrance or at a prominent location within the room. Present from ten to twelve table wines, both red and white, with a variety of fresh grapes and some colorful seasonal fruit, such as red apples.
2. Head the listing of wines on food menus with the phrase "To Make a Meal a Feast." This reminder suggests that wine enhances any meal and will add to the guests' enjoyment (and thereby build wine sales).
3. A good merchandising gimmick is to feature a "Wine of the Week." The wine can be called to the guests' atten-

tion by menu "clip-ons," table tents, and especially by the service person, who informs the guest of the particular wine for the week and also extolls its qualities. A variation of this is wines of the week—a red and a white wine, which allows guests to have the wine special no matter what food they order.

4. Incentives to service employees are also productive contributors to wine sales. They might receive, for example, one dollar for every bottle they serve or fifty-five cents for every half bottle. Such a program will be more active and more productive if the bonus is paid daily.

5. The demand for champagne and other sparkling wines is growing in the United States. This is partly due to advertising and promotion through magazine and promotional programs conducted by wine organizations. Restaurants can profitably capitalize on this trend.

6. "Treasure Chest of Wines." A certain restaurant with a healthy clientele had a special wine book entitled "Treasure Chest of Wines," which listed a selection of the finest wines available. Many of this restaurant's customers wore Johnson and Murphy shoes, which are very expensive. The service personnel were instructed to look at the customer's shoes; if they saw they wore Johnson and Murphy shoes, the servers brought out this special wine list. Sales were excellent. This is an example of an unusual but effective sales technique.

7. Remember to suggest the after-dinner brandy.

Wine sales promote "happiness." First, wine helps make the guests happy. Then the waiter shares in their happiness. Certainly increased wine sales make the restaurant manager happy—and the food and beverage manager of the hotel (if the restaurant is in a hotel), and the general manager of the hotel. Such "happiness" can go further if the restaurant or hotel is part of a chain—the parent company is the last to partake in this happiness (aside from, possibly, the tax collector).

## Wine Bars

This type of hospitality operation is fairly new in America, but it is not a new concept at all in Europe. Wine bars are especially popular in Germany, where the wine bar is called a *weinstube*. In a specialty shop like a wine bar (the specialty is wine by the glass) a wide variety of products should be available. Offer at least twenty different wines to sell by the glass. Because many wines are not readily available by the glass, a visit to a wine bar can be an adventure and perhaps an educational experience.

Wine bar lists differ from wine lists in a restaurant. Restaurant wine lists supplement the food offerings. Wine bar lists stand alone—the guest is there for the wine itself. It is good to offer guests a variety of cheeses to eat with the wines. Half bottles and bottles should be available for couples and groups to purchase. Bottles of the same variety as those sold by the glass should be available plus another twenty to twenty-five wines in bottles alone.

To add to guests' education and experience of adventure, wines sold by the glass and bottle should come from a wide variety of wine sources. American, French, and German wines are the traditional offerings, but a wine bar should include wines from Italy, Spain, Portugal, South America, and Australia.

Keep a wine bar list current like they do in the *weinstubes* of Germany—merely red-line out-of-stock items and write in additions. Whether you sell houses, automobiles, lawn mowers, foods, or beverages, observe one common principle: Sales are made only when customers are asked to buy.

# 17 Serving Healthful Food

**Purpose:** To suggest a sensible (but nonmedical) approach to meeting a relatively new but continuing and increasing trend in the eating habits of restaurant customers.

That diet is important to general good health has been evidenced in the United States by recent regulations requiring a list of ingredients on product packaging and by more rigorous inspections of raw foods. Exhibit 17-1 is a menu from a sports/fitness complex that complements the exercise-for-health regimen with food selections consistent with the theme. Note their promotion of the health idea in their introductory words of greeting: "... freshest ingredients and healthiest cooking techniques possible.... great food that's good for you, too."

The trend toward healthier foods may have peaked, however, as evidenced by the statistics on the fastest growing categories of foods currently being sold in the supermarkets. According to a report of Chicago-based Information Resources, Inc., carbonated beverages passed milk as the number one selling packaged product. The second fastest-growing category of foods is dinner sausage, followed by fresh eggs, butter, and frozen desserts and toppings.

Restaurateur take notice!

## Health Foods on Menus

The considerations for choosing what "health" foods to offer on a menu are no different from the basic considerations in choosing any menu items: Who are the potential customers? What do they want to eat? How much are they willing to pay? How does one find out what customers want? The best way to find out what customers want is to directly ask them when it is possible to engage them in conversation. Another way is to prepare a card containing several questions about the information desired, in this case health food. Such a questionnaire involves the people in the operation. This can be an interesting experience for many and a subtle promotional gimmick.

Successful businesspeople are aware of current political, economic, and social events. If you read, watch, or listen to the news every day, you will learn the latest on health and health foods.

Also look at what is being advertised. When we see the thousands of ads being thrust before us, sometimes consecutive ads for competing products, we might wonder if advertising pays. Are people influenced by what they

# Appetizers

Jumpin' Jacks menu items are prepared using the freshest ingredients and with the healthiest cooking techniques possible. Jacks' Classics* are some of our customer favorites — try 'em for a taste of hometown specialties. Or, see how flavorful and satisfying healthy cuisine can be with a light selection from our menu. Whatever you choose, you'll be assured of great food that's good-for-you, too. Enjoy!

## SESAME CHICKEN STRIPS
Sesame-crusted chicken tenders
with BBQ teriyaki sauce and cilantro lime dipping sauce
$5.00

## QUESADILLA
Wisconsin cheddar cheese, roasted
tomatoes, peppers, and onions, served:
with salsa and cilantro sour cream $3.95
with grilled chicken $4.50

## TWICE BAKED POTATO SKINS
Filled with sour cream and chive
mashed potatoes, served with cheddar and beer sauce
$3.50

## JACKS' PIZZA BREAD
Mozzarella and parmesan cheese, roasted tomatoes, with
fresh basil and oregano on crisp cracker bread
$4.50

## SHRIMP EGG ROLL
Shrimp with stir fried vegetables in a
crispy egg roll served with BBQ teriyaki sauce
$3.25

**Exhibit 17-1**
**Menu from Jumpin' Jacks**
*Reprinted with permission of Sports Core, Kohler, Wisconsin*

# Soups & Salads

### JACKS' HOMEMADE SOUPS

**Signature "Down Home" Chicken Dumpling**
bowl $2.50
cup $1.75

**Jacks' Soup of The Day**
bowl $2.50
cup $1.75

### ROASTED CASHEW CHICKEN SALAD*
Diced tender chicken with honey-roasted
cashews and pineapple served on a bed of greens
$6.25

### SPINACH SALAD*
Fresh spinach with mushrooms, tomatoes, cucumbers
and feta cheese served with warm bacon dressing
$6.95

### CAESAR SALAD
Romaine lettuce tossed with creamy garlic dressing,
parmesan cheese and herb croutons
$5.75
w/ chicken or tuna $6.95

### VEGETABLE PASTA SALAD
Curly pasta and fresh vegetables mixed in a
creamy corn and mustard dressing
$5.95

### FRESH FRUIT PLATE
Seasonal fresh fruit with lemon poppy seed dipping sauce
$6.75

### SIDE SALAD
Romaine lettuce, tomato wedge and herb croutons,
served with your choice of dressing
$2.50

### SOUP AND SALAD COMBO
Bowl of soup with a side salad, choice of dressing
$5.00

*Exhibit 17-1, continued*

# Sandwiches

All sandwiches served with your
choice of fresh fruit, pasta salad, mac & cheese or chips.

## WRAPPERS
The latest rage in food! Wrappers are large,
thin flour tortillas wrapped around some of your favorite foods:

### Sheboygan Wrapper
Sliced Sheboygan brats with
beer-glazed onions and mustard
$5.75

### BBQ Pork Wrapper
Thin sliced pork stewed in our
own BBQ sauce and cole slaw
$5.95

### Chicken Fajita Wrapper
Marinated chicken, sauteed
onions and peppers with
cilantro sour cream and salsa
$6.25

### Veggie Wrapper
Roasted zucchini, summer squash,
carrots and onions with mozzarella
cheese and herb mayo
$5.50

## TUNA SALAD SANDWICH*
White tuna in Jacks' homemade sauce topped with sprouts, cheddar
and tomatoes on whole wheat bread
$5.75

## GRILLED CHICKEN BREAST
Served on rosemary focaccia bread, this lemon-marinated chicken
breast is complemented with a roasted garlic caper mayonnaise,
tomatoes and lettuce
$6.25

## TURKEY CLUB
This traditional club favorite is made with herb-roasted turkey, lean pork
bacon, lettuce, tomato, and herb mayo, served on toasted sundried
tomato bread
$6.25

## THE BIG JACK
Lean ground beef burger piled high with lettuce, red onions, tomato,
and Jacks' special sauce on a whole wheat hard roll
$5.95

## ROASTED VEGGIE BAGEL
A warm bagel - spread with sun-dried tomato cream cheese, topped
with roasted summer squash, zucchini, carrots, red onions,
sweet bell peppers, and spinach
$5.00

*Exhibit 17-1, continued*

# Entrees

*All entrees served with your
choice of Jacks' homemade soup or side salad.*

## SHRIMP LINGUINE*

Gulf shrimp and tender linguine mixed with roasted
tomatoes and served in a light garlic cream sauce
$8.95

## CHICKEN ALMONDINE*

Tender diced chicken breast sauteed with mushrooms, peppers,
onions and almonds in a cream sauce served over puff pastry
$7.50

## SIRLOIN STEAK

A regional favorite grilled to your preference and served
with garlic mashed potatoes and roasted vegetables
$8.50

## WOK-SEARED CHICKEN BREAST

Tender seared chicken breast accompanied by
stir fried vegetables and rice pilaf
$7.25

## ORIENTAL STIR FRY

Fresh wild mushrooms, pea pods, zucchini and sweet bell
peppers stir fried with garlic, ginger and scallions served over rice pilaf
with beef $7.25
with shrimp $9.25

## VEGETABLE PRIMAVERA

Carrots, zucchini, broccoli, and red pepper -
tossed with a cream sauce over gourmet pasta
$6.95

*Exhibit 17-1, continued*

hear? The Tampa General Hospital cafeteria found that many people do take advertising to heart. Before a cereal company began promoting the fabulous health benefits of bran, this large-volume cafeteria was selling fifty bran muffins daily. Within three weeks after the television advertising on bran began, the cafeteria was selling eight hundred bran muffins each day. Volume rose sixteen times. This example may not represent what always *does* happen, but it shows what *can* happen. Tampa General's experience also indicates that you should consider what is being advertised as a clue to what health item you should feature next.

## Menu Copy

When featuring selections designed to appeal to guests who desire "health" foods, do not promise any health improvements. Such customers know what they want and will so order. Nevertheless, descriptions of cooking methods will appeal to these customers, if they are true. For example, if vegetables are steamed, mention this. If you fry using a cooking oil that has no cholesterol, salt, or additives, this will attract the health conscious to your fried foods, which most people eating "healthy" will usually avoid. Note the use of such a product in the menu description of a fried-food item.

## Low-Calorie Foods

It is common to find on menus, especially luncheon menus, foods for weight-conscious patrons. It is quite possible to offer a balanced list of items from the available local convenience foods. But attractive selections can be developed from scratch with a little research in the calorie tables and imagination. An item on many luncheon menus in France, Germany, Switzerland, and Austria is a vegetable plate with a poached egg, which usually includes six vegetables. It is an interesting challenge to a menu writer to prepare a low-calorie section on a menu that includes items most people like. This can be done simply by taking items from the regular menu and changing the cooking method and eliminating sauces and stuffings.

## The Restaurant's Responsibility for Nutrition

The restaurateur has no legal responsibility to serve customers meals that provide all the nutrients required for a healthy life. Since most people eat only a few of their meals in restaurants, their own diets are their personal responsibility. However, the food service operator of a full-service establishment should consider it a moral responsibility to provide nutritionally balanced meals in the menu offerings. To assume this moral responsibility you must acquire a basic knowledge of nutrients, what they are, and their principal sources.

### Nutrients

The five essential nutrients are fats, proteins, carbohydrates, minerals, and vitamins. They must be combined with a sixth item—water—to perform their nutritional functions. Vitamins, minerals, and water are micronutrients and do not provide energy. Carbohydrates, fats, and proteins are macronutrients and do directly furnish energy to the body. But they can provide energy only if the micronutrients are present and sufficiently balanced to act as a release mechanism. The process by which this happens is called digestion.

### The Macronutrients

*Protein.* Protein is one of the direct sources of energy, but it is primarily a source of body-building material. Protein is found in many foods, but not all have the same nutritive value. The proteins found in meat, fish, milk, cheese, and eggs are of superior quality. Fruits and vegetables contain some protein. Greater amounts are found in nuts, cereals, and dried beans. You need not eat meat to ingest sufficient protein. Many Eastern religions forbid meat eating, and many Westerners are "vegetarians" for moral or health reasons. Most Americans, however, eat fish, meat, and especially poultry as their principal sources of protein.

*Carbohydrates.* The so-called starchy foods are another of the macronutrients that provide energy and heat to the body. Carbohydrates are plentiful in pasta (a staple in the Italian diet) and in corn (a staple in the Mexican diet). They are also found in potatoes (both sweet and white), rice, cereal grains, and those sweets forbidden to dieters. The important characteristic about carbohydrates is that the human body needs more carbohydrates than any of the other nutrients to function properly. Over 50 percent of the calories (a unit of heat energy) eaten should come from foods that supply carbohydrates. And those foods should be starches rather than sweets.

*Fats.* Fats are found principally in those foods that help make a meal a pleasure—butter, cream, salad oils, and meats. These foods contain more calories, ounce for ounce, than the protein and carbohydrate foods. We need fats for body growth and maintenance, but they should constitute no more than about one-third of the calories we consume. Fatty foods satisfy hunger more quickly than other foods and delay hunger longer because they are digested more slowly. Cholesterol, the substance reported to be a cause of heart disease, is a steroid alcohol principally derived from fatty foods. Definitive knowledge on the effects of cholesterol on health is not yet available, but many people consider it prudent to avoid eating a lot of fatty meats, eggs, butter, and other dairy products, which are known to raise the cholesterol level in the blood.

**The Micronutrients**

*Minerals.* Minerals do not contribute directly to growth and energy, but they are needed in the digestive processes that result in growth and energy. We need about twenty minerals in varying amounts. The only minerals that we must make sure to consume in a balanced diet are calcium, phosphorus, and iron. The other minerals come from the foods that furnish calcium, phosphorus, and iron. Cereals and leafy vegetables provide calcium, as does the most prominent source—milk. Phosphorus is found in protein-rich foods. Meat, eggs, vegetables, and cereals all contain iron. An important function of minerals in the body is to help maintain the balance between acids and alkalines. However, people who eat a normal diet seldom need be concerned about this.

*Water.* Water has many important functions in promoting growth and body building. It is very plentiful and most people drink enough of it. Perhaps this is why the literature on nutrition does not emphasize water consumption. Nevertheless, it is absolutely necessary: it supplies liquid for the blood, the digestive juices, and the elimination of waste products. Drinking water with meals aids in digestion.

*Vitamins.* There are about a dozen known vitamins plus another dozen in the so-called "B" complex. The vitamin experts tell us that there are probably many more vitamins to be discovered. Most of the vitamins have been named during the past twenty years. When vitamins were first discovered, their chemical structure was not known; hence they were designated by letters. We should be sure to include vitamins A, $B_1$, C, and G (or $B_2$) in our diets. If we eat food with these four vitamins, then we will probably get enough of the other vitamins. Vitamin D, the "sunshine" vitamin, does not occur in large quantities in any foods, but adults need only receive a little sunlight for their bodies to manufacture enough of this vitamin.

*Vitamin A* (called "carotene") is found in leafy green vegetables like spinach, watercress, kale, and the outer leaves of cabbage. Carrots, tomatoes, whole milk, cream, butter, eggs, poultry, and fish oils also contain this vitamin.

*Vitamin B₁* (called "thiamine") is provided by lean meat, yeast, cereals, beans, peanuts, milk, oranges, pineapples, grapefruit, tomatoes, peas, potatoes, and leafy green vegetables.

*Vitamin C* (called "ascorbic acid") can be found in oranges, grapefruit, tomatoes, pineapples, raw vegetables, green peppers, asparagus, turnips, bananas, watermelons, and cantaloupes.

*Vitamin G* (called "riboflavin") is plentiful in milk, leafy green vegetables, eggs, lean meat, whole wheat cereals, and yeast. Vitamin B₂ is also riboflavin.

Many books have been written on vitamins. Some stress the importance of a particular-type diet; others emphasize supplements to the diet. But they all have one thing in common. They each list the same food sources for the several vitamins as we did in the brief outline above.

We want to point out that if normally healthy persons exercise common sense in choosing foods to eat, they will get all the necessary nutrients.

## The Menu and Nutrition

A review of the foods that supply the nutrients needed for good health suggests that any full-service restaurant whose menu has some variety in its selections of appetizers, entrées, potatoes, vegetables, salads, and desserts will supply nutritional food. However, faulty preparation procedures can cause a loss in the nutritive value of the raw product. Vegetables can be steamed instead of excessively boiled. Fried foods can be cooked in nonsaturated fats. Holding prepared foods too long can also harm their nutritional value. If full-service restaurant operators assume moral responsibility to furnish healthy food, they must see that they meet these minimum requirements of providing a varied menu and preparing foods correctly.

## Preserving Food Value

Steam pressure cooking methods best preserve the vitamins in vegetables. If you choose to boil vegetables, use as little water as possible. The water in which vegetables have been boiled can be used in gravies and soups, which will add vitamins to these items.

The cooking of frozen foods is best begun while they are still frozen because the exposure to air during thawing affects the quality of some vitamins.

Foods containing vitamin A should not be fried because fats dissolve this vitamin. Loss of vitamin A due to frying is usually not a problem because vegetables are the most common source of this vitamin, and they are rarely fried. However, poultry and eggs, which also contain vitamin A, are favored foods for frying. A diet-conscious person is very likely to order breakfast eggs boiled, poached, shirred, or in an omelette. From the standpoint of vitamin preservation, these cooking methods are all preferable to frying.

Storing foods at low temperatures preserves vitamins. Foods stored in a refrigerator, especially fruits and vegetables, should be covered to prevent drying out and loss of vitamin freshness.

Try to cook fruits and vegetables as soon as possible after cutting. Allowing them to stand in water also causes loss of vitamins.

Serving food promptly after cooking provides restaurant patrons with not only more vitamins but also a more satisfying and attractive meal.

## Fast Food

These operations specialize in a limited number of items and make no pretense that they are providing their clients with a well-balanced diet. Most adults know that foods other than those provided in a fast food store are necessary for a balanced diet and will make sure to round out their diets in meals taken at home or elsewhere. Parents must assume this responsibility on behalf of their children.

## Special Diets

The commercial restaurant is not in the business of prescribing special diets. However, the active restaurant will have a number of customers who are diabetics and others who are on low-sodium diets. These customers know their needs. To satisfy them, all you must do is try to meet their requests. Service personnel should be familiar with the cooking procedures and know which foods are prepared without salting. Allowing diabetics to make an unusual substitution that will reduce the carbohydrates in their meal is an example of how you can cooperate to win the favor and business of these special-diet customers.

## Macrobiotic Diets

*Macrobiotics* is a term, first used by a Japanese philosopher George Ohsawa, that describes a specific approach to dieting rather than a particular diet itself. The general dietary recommendations are the basis for eating in many Asian cultures. Ohsawa related the selection of foods to the study of yin and yang, which is the foundation of all Asian medicine. After Ohsawa's death in the 1960's, Michio Kushi of the Boston area has promoted this philosophical basis for diet. Kushi has given more than 5,000 lectures and seminars in America and Europe. Over 10,000 stores as well as a few hundred restaurants in the United States carry natural foods. The restaurants are able to produce a variety of entrées in spite of the limited number of food products used. The macrobiotic approach to diets has spread to most major countries.

Macrobiotic diets vary, but they generally consist of about 50 percent whole cereal grains, 5 percent soups, 25 to 30 percent vegetables, 10 percent beans, and 5 percent sea vegetables.

The regular cereal grains are brown rice, millet, barley, corn, whole oats, and rye. Soups can be prepared with a variety of ingredients, including seasonal vegetables, seaweed, grains, and beans. Vegetables include green and leafy types (broccoli, Brussels sprouts, bok choy, collard greens, Chinese cabbage), stem or root types (carrot, radish, onion, turnip), and ground (pumpkin, cauliflower, acorn squash, butternut squash). Beans used regularly are lentils, chickpeas, and azuki. Those for occasional use are black-eyed peas, split peas, navy beans, and lima beans. Sea vegetables are uncommon in our American diet and usually found in only health-food stores. Common ones are kombo, wakame, nori, agar agar, and hiziki.

The macrobiotic diet can be supplemented once or twice a week with white meat fish and some seafoods. Native fruits (no bananas in Chicago) may be eaten as dessert items, as can sweetened vegetables. Beverages include several different teas, and beer is recommended for occasional consumption.

Foods to be avoided are animal products, including eggs, dairy foods, processed foods, sugar, coffee, and most of those not mentioned in the listing above of macrobiotic foods.

## Summary

The trend in the United States to keep fit through exercise and eating healthily may at times seem to some ludicrous or even hedonistic. But this trend, if it continues, is bound to result in a healthier and probably happier and more prosperous population. These are admirable goals. Food service operators have the obligation to supply what clients want, and they should welcome the opportunity to gain a reputation (and thereby increase their sales volume) for making the effort to know these wants and offer them attractively.

# 18 The Computer and the Menu Writer

**Purpose:** To investigate the ways computers can be used effectively in the different functions of a food service operation. To discuss how these uses apply to the menu writer.

Since the last edition of this book, there have been great changes in computer technology. It seems that the construction of the "information superhighway" provided by Internet services has fascinated half the population and mystified the other half. The most significant change for the food service industry has been the large reduction in the price of computers. This has made computer service available to even small restaurants. Restaurant patrons are reminded of this by the change in the form of restaurant checks. The change noticeable to the credit card user is that the check and the receipt have been wedded into one. This is only overt evidence of the simultaneous accumulation of information for use by purchasing, production, sales, and control and by the menu-writing team that is composed of representatives of each of these departments. Use of the computer in the business world, including the food service industry, will continue to increase in the coming years.

## Cost Justification

Computers can do millions of calculations in "nanoseconds" (on billionth of a second) and store great quantities of information. Food service operators might naturally look to computers as useful in control procedures. Using them to keep track of heretofore almost unmanageable inventories would seem like a good starting point. A story from a few years ago about the effectiveness of inventory control by computer told about a manufacturing company that gained such pin-point inventory control with computers that it was able to reduce its inventory storage space by 33 percent. The intriguing point was not that the company managers discovered that they could manage with less inventory, which contributed to saving, but that ordering became so refined that a considerable portion of the inventory was "stored" in rail cars that were rolling toward the plant with supplies. Less storage space was needed, and less money was tied up in inventory.

Irrespective of the glowing report of computers' contribution to improvements in the food service industry and other facets of the business world, computers in food service must be more than effective—they must be *cost* effective if they are to help increase profits. This can mean choosing the correct system for the operation; or in the case of small operations, whether or not to select any system.

In evaluating a computer system, we are faced with a dichotomy—evaluation by quantification or evaluation by judgment based on observation and experience. There are five basic questions to ask in evaluating a computer system:

1. Are there payroll savings?
2. Does the prompt availability of information provide a nonquantifiable advantage?
3. Is added accuracy a significant factor?
4. Is there a positive effect on customer satisfaction?
5. Is there a positive or negative effect on the morale of employees?

The information in this chapter will give directions in which to go for finding the answers to these questions.

## Food Control

Food service operators would be wise to take the consultants' advice. You must first define the basic elements of a food control system. To do this five questions must be answered.

1. How much did we buy?
2. How much did we prepare?
3. How much did we sell?
4. How much did we have left over?
5. If it doesn't check out, where did it go?

We will next analyze what is involved in each of these basic elements.

### How Much Did We Buy?

The first question involves purchasing, receiving, and keeping inventory. These func-

tions seem ideal for control by computer. They involve numbers and units and can be easily quantified. However, computers might not be useful in all applications.

The average restaurant and hotel food operation, for example, uses the different categories of food in about the following proportions:

Meat (beef, veal, pork, lamb)—33%
Poultry—8%
Fish and shellfish—12%
Fruits and vegetables—15%
Dairy—15%
Groceries, breads, frozen food—17%

A few years ago, groceries, breads, frozen foods, and some dairy items were the only items that could benefit in purchasing through use of the computer because of the standardized packaging. Meat items (for example, the strip loin, IMPS Code 180, mentioned in Chapter 6 in the discussion on cost factors) were ordered in the conventional way because not all purveyors were equipped to receive computer orders. Now a system of item numbers has been developed between vendor and customer that allows this and other meat items, produce, and all but a few specialty items to be ordered by computer with no direct contact between customer and supplier.

Once an order is placed, the computer can furnish the receiving department with copies so that the department can be prepared for incoming merchandise. At the same time, the computer can indicate any item ordered that does not conform to accepted purchase specifications.

### How Much Did We Prepare?

In finding the answer to this question, the computer provides a complete service. Control of preparation begins with forecasting what will be needed, and the sales histories compiled by the computer are vital to this forecasting procedure. Given the menus, house counts, and number of covers expected at a particular meal, the computer can project the probable number of each item on the menu to be served and suggest the quantities needed to take care of the indicated business.

## How Much Did We Sell?

The sales histories provided by the computer answer this question.

## How Much Is Left Over?

Here, too, the computer can be useful. The answer measures the effectiveness of the portion control system. The key to a good food cost rests with portion control. Appendix D lists 1,001 possible food selections. With so many items to choose from, portion control would seem to be an impossible task. Actually, a day-to-day count of about twenty items in a tight portion control procedure will provide a "hands-on" control of 80 percent or more of the dollars involved for items that are most susceptible to loss from overproduction and theft.

The procedure is simple. Exhibit 18-1 is a typical portion control sheet. It provides for a listing of high-cost items issued from the butcher shop to the kitchen, or in the case of portion-cut items, issued from the storeroom. Sales of these items recorded on checks, ascertained by manual count or from a computer register, are recorded by outlet. The difference, if any, is recorded in the final column.

## If It Doesn't Check Out, Where Did It Go?

To find this answer, you must be personally involved, or all that occurred before was a waste in relation to food control.

We have an interesting story about one business's experience with "where it went." A few years ago, at a resort property in the Adirondack Mountains that operated only four months each year, there was a graveyard of a peculiar variety. Behind the kitchen were markers, made from logs, with dates on them. They commemorated six consecutive years. Next to the most recent marker was a pit. It measured about eight-feet square and about ten-feet deep.

There was nearly an annual turnover of chefs because of the short season of operation. The new chef, who assumed his duties the year in question, was strolling about the property with the owner to get the lay of the land. When they neared the unusual graveyard, he asked what the dated markers meant. He was told that since the resort was situated in a rather remote location, there was no garbage collection. So a pit was dug at the beginning of the year to accommodate the garbage—the leftovers. He explained that the temporary employees from nearby colleges ceremoniously closed the pit at the close of the season and duly marked it for posterity.

When the season was about half over, the owner came to the chef and remarked that the pit had only about ten inches of garbage in it. How come? The chef explained that he kept a close watch on preparation to keep leftovers to a minimum, and made sure that the few leftovers that did occur were salvaged and used. At the end of the season, the pit still had less than two feet of garbage fill. The owner realized that there really was a graveyard on his property—his potential profits were buried there! Subsequently, pits were never more than three feet deep.

As mentioned above, only about twenty items need close portion control because they are the most likely to be overproduced or stolen. Theft is a two-edged sword. It can cut profits through the theft itself, and it can hide overproduction, which increases as the thief becomes more proficient. There was a chef a few years ago, maybe the same one who failed to fill the pit, who watched employees as they came from home to the job. He considered anyone wearing a loose raincoat, especially if it was not raining, a suspicious character. When the chef was asked why he considered

Hotel _____ Location _____ Date _____ 19____

| Item | Portion Size | Number Used | NUMBER SOLD | | | | Total Sold | Difference |
|------|-------------|-------------|-------------|--------------|--|---------|-----------|-----------|
| | | | Town Room | Special. Rest. | | Banquet | | |
| | | | | | | | | |
| | | | | | | | | |
| | | | | | | | | |
| | | | | | | | | |
| | | | | | | | | |
| | | | | | | | | |
| | | | | | | | | |
| | | | | | | | | |
| | | | | | | | | |
| | | | | | | | | |
| | | | | | | | | |
| | | | | | | | | |
| | | | | | | | | |
| | | | | | | | | |
| | | | | | | | | |
| | | | | | | | | |
| | | | | | | | | |
| | | | | | | | | |
| | | | | | | | | |
| | | | | | | | | |
| | | | | | | | | |
| | | | | | | | | |
| | | | | | | | | |
| | | | | | | | | |
| | | | | | | | | |
| | | | | | | | | |

_____
Chef's Signature

**Exhibit 18-1**
**Food Portion Control Sheet**

this "peculiar," he expounded on the storage capacity of raincoat pockets. Good control needs all the help it can get from numbers provided by the latest in technology, but numbers are useless unless they supplement good judgments and keen observations.

## Basic Controls and the Menu Writer

All areas of a well-fashioned food service organization are interrelated. In fact, if any section attempts to act as an isolated unit, it can lead to the breakdown of the integrity of organization. As you might expect, the menu writer is involved in all the elements of the basic control system outlined above. The primary responsibility of the menu writer is to produce a menu with items the customers want and at the prices they are willing to pay. What might be called the co-primary responsibility is that the menu yield a profit.

The first basic element of control relates to buying. In Chapter 5 we showed that menu writing is the task of a team. One member of this team is the food purchaser, who guides the team as they select items that the customers want while at the same time considering product availability and cost.

The second basic element is control of the preparation of items. The most common concern is preparing the proper quantities of food—not too much and not too little—to meet anticipated volume. The menu writer's responsibility in control of preparation is to write a menu properly balanced between items that can be prepared in advance and items prepared to order. Unfortunately, oftentimes customers order an item, say broiled fish, and receive food that by all indications has sat in a steam table for too long. Instead of receiving a freshly broiled fish, they receive a rubbery lukewarm fish. This can be the result of an imbalance in menu selections that prompts the cook to "get ahead" on a few items so that he or she will be able to keep up with the incom-

ing orders. The skilled menu writer anticipates such situations and builds the menu to eliminate such problems.

In relation to how much was sold, the menu writer's concern is obvious. How much was sold can be an affirmation of the quality of the menu or a negative judgment against it. Knowing how well menu items sell is also necessary information for making timely revisions. This information is also essential to making effective forecasts for food preparation and provisions for service.

Leftovers can result from preparing too much or from the waning popularity of a usually favored dish. For whatever reason, you will have some leftovers from time to time. The menu writer knows this and provides for their judicious use in specials, employees' meals, or whatever retrieves the most value from the remaining product. Unlike the leftovers that were considered garbage in the "pit" story, the menu writer sees value in them and acts accordingly.

## Point-of-Sale Technology

Of all the different ways in which computers can be used, this phase is the most familiar to lay persons. The supermarket check-out counter and the cashier's desk in department stores put the buyer within arms' length of this electronic phenomenon. If you visit the nearest McDonald's, Wendy's, Burger King, or other fast food operation, you can see that when the clerk merely presses one key the order is recorded and the price displayed. This technology is certainly different from the registers with "clunking" keys and a cranking handle of years past, but it is a great stride in efficiency and a great deal easier on the arm.

This technology has been most effectively adapted to classical, signature, and family restaurants, as well as to the fast food operations.

## Forecasting

The importance of forecasting to food cost was briefly mentioned above in the discussion of how much was prepared. The procedure in forecasting calls first for estimating the total number of covers to be served at a particular meal. To do this you must consider the season of the year, the day of the week, and other things that affect volume. You must know how many covers will be served in order to determine the number of staff required to give the good service customers expect. In most restaurants, service staffs include full-time and part-time employees, which gives the flexibility necessary to increase and decrease the number of servers depending on anticipated business. The regulation of days off also plays a part in the fluctuating size of the staff. The size of the preparation staff, which is ordinarily all full-time employees, is also adjusted in this way. Overtime is also a consideration when staffing.

The next step in forecasting is to estimate the numbers of the various menu selections to be served. This, of course, relates to preparation estimates and control of overproduction.

## Precheck Systems

The computer/register technology has various capacities and can be used to advantage depending on the type of operation. It is especially useful in a large restaurant operation with food coming from several stations in the kitchen.

The waiter or waitress takes orders in the usual manner on an order (scratch) pad. The order is then recorded at a point-of-service terminal along with the server's number and the number of the table. The items recorded are instantly printed in check form, with items and amounts for use as the check, but it is also recorded by remote printers at the preparation stations in the kitchen. In some operations, the person taking the orders never leaves the dining room; the orders are collected and delivered by persons whose work is restricted to this function. The printed order shows the table number and the server's number, so delivery can be made without further inquiry. The orders are also placed using a system that identifies the location at the table of each order. We explained such a system of writing orders in Chapter 2. The precheck system should offer great satisfaction to the guest whose server is always in the kitchen or otherwise out of sight when needed. For the many restaurants with "display kitchens," the precheck system has little value.

This brief summary of forecasting points to the value of the sales history. The point-of-sale computer/register helps to compile this information. Prior to this technology, sales histories had to be compiled by laborious and cumbersome manual abstracts of restaurant checks. The accuracy of computerized sales history compilations is also greater than those compiled manually.

## Potential Costs

For the software program used with the computer to produce the information described above, the computer/register keyboard must be configured to list the menu items and prices. After the simple input by the server, the computer, using the appropriate program, tabulates the number of covers for each item and the dollar values of the sales of each item. This plus the computation of taxes is sufficient to produce guest checks. In addition to entering the menu items and prices, costs of the several items can also be entered. With the appropriate program the computer can provide a daily report of covers, sales, and costs of the items sold. The total cost, as a percentage and in dollars, will be a potential cost. This can be compared to the actual cost of food consumed, calculated in the conventional manner of adding opening inventory with purchases and subtracting closing inventory.

Many companies that produce this type of equipment might propose that you include a very elaborate computer system to compile the costs of the individual items. This involves entering the entire food inventory reduced to measures used in recipes and including all the recipes and the various computer instructions that relate to this multiplicity of items. The manual computation of costs by an experienced food service manager or food controller is more simple and used by virtually all restaurants and hotels. Appendices A and B explain how to compute costs by using cost factors and make-up costs, and they also include schedules showing standard packaging and yields. Organized manual calculations greatly reduce the complexity of costing.

## Billing to Hotel Accounts

Another way point-of-sale technology saves on labor costs is in the linking of the restaurant terminals to the front-office system. When guests eat at the hotel restaurant they normally charge their meals to their room account. This linking of computer components allows the cashier in the restaurant to instantly post the meal charges to the guest's room account. This saves on the labor required to transfer the checks to the front desk. This might not normally be of great importance because the transfer is often done by pneumatic tube. However, at the breakup of a convention in a large hotel when there is a heavy morning checkout, this computer capacity guarantees that the customers' accounts will be complete, with the transfer of checks and the posting to the individual accounts accomplished simultaneously as the restaurant cashier "rings" the check.

## Effectiveness of Menus

The capacity of the computer/register to produce a schedule that shows a sales history, that is, how the menu items sell in relation to total covers served, and how they move in different groupings of menu items, was mentioned above in the discussion of forecasting. To evaluate the effectiveness of the menu, you must compare it against a standard. The standard here is what was planned when the menu was written. The selection of items was, of course, anticipated to be what the customers desired in items and prices. In addition, the individual items were expected to be balanced in popularity so that the workload in the kitchen would be divided in a reasonably even fashion and the overall potential cost would meet budget expectations.

When you make such comparisons, you almost inevitably will find variations from the original concept. Some will be pleasant surprises; others, not so pleasant. The virtue in making menu evaluations is that they will help you to avoid making rash decisions such as eliminating an item that has had a disappointing performance. What you think should be attractive items to the customers, but which do not move well, often sell better if they are given a different menu location or an adjusted price—sometimes a price adjustment upward.

In any series of menus, certain popular items will appear several times. You should notice how these items move in the different combinations, and how they affect the movement of other selections.

To evaluate whether or not an item is contributing a sufficient number of covers or the percentage of the item sold to the total number of covers sold, we suggest you use a standard formula that has been proven very effective over the years.

1. Take 75 percent of the covers served.
2. Divide by the number of items on the menu. The result is an "acceptable" sales number for each item.
3. To get the "acceptable" sales percentage, divide the acceptable number by the total covers.

*Example:* The menu has 10 items and 200 covers are served.

1. 200 covers times 75 percent equals 150 covers.
2. 150 covers divided by 10 menu items equals 15. This is the acceptable sales number.
3. 15 divided by 200 equals 7.5 percent. This is the acceptable sales number expressed as a percentage.

In Chapter 6, on menu pricing, we illustrated that cost of sales is but one criterion in pricing menu selections. More important is the gross profit (sales less food cost) resulting from the sale of an item. The gross profit should be sufficient to cover other costs. In Chapter 6 we noted five items with low selling prices and very low food costs. The expensive items ran higher food costs. We called attention to the fact that as the food cost percentage rose the gross profit increased. That example showed that expensive items can be sold at higher food cost percentages and still yield desired gross profits.

In addition to comparing the actual number of items sold with an "acceptable" number, you should use a second test to evaluate the effectiveness of a menu. This is a check on the gross profits produced by the several items. Use this standard formula to determine the gross profits (see example A):

1. Calculate the gross profit of each item. (Selling price less food cost.)
2. Multiply each gross profit by the number of covers served.
3. Take 75 percent of the sum of the gross profits.
4. Divide by the number of menu selections. This is the "acceptable" gross profit for each item.

Example B compares the number of covers served for each item with the "acceptable" number of covers, and the gross profit realized on each item with the "acceptable" gross profit.

In the first four items, both the covers and the gross profits exceed the "acceptable" levels by healthy margins. The same is true of the half chicken. These are items to keep on the menu. The veal cutlet, the flounder, and the shrimp platter are deficient in both covers sold and gross profit when compared to the standards. These are items to replace.

The halibut slightly exceeds the standard in covers, but falls short of producing the gross profit desired. This is a candidate for a price increase. By increasing the price to $8.95 you will probably still sell as many covers, and the additional price ($3.20) will make the gross profit slightly exceed the standard.

The lobster tail sold fewer covers than the standard, but produced a higher gross profit than the standard gross profit. This item certainly should be retained. However, more covers might be sold if the item were relocated on the menu.

These decisions to keep, drop, raise the price of, or relocate items were made strictly on the basis of the numbers. These are only possible actions to take when item sales produce such results. Such decisions must be tempered by judgment. For example, you might decide to relocate the veal cutlet and feature it in a different way on the menu.

All of the above schedules and computations can be produced by special software used with the point-of-sale computer register. Whether or not to buy this software would depend on its cost. Such evaluations are made only quarterly during the usual course of business. A point-of-service machine can give you the number of covers served by item, the selling prices, and costs. By doing manual calculations you can produce the balance of the figures for the comparisons in a few minutes, and thus buying the capacity to have the computer supply these could probably not be justified. However, if the capacity requires little or no extra cost, use it. Food service management requires long working hours, so welcome any help.

## Glossary

Following is a brief glossary of terms that appear in proposals for computer systems designed for hotel and restaurant food operations.

*Application software.* Software individually purchased and developed to perform specific functions.

*Example A*:

| Item | Covers | Selling Price | Cost | Gross Profit |
|---|---|---|---|---|
| Prime rib | 40 | $12.00 | $5.25 | $6.75 |
| Rib eye steak | 24 | 10.50 | 4.25 | 6.25 |
| New York steak | 24 | 11.50 | 4.95 | 6.55 |
| Ground sirloin | 32 | 8.00 | 1.95 | 6.05 |
| Veal cutlet | 10 | 9.75 | 3.50 | 6.25 |
| Half chicken | 30 | 8.50 | 2.25 | 6.25 |
| Lobster tail | 14 | 12.50 | 5.40 | 7.10 |
| Flounder | 6 | 9.00 | 3.25 | 5.75 |
| Halibut | 16 | 8.75 | 2.95 | 5.80 |
| Shrimp platter | 4 | 9.50 | 3.60 | 5.90 |
| Total | 200 | | | |

1. Determine the gross profits per cover on each of the menu selections, as on the above schedule.
2. Multiply the number of covers sold *by* their gross profits. Add these totals (equals $1,267.70).
3. Seventy-five percent of $1,267.70 equals $950.78.
4. Divide $950.78 by the number of menu items (10). The "acceptable" gross profit for each of the items is therefore $95.08.

*Example B*:

| Item | Covers | Gross Profit | Total | Compare Covers | Compare Gross Profit |
|---|---|---|---|---|---|
| Prime rib | 40 | $6.75 | $270.00 | 40 > 15 | $270. > $95. |
| New York strip | 24 | 6.55 | 157.20 | 24 > 15 | 157. > 95. |
| Rib eye steak | 24 | 6.25 | 150.00 | 24 > 15 | 150. > 95. |
| Ground sirloin | 32 | 6.05 | 193.60 | 32 > 15 | 194. > 95. |
| Veal cutlet | 10 | 6.25 | 62.50 | 10 < 15 | 63. < 95. |
| Half chicken | 30 | 6.25 | 187.50 | 30 > 15 | 188. > 95. |
| Lobster tail | 14 | 7.10 | 99.40 | 14 < 15 | 99. > 95. |
| Flounder | 6 | 5.75 | 34.50 | 6 < 15 | 35. < 95. |
| Halibut | 16 | 5.80 | 92.80 | 16 > 15 | 93. < 95. |
| Shrimp platter | 4 | 5.90 | 23.60 | 4 < 15 | 24. < 95. |

*Configuration.* The relative arrangement and design of parts in a computer system.

*Cost effective.* Means that a system has benefits that outweigh the involved costs.

*Display terminal.* A video screen that presents "soft copy" information.

*Feedback.* Information that explains the difference between actual and potential performance.

*Flexible system.* A system that can be modified and can accommodate additions.

*Food service Information System (FIS).* Presents food service data designed to increase the effectiveness of management.

*Hard copy.* A printed copy of information produced.

*Hardware.* The physical components that make up computer systems.

*Input.* To introduce data into the computer system.

*Interface.* A common line or boundary between two systems.

*Menu explosion.* Breaking down of menu items into ingredients.

*Output.* Processed data made available for use.

*Point-of-sale (POS) terminal.* A device employed by a cashier to record sales for later accounting use and to service the immediate needs of waiting customers.

*Precheck system.* Requisitioning of menu items from the food preparation areas using a terminal remote to the kitchen that simultaneously records the information to compile guest checks.

*Preset.* A computer/register keyboard with keys assigned to individual items, which when pressed produce information on the item and price.

*Remote printer.* A device remote to the input terminal in a precheck system that produces "hard copy" instructions to food preparation personnel.

*Soft copy.* Information for viewing on a video screen.

*Software.* Programs of instructions to extend the capabilities of the basic computer.

*System.* An orderly arrangement of units of data in an interrelated series.

# 19 Accuracy in Menus

**Purpose:** To establish the importance of a menu that elicits customer confidence in the integrity of a restaurant.

The common expression "What you see is what you get" is a compliment when applied to a restaurant if what the guest expects an item to be like from its menu listing and description is what he is served. A food operation has a duty to its customers to be worthy of this compliment. Adhering to total honesty in a menu has the further advantage of being sound salesmanship.

## Quality Claims

Marketing includes the advertising of products on television, on radio, and in the print media. It also includes the packaging of products. Both of these facets of marketing attempt to make the product as attractive as possible. Media advertising uses all means available to extol the advantages of the product and at the same time sublimate any possible negative feature of the product. The technique often borders on being deliberately deceitful. In the packaging of products, color and design, like media advertising, present a wholly positive image. However, legal regulations governing packaging strive to ensure complete honesty in stating ingredients, food values, and items relating to quantities, weights, and quality claims.

In a sense, the menu packages the product of a restaurant, and the words and phrases used to describe the selections should be completely honest. To do less is not only dishonest but insults your guests' intelligence.

It is a good practice in menu writing to describe food selections by using government-controlled quality grades, sizes, counts, and weights, but they should be used with complete honesty. The following tables and narrative give a complete list of grades, sizes, weights, and counts.

### Grade Standards—Meat

Differences in quality and yield of meat are indicated by United States Department of Agriculture (USDA) grade standards.

#### Quality Grades of Beef

| Steer and Heifer | Bullock |
|---|---|
| U.S. Prime | U.S. Prime |
| U.S. Choice | U.S. Choice |
| U.S. Select | U.S. Select |
| U.S. Standard | U.S. Standard |
| U.S. Commercial | U.S. Utility |
| U.S. Utility | |
| U.S. Cutter | |
| U.S. Canner | |

## Quality Grades of Lamb and Sheep

| *Lamb and Yearling* | *Sheep* |
|---|---|
| U.S. Prime | U.S. Choice |
| U.S. Choice | U.S. Good |
| U.S. Good | U.S. Utility |
| U.S. Utility | U.S. Cull |

*Yield grades* refer to the amount of usable meat in proportion to fat and bone in a carcass. Yield grades for beef and lamb in ascending order of fat content are 1, 2, 3, 4, and 5.

## Quality Grades of Pork

| *Barrow and Gilt* | *Sow* |
|---|---|
| U.S. No. 1 | U.S. No. 1 |
| U.S. No. 2 | U.S. No. 2 |
| U.S. No. 3 | U.S. No. 3 |
| U.S. No. 4 | U.S. Medium |
| U.S. Utility | U.S. Cull |

## Quality Grades for Veal

U.S. Prime
U.S. Choice
U.S. Good
U.S. Standard
U.S. Utility

Pork and veal are not graded separately for quality and yield, but *conformation*—the general shape of the animal, which partly determines the yield—is incorporated in the quality grade.

Hotels and restaurants will ordinarily use only U.S. No. 1 grade pork and USDA Prime and USDA Choice grades of beef, lamb, and veal. Yield grade 3 of beef is the preference of these operations.

## Quality Grades—Poultry

USDA quality grade designations for poultry are A, B, and C. Except for use in soup stocks, good hotels and restaurants will use Grade A exclusively.

## Quality Grades—Fresh Shell Eggs

The following U.S. government grades have been established for fresh eggs: U.S. AA, A, B, C, Dirty, and Checks. Eggs are graded on an individual basis, and then a grade is assigned to a case or lot based on the percentages of individual eggs of a particular grade that are in the unit. Specific standards are applied for U.S. Consumer, U.S. Wholesale, and U.S. Procurement grades and for quality at point of origin and at destination. U.S. Consumer grades in general have higher percentages of higher grades of individual eggs than do U.S. Wholesale grades. For example, a case of U.S. AA Consumer grade eggs must be 85 percent AA at the place of origin, but up to 15 percent may be A or B grade, and not over 5 percent may be C or Check grade. At the point of destination, 80 percent must be AA grade, 20 percent may be A or B grade, and not over 5 percent may be grade C or Check.

In menu writing, the size of the egg is often included in the description of the selection. Following are egg sizes determined by the weight of a dozen.

### U.S. Weight Classes

| | *Min. per Dozen* | *Min. per 30 Dozen Case* |
|---|---|---|
| Extra large | 27 oz. | 50.5 lbs. |
| Large | 24 oz. | 45.3 lbs. |
| Medium | 21 oz. | 39 lbs. |
| Small | 18 oz. | 33.5 lbs. |

Hotels and restaurants normally use Grade A, Large, or Extra Large eggs.

## Seafood Grading

The U.S. Department of Commerce and the National Maritime Fishery Service under the direction of the Department of the Interior have the responsibility of grading seafood. The U.S. Department of Health provides an additional protection in its responsibility for inspecting the sources of fresh seafood. Fresh seafood is sold only in A and B grades, but there are four grades for processed seafood—A, B, C, and Substandard. Grade A is the standard for hotels and restaurants.

Grade A indicates the best quality and top grade. The Grade A products are uniform in size and color, free from most blemishes and defects, and of good typical flavor.

Grade B represents a good-quality product, but the product may not be quite so uniform in size, can have a few blemishes, and may not present as appealing an appearance as the Grade A products. This grade indicates that the seafood is of good quality and is quite acceptable for most purposes.

Grade C and substandard grades are wholesome and safe to eat but have variations in size and appearance, and are generally used for export or for soup or processed fish dishes.

## Grades—Fresh Fruits and Vegetables

U.S. government grade standards are available for most fresh fruits and vegetables but are not mandatory for use. The designations vary from product to product. For example, lettuce grades are U.S. Fancy, U.S. No. 1, and U.S. No. 2. For potatoes the grades are U.S. Extra No. 1, U.S. No. 1, U.S. Commercial, and U.S. No. 2. Weight and diameter are factors in potato grading. For apples the grades are well defined and include U.S. Extra Fancy, U.S. Fancy, U.S. No. 1, and U.S Utility. There is no U.S. grade standard for bananas, most of which are imported into the United States. U.S. grades for Florida grapefruit are U.S. Fancy, U.S. No. 1 Bright, U.S. No. 1 Golden, U.S. No. 1 Bronze, U.S. No. 1 Russet, U.S. No. 2, U.S. No. 2 Bright, U.S. No. 2 Russet, and U.S. No. 3. Sizes and counts of Florida grapefruit are indicated in U.S. grade standards. In terms of a 4/5 bushel box, these are 14, 18, 23, 27, 32, 36, 40, 48, 56, and 64. Packs of grapefruit from Florida, California, and Arizona are generally similar, but a 4/5 bushel of Florida grapefruit will generally weigh considerably

more than a 4/5 bushel of California and Arizona fruit. A difference in weight generally reflects a difference in the juice content of the fruit.

## Grades—Processed Fruits and Vegetables

United States Department of Agriculture grade standards are not mandatory for use by a food processor and infrequently appear on the labels of canned fruits and vegetables in retail markets. Grocery suppliers serving hotels and restaurants often designate the first, second, and third grades of their products by using different-colored labels. Grade designations are not consistent among commodities but in general are A, B, C, and Substandard. A may also be termed "Fancy"; B, "Choice"; and C, "Standard." In some instances grade B is termed "Extra Standard."

Contents of containers may be stated as drained weight, fill weight, or net weight. Traditionally, cans have been labeled for net weight, which means the weight of the total can content including solid content and liquid packing medium. From net weight labeling, a buyer can have no knowledge of the part of total weight that is solid content, such as peach halves or canned tomatoes, and the part that is liquid. Drained weight is the weight of the solid material in a can after the liquid has been drained away.

## Grades—Dairy Products

These products are used principally in food preparation in conjunction with other products and, except for "sweet cream butter," are seldom referred to in terms of quality. However, hotels and restaurants with reputations for serving the finest foods usually become famous for excellence because they use more butter, eggs, and cream than other establishments. We noted the quality grades and sizes of eggs in a separate category above, although they are usually included in the dairy product group.

The health standards under which dairy products are handled are of primary importance. In the United States the high standards of manufacturing and inspection relieve the consumer of any anxiety about sanitation.

Federal and state graders score butter on the basis of flavor, body, salt, color, and packaging. Flavor is the main determinant of the quality of butter. Normally butter is scored AA (93 score), grade A (92 score), grade B (90 score), and grade C (89 score). Lower-score butters are generally used in manufactured products.

## Quantity Claims

In menu writing, reference to size and weight is often part of the description of particular items such as steaks, lobsters, and eggs. Accurately stating such dimensions is as important as truthfully claiming the quality of products. For example, the weight classes of eggs are Extra Large, Large, Medium, and Small. Large-size eggs are the most acceptable for general use. They are big enough to be attractive if served fried or poached, and if used for other purposes, fewer are needed to obtain a particular volume. The term "jumbo" is found on some menus, but there is no standard U.S. grade so designated.

### Seafood

**Lobster.** Fish markets in certain areas of the Middle East offer "rich man's fish" and "poor man's fish." Heading the list of rich man's fish are lobsters and lobster tails. In the U.S., too, lobster is a food that few people can afford. The true lobster and the spiny lobster are close to becoming endangered species, and they are already priced higher than any other items on menus, including prime fillet of beef.

The true New England lobster is a two-claw lobster found primarily from Cape Cod north to the Maritime Provinces of Canada.

Two-claw lobsters are also found off the shores of Denmark and Scandinavia, and some are taken from the Sea of Marmara near Turkey, where the clawless spiny lobsters are also found.

Lobsters are normally available year round; however, the harvest during February, March, and early April is usually curtailed due to bad weather. By law, lobsters cannot be harvested during their molting season. Molting happens during the inclement weather of spring, which naturally decreases the supply of lobsters tremendously.

The New York seafood market classifies lobsters as follows:

*Jumbo*—3 pounds and up
*Large*—1.5 to 2.5 pounds
*Quarters*—1 to 1.5 pounds
*Chicken*— .75 to 1 pound

Usually a 1- to 1.25-pound lobster is considered a portion. However, a real lobster lover goes for the large lobster, which weighs from 1.5 to 2.5 pounds. Lobsters sometimes lose one claw. If this happens, they must be sold as culls and are generally used for cooked lobster meat.

The rock or spiny lobster can be found almost anywhere in coastal waters. The sources of rock lobster tails from the United States are the coast of Florida, the Gulf of Mexico, the Cuban coastal waters, and the lower coast of California. The majority of lobster tails, however, are imported from other countries. The principal sources of supply are South Africa, New Zealand, and Australia. Rock lobster tails generally average about 8 ounces each, with some reaching considerably over 1 pound. The New York seafood market grades for lobster tails are as follows:

*Jumbo*— 1 pound and up
*Large*—12 ounces to 1 pound
*Medium*—9 to 12 ounces
*Small*—6 to 9 ounces

If you are writing a menu for a restaurant

in the states of Maine or Massachusetts, do not include lobster tails in your selections. These two states prohibit the marketing of what is called a "mutilated lobster," which rules out tails from the rock lobster, crayfish, and the small Danish lobster.

**Oysters.** Some lovers of shellfish expound on the wonders of "oysters on the half shell" as providing a taste thrill that cannot be duplicated by any other type of seafood. Although people who like raw oysters are in the minority, their numbers are substantial, and so the menu planner should consider including oysters on a seafood menu.

An unfortunate circumstance of the twentieth century is the pollution of waters, both fresh and salt. This has led to regulations that allow oysters sold through regular food channels in the United States to come from only those shellfish beds that have been approved as sanitary by the U.S. Public Health Service. Oysters harvested from these areas are given labels with a certification number that designates an approved area.

Oysters from the eastern shore of the United States are harvested from the Canadian Maritimes in the north to the Gulf of Mexico in the south. The premium oyster is the bluepoint from the Chesapeake Bay. The Long Island oyster is a very close second. The Gulf of Mexico produces a large, very dark oyster that is very strong in iodine but highly prized in Creole cooking.

Many varieties are sold for serving raw on the half shell, but most are shucked and sold by the pint, quart, or gallon to the retail and commercial trade. Shucked oysters, regardless of size, weigh about 8 pounds per gallon. They are sold fresh and must be well iced because they deteriorate very rapidly. Oysters in the shell are usually sold by count or by the bushel. The Chesapeake Bay bluepoints and the Long Island oysters run about 250 to 300 per bushel. Cape Cod oysters run about 200 to 250. The small Chincoteagues average 300 to 350 per bushel. All sizes weigh about 65 to 70 pounds per bushel gross and about 3 pounds less net weight.

Federal standards for shucked oysters list the following sizes per gallon.

*Eastern Oysters*
Extra large—Up to 160 per gallon
Large—160 to 210
Medium—210 to 300
Small—300 to 500
Very small—500 and up
*Pacific Oysters*
Large—Up to 64 per gallon
Medium—65 to 96
Small—97 to 144
Very small—144 and up

The Pacific oysters include the Olympia oyster and the Japanese oyster. The latter is generally cooked. The former is used in cocktails.

**Clams.** There are two types of clams harvested from the shores of the United States that are of commercial importance and of importance to the menu writer: hard-shell clams and soft-shell clams. Types of clams are the New England soft-shell clam, the littleneck hard-shell clam, the cherrystone hard-shell clam, and the quahog. All four of these clams are usually bought by the bushel, which weighs 75 to 78 pounds.

The counts per bushel of these clams are as follows:

New England soft-shell clam—700 to 800
Littleneck clam—650 to 700
Cherrystone clam—325 to 350
Quahog—175 to 200

The New England soft-shell clam is the clam generally eaten at clambakes and shore dinners. New Englanders call them steamer clams, true clams, or long-neck clams.

The large quahogs are tough and are generally cut up to fry or to use in chowders and similar dishes. The smaller three types of clams can be eaten raw.

There are also four Pacific clams. The large Pismo clam is tough like the quahog and similarly used in chowders and seafood dishes. The butter clam is about the size of the Eastern littleneck, and the Pacific littleneck is the size of the cherrystone. The Pacific soft-shell clam is called the razor clam. It measures 3 to 4 inches in length and is usually served deep-fried.

Shucked clams, like shucked oysters, can be purchased by the gallon either fresh or frozen. The fresh clams are quite delicate and should be packed in ice immediately after shucking. Frozen shucked clams should be frozen within an hour after shucking.

**Crabs and Crabmeat.** The menu writer should know about the different types of crabs in order to properly identify them.

The blue crab (Eastern shore crab) has made a comeback after nearly becoming extinct because of heavy harvesting and pollution. Like oysters on the half-shell, the blue crab provides what many gourmets consider a unique taste thrill. Before the blue crab has molded its hard shell, it is known as a soft-shell crab. It is very much in demand from early spring to mid summer. After the hard shell is formed, it is harvested for crabmeat.

Eastern shore crabmeat is graded for size as follows:

*Jumbo lump or backfin lump*—the most desirable and is all large lump and white in color.
*Lump*—consists of small chunks from the body and is white and fine tasting.
*Special or mixed crabmeat*—50 percent lump with the remainder being flake.
*Flake*—all white meat from the body of the crab; often contains considerable "bone."
*Clawmeat*—meat from the claw; brownish in color and also may contain considerable "bone."
*Rock crabmeat*—very fine, on the watery side, rather "bony"; used primarily in convenience food items such as crab imperial and inexpensive crab cakes.

The West Coast crabs of commercial interest are the dungeness, king, rock, tanner, and snow. Of this group, the dungeness crab and the king crab are the most desirable and the most expensive.

The dungeness crab is found all along the Pacific Coast from Mexico to Alaska. The crabmeat is usually marketed cooked and is generally sold frozen. The dungeness crabmeat is tender and sweet, but the lumps of the meat are small and rather moist, and the flavor does not compare favorably with the lump crabmeat of the eastern shore blue crab.

King crabs are caught only in Alaskan waters and became popular when the supply of eastern shore crabmeat was scarce. It is now the largest source of crabmeat in the United States and also the most expensive. King crab is normally marketed as cooked crab legs and cooked shucked king crabmeat. The supply of king crab is being rapidly depleted, and the crab may be put on the endangered list unless prudence is introduced into the harvesting practices.

Tanner crabs are mostly marketed locally, primarily for their claws. Snow crabs are found mostly in Alaskan waters, and are also sold primarily for their claws. Almost all snow crabment is marketed cooked and frozen.

**Shrimp.** The great popularity of this shellfish is leading to a rapid depletion in its supply worldwide. Prices have been on a steady increase, but the demand has not been greatly affected. About 50 percent of the shrimp consumed in the United States is from domestic harvesting. The other 50 percent come principally from the Mediterranean and Indonesian ocean waters. Some shrimp are imported from as far away as Australia.

The principal types of shrimp are the pink, white, and brown. The quality and taste do not depend so much on the variety of shrimp as on their source. For example, brown shrimp harvested along the shores of the Gulf of Mexico have a rather strong iodine taste, while those taken from the deeper waters of the Gulf do not and are among the best-tasting shrimp available. Cooking tests of pink, white, and brown shrimp reveal that brown shrimp shrink less, and the 21 to 25 count are indistinguishable from the 16 to 20 count white and pink shrimp when cooked.

The size of shrimp is determined by the

number of shrimp per pound. The smaller the size, the less the cost. Shrimp is marketed under different names for the various sizes depending on the part of the country where they are marketed. Most green headless shrimp are marketed in the following sizes: under 10s, which means there are from 8 to 10 of these extremely large shrimp per pound; 10 to 15s; 16 to 20s; and 21 to 25s. All these sizes can be designated as *jumbo* shrimp. *Medium* shrimp are from the next four size categories: 26 to 30s; 31 to 35s; 36 to 42s; and 43 to 50s. The count for *small* shrimp are 51 to 60, and 61 and up.

**Scallops.** The menu writer need be concerned about only two varieties of scallops: the small bay scallop and the larger sea scallop. A gallon of either variety weighs about 8 pounds. The count per gallon for bay scallops is from 480 to 850. Sea scallops run from 100 to 185 per gallon. Cape scallops are considered to have the finest taste. They are about the same size as other bay scallops but are creamy white, tender, and full of flavor.

The New York seafood market lists bay scallops in three sizes: *large* are 3/4 inch in diameter; *medium* are 1/2 to 3/4 inch; and *small* are 1/2 inch or less in diameter.

*Caveat.* Some not-so-reputable seafood dealers will cut halibut into scallop-sized pieces as a substitute for sea scallops or to mix with the authentic product. Cut shark meat is sometimes used in this same fraudulent manner.

### Steak and Bacon

Size is sometimes used in describing steaks. Restaurants specializing in steaks often feature the 1-pound sirloin and the 24-ounce porterhouse steaks. Other steakhouses sell by the ounce, beginning at about 15 ounces down to 8 ounces for the strip sirloin steaks and 10 ounces to 6 ounces for the tenderloin steaks. Steaks cut from the sirloin butt may be sold in this manner also. In the interest of writing an accurate menu, the menu writer should be

sure that the weights advertised are the same as those sold.

In steak descriptions, it is common to see terms such as Texas-sized and king-sized, which mean large. These are honest descriptions if the average steak customer perceives the cut of meat as large. *King-sized* and *queen-sized* are sometimes used to designate the larger and the smaller steak. With respect to strip sirloin steaks, these terms would be deceptive if the king-sized were 10 ounces and the queen were 8 ounces. The 8-ounce steak is certainly small, but the 10-ounce steak is not a large sirloin steak. *Minute steak* is another term used to designate a smaller steak. It is meaningless insofar as actual size is concerned, but it is harmless and its use will not diminish a menu's integrity. *Delmonico* is often used to describe a steak. This word has a real meaning when applied to potatoes, but like club steak it has nearly as many different meanings as there are restaurants using the name. New York and Kansas City (K.C.) steaks also have a variety of interpretations. "Prime steak cut to order from an aged sirloin strip . . ." is a true statement that will have meaning and appeal to steak lovers everywhere.

The use of *rasher of bacon* to denote a certain quantity is quite controversial among restaurant operators. We can find only that it means more than one slice. If a standard order of bacon with two eggs is three slices in a particular restaurant, perhaps three slices constitutes a rasher in that restaurant.

In the interest of variety in expression, the menu writer can use any word that has a definite meaning regarding an item's size or quantity, such as *pair* or *brace*. Such words not only are acceptable to a policy of writing accurate menus, but they should be used at times to avoid monotony.

## Sources of Origin of Menu Selections

Menu claims of quality and quantity are subject to immediate judgment by customers.

Such menu descriptions, therefore, are usually accurate. This is not the case, however, in descriptions of items' *sources of origin*. Who can tell the difference between a Wisconsin turkey and a North Carolina turkey? Both states grow very fine turkeys, as do many other states. These are usually harmless but unnecessary statements. However, say the turkey was grown in Wisconsin. A Milwaukee restaurant might want to highlight this to appeal to the state pride of its regular, local customers. In this case the operator is exercising good merchandising judgment by engaging in provincial bragging. So what! It is another thing if a restaurateur indicates that the country ham on the menu is a Smithfield ham. If it is not, it is a misrepresentation.

A number of terms that seemingly indicate a geographic origin do not necessarily guarantee that the item is from that area. These terms indicate type rather than source place. These are consistent with truth-in-menu presentation, and include among many others New England clam chowder, Danish pastry, Irish stew, French fries, German potato salad, and Denver sandwich.

## Descriptive Terms

A twenty-third century anthropologist stumbling on the scripts of today's radio and television commercials would properly name the twentieth century the "Age of Advertising Exaggerations." In menu writing, exaggerations can be tolerated as long as they do not deceive. A menu-writing team, in the course of writing creative and persuasive text, gets "pumped up," and the superlatives flow fast and furiously. At such times it is harder to control ideas than to generate them.

It has become a fairly common but effective merchandising method, especially in family restaurants, to have photographic representations of menu items. Clearly the picture should be true to the actual presentation of the item if menu accuracy is not to be violated. In addition to the general appearance of the

plate, counts and sizes indicated in the picture should agree with the delivered meal. Likewise there should be no omissions or additions. Colors in photographs may stray from reality at times but this is acceptable since it is not a predetermined deception.

## Preparation Style

Among the clientele of any restaurant will be many health-conscious guests. These folks pay particular attention to how items are prepared when making their selections from a menu. Many people, for example, avoid fried foods. The description of items should include their preparation style, and the stated preparation method must be as accurate. The following terms are common, and the menu writer can properly assume that customers will understand them:

Baked
Barbecued
Braised
Broiled
Charcoal broiled
Deep fried
Fried in butter
Poached
Roasted
Sautéed
Smoked
Steamed

## General Descriptive Terms

The following descriptive terms are some of the most commonly used in menus.

*Fresh.* Free of preservatives and not previously canned, bottled, packaged, dried, processed or frozen. When the word *fresh* precedes such words as baked, ground, made, roasted, and so on, it must meet the definition of *freshly*.

*Freshly.* Denotes the process was completed on the premises and that there is no deterioration in the characteristics of color, texture, and bouquet.

*Geographic origin.* Grown, harvested, processed, or packed at the location specified. Examples would include Maine lobster, Idaho potato, Western beef, imported Swiss cheese, and Danish blue cheese.

*Homemade.* Prepared on the premises in a manner that involves more than heating and adding spices or flavoring to commercially processed foods.

*In season.* Available as a fresh product in the location of the restaurant.

*Kosher.* Prepared or processed to meet the requirements of the orthodox Jewish religion. The product is identified by the presence of Hebrew lettering or symbols on the tag, label, or wrapping.

*Kosher style.* No religious significance.

*Our own or house brand.* The product is prepared on the premises, is commercially prepared to an exclusive specification, or bears the establishment's label.

## Product Identification

### Pork

*Baked ham.* A ham that has been heated in an oven for a specified time. It may exhibit a crust and have a residual of syrup or a carmelization of sugar apparent on the surface.

*Country ham.* A dry-cured ham that is prepared in the country.

*Smithfield ham.* A dry-cured ham from Smithfield, Virginia, that has been smoked.

### Beef

*Chopped or ground beef.* Prepared from the exclusive grinding of a cut of round steak.

*Chopped or ground sirloin.* Derived from the grinding of trimmings or pieces of meat from the beef loin.

*Beef loin.* That portion of the hindquarter remaining after removal of the round and the flank. It is composed of the strip loin, tenderloin, and top butt or butt sirloin.

*Beef rib (Prime rib).* A beef cut from the fore-

quarter, which contains seven ribs (sixth through twelfth inclusive), and the plate is removed.

### Lamb

*Spring lamb.* A lamb born during early winter and slaughtered between March and early October. The lamb carcass is identified and stamped "Spring Lamb" on the leg by the USDA at the time of grading.

### Veal

*Veal.* A "calf" slaughtered between three to six weeks of age; seldom over three months.

*Calf.* Not over ten months of age.

### Poultry

*Capon.* A castrated male chicken usually under eighteen months of age.

*Rock Cornish hen.* A small breed of chicken slaughtered between five to seven weeks and which seldom exceeds 1 1/2 pounds dressed ready to cook.

### Flatfish

*Brook trout.* A fresh-water fish distinguished by its dark gray or olive color with small gray or red spots.

*Rainbow trout.* A fresh-water fish characterized by a broad reddish band, or "rainbow," that runs along the side of the fish from head to tail. This band blends into a dark olive green on the back and pure white or silver on the belly.

*Dover sole.* A flatfish found in the Pacific coastal waters off Washington, Oregon, California, and Alaska that can reach ten pounds. This fish is also known as the slipper sole or short-finned sole. It is characterized by one eye, a small mouth, an abundance of slime, and a uniform light- to dark-brown color on the same side as the eye.

*English sole.* A small-mouthed flatfish characterized by one eye and a yellowish brown color on the same side as the eye. It is slightly smaller than Dover sole and is second only to the Petrale sole in desirability.

It is found in waters from southern California to northwestern Alaska. English sole is also known as the California or common sole. (A different species of English sole is found only in European waters. This sole is marketed as either imported English sole or imported Dover sole.)

*Gray sole.* An east coast flatfish of the New England area; usually marketed as fillets.

*Lemon sole.* A flatfish found off the New England areas; closely related to the blackback or winter flounder. It does not have as high a market value as its Pacific coast counterpart (English sole).

*Petrale sole.* The most important and highly valued flatfish found in the coastal waters from southern California to northwestern Alaska. Petrale sole is olive brown on one side and white on the other and has scales on both sides. It has a large mouth with two rows of teeth on each side of the upper jaw. This sole is also known as the pet sole.

*Fillet.* The side of a fish cut lengthwise away from the ribs and back bone. Usually they are boneless.

*Scrod.* The smaller sizes of cod, haddock, or pollock, weighing from one to four pounds.

## Shellfish

*King crab.* One of the largest crabs found in the north Pacific waters off Alaska. The legs measure an average of 3 1/2 to 4 feet from tip to tip, and the whole crab weighs approximately 11 pounds. It is sold as cooked claws, legs, or picked king crabmeat. It is generally more expensive than snow crab.

*Snow crab.* Smaller than the king crab, with legs that measure an average of 2 1/2 feet from tip to tip. Although found in the same general area as the king crab and marketed in the same manner, it is generally less expensive.

*Prawn.* A shrimp-like crustacean that completes its life cycle in fresh water.

## Dairy Products

*Cream.* A product derived from fresh milk; contains a minimum of 18 percent butter fat. The two grades of cream generally avail-

able to the consumer are light (table or coffee) and heavy (whipping or pastry) cream. Light cream must meet the minimum butterfat standard for cream. Heavy cream contains approximately 36 percent butterfat.

*Half and half.* A homogenized mixture of milk and cream that contains approximately 12 percent butterfat.

*Roquefort cheese.* A semi-hard cheese that derives its name from the village of Roquefort, France. Roquefort is made from sheep's milk and has a stronger flavor than blue cheese.

*Butter.* Federal standards require that butter contain not less than 80 percent milk fat with 15 percent moisture and the remaining 5 percent milk solids, salt, coloring, and a small amount of stabilizer.

*Margarine.* A fatty food made by blending fats and oils with other ingredients such as milk solids, salt, flavorings, vitamins, and coloring products. Good margarine contains at least 80 percent approved fats and not more than 15 percent moisture and 4 percent salt.

*Ice cream.* The states have individual standards for this product, but generally ice cream must have a butterfat content of 10 percent or more. Ice milk is usually 8 to 10 percent butterfat. In the past premium ice cream contained 18 percent butterfat, 40 percent milk solids, and had an overrun of 60 to 80 percent. (Sixty to 80 percent overrun means that a gallon of ice cream mix, when frozen, produces 1.6 to 1.8 gallons of ice cream because of the air mixed in during the freezing process.) Today any ice cream with a butterfat content of 14 percent or more is considered a premium ice cream, but there are still a number of premium ice creams that have a butterfat of 16 to 18 percent with as high as 35 percent milk solids and 60 to 80 percent overrun. Richness beyond 18 percent, while giving a wonderful taste thrill as it is, tends to produce a film in the mouth and an unpleasant aftertaste. A satisfying ice cream is not wholly dependent on high butterfat content. Flavoring is an important element, and an otherwise good product can be poor eating if a substandard flavoring ingredient is used.

*Maple syrup.* One of the most genuine American products is maple syrup. Indians taught the first settlers on this continent how to prepare it. Maple syrup is the processed sap of the *acer saccharum*. These trees are found largely in the northeastern United States and in southeastern Canada. The sap is obtained by tapping the trees in the early spring, which causes the sap to flow for a short period of time. The slow growth of this tree combined with high production costs and a firm demand has made maple syrup a highly valued product. Since it is relatively expensive, it is used primarily as a flavoring for other syrups and in fine candles. Blends and imitations may be called table syrup or otherwise appropriately described.

## Nutrition

Ordinarily, customers make their own selections from a menu, so the menu writer cannot guarantee that they will receive a nutritional meal. However, a menu should contain a balance of offerings from which customers can select a nutritional meal. Variety in a menu does not mean that the necessary nutritional elements will be present. For example, a menu may contain beef, veal, pork, lamb, fish, poultry, cheese, and eggs. This is a wide variety of items, but they are all protein dishes. Variety is primarily concerned with the public taste. Balance provides the nutritional benefits—bulk, protein, starch, alkaline foods, fats, and vitamins. A restaurant's menu-writing team does not require a dietitian, but the basic rules of nutrition, which are really only common sense in eating, should guide the team in its selection of items.

## Dietary Claims

"Slim and trim" seems to be the order of the day. A look around at almost any group of people will show that there is more conversation about this than achievement. Nevertheless, it is good merchandising to include low-calorie meals on menus. All the dietary background you need to develop such items can be found in a book of calorie counts. It is not necessary or prudent to go beyond this in menu writing.

# 20   Brainstorming a Sales Program

**Purpose:** To emphasize the main function of the menu—to sell.

In the first chapter of this text were charts that showed the steady increase in the number of meals taken outside the home. In this final chapter we review the selling efforts that have contributed to this growth and present ways of producing novel ideas for further promotional efforts. As we have mentioned, the menu can be at the forefront in promoting sales.

## The Brainstorming Session

*Synergism* (n). Cooperative action of discrete agencies such that the total effect is greater than the sum of the effects taken independently.
— *Webster's New Collegiate Dictionary*

This definition is the basis of the brainstorming session. If two men can each lift 100 pounds, then by working together they can lift 225 pounds. "2 + 2 = 5" is the catch phrase to describe synergism, or the brainstorming session.

The discrete agents in the session are the minds of the participants. One mind stimulates another. The idea is that no one person has as much knowledge and experience as the total group, so when knowledge and experiences are exchanged with 100 percent partici-

pation, successful answers will emerge. A few years ago someone resurrected the word *serendipity*. There were jokes based on its meaning, songs written about it, a singing team named after it, and an office complex bore and perhaps still bears the name. Serendipity refers to important concepts or discoveries that come about accidentally or otherwise without being purposefully sought after. A better definition of serendipity is "what happens when preparation meets opportunity." The brainstorming session is serendipitous—it invites the unexpected. The stimulated "discrete agents" become creative. They keep looking for new ideas and opportunities, never becoming mired in the status quo but always looking for what is possible.

Their minds should roam freely. Beyond the general purpose of the session, to develop sales in this instance, little in the way of rules are needed or desired. Each additional rule narrows perspective, and unconsciously suggestions are made within a particular frame of reference determined by past experience, individual wants, and so on. In the brainstorming session the idea is to break through the frames of reference. The frames of reference are turned upside down by asking such questions as: Suppose cause and effect were reversed? What if this or that factor or element were reversed? Does it have to be this way?

In such a session it is easy to become quite Bohemian, so the ideas must be directed at the purpose or an unintelligible mess develops. As the venerable baseball manager Casey Stengel put it, "If one doesn't know where he is going, he might arrive somewhere else."

## What Can Happen?

A menu-writing team held a brainstorming session to come up with some garnishes for the "Sandwich of the Week," which was a promotion for a restaurant with a large clientele of businesspeople. The session yielded the following list of suggestions.

A simple spray of watercress or parsley
Leaves of curly endive or romaine
Leaves of lettuce and tomato boat
Celery stalks or scallions with leafy parts
Asparagus tips or fresh broccoli
Pickled beets, onions, cucumbers
Raw-carrot curls or cauliflowerettes
Cherry tomatoes or tomato wedges
Sliced cucumber wedges/slices or green
    pepper rings
Dill pickle spear or slices, or gherkins
Shredded salad greens with mandarin orange
    slices
Stuffed olives, green or black
Fresh mushrooms
Whole stuffed or sliced red pimiento strips
Devilled eggs
Sieved curled anchovies or anchovy fillets
Flutes of cream cheese or egg-butter
Cheese slices (rolled) or wedges
Fruit kabobs (cherries, grapes, pineapple
    chunks, melon balls)
Cinnamon apple rings with sour cream
Minted fruit cup with fresh fruits
French fried potatoes
Onion rings or zucchini slices
Potato salad, cole slaw, macaroni salad
Three bean salad
Popcorn and mixed nuts

## A List of Promotional Ideas (for Starters)

A large part of this list of promotional ideas very likely came out of brainstorming sessions in restaurants and hotels.

Sunday brunch—Cooked-to-order omelettes
Sunday family dinners—Sell ten kinds of
    chicken
Gala holiday dinners—See Chapter 10
Happy hours
Make your own sandwiches
Make your own sundaes
Buffet crepes cooked to order
Ham biscuits served from a cart
"First" drink free for secretaries
Ethnic dances on Saturday night
Free meal privileges to certain
    people—radio, newspaper
Bar maids
Big portions
Big baked potatoes
Wine of the week
Imported (well-known) wines as house wines
Big-screen television in the bar
Display tables at dining room entrance
Wine, coffee, liquor bar in banquet office
Better breakfast program
Appetizer—salad bars
Animal crackers and balloons for kids
Fashion shows—both men and women
Back local teams—softball, bowling, etc.
"Grazing"
Wine bars—forty to fifty selections
Free breakfast with room
Express breakfast—service kitchen in
    elevator
Buffet breakfast bars
Continental breakfast in lobby

## Weekly Promotions

The value of continuous weekly promotions has been demonstrated for both hotel restaurants and free-standing units. They tend to increase sales not only on the night of the promotions but on the other evenings of the week as well. They are good public relations, and free publicity results. Weekly promotions introduce new people to the operations and generally build a greater community awareness of the restaurant. Listed on the next several pages are some promotions that have a proven track record of success.

## Family Country Dinner

**Theme.** Although the United States is now the most highly industrialized country in the world, for a great part of the first half of the twentieth century the United States was rural and family oriented. Social life revolved around the family to a much greater degree than it does in these waning years of the

century. Sunday afternoon was the time to gather, to socialize, and to eat hearty home-cooked food.

**Market.** Advertising and promotional efforts should be directed primarily to young married couples who are beginning families.

**Service.** All food should be served family style, on platters and in large bowls.

### Decor and Special Features
1. Table centerpiece of flowers, fruit, or foliage.
2. Checked (or otherwise informal) table-cloths for all tables.
3. Old-fashioned candy table at door. Set up like the old general store with jars of penny candy for the children to take.
4. Take-home boxes for all the leftovers

---

**Family Country Dinner**
**Sample Menu**
Tuna Salad on Tomato Slices
Fresh Fruits of the Season
Chilled Fruit Juice with Sherbet
Seafood Cocktail • A Cut of Melon

Bowls of Relishes

Cream of Chicken Soup • Fresh Vegetable Soup

Pot Roast of Beef with Natural Gravy
Fried Young Chicken, Currant Jelly
Texas Barbecue with Ribs

Whipped Potatoes • Baked Beans • French Fries
String Beans • Applesauce
Cole Slaw • Buttered Peas
Sliced Tomatoes

Hot Rolls

Strawberry Ice Cream Sundae • Apple Pie with Cheese
Chocolate Layer Cake

Coffee • Tea • Milk

that customers may want to take home.

5. Attractive, young hostess dressed in a long, frilled calico dress, giving out comic books and small games or toys to the children.
6. Have souvenir menus printed on the back of a 1920 newspaper front page.
7. Hand out candy at the tables after the meal.
8. Have a special drink—"buckets of beer" for 50 cents. Use old tin buckets.

## Sunday Brunch

**Theme.** A large varied buffet offered on Sunday from 11:00 A.M. to 3:00 P.M.

**Market.** Family groups, city residents, young couples, hotel guests if the restaurant is in a hotel.

**Menu and Service.** The Sunday brunch is a well-decorated buffet consisting of items from the following groups:

1. *Breakfast items*—An egg dish and sausage, sweet rolls, lox, bagels, juice, and fruits.
2. *Hot luncheon items*—A hot sauce item such as shrimp creole, creamed chicken, or beef stroganoff.
3. *Cold luncheon items*—Cold cuts, potato salad, cole slaw, tossed salad, bread, and rolls.
4. *Soup*—Have one or two soups.
5. *Salads*—Offer a variety such as chicken, molded gelatin, tuna, and tossed.
6. *Dessert*—Pie, pudding, or a gelatin item as well as pastry items.

Note: A Bloody Mary is a good item to include in the price.

A champagne fountain is also an effective conversation piece.

**Decor and Special Features.** This promotion has worked especially well in restaurants located near churches. The buffet must be attractive, well garnished, and well stocked at all times. The host or hostess must be willing to watch the buffet line, and explain items to people and guide them through.

The price should be moderate and the menu must show variety. Promotion can be done internally using tent cards and posters, or externally with small newspaper ads.

## Shakespearian Festival

**Theme.** This promotion is for restaurants with English decor, a Tudor-type room, or with heavy paneling. Such a decor lends itself well to this promotion. The bawdy times of Elizabethan England have great romantic appeal. The works of Shakespeare convey the feeling of everyday life in those times, but also cover a great deal of countries and characters that lend themselves to a varied cuisine. These works are the central theme of this promotion.

**Market.** Mid-week diners, special family and local groups, and hotel guests if the restaurant is located in a hotel.

**Menu and Service.** All food to be displayed in buffet style, with the exception of desserts.

### Decor and Special Features

1. Special costumes of Elizabethan design for the hostess and service personnel.
2. A strolling minstrel or bard reading from Shakespeare and moving from table to table.
3. A special souvenir menu printed on parchment in Old English.
4. Special beverage service
   a. Tankards of beer.
   b. All mixed drinks served in stemmed glasses and garnished with abundant fruit.
   c. A house claret wine offered in a carafe.
5. Special table setting with goblets and colored linen.

<table>
<tr><td></td><td>

**Shakespearean Festival**
**Sample Menu**
</td></tr>
</table>

|            | **Shakespearean Festival**<br>**Sample Menu** |
|------------|-----------------------------------------------|
| *Act I*    | Chilled Fruits from Caesar's Conquests<br>"Tempest" Cocktail of Shrimp<br>Relishes from the Venetian Merchant<br>Assorted Herring from Hamlet's Denmark<br>Marinated Vegetables from the Mermaid Tavern |
| *Act II*   | Lamb and Veal Pie—Macbeth<br>Italian Casserole au Brutus (Lasagne)<br>Huntsman's Stew of Bernum Wood<br>Hot Seafood in the Witches' Brew<br>Roast Beef from the Coals of King Lear's Hearth<br>Roast Chicken as Othello Liked it |
| *Act III*  | Romeo and Juliet Salad<br>Roast Potatoes from the Bard's Table<br>Elizabethan Assorted Vegetables |
| *Encore*   | Midsummer Night's Dream — Ice Cream Pie — Decorated in a Mold<br>Cleopatra's Jewels — Pastry<br>Assorted Pies of Merry England<br>Falstaff's Favorite — Assorted Cheeses and Fresh Fruits<br>(Passed at the table) |

## Roast Beef Buffet

**Theme.** A roast beef buffet is "The Great Meal Deal."

**Market.** Local residents and social groups and hotel house guests if the restaurant is located in a hotel.

**Menu and Service.** Consistent with the atmosphere and decor of the room, set up a special table featuring the following menu.

**Special Feature.** The table should be manned by a cook in whites, carving the beef.

## Fish Smorgasbord

**Theme.** A good promotion for Friday night. Fish lovers will appreciate good, fresh fish.

**Market.** Families and regular diners.

**Menu and Service.** The following are some menu ideas that can be used in this promotion.

**Decor and Special Features**
1. Have a bowl of saltwater taffy at the door.
2. Give the kids nautical toys like a bo'sun's whistle or spyglasses from Japan.
3. Dress the waiters in striped Jerseys and white trousers.

## Diamond Jim Brady Night

**Theme.** Diamond Jim Brady is a symbol of luxurious and impassioned dining. Being very wealthy, Jim Brady had a palate for beef,

---

**Roast Beef Buffet**
**Sample Menu**
An Assortment of Fresh Fruits
Tossed Garden Greens with French or Blue Cheese Dressing
Celery Stuffed with Blue Cheese
Mixed Bean Salad with Vinaigrette
Fresh Sliced Tomatoes • Onion Rings
Assorted Relishes—Iced • Marinated Beet Salad
Fancy Devilled Eggs • Kosher Dill Pickles

---

Roast Prime Ribs of Beef
or
Steamship Round Au Jus, Carved to Order
or
Barbecued Spare Ribs

Julienne of Beef Stroganoff, Rice Pilaf

Pepper Steak—Maison

---

Au Gratin Potatoes • Parisienne Potatoes
Fresh String Beans with Almonds • Glazed Baby Carrots

A separate dessert table featuring Black Walnut Pecan Pie, Old-Fashioned Blueberry Cobbler, and Bread and Butter Pudding.

---

huge salads, fancy desserts, oysters by the dozen, and any available thing that appealed to him at the moment. Well-stocked buffets and large portions from the menu are a "Brady trademark," along with the color red and the bold typefaces and printing of the gay nineties period.

**Market.** Local diners and hotel guests if the restaurant is located in a hotel.

**Decor and Special Features**
1. Costumes from the 1890's for the service personnel
   a. Men—Red striped shirts, bowlers, and arm garter.
   b. Women—Long dresses of the era.
2. A barbershop quartet to entertain in the room.
3. Checkered tablecloths to cover the tables.
4. Garters for the ladies.

5. Candy wrapped in gold for the ladies.
6. Souvenir menus printed on the back of a newspaper of the day.

**Menu and Service (see page 256)**

## Selling Opportunities for Hotel Restaurants

In the United States many hotel restaurant operators wrongly assume that hotel guests are a "captured market." Although they could eat elsewhere, these guests are the greatest potential customers for the hotel's food outlets. They are already in the hotel, generally have the money to spend, and of course must eat. Judging from sales records, attracting the guests to the hotel's restaurant is not as easy as it seems. In this case a brainstorming session with hotel management as participants could lead to a creative, effective promotional campaign that will attract

**Fish Smorgasbord**
**Sample Menus**

*Cold*

King Crab Legs, Alaskan Mariniere
Fresh Columbia River Salmon in Aspic Cucumber Sauce
Herring Filet in Sour Cream
Jumbo Shrimp on Horseback, Oscar Sauce
Fresh Clams and Oysters on Half Shell
Smoked Eel, Egg Sauce
Smoked Oysters
Fresh Salmon Marinated in Dill
Roll-Mopps
Tuna Salad, Garni
Seafood Tidbits
King Crabmeat Salad
Herring Marinated in Wine

*Hot*

Spanish Seafood Creole, Rice Pilaf
Sweet and Sour Shrimp
Indian Lobster Curry, Chutney Sauce
Fresh Scallops Veronique with White Wine and Grapes
Salmon Patties, Tomato Sauce
Baked Halibut, Garni
King Crab a la Newburg
Crabmeat Tetrazzini
Fresh Oyster Stew
Shrimp Chow Mein
Deep Fried Filet of Sole, Lemon Sauce

*Beverages*. Add special drinks to the menu: Navy Grog Punch, Hot-Buttered Rum, Gin and Fresh Fruit. Serve in large tankards or tall frosted glasses.

hotel guests to the hotel's restaurant. Following are some ideas that might result from such a session.

## Internal Promotion

Make use of signs and posters in public spaces, especially the main lobby and the elevator lobbies. The elevators are good places to post ads for the restaurants, bars, and lounges. In addition to directory listings, place tent cards in the guests' rooms. Tent cards should have a special message or an attractive picture of the outlet advertised.

Another effective internal promotion is the "Bellman Referral." When a bellman spends three to five minutes with a guest, it is three minutes of opportunity, not just duty. A well-trained bellman who is comfortable being with and talking to guests can better promote the facilities than the radio station down the street that you have paid to run an ad. To realize this opportunity and to properly emphasize the selling potential to the bellmen, you will need to train and to motivate them. Meet with the bellmen in the outlets to be promoted and explain the menu and service. Invite them to come in when off duty with a guest for a

**Sample menu—Diamond Jim Brady night**

### Beverages

- Lillian Russell— A jumbo mixture of essence of fruit and blended spirits in the old-fashioned manner.
- The Iron Horse Sour—A favorite of the hearty men who sped over the steel rails. Concocted in "locomotive" proportions of bourbon, lemon, and a sweet touch.
- Remember the Maine—A drink of battleship size and firepower. Made with blended rums and the fruits of the rebellious Caribbean.

### Food

"Diamond Jim breaks the bank"—*A perfectly ridiculous offer*
The Gulf's Most Tender Shrimp
Clams from the Great Ipswich Bay
Oysters from the Chesapeake's Shallows
*10 Cents Each"—A price that caused the great crash."*

A parade of hot gems will pass gratis before you as you dine.
Partake freely of these morsels—egg rolls, chicken in a blanket, pâte in bacon or tiny cheese puffs.

### The Height of Festivities

- Prime Rib of Beef—From Jim's private stockyard. Carved before you and served with the rib for relaxed nibbling of the sweeter meat.
- A Huge Sirloin Steak with Jim's respects—He admired men who could eat well and long. Broiled tenderly to your taste.
- Baked Jumbo Diamond Shrimp—Large pearl pink gems of seafood stuffed with Jim's private formula.
- The Breasts of Chicken that made men fly—Tender white meat from the breast of an admired bird, sauce supreme.
- Lillian's Favorite Vintage Beef Casserole—Chunks of young prime beef simmered in her favorite wine of Burgundy. Tender and hearty like the men she admired.
- Harvest's Love of Pork—Like the virile men of the land, a succulent meat garnished with the love of apples and spicy dressing.
- A Treat of Sole from Davy Jones—Jim even knew the sea and the best that it offered. Light white fish fried in corn batter.
- The Red King Lobster Visits—Of all the royalty that Jim greeted he much preferred the lobster boiled . . . the royalty of New England at 1 1/2 pounds.

———————

All of the above served with Delmonico Diamond Potatoes, Roast Crackling Potatotes, Creamed Pearl Onions, Fresh Gems of the Garden in Salad and Spring Vegetables.

A loaf of Jim's favorite bread from the stove hearth.

A pause in tribute—a small cup of special sherbet to clear the palate for . . .
"The Close of the Century"
Assorted Cheeses from Jim's Foreign Holdings
Ice Cream Pie from the Mold of Royalty, Sauce of Raspberry

The Lillian Russell Sundae—Ice Cream Toppings for Her Sweet Tooth (Creme de Menthe)

Freshly Baked Pies . . . loved by Jim's common friends

complimentary dinner. Let them discuss their ideas on how best to promote from their peculiar position with the guests. Also encourage the bellmen to volunteer some of the comments that they have, no doubt, heard from the guests about the food outlets. Their association with guests allows them to sell as the guests' friend in a casual, friendly manner rather than the pressure pitch the guest usually receives from ordinary advertising. An incentive program for the bellmen is a must. They can give guests a personal card good for a cocktail; these will provide the accounting for the sale.

A more obvious program of selling by bellmen is to provide them with half-dollar-sized coins that entitle the guest to a complimentary drink. The bellman can give the hotel guest a "tip." This is sort of a "man bites dog" approach.

## It's the Little Things That Count

From poll after poll of restaurant guests, we have discovered that patrons prefer to be "pampered" rather than "processed." When guests are asked about the little extra services that they did not expect, they respond that the things they most appreciate are included in the following:

1. A second cup of coffee offered without the guests' asking.
2. Attention from the manager who stops by the table to see that everything is satisfactory.
3. "Piped-in" or soft music in the background.
4. Appetizers to munch on while waiting to be served.
5. A dessert cart from which to select desserts.
6. A small decorated cake provided free when it is learned a birthday or anniversary is being celebrated.
7. A fruit juice for guests waiting to be seated.
8. Large soft facial-quality napkins where paper is used.
9. Low-calorie sugar substitute provided in sugar bowl for guests watching calories.
10. A small loaf of bread, cutting board, and knife provided with the meal.
11. Uncluttered entrance to the dining room.
12. Well-ventilated dining room at a comfortable temperature: no food or smoke odors.
13. Well-groomed host or hostess with genuine smile and pleasant manner.
14. A bread basket containing a complete assortment of individually cellophane-wrapped crackers.
15. Neatly set table with gleaming silver and shining glassware.
16. Low lights for dinner—candlelight where permitted.
17. Comfortable, well-dusted chairs—no crumbs.
18. Clean menus with easy-to-read print.
19. A helpful salesperson with congenial enthusiasm, courteous greeting, suggestive selling, and prompt, efficient service.
20. Plenty of ice in the drink.
21. The aroma of freshly baked rolls coming from the full roll basket.
22. Specially split and toasted rolls carefully wrapped in a napkin to retain the heat.
23. Dairy-fresh butter untainted by other icebox foods.
24. Ice-cold water in a crystal clear glass . . . and keep the glass full.
25. Remembering to repeat guest's name.
26. Hot foods served piping hot: hot the pot!
27. Cold foods served cold: chill the dish!
28. Home-baked pastry served warm.
29. Cream in sizable pitcher, giving the impression of generosity.
30. A variety of well-prepared and pre-

sented hors d'oeuvres, at a banquet reception to start the evening off right.

31. A well-tossed salad gives superior flavor to the salad and "class" to the meal. When tossed at tableside, glamour is added.

32. Markers for steak—rare, medium, or well. These let the guest know that an effort is made to please.

33. Unusual garnitures cause verbal comments that "snowball." (There is nothing more valuable than word-of-mouth advertising.)

34. Mints and candies passed after dinner.

35. Waiter! You had better smile when you say, "It's not my table."

36. Moving objects claim interest:
Salad cart or buffet
Dessert cart
Coffee server
Bread and roll server
Roast beef wagon
Sizzling platters
Flaming swords
Chafing dishes

37. Make the dessert generous enough to be impressive. It provides the final impression of the meal.

38. Service of condiment basket or at least offer an appropriate sauce.

39. Use of magnetic crumber (instead of dusting crumbs on the floor.)

40. Amusement for children—toys, games, or balloons.

41. Prompt presentation of check at the end of the meal.

42. Liquor and food on one check.

43. The bowl of fruit, the barrel of apples, or the plate of mints from which the guests may help themselves when leaving the dining room.

Perhaps this list of hints to gain customer satisfaction can be summed up in this definition of good service from a pioneer hotelier: "Anticipating the customers' needs before the customers themselves know."

All these things will help smooth the path to your door. Remember the words of Michelangelo, "Trifles make perfection, but perfection is no trifle."

# Appendix A
## Cost Factors

In Chapter 6, a sample list of cost factors appeared as Table 6-1, for which we gave a column-by-column explanation. An example of the application of a cost factor was also included. To develop these cost factors requires butcher tests of the various meat, fish, and poultry items and some pricing of recipes.

Figure A-1 is a copy of a butcher test on an IMPS 180 striploin, which produced the cost factor 1.24 for the 14-ounce steak priced in the example in Chapter 6.

The headings on the Butcher Test Card are self-explanatory. The entries on the lower lines are gathered in the reverse order in which they appear. In trimming the striploin, the fat cover and a piece of the flank are removed. The fat weighs 7 pounds, 7 ounces from the two pieces, and the trimmed meat for use as hamburger meat, or more likely as consommé meat in making stock, weighs 12 ounces. Hamburger meat purchased at the time of the test was $1.25 per pound. This price is used as a recovery cost. At the butt end of a striploin is a vein, which makes this part of the strip unusable for first-grade steak meat in a fine restaurant. However, some lesser operations do not make this differentiation. Other than this small tough vein, the meat is of the same quality as the balance of the strip. The purchase price of vein steak meat was $2.40 per pound, as shown on the card; the 2 ¼ pounds amounts to $5.40. The cost of this vein steak meat plus the hamburger meat amounts to $6.34. This is deducted from the total cost of the two striploins, which is $68.15. The remaining $61.81 is chargeable to the 18 pounds, 9 ounces to be used for steaks. The cost of the steak meat thus rises to $3.33 per pound—$61.81 divided by 18 pounds, 9 ounces. This amounts to 20.8 cents per ounce. To develop cost factors, the size of the steak is multiplied by the cost per ounce and divided by the purchase price per pound. To illustrate:

```
 8 ounces × 20.8 cents = $1.66 divided by $2.35 =  .71
10 ounces × 20.8 cents = $2.08 divided by $2.35 =  .89
12 ounces × 20.8 cents = $2.50 divided by $2.35 = 1.06
14 ounces × 20.8 cents = $2.91 divided by $2.35 = 1.24
16 ounces × 20.8 cents = $3.33 divided by $2.35 = 1.42
```

This test of two striploins illustrates how cost factors are developed; however, each piece of meat will vary slightly in trim, so to develop sound cost factors, multiple tests (at least ten pieces) should be subjected to butcher tests. The average of these tests will be reliable because it will reflect the different yields.

To develop a cost factor for foods that are portioned from cooked meat, the butcher test must be supplemented by a cooking test. Figure A-2 shows copies of two such tests. Note that on this Butcher Test Card there is less trim and fat loss than in the test shown above. The vein end has not been removed and more fat cover is allowed to remain. On the reverse side of the Butcher Test Card is the form needed to complete the cooking test. Note the first three lines are carried over from the butcher test. The next line shows the weight after cooking, and the cost per pound is computed; that is, $68.95 divided by the cooked weight of 16 pounds. The ratio shows that about one-third of the trimmed weight is lost in cooking. Before slicing into portions of roast sirloin, another 1 pound of fat is trimmed from the meat. Finally, there are 15 pounds of saleable meat, and the $68.95 is chargeable to this amount, which amounts to $4.67 per pound of cooked meat ready for slicing or 29 cents per ounce. The cost factor per pound is 1.87. An 8-ounce portion costs $2.34 and has a cost factor of .936 ($2.34 divided by $2.50, the value per pound of the original weight).

### Table A-1. Portion and Yield Factors for Meats, Poultry, Fish, and Shellfish

| Wholesale Cut | IMPS Code Number | Entree | Yield Factor (percent) | Portion Factors | | |
| --- | --- | --- | --- | --- | --- | --- |
| | | | | Size and State | Cost | Average Number of Servings |
| **MEATS** | | | | | | |
| **Beef** | | | | | | |
| Rib, primal (regular, 34 to 38 lb.) | 103 | Roast ribs of beef | 26 | 15 oz., cooked | 3.60 | 10 |
| | | | | 11 oz., cooked | 2.64 | 14 |
| | | | | 9-½ oz., cooked | 2.23 | 16 |
| | | | | 8-½ oz., cooked | 2.04 | 18 |
| Oven ready (20 to 22 lb.) | 109 | | 44 | 15 oz., cooked | 2.10 | 10 |
| | | | | 11 oz., cooked | 1.49 | 14 |
| | | | | 9-½ oz., cooked | 1.32 | 16 |
| | | | | 8-½ oz., cooked | 1.17 | 18 |
| Top round (roast ready), 19 to 23 lb.) | 168 | Pot roast | 55 | 8 oz., cooked | .91 | 23 |
| | | | | 6 oz., cooked | .68 | 30 |
| | | Round steak | 65 | 10 oz., raw | .96 | 21 |
| | | | | 8 oz., raw | .77 | 27 |
| | | Roast round | 57 | 8 oz., cooked | .88 | 23 |
| | | | | 6 oz., cooked | .66 | 31 |
| | | | | 4 oz., cooked | .44 | 47 |
| Bottom round (25 to 28 lb.) | 170 | Pot roast | 55 | 8 oz., cooked | .91 | 28 |
| | | | | 6 oz., cooked | .68 | 37 |
| | | Hamburger | 90 | 8 oz., raw | .55 | 47 |
| | | | | 6 oz., raw | .42 | 63 |
| | | | | 5 oz., raw | .35 | 76 |
| Strip loin (bone in, 10-inch trim, 18 to 20 lb.) | 175 | Sirloin steak (2-inch tail, 1/8-inch fat) | 50 | 16 oz., raw | 2.00 | 10 |
| | | | | 14 oz., raw | 1.75 | 12 |
| | | | | 12 oz., raw | 1.50 | 14 |
| | | | | 10 oz., raw | 1.25 | 16 |
| | | | | 8 oz., raw | 1.00 | 20 |
| Strip loin (boneless, 12 to 14 lb.) | 180 | Sirloin steak (2-inch tail, 1/8-inch fat) | 70 | 16 oz., raw | 1.42 | 10 |
| | | | | 14 oz., raw | 1.24 | 12 |
| | | | | 12 oz., raw | 1.06 | 14 |
| | | | | 10 oz., raw | .89 | 16 |
| | | | | 8 oz., raw | .71 | 20 |
| Top sirloin butt (boneless, 12 to 14 lb.) | 184 | Top butt steak | 62 | 10 oz., raw | 1.01 | 12 |
| | | | | 8 oz., raw | .81 | 16 |
| | | | | 6 oz., raw | 1.01 | 20 |
| | | Roast top sirloin | 75 | 8 oz., cooked | .67 | 20 |
| | | | | 6 oz., cooked | .50 | 26 |
| | | | | 4 oz., cooked | .34 | 38 |

*Table A-1, continued*

| Wholesale Cut | IMPS Code Number | Entree | Yield Factor (percent) | Portion Factors | | |
|---|---|---|---|---|---|---|
| | | | | Size and State | Cost | Average Number of Servings |
| Tenderloin (full, 7 to 9 lb.) | 189 | Tenderloin steak | 50 | 10 oz., raw | 1.25 | 5 to 7 |
| (short, 5 to 6 lb.) | 192 | | | 8 oz., raw | 1.00 | 7 to 9 |
| | | | | 6 oz., raw | .75 | 9 to 12 |
| | | Roast tenderloin | 40 | 8 oz., cooked | 1.25 | 5 to 7 |
| | | | | 6 oz., cooked | .94 | 7 to 9 |
| | | | | 4 oz., cooked | .63 | 11 to 14 |
| Corned brisket (kosher style, 12 to 14 lb.) | 120 | Corned beef | 45 | 8 oz., cooked | 1.11 | 10 to 12 |
| | | | | 6 oz., cooked | .83 | 14 to 16 |
| | | | | 4 oz., cooked | .56 | 21 to 25 |
| Fresh brisket | 120 | Same as corned brisket | | | | |
| Chuck (square cut, boneless, 62 to 72 lb.) | 116 | Pot roast | 66 | 8 oz., cooked | .76 | 82 to 95 |
| | | | | 6 oz., cooked | .57 | 109 to 126 |
| | | | | 4 oz., cooked | .38 | 163 to 190 |
| | | Stew meat or hamburger | 90 | 8 oz., raw | .56 | 111 to 129 |
| | | | | 6 oz., raw | .42 | 148 to 172 |
| | | | | 4 oz., raw | .28 | 220 to 380 |
| **Veal** | | | | | | |
| Veal leg (single, 25 to 28 lb.) | 334 | Roast leg | 40 | 8 oz., cooked | 1.25 | 20 to 22 |
| | | | | 6 oz., cooked | .94 | 26 to 28 |
| | | | | 4 oz., cooked | .63 | 40 to 42 |
| | | Veal cutlets | 47 | 8 oz., raw | 1.06 | 23 to 26 |
| | | | | 6 oz., raw | .80 | 31 to 35 |
| | | | | 4 oz., raw | .64 | 47 to 52 |
| | | Veal stew | 68 | 12 oz., raw | 1.10 | 22 to 25 |
| | | | | 10 oz., raw | .92 | 27 to 30 |
| Veal rack (double, trimmed, 10 to 12 lb.) | 306 | Veal chops | 60 | 10 oz., raw | 1.08 | 9 to 11 |
| | | | | 8 oz., raw | .86 | 12 to 14 |
| | | Roast loin | 38 | 8 oz., cooked | 1.32 | 7-½ to 9 |
| | | | | 6 oz., cooked | .99 | 10 to 12 |
| | | | | 4 oz., cooked | .66 | 15 to 18 |
| Veal chuck (square cut, 8 to 12 lb.) | 309 | Veal stew | 68 | 12 oz., raw | 1.10 | 7 to 10 |
| | | | | 10 oz., raw | .92 | 8 to 13 |
| | | | | 8 oz., raw | .74 | 10 to 16 |
| | | Roast shoulder | 40 | 6 oz., cooked | .94 | 10 to 12 |
| | | | | 4 oz., cooked | .63 | 14 to 16 |
| Calves liver (3 to 5 lb.) | Fresh | Calves liver | 85 | 6 oz., raw | .44 | 4 to 6 |
| | | | | 4 oz., raw | .30 | 6 to 10 |
| Sweetbreads (12 to 16 oz. a pair) | Frozen | Sweetbreads | 50 | 6 oz., raw | 1.00 | 1 |
| | | | | 6 oz., raw | .75 | 1 |
| Veal kidneys (4 to 5 oz. each) | Fresh | Veal kidneys | 40 | 8 oz., raw | 1.25 | 4 per serving |
| | | | | 6 oz., raw | .94 | 3 per serving |
| **Lamb** | | | | | | |
| Lamb chuck (15 to 17 lb.) | 206 | Lamb stew | 55 | 12 oz., raw | 1.37 | 11 to 13 |
| | | | | 10 oz., raw | 1.14 | 13 to 15 |
| | | | | 8 oz., raw | .91 | 16 to 18 |
| Lamb rack (6 to 8 lb.) | 204 | Lamb chops | 50 | 8 oz., raw | 2.00 | 6 to 8 |
| | | | | 6 oz., raw | .87 | 8 to 10 |
| | | | | 4 oz., raw | .50 | 12 to 16 |
| | | Roast rack | 45 | 8 oz., cooked | 1.11 | 5 to 7 |
| | | | | 6 oz., cooked | .83 | 7 to 9 |
| | | | | 4 oz., cooked | .56 | 10 to 14 |
| Lamb leg (16 to 18 lb.) | 233 | Roast leg | 44 | 8 oz., cooked | 1.14 | 14 to 16 |
| | | | | 6 oz., cooked | .85 | 18 to 21 |
| | | | | 4 oz., cooked | .57 | 28 to 31 |
| **Pork** | | | | | | |
| Ham (fresh, 12 to 14 lb.) | 401 | Baked ham | 55 | 8 oz., cooked | .91 | 14 |
| | | | | 6 oz., cooked | .68 | 19 |
| | | Ham steak | 80 | 10 oz., raw | .78 | 16 |
| | | | | 8 oz., raw | .62 | 21 |
| Ham (pullman, 7 to 9 lb.) | Trade | Ham, ready to eat | 85 | 8 oz., raw | .59 | 12 to 15 |
| | | | | 6 oz., raw | .44 | 16 to 20 |
| Prosciutto (bone in, 12 to 14 lb.) | Trade | Hors d'oeuvres | 50 | 4 oz., raw | .50 | 24 to 28 |
| | | | | 2 oz., raw | .25 | 48 to 56 |

Table A-1, continued

| Wholesale Cut | IMPS Code Number | Entree | Yield Factor (percent) | Portion Factors | | |
|---|---|---|---|---|---|---|
| | | | | Size and State | Cost | Average Number of Servings |
| Shoulder (4 to 8 lb.) | 404 | Roast shoulder | 40 | 8 oz., cooked | 1.25 | 3 to 6 |
| | | | | 6 oz., cooked | .94 | 4 to 8 |
| | | | | 4 oz., cooked | .63 | 6 to 12 |
| Pork loin (10 to 12 lb.) | 411 | Pork chops | 82 | 8 oz., raw | .61 | 16 to 19 |
| | | | | 6 oz., raw | .46 | 22 to 26 |
| | | Roast loin | 50 | 8 oz., cooked | 1.00 | 10 to 12 |
| | | | | 6 oz., cooked | .75 | 13 to 16 |
| | | | | 4 oz., cooked | .50 | 20 to 24 |
| **POULTRY** | | | | | | |
| Roasting chicken (3 to 4-½ lb.) | N.A. | Roast chicken | 30 | 4 oz., cooked | .83 | 3 to 5 |
| | | | | 3 oz., cooked | .75 | 4 to 7 |
| | | | | 2-½ oz., cooked | .53 | 5 to 8 |
| | | Breast of chicken | — | 11 oz., raw | 1.43 | — |
| | | | | 10 oz., raw | 1.30 | — |
| | | | | 9 oz., raw | 1.17 | — |
| | | Chicken leg | — | 11 oz., raw | .73 | — |
| | | | | 10 oz., raw | .66 | — |
| | | | | 9 oz., raw | .59 | — |
| Fowl (5-½ to 6-½ lb.) | N.A. | Chicken pot pie | 25 | 4 oz., cooked | 1.00 | 5 to 6 |
| | | | | 3 oz., cooked | .90 | 7 to 8 |
| Turkey (22 to 26 lb.) | N.A. | Roast turkey or turkey salad | 23 | 6 oz., cooked | 1.63 | 13 to 16 |
| | | | | 4 oz., cooked | 1.08 | 20 to 24 |
| | | | | 3 oz., cooked | .98 | 26 to 32 |
| Duckling (4-½ to 5 lb.) | N.A. | Roast duckling | — | ½ per serving | 2.38 | 2 |
| Broiling chicken | N.A. | Broiled or fried chicken | — | 1 per serving | — | — |
| **FISH** | | | | | | |
| Bass, sea (whole, 1 to 1-¼ lb.) | N.A. | Sea bass, fillet | 48 | 8 oz., raw | 1.04 | 1 |
| | | | | 6 oz., raw | .78 | 1-½ |
| Bass, striped (whole, 8 to 12 lb.) | N.A. | Striped bass, fillet | 40 | 8 oz., raw | 1.25 | 6 to 9 |
| | | | | 6 oz., raw | .94 | 8 to 12 |
| Bluefish (whole, 3 to 8 lb.) | N.A. | Bluefish, fillet | 40 | 8 oz., raw | 1.25 | 2-½ to 6 |
| | | | | 6 oz., raw | .94 | 3 to 8-½ |
| Codfish (whole, 5 to 8 lb.) | N.A. | Codfish, fillet | 40 | 8 oz., raw | 1.25 | 4-½ to 6 |
| | | | | 6 oz., raw | .94 | 6 to 8-½ |
| Flounder (whole, ¾ to 2 lb.) | N.A. | Flounder, fillet | 33 | 8 oz., raw | 1.52 | ½ to 1 |
| | | | | 6 oz., raw | 1.14 | ½ to 1-½ |
| Haddock (whole, 3 to 8 lb.) | N.A. | Haddock, fillet | 36 | 8 oz., raw | 1.39 | 2 to 5-½ |
| | | | | 6 oz., raw | 1.04 | 3 to 7-½ |
| Halibut (whole, 10 to 12 lb.) | N.A. | Halibut, fillet | 55 | 8 oz., raw | .91 | 11 to 13 |
| | | | | 6 oz., raw | .68 | 15 to 17 |
| | | Halibut, steak | 81 | 8 oz., raw | .91 | 16 to 19 |
| | | | | 6 oz., raw | .68 | 21 to 25 |
| Mackerel (whole, 1 to 2 lb.) | N.A. | Mackerel, fillet | 50 | 8 oz., raw | 1.00 | 1 to 2 |
| | | | | 6 oz., raw | .75 | 1 to 2-½ |
| Pompano (whole, 1 to 1-¼ lb.) | N.A. | Pompano | 40 | 8 oz., raw | 1.25 | 1 |
| | | | | 6 oz., raw | .94 | 1-¼ |
| Red snapper (whole, 8 to 12 lb.) | N.A. | Red snapper, fillet | 40 | 8 oz., raw | 1.25 | 6 to 9 |
| | | | | 6 oz., raw | .94 | 8 to 12 |
| Salmon (head off, 8 to 12 lb.) | N.A. | Salmon, fillet | 65 | 8 oz., raw | .77 | 10 to 15 |
| | | | | 6 oz., raw | .58 | 14 to 20 |
| | | Salmon, steak | 85 | 8 oz., raw | .59 | 13 to 20 |
| | | | | 6 oz., raw | .44 | 18 to 27 |
| Scrod (whole, 5 to 7 lb.) | N.A. | Scrod, fillet | 40 | 8 oz., raw | 1.25 | 4-½ to 5 |
| | | | | 6 oz., raw | .94 | 6 to 6-½ |
| Shad (fillet, ½ to 1 lb.) | N.A. | Shad, fillet | 100 | 8 oz., raw | .50 | 1 to 2 |
| | | | | 6 oz., raw | .37 | 1 to 2-½ |
| Shad, roe (pair, 6 to 14 oz.) | N.A. | Shad roe | 100 | 8 oz., raw | .50 | 1 to 1-½ |
| | | | | 6 oz., raw | .37 | 1 to 2 |
| Sole, English (whole, 1 to 2 lb.) | N.A. | Dover sole | 100 | 1-½ lb., raw | 1.50 | 1 |
| | | | | 1 lb., raw | 1.00 | 1 |
| Swordfish (center cut) | N.A. | Swordfish, steak | 90 | 8 oz., raw | .55 | — |
| | | | | 6 oz., raw | .42 | — |
| Whitefish (whole, 2 to 3 lb.) | N.A. | Whitefish, fillet | 50 | 8 oz., raw | 1.00 | 2 to 3 |
| | | | | 6 oz., raw | .75 | 2½ to 4 |

*Table A-1, continued*

| Wholesale Cut | IMPS Code Number | Entree | Yield Factor (percent) | Portion Factors | | |
|---|---|---|---|---|---|---|
| | | | | Size and State | Cost | Average Number of Servings |
| **SHELLFISH** | | | | | | |
| Clams, cherrystone (320 to 360 per bu.) | N.A. | Clams, fresh | 95 | 6 per serving | .019 | 50 to 55 |
| Clams, little neck (600 to 700 per bu.) | N.A. | Little neck clams | 95 | 12 per serving | .019 | 48 to 55 |
| | | | | 6 per serving | .009 | 95 to 110 |
| Crab meat (1 lb. tin) | N.A. | Cocktail or entree | 95 | 5 oz. | .33 | 3 |
| | | | | 3 oz. | .24 | 5 |
| Crab meat (frozen) | N.A. | Cocktail or entree | 95 | 6 oz. | .39 | 2-½ |
| | | | | 4 oz. | .26 | 4 |
| Live lobster | N.A. | Whole lobster | 100 | 2 lb., raw | 2.00 | — |
| | | | | 1-½ lb., raw | 1.50 | — |
| | | | | 1-¼ lb., raw | 1.25 | — |
| | | Lobster cocktail or lobster meat | 20 | 6 oz., cooked | 1.87 | — |
| | | | | 4 oz., cooked | 1.25 | — |
| | | | | 2 oz., cooked | .63 | — |
| Lobster meat (fresh) | N.A. | Lobster cocktail or lobster meat | 95 | 6 oz., cooked | .39 | 2-½ |
| | | | | 4 oz., cooked | .26 | 4 |
| | | | | 2 oz., cooked | .13 | 8 |
| Lobster meat (frozen, 14 oz. can) | N.A. | Lobster meat | 80 | 6 oz. | .47 | 2 |
| | | | | 4 oz. | .31 | 3 |
| Oysters, Chatham | N.A. | Oysters in half shell | 95 | 12 per serving | .52 | 15 to 20 |
| | | | | 6 per serving | .26 | 30 to 40 |
| Scallops, Long Island (480 to 640 per gal.) | N.A. | Cape Cod scallops | 100 | 24 per serving | .04 | 20 to 26 |
| | | | | 18 per serving | .03 | 26 to 35 |
| Scallops, sea (8 lb. per gal.) | N.A. | Sea scallops | 95 | 6 oz., raw | .05 | 20 |
| | | | | 5 oz., raw | .04 | 24 |
| Shrimp (headless, frozen, 16 to 20 lb.) | N.A. | Shrimp cocktail or entree | — | 10 per serving | .55 | 1-½ to 2 |
| | | | | 7 per serving | .39 | 2 to 3 |
| | | | | 5 per serving | .27 | 3 to 4 |

*Note:* N.A. indicates not applicable. Lines indicate that there is too much variation to be specific.

PRINTED IN U.S.A.

## BUTCHER TEST CARD

S.L. 500-2/79

ITEM _180 Striploin_    GRADE _Choice_    Y/15/8 3

PIECES _2_ WEIGHING _39_ LBS. _O_ OZ.    AVERAGE WEIGHT _14 lb. 8 oz_ DATE

TOTAL COST $ _88.15_ AT $_2.25_ PER _lb._    SUPPLIER _—_    HOTEL _—_

| BREAKDOWN | NO. | WEIGHT | | RATIO TO TOTAL WEIGHT | VALUE PER LB. | TOTAL VALUE | | COST OF EACH | | PORTION | | COST PER FACTOR | |
|---|---|---|---|---|---|---|---|---|---|---|---|---|---|
| | | LB. | OZ. | | | | | LB. | OZ. | SIZE | COST | LB. | PORTION |
| Steak Meat | | 18 | 9 | 44.0 | 3.33 | 61 | 81 | 3.33 | 2.08 | 14oz | 2.91 | 1.46 | 1.74 |
| Vein Steaks | | 2 | 4 | 7.8 | 2.40 | 5 | 40 | | | | | | |
| Hamburger | | — | 12 | 2.6 | 1.75 | | 94 | | | | | | |
| Suet (waste) | | 7 | 7 | 25.6 | — | — | | | | | | | |
| | | | | | | | | | | | | | |
| | | | | | | | | | | | | | |
| | | | | | | | | | | | | | |
| | | | | | | | | | | | | | |
| | | | | | | | | | | | | | |
| TOTAL | | 29 | 0 | 100.0 | 2.35 | 68 | 15 | | | | | | |

ITEM    PORTION SIZE _14 oz_ X COST FACTOR PORTION _1.74_

**Figure A-1. Butcher Test Card**

PRINTED IN U.S.A.

## BUTCHER TEST CARD

S.L. 500-2/79

ITEM _Strip loin_  GRADE _____ DATE _____

PIECES _2_ WEIGHING _28_ LBS. _—_ OZ. AVERAGE WEIGHT _____

TOTAL COST $ _7P,_ AT $ _7.5¢_ PER _#_ SUPPLIER _____ HOTEL _____

| BREAKDOWN | NO. | WEIGHT | | RATIO TO TOTAL WEIGHT | VALUE PER LB. | TOTAL VALUE | | COST OF EACH | | | PORTION | | | COST FACTOR PER | |
|---|---|---|---|---|---|---|---|---|---|---|---|---|---|---|---|
| | | LB. | OZ. | | | | | LB. | OZ. | | SIZE | COST | | LB. | PORTION |
| Ready To Cook | | 24 | 4 | 86.1 | 2.84 | 48 95 | | | | | | | | | |
| Trim | | 1 | — | 2.6 | 1.40 | 1 05 | | | | | | | | | |
| Fat | | 3 | — | 10.5 | — | — | | | | | | | | | |
| | | | | | | | | | | | | | | | |
| | | | | | | | | | | | | | | | |
| | | | | | | | | | | | | | | | |
| TOTAL | | 28 | — | 100.0 | | 7P — | | | | | | | | | |

PORTION SIZE _____ PORTION COST FACTOR _____

ITEM _____

**Figure A-2. Butcher Test Card, with Cooking Test**

## COOKING LOSS

Strip loin
2 pc.
28 lbs.
2.50 per #

COOKED _____ HOURS _____ MINUTES AT _____ DEGREES
_____ HOURS _____ MINUTES AT _____ DEGREES

| BREAKDOWN | NO. | WEIGHT LB. | WEIGHT OZ. | RATIO TO TOTAL WEIGHT | VALUE PER LB. | TOTAL VALUE | COST OF EACH LB. | COST OF EACH OZ. | PORTION SIZE | PORTION COST | COST FACTOR PER LB. | COST FACTOR PER PORTION |
|---|---|---|---|---|---|---|---|---|---|---|---|---|
| ORIGINAL WEIGHT | | 28 | - | 100 | 2.50 | 70.- | | | | | | |
| TRIMMED WEIGHT | | 24 | 4 | 86.6 | 2.84 | 68.97 | | | | | | |
| LOSS IN TRIMMING | | 3 | 11 | - | - | 1.05 | | | | | | |
| COOKED WEIGHT | | 16 | - | 57.c | 4.3c | 68.97 | | | | | | |
| LOSS IN COOKING | | 8 | 4 | 34.0 | - | - | | | | | | |
| BONES AND TRIM | | 1 | -0 | - | - | - | | | | | | |
| LOSS IN SLICING | | - | - | | - | - | | | | | | |
| SALABLE MEAT | | 15 | 0 | 53.6 | 4.61 | 68.97 | 4.61 | .79 | 8 oz | 7.34 | 1.87 | .936 |
| SALABLE MEAT | | | | | | | | | | | | |
| REMARKS: | | | | | | | | | | | | |

ITEM     PORTION SIZE 8 oz   COST FACTOR   PORTION COST FACTOR .936

# Appendix B
## Product Testing

In making menu revisions the menu writer replaces items that do not meet expectations in volume, reprices items that should be more attractive at lower or higher prices, and relocates items that can gain improved acceptance if featured in different groupings. Items to replace nonattractive items may come from other menus in the cycle that have proved popular and will bear another featuring, or they may be new items. Some of the new items are standard features on many menus but have not been used on the one being revised. However, in today's world of expanding product choices, especially in the convenience food line, a new menu selection may be one of these. You must test such products before you put them into use. There are usually competitive products and you must choose among them. The best tests are *competitive* and *blind*.

Opportunities for promotion should never be wasted. They exist even in testing new products to add to a restaurant menu. This testing of new products need not be done by the hotel or restaurant personnel exclusively. Food editors of the local newspapers and magazines are delighted to be included in such tests, and they will certainly have something to say in a column about the experience. Regular customers are flattered to be asked to cooperate in such testings. Inviting customers on a random basis is another approach. As the title of this text suggests, they are related functions. Few people buy without incentives. Merchandising and promotions supply incentives. Figure B-1 illustrates a score sheet for use in testing food products. It is designed for use by individuals participating in a test to rate the competitive products, and it can be used for tabulating the results of the individual scores.

### Costing Menus

Appendix A includes an extensive list of cost factors, which help considerably in rapidly costing many entrée items. We mentioned that the costing of recipes was needed to supplement the cost factors in costing menus. Table B-1 consists of packaging information; portion sizes; and portions per pound or per packaging unit for fruits, vegetables, and grocery items (fresh, frozen, canned, dried, and dehydrated). This is an invaluable aid in costing recipes. Also included are standard measures, equivalency measures, and conversion tables.

## Table B-1. Approximate Quantities Required for Some Common Fruits and Vegetables

| Item | Shipping Container | Approximate Net Weight in Pounds, as Purchased per Container | Miscellaneous Shipping or Portioning Data | Portion Size as Served | Portions per Pound as Purchased | Approximate Amount to Purchase as Purchased for 100 Portions |
|---|---|---|---|---|---|---|
| **FRUITS** | | | | | | |
| Apples, whole | Western box, 113's | 44 | | 1 each | 2.3 | 44 lbs. (1 box) |
| Apples, baked | Western box, 88's | 44 | | 1 each | 1.8 | 55 lbs. (1-¼ box) |
| Apples, for pies | Bu. basket | 48 | 20 pies per bu.; 2-½ lbs. used per 9-in. pie | 1 pie slice[a] | 2.5 | 40 lbs. |
| Apples, rings | Western box, 113's | 44 | 5 rings per apple | 2 rings | 6.7 | 15 lbs. (⅓ box) |
| Apple salad, Waldorf | Western box, 113's | 44 | | ½ C. diced | 4.5 | 22 lbs. (½ box) |
| Apple slices, small | Western box, 113's | 44 | 15 slices per apple | 3 slices | 14.0 | 7-½ lbs. (20 apples) |
| Applesauce | Bu. basket | 48 | 16 to 20 qts. per bu. | ½ C. | 2.8 | 36 lbs. (¾ bu.) |
| Apricots, whole | Till, 60's | 5 | 8 to 12 per lb. | 2 each | 5.0 | 20 lbs. (4 till) |
| Apricots, whole | Los Angeles lug | 20 | 100 apricots per lug | 2 each | 2.5 | 40 lbs. (2 lugs) |
| Avocados, half | Flat, 18's | 13 | | half | 2.0 | 52 lbs. (4 flats) |
| Avocados, sliced | Flat, 24's | 13 | 30 slices per avocado used in grapefruit salad | 4 slices | 25.0 | 4 lbs. (8 avocados) |
| Bananas, whole | Box | 40 | 3 per lb. | 1 each | 3.0 | 33 lbs. (.8 box) |
| Bananas, sliced | Box | 40 | 2 to 2-½ C. per lb. or 30 slices per banana | ½ C. | 4.0 | 25 lbs. |
| Blackberries | Crate, 24 qts. | 30 | (use 1 qt. per pie for pies) | ½ C. with cream | 6.0 | 17 lbs. (13 boxes) |
| Blueberries, for pies | Crate, 12 qts. | 8 | ¾ qt. per 9-in. pie | 1 pie slice[a] | 7.0 | 15 lbs. (24 pts.) |
| Blueberries, pudding | Crate, 24 qts. | 30 | | ½ C. | 12.1 | 8-¼ lbs. (6-½ qts.) |
| Cherries, sweet, whole | Lug | 15 | | 12 cherries | 5.0 | 20 lbs. (1-⅓ lug) |
| Cherries, sour, pie | Bushel | 54 | 1-¼ qt. per 9-in. pie | 1 pie slice[a] | 3.3 | 33 lbs. (⅔ bu.) |
| Cranberries, sauce | Box | 25 | Cooked sauce | ¼ C. | 3.5 | 7-½ lbs. |
| Cranberries, sauce | Box | 25 | Chopped raw | ½ C. | 6.0 | 17 lbs. |
| Figs | Flat, 48's | 6 | | 3 medium figs | 2.8 | 36 lbs. (6 boxes) |
| Grapes, Concord, whole | Basket | 6 | | ¼ lb. | 4.0 | 25 lbs. (4 baskets) |
| Grapes, European, whole | Box | 28 | 70 grapes per lb. | ½ C. | 3.6 | 28 lbs. (1 box) |
| Grapefruit | ⅘ bu. carton, 32's | 40 | | Half | 0.8 | 125 lbs. (3-⅛ boxes) |
| Grapefruit, sections | ⅘ bu. carton, 32's | 40 | 12 sections per grapefruit | 6 sections (salad) | 0.8 | 125 lbs. (3-⅛ boxes) |
| Grapefruit, juice | ⅘ bu. carton, 40's | 40 | 6-½ qts. juice per carton | 4 oz. | 1.3 | 80 lbs. (2 boxes) |
| Lemons, juice | ⅘ bu. carton, 85's | 38 | For lemonade: 1 pt. juice per dozen; 8 qts. per carton | 2 oz. juice | 3.6 | 28 lbs. (12 doz.) |
| Lemons, slices | ⅘ bu. carton, 85's | 38 | 8 slices per lemon | 1 slice | 40.0 | 2-¼ lbs. (1 doz.) |
| Lemons, wedges | ⅘ bu. carton, 85's | 38 | 6 wedges per lemon | 1 wedge | 25.0 | 3-½ lbs. (1-½ doz.) |
| Limes, juice | Dozen | | For limeade | 1-¾ oz. (1 lime) | | 9 doz. |
| Limes, wedges | Dozen | | 4 to 5 wedges per lime | 1 wedge | | 2 doz. |
| Melons | | | | | | |
| Cantaloupe[b] | Crate, 45's | 70 to 80 | | half | 8 to 1.0 | 90 lbs. (1.2 crates) |
| Cantaloupe, rings | Crate, 45's | 70 to 80 | 8 rings per melon, each ring used to hold chopped fruit for salad | 1 ring | 4.0 | 22 lbs. (13 melons) |
| Cantaloupe, balls | Crate, 45's | 70 to 80 | 30 balls per melon; used for melon ball cup | 9 balls | 1.8 | 51 lbs. (30 melons) |

| | | | | | | |
|---|---|---|---|---|---|---|
| Cantaloupe, diced | Crate, 45's | 70 to 80 | 10 oz. meat per melon | 3 oz. | 1.8 | 51 lbs. (30 melons) |
| Casaba, wedge[c] | Crate, 8's | 50 | | ⅛ melon | 1.3 | 82 lbs. (13 melons) |
| Watermelon, slice | Individual melon | 35 | | 1 lb. | 1.0 | 100 lbs. (3 melons) |
| Nectarines, whole | Lug, 120's | 20 | | 2 whole | 2.4 | 34 lbs. (1-⅔ lug) |
| Oranges, whole | Carton, 88's | 38 | | 1 whole | 2.3 | 43 lbs. (8-⅓ doz.) |
| Oranges, juice | Carton, 88's | 45 | 10-½ qts. per carton | 4 oz. | 2.2 | 55 lbs. (1-¼ cartons) |
| Oranges, slice | Carton, 88's | 45 | 6 slices per orange for salad | 3 slices | 4.0 w | 26 lbs. (50 oranges) |
| Oranges, sections | Carton, 88's | 38 | 9 sections per orange | 6 sections | 3.6 | 28 lbs. (5-½ doz.) |
| Peaches, sliced | Lug | 20 | 4 per lb.; 6 C. sliced per lb.; 8-½ qts. sliced per lug | ½ C. | 1.7 | 60 lbs. (3 lugs) |
| Peaches, pie | Basket, 20's | 5 to 6 | 3 pies per basket; 2 C. per pie | 1 slice pie[a] | 3.4 | 30 lbs. (5 to 6 baskets or ⅔ bu.) |
| Peaches, pudding | Bushel | 45 | | ½ C. | 5.5 | 18 lbs. |
| Pears, whole | Box, 120's | 40 | 3 per lb. | 1 whole | 3.0 | 34 lbs. |
| Pears, diced | Bushel | 48 | | ½ C. | 3.0 | 32 lbs. (¾ bu.) |
| Persimmons, whole | Flat, 28's | 14 | (6 sections can be obtained per persimmon) | 1 each halved | 2.0 | 50 lbs. (8-⅓ doz.) |
| Pineapple, diced | Crate, 24's | 70 | 20 oz. diced per pineapple | ½ C. | 1.7 | 60 lbs. (20 pineapples) |
| Pineapple, sliced | Crate, 24's | 70 | 10 round slices per pineapple | 1 slice | 3.3 | 30 lbs. (10 pineapples) |
| Plums, whole | Basket, 5 x 5 | 5 | 18 to 24 medium per basket | 3 medium | 4.4 | 22-½ lbs. (4-½ baskets) |
| Plums, pie | Basket, 4 x 5 | 5 | 2-½ to 3 9-in. pies per basket | 1 pie slice[a] | 3.3 | 30 lbs. (6 baskets) |
| Raspberries | Crate, 24 pts. | 18 | | 3 oz. (⅔ C.) | 6.3 | 16 lbs. (20 pts.) |
| Raspberries, pie | Crate, 16 qts. | 20 | ¾ qt. per pie | 1 pie slice[a] | 6.0 | 17 lbs. (13 qts.) |
| Raspberries, cobbler | Crate, 16 qts. | 20 | | ½ C. | 10.0 | 10 lbs. (8 qts.) |
| Rhubarb, hothouse | Flat | 5 | Used for sauce | ½ C. | 4.0 | 20 lbs. |
| Rhubarb, pie | Crate | 40 | 3 C. rhubarb sliced per pie | 1 pie slice[a] | 6.6 | 15 lbs. |
| Strawberries | Crate, 24 qts. | 30 | 6 servings to qt. | ⅔ C. | 5.0 | 20 lbs. (17 qts.) |
| Strawberries, pie | Crate, 24 qts. | 30 | 1 qt. per pie | 1 slice pie[a] | 5.0 | 20 lbs. (17 qts.) |
| Strawberries, sauce | Crate, 24 pts. | 18 | | ¼ C. | 10.0 | 10 lbs. (13 pts.) |
| Tangerines | Crate, 125's | 40 | | 1 tangerine | 3.0 | 35 lbs. |
| Tangerines, sections | Crate, 125's | 40 | 10 sections per tangerine; used for salad | 5 sections | | 16 lbs. (4-¼ doz.) |
| **VEGETABLES** | | | | | | |
| Artichoke, globe | Artichoke box, 72's | 40 | | 1 each | 1.8 | 56 lbs. (8-⅓ doz.) |
| Asparagus | Crate | 29 | 1 bunch is 2-½ lbs. and contains 24 stalks | 3 oz. (3-4 stalks) | 2.6 | 38 lbs. |
| Beans, lima, Fordhook | Bu. basket | 30 | Yields 8 qts. shelled | 3 oz. (½ C.) | 2.1 | 48 lbs. |
| Beans, lima, baby | Bu. basket | 28 | Yields 8 qts. shelled | 3 oz. (½ C.) | 2.2 | 45 lbs. |
| Beans, lima, fava | Bu. basket | 28 | Yields 8 qts. shelled | 3 oz. (½ C.) | 2.1 | 48 lbs. |
| Beans, lima, shelled | Basket | ¼ | | 3 oz. (½ C.) | 5.3 | 19 lbs. |
| Beans, snap | Bu. basket | 30 | | 3 oz. (½ C.) | 4.5 | 22 lbs. |
| Beets, with tops | Crate, 36 bunches | 45 | | 3 oz. (½ C.) | 2.1 | 46 lbs. |
| Beets, topped | Bu. basket | 52 | | 3 oz. (½ C.) | 4.0 | 25 lbs. |
| Beet greens | Bu. basket | 18 | | 3 oz. (½ C.) | 2.3 | 43 lbs. |
| Broccoli | Crate, 18 bunches | 63 | 1 bunch is 2 to 2-½ lbs. | 3 oz. (½ C.) | 2.9 | 35 lbs. |
| Brussels sprouts | Drum | 27 | | 3 oz. (½ C.) | 4.1 | 24 lbs. |
| Cabbage, shredded | Bag | 50 | Cooked 1 lb. shredded cabbage yields 2-½ C. | 3 oz. (½ C.) | 4.0 | 25 lbs. |

*Table B-1, continued*

| Item | Shipping Container | Approximate Net Weight in Pounds, as Purchased per Container | Miscellaneous Shipping or Portioning Data | Portion Size as Served | Portions per Pound as Purchased | Approximate Amount to Purchase as Purchased for 100 Portions |
|---|---|---|---|---|---|---|
| Cabbage, shredded | Bu. basket | 40 | Raw 1 lb. shredded cabbage equals 3-½ C. | ½ C. slaw | 6.5 | 15 lbs. |
| Cabbage, Chinese | Bu. basket | 40 | Diced raw | 2-½ oz. (½ C.) | 4.0 | 25 lbs. |
| Carrots, with tops | Crate, 36's (bunches) | 45 | | 3 oz. (½ C.) | 2.8 | 35 lbs. |
| Carrots, with tops | Crate, 36 bunches | 45 | Strips raw | 2 oz. (4 strips) | 4.3 | 23 lbs. |
| Carrots, topped | Bag | 50 | | 3 oz. (½ C.) | 3.9 | 26 lbs. |
| Carrots, topped | Bag | 50 | Strips raw | 2 oz. (4 strips) | 5.8 | 17 lbs. |
| Cauliflower | Crate, 12's | 24 | | 3 oz. (½ C.) | 2.0 | 50 lbs. |
| Chard | Bu. basket | 18 | | 3 oz. (½ C.) | 3.7 | 27 lbs. |
| Celery | Crate, 30's | 30 | | 3 oz. (½ C.) | 3.7 | 27 lbs. |
| Celery | Crate, 30's | 30 | Stalk pieces raw (small) | 2 oz. (2 stalks) | 6.0 | 17 lbs. |
| Cucumbers, pared | Bu. basket | 45 | 75 cucumbers; 1 9-in. cucumber yields 25 to 30 slices | 2-½ oz. (5 slices) | 5.8 | 18 lbs. |
| Cucumbers, unpared | Bu. basket | 45 | 15 to 25 heads | 2-½ oz. (5 slices) | 7.6 | 13 lbs. |
| Endive, Belgium, chopped | Basket | 5 | | 2 oz. (½ C. or ⅓ head) | 7.1 | 14 lbs. |
| Collards | Bu. basket | 20 | 12 bunches | 3 oz. (½ C.) | 4.3 | 23 lbs. |
| Corn, on the cob | Wirebound crate | 40 | 5 doz. ears each ear approximately 10 to 12 oz. as purchased | 7 oz. (1 ear) | 1.7 | 60-75 lbs. (8-⅓ doz.) |
| Corn, kernels from cob | Wirebound crate | 40 | | 3 oz. (½ C.) | 1.5 | 66 lbs. |
| Eggplant | Bu. basket | 40 | 24 to 30 eggplant; eggplant pared and steamed | 3 oz. (½ C.) | 4.0 | 25 lbs. |
| Eggplant, sliced | Bu. basket | 40 | Unpared, batter-fried | 3-½ oz. (1 slice) | 4.3 | 23 lbs. |
| Escarole, diced, raw | Bu. basket | 25 | 2 doz. heads | 2 oz. | 5.8 | 17 lbs. |
| Chicory, curly leaf | Bu. basket | 22 | 2 doz. heads | 2 oz. | 6.0 | 17 lbs. |
| Kale | Bu. basket | 19 | | 3 oz. (½ C.) | 3.7 | 27 lbs. |
| Kohlrabi | Bu. basket | 22 | 3 to 5 per lb. | 3 oz. (½ C.) | 2.9 | 35 lbs. |
| Leeks | Bu. basket | 18 | 18 bunches, 3 to 5 per bunch | 3 oz. (½ C.) | 2.2 | 45 lbs. |
| Lettuce, iceberg | Carton, 24's | 25 | Chopped raw | 2 oz. (½ C.) | 5.9 | 17 lbs. |
| Lettuce, iceberg | Carton, 24's | 25 | Underliners for salad; 12 per head average | | 11.1 | 9 lbs. |
| Lettuce, leaf | Bu. basket | 18 | Raw | 2 oz. | 5.3 | 19 lbs. |
| Lettuce, Boston or Bibb | Bu. basket | 24 | Raw | 2 oz. | 5.1 | 20 lbs. |
| Mushrooms, chopped | Carton | 1 | | 1 oz. (2 T.) | 11.1 | 9 lbs. |
| Mustard greens | Bu. basket | 18 | | 3 oz. (½ C.) | 3.1 | 32 lbs. |
| Okra | Bu. hamper | 38 | Diced and cooked | 3 oz. (½ C.) | 5.1 | 20 lbs. |
| Onions, dry | Sack | 50 | | 3 oz. (½ C.) | 4.0 | 25 lbs. |
| Onions, dry | Sack | 50 | French-fried | 2-½ oz. | 5.0 | 20 lbs. |
| Onions, dry | Sack | 50 | Raw diced or sliced | 2 oz. | 7.1 | 14 lbs. |
| Onions, green | California ⅔ crate | 50 | 8 doz. bunches to the crate | 1-½ oz. (2 onions) | 3.9 | 25 lbs. |
| Parsnips | Bu. basket | 45 | | 3 oz. (½ C.) | 4.2 | 24 lbs. |
| Peas, green | Bu. basket | 28 | 8 qts. shelled | 3 oz. (½ C.) | 1.9 | 53 lbs. |

| | | | | | | |
|---|---|---|---|---|---|---|
| Peppers, green | Sturdee crate, 1-¼ bu. | 30 | Chopped raw | 1 oz. | 13.1 | 8 lbs. |
| Peppers, green | Sturdee crate, 1-¼ bu. | 30 | Halves steamed | 2 halves | 4.0 | 25 lbs. |
| Potatoes, Irish | Sack | 100 | Whole, pared | 1 (5 oz.) | 2.6 | 39 lbs. |
| Potatoes, Irish | Sack | 100 | Baked | 1 (7 oz.) | 2.1 | 47 lbs. |
| Potatoes, Irish | Sack | 100 | Hash brown | 4 oz. | 2.3 | 44 lbs. |
| Potatoes, Irish | Sack | 100 | Mashed | 4 oz. | 3.3 | 30 lbs. |
| Potatoes, Irish | Sack | 100 | Raw-fried | 4 oz. | 1.7 | 59 lbs. |
| Potatoes, Irish | Sack | 100 | French-fried | 3 oz. | 2.7 | 37 lbs. |
| Potatoes, sweet | Bushel | 50 | 140 potatoes; mashed | 4 oz. | 3.3 | 30 lbs. |
| Potatoes, sweet | Bushel | 50 | Candied | 4 oz. | 3.4 | 30 lbs. |
| Potatoes, sweet | Bushel | 50 | Baked | 6 oz. | 2.7 | 36 lbs. |
| Pumpkin | Bushel | 40 | | 3 oz. (½ C.) | 3.4 | 30 lbs. |
| Radishes | Dozen bunches | 10 | Raw | 1 oz. | 10.0 | 10 lbs. |
| Rutabagas | Bushel | 45 | | 3 oz. (½ C.) | 3.8 | 27 lbs. |
| Spinach | Bushel | 18 | | 3 oz. (½ C.) | 3.2 | 31 lbs. |
| Spinach, trimmed and washed | Bushel | 18 | | 3 oz. (½ C.) | 4.0 | 25 lbs. |
| Squash, summer | Bushel | 40 | | 3 oz. (½ C.) | 4.2 | 24 lbs. |
| Squash, acorn | Bushel | 50 | 50 squash | 1 half | 2.0 | 50 lbs. |
| Squash, Boston marrow | Pound | | Mashed | 3 oz. (½ C.) | 4.1 | 24 lbs. |
| Squash, Boston marrow | Pound | | Baked | 4 oz. | 2.9 | 35 lbs. |
| Squash, butternut | Pound | | Mashed | 3 oz. (½ C.) | 2.4 | 41 lbs. |
| Squash, butternut | Pound | | Baked | 4 oz. | 1.7 | 59 lbs. |
| Squash, Hubbard | Pound | | Mashed | 3 oz. (½ C.) | 3.1 | 33 lbs. |
| Squash, Hubbard | Pound | | Baked | 4 oz. | 2.2 | 46 lbs. |
| Tomatoes, unpeeled | Lug, 5 x 5 | 30 | 75 tomatoes; raw | 3 oz. | 4.9 | 20 lbs. |
| Tomatoes, peeled | Lug, 5 x 5 | 30 | Raw | 3 oz. | 4.7 | 21 lbs. |
| Turnips, topped | Bushel | 50 | | 3 oz. (½ C.) | 4.0 | 25 lbs. |
| Turnips, with tops | Crate, 18's | 36 | | 3 oz. (½ C.) | 3.3 | 31 lbs. |
| Watercress | Basket, 14 bunches | | Raw | 2 oz. | 5.9 | 17 lbs. |

Note: All vegetables cooked unless otherwise noted.

[a] Each pie cut 6.

[b] Yield on honeyball melons is same as for cantaloupes if 45 per crate.

[c] Yield on honeydew and Persian melons is same as for casabas if 8 per crate.

*From U.S. Department of Agriculture*

Product: _____    Date:_____

| Item | First Choice 3 Points | Second Choice 2 Points | Third Choice 1 Point | Total Points |
|------|------------------------|-------------------------|----------------------|--------------|
| A    |                        |                         |                      |              |
| B    |                        |                         |                      |              |
| C    |                        |                         |                      |              |
| D    |                        |                         |                      |              |
| E    |                        |                         |                      |              |
| F    |                        |                         |                      |              |
| G    |                        |                         |                      |              |
| H    |                        |                         |                      |              |
| I    |                        |                         |                      |              |
| J    |                        |                         |                      |              |
| K    |                        |                         |                      |              |

Remarks (Taste, Color, Appearance, etc.): _____

_____

_____

_____

Signature

**Figure B-1.  Score Sheet for Taste-Testing Products**

## Make-up Costs

When you cost menus you should remember that a purpose of doing so is to construct a guide for establishing selling prices. Costing is also an aid in evaluating results; that is, to check food costs to see if desired or budgeted standards are being met. At no times are menu costings to be taken as accounting numbers that must be ledger balanced or evaluated by some other such accounting procedure. Menu costs need be only close approximates to actual costs. Consequently, elaborate, computer-based systems that are purported to account for every crumb are usually extra baggage even if all the computer input is current, which is not often the case in our observations. The entreé cost, as measured by portion cost factors plus make-up costs, gives sufficiently accurate information for cost control purposes.

Table B-2 gives a list of estimated portion costs that can be used in calculating make-up costs.

This short list will be sufficient in a surprisingly large number of cases. Items such as shrimp or crabmeat cocktail, smoked salmon, and marinated herring are easily costed as added items when necessary. A few cents additional is also necessary to cover garnishes with entrées on some items.

To illustrate the use of the "make-up" costs, let us assume that the entrée includes a potato, vegetable, salad, and rolls and butter.

| | |
|---|---|
| Potato | .20* |
| Vegetable | .20 |
| Side salad | .22 |
| Rolls & butter | .16 |
| Subtotal | .78 |
| Plus nonproductive costs 5% | .04 |
| Total | .82 |

* The .20 cost for the potato is about an average of the three potato costs listed – .25 + .18 + .15 = .58 divided by 3 = 19 ⅓ cents or rounded up to .20.

If a striploin costs \$3.00 per pound and a 14-ounce steak is served (recall the cost factor for this item is 1.24), then \$3.00 × 1.24 = \$3.72 + .82 (make-up cost) = \$4.54 (menu cost). If the selling price is \$11.00, the food cost is 41.3 percent. The gross profit (\$11.00 − \$4.54) is \$6.46.

If soup, coffee, and dessert are included for a full table d'hôte meal, you should add the appropriate costs.

The central idea is to keep menu costing simple and rapid to best serve its purposes. With the tools provided in these appendices, you can accomplish this.

### Table B-2. Estimated Portion Costs for Selected Items

| | | | |
|---|---|---|---|
| Fresh fruit cup | .28 | Cole slaw | .08 |
| Stock soup (cup) | .12 | Pies—homemade | .22 |
| Cream soup (cup) | .16 | French pastry | .40 |
| Potato—Baked | .25 | Fruit jello | .15 |
| French fry | .18 | Puddings | .18 |
| Other | .15 | Bought pies (whole) | 2.00 |
| Frozen vegetables | .15 | Ice cream (#12 scoop) | .20 |
| Fresh vegetables | .20 | Rolls and butter | .16 |
| Side salads (dinner) | .22 | Coffee (incl. cream) | .15 |
| Salad bar | .60 | Toast and jelly | .12 |

Nonproductive costs are 5 percent of other items

# Appendix C
# Guides to Food Production and Purchasing

### Table C-1. Amounts of Foods for 50 Servings

| Food and Purchase Unit | Amount per Unit | Approximate Serving Size | Servings per Pound (AP) | Amount to Buy for 50 Servings | Comments |
|---|---|---|---|---|---|
| **MEATS** | | | | | |
| **Beef** | | | | | |
| Rib roast, rolled, boned, 7-rib | 12 to 15 lbs. | 2-½ to 3 oz. cooked (3-½ to 4-½ inch slice) | 2-½ to 3 | 17 to 20 lbs. | May use sirloin butt, boned |
| Rib roast, standing, 7-rib | 16 to 25 lbs. | 3 to 3-½ oz. cooked | 2 to 2-½ | 20 to 25 lbs. | |
| | | 4 to 5 oz. cooked | 1-⅓ to 1-⅔ | 27 to 36 lbs. | |
| Chuck pot roast, bone-in, top | 9 to 12 lbs. | 3 to 3-½ oz. cooked | 2 to 2-½ | 20 to 25 lbs. | |
| Chuck pot roast, bone-in, crossarm | 6 to 9 lbs. | 3 to 3-½ oz. cooked | 2 to 2-½ | 20 to 25 lbs. | Top chuck is more tender |
| Round steak | | 4 to 4-½ oz. clear meat, un-cooked | 2-½ to 3 | 17 to 20 lbs. | Bottom round requires longer cooking than top round |
| Stew, chuck and plate, clear meat | | 5 oz. stew | 3 to 5 | 10 to 17 lbs. | Yield per lb. of raw meat depends on amount of vegetables added to stew |
| **Lamb** | | | | | |
| Leg roast | 6 to 8 lbs. | 2-½ to 3 oz. cooked (3-½ to 4-½ inch slice) | 1-½ to 2-½ | 20 to 35 lbs. | Great variation is due to difficulty in carving |
| Shoulder roast, boneless | 4 to 6 lbs. | 2-½ to 3 oz. cooked (3-½ to 4-½ inch slice) | 2-½ to 3 | 15 to 20 lbs. | |
| Stew, shoulder and brisket, clear meat | | 5 oz. stew | 2-½ to 3 | 17 to 20 lbs. | Yield per lb. of raw meat depends on amount of vegetables added to stew |
| **Pork** | | | | | |
| Loin roast, trimmed | 10 to 12 lbs. | 2-½ to 3 oz. cooked (3-½ to 4-½ inch slice) | 2 to 2-½ | 20 to 25 lbs. | |
| Ham | | | | | |
| Fresh, bone-in | 12 to 15 lbs. | 3 to 3-½ oz. cooked | 2 to 2-½ | 20 to 25 lbs. | |
| Smoked, ten-derized, bone-in | 12 to 15 lbs. | 3 to 3-½ oz. cooked | 2-½ to 3 | 17 to 20 lbs. | Smoked shoulder may be substituted for ground or cubed ham in recipes |
| Canned, boneless, ready-to-eat | 2 to 9 lbs. | 3 oz. cooked | 4 to 5 | 10 to 12 lbs. | |

*Table C-1, continued*

| Food and Purchase Unit | Amount per Unit | Approximate Serving Size | Servings per Pound (AP) | Amount to Buy for 50 Servings | Comments |
|---|---|---|---|---|---|
| Loaf or extended patties | 1 lb. raw meat measures 2 C. packed | 4 to 4-½ oz. cooked | 3-½ to 4 | 12 to 15 lbs. | May use one kind of meat or a combination |
| **Bacon** | | | | | |
| Sliced | 30 to 36 medium or 15 to 20 wide strips per lb. | 3 strips | 10 to 12 | 5 to 6 lbs. | 1 lb. cooked and diced measures 1-½ C. |
| | | 2 strips | 7 to 10 | 5 to 7 lbs. | |
| Canadian, sliced | 12 to 16 slices per lb. | 2 or 3 slices | 5 to 8 | 7 to 10 lbs. | |
| **Liver** | | 4 oz. cooked | 3 to 4 | 13 to 17 lbs. | |
| **Sausage** | | | | | |
| Links | 8 to 9 large per lb. | 3 links | 3 | 17 to 20 lbs. | Yield varies with proportion of fat that fries out in cooking |
| Cakes | | 6 to 8 oz. raw (2 cakes) | 2 to 2-½ | 20 to 25 lbs. | |
| **Wieners** | 8 to 10 per lb. | 2 wieners | 4 to 5 | 10 to 11-½ lbs. | |
| **POULTRY** | | | | | |
| **Chicken** | | | | | |
| Fryers, dressed | 2-½ to 3-½ lbs. | ¼ fryer | | 35 to 40 lbs. | Dressed means bled and with feathers removed |
| Fryers, eviscerated | 1-¾ to 2-½ lbs. | ¼ fryer | | 25 to 30 lbs. | Eviscerated means ready to cook |
| **Fowl** | | | | | |
| For fricassee, dressed | 3-½ to 6 lbs. | 4 to 6 oz. bone-in | 1 to 1-½ | 35 to 50 lbs. | |
| For fricassee, eviscerated | 2-½ to 4-½ lbs. | 4 to 6 oz. bone-in | 1-¼ to 2 | 25 to 35 lbs. | |
| For dishes containing cut-up cooked meat, dressed | | 1 to 2 oz. clear meat | 2-½ to 3 | 17 to 20 lbs. | 4 lbs. raw yield about 1 lb. cooked boned meat |
| For dishes containing cut-up cooked meat, eviscerated | | 1 to 2 oz. clear meat | 3 to 4 | 13 to 17 lbs. | 3 lbs. raw yield about 1 lb. cooked boned meat |
| **Turkey** | | | | | |
| Young tom, dressed | 12 to 23 lbs. | 2 to 2-½ oz. clear meat | 1 to 1-½ | 35 to 50 lbs. | 1 lb. raw yields 4 to 5 oz. sliced clear meat or 5 to 6 oz. cooked boned meat |
| Young tom, eviscerated | 10 to 18 lbs. | 2 to 2-½ oz. clear meat | 1-½ to 2 | 25 to 35 lbs. | Yields of all turkeys depend on type and size of bird: broad-breast and larger birds yield more than standard type and smaller birds |
| Old tom, dressed | 20 to 30 lbs. | 2 to 2-½ oz. clear meat | 1 to 1-½ | 35 to 50 lbs. | |
| Old tom, eviscerated | 16 to 25 lbs. | 2 to 2-½ oz. clear meat | 1-½ to 2 | 25 to 35 lbs. | |
| **Veal** | | | | | |
| Leg roast | 15 to 20 lbs. | 3 to 3-½ oz. cooked | 1-½ to 2-½ | 20 to 35 lbs. | Great variation is due to difficulty in carving |
| Shoulder roast, boneless | 8 to 14 lbs. | 3 to 3-½ oz. cooked | 2-½ to 3 | 17 to 20 lbs. | |
| Cutlet | | 4 to 5 oz. uncooked | 3 to 4 | 12 to 17 lbs. | May use frozen cutlets |
| **Ground Meat** | | | | | |
| Patties | 1 lb. raw meat measures 2 C. packed | 4 to 5 oz. uncooked (1 or 2 patties) | 2-½ to 3 | 17 to 20 lbs. | May use one kind of meat only or combinations, such as 10 lbs. beef and 5 lbs. veal or pork, or 10 lbs. fresh pork and 5 lbs. smoked ham |

*Table C-1, continued*

| Food and Purchase Unit | Amount per Unit | Approximate Serving Size | Servings per Pound (AP) | Amount to Buy for 50 Servings | Comments |
|---|---|---|---|---|---|
| **FISH** | | | | | |
| **Fresh or Frozen Fillets** | | 4 to 5 oz. | 3 to 4. | 14 to 17 lbs. | |
| **Oysters** | | | | | |
| For frying | 24 to 40 large per qt. | 4 to 6 oysters | | 7 to 8 qts. | |
| For scalloping | 60 to 100 small per qt. | | | 4 to 5 qts. | |
| For stew | 60 to 100 small per qt. | 4 to 6 oysters | | 3 qts. | |
| **VEGETABLES\*** | | | | | |
| Asparagus, by lb. or in bunches | 2 to 2-½ lbs. per bunch; 32 to 40 stalks per bunch | 3 oz. or 4 to 5 stalks | 3 to 4 | 12 to 16 lbs. | Yield may be increased if tough part of stalk is peeled |
| Beans, green or wax, by lb. | 1 lb. measures 1 qt. whole or 3 C. cut up | 2-½ to 3 oz. or ½ C. | 4 to 5 | 10 to 12 lbs. | |
| Beets | | | | | |
| by lb. | 4 medium per lb. (1-½ to 2 C. cooked and diced) | 2-½ to 3 oz. or ½ C. | 4 to 4-½ | 12 to 14 lbs. | |
| by bunch | 4 to 6 medium per bunch | 2-½ to 3 oz. or ½ C. | 4 to 4-½ | 12 to 14 lbs. | |
| Broccoli, by lb. or in bunches | 1-½ to 2-½ lbs. per bunch | 2-½ to 3 oz. | 2-½ to 3 | 17 to 20 lbs. | Yield may be increased if tough part of stalk is peeled |
| Brussels sprouts, by qt. berry basket | 1 to 1-¼ lbs. per basket | 2-½ to 3 oz. | 4 to 6 | 10 baskets or 12 lbs. | |
| Cabbage, by lb. | | | | | |
| Raw | 4 to 6 C. shredded per lb. | 1 to 2 oz. | 8 | 8 to 10 lbs. | |
| Cooked | 2 qts. raw shredded per lb. | 2-½ to 3 oz. or ½ C. | 4 | 12 to 15 lbs. | |
| Carrots, by lb. | | | | | |
| Cooked | 6 medium per lb. | 2-½ to 3 oz. or ½ C. | 3 to 4 | 14 to 16 lbs. | 1 lb. raw yields 2 C. cooked and diced; after cooking, 3-¼ C. diced weigh 1 lb. |
| Raw | | strips, 2 to 3 inches long | | 2 to 2-½ lbs. | 3-½ C. diced raw weigh 1 lb. |
| Cauliflower, by head, trimmed | 1 to 3 lbs. per head | 3 oz. or ½ C | 2 | 28 to 32 lbs. | A 3-lb. head yields 3 qts. raw flowerets |
| Celery, pascal, by bunch | | | | | |
| Cooked | 1 medium bunch weighs 2 lbs. | 2-½ to 3 oz. or ½ C. | 3 to 4 | 7 to 10 bunches | 1 medium bunch yields 1-½ qts. raw diced |
| Raw | 1 medium bunch weighs 2 lbs. | | 8 to 10 | 3 to 4 bunches | 1 qt. raw diced weighs 1 lb. |
| Cucumbers, single | 1 cucumber weighs 10 to 14 oz. | 5 to 7 slices (¼ C.) | | 8 to 9 cucumbers | 1 medium yields 1-¾ to 2 C. of peeled slices |

*Table C-1, continued*

| Food and Purchase Unit | Amount per Unit | Approximate Serving Size | Servings per Pound (AP) | Amount to Buy for 50 Servings | Comments |
|---|---|---|---|---|---|
| Eggplant, single or by dozen | 1 small eggplant weighs 1 lb. | 2-½ oz. (1-½ slices) | 4 | 10 to 12 | A 1-lb. eggplant yields 8 to 9 slices |
| Lettuce, by head | 1 medium head weighs 1-½ to 2-½ lbs. before trimming | ⅙ to ⅛ head | | 4 to 5 heads for garnish; 6 to 8 heads for salad | 10 to 12 salad leaves per head; 1 head untrimmed yields 1-½ to 2 qts. shredded; 2 qts. shredded weigh 1 lb. |
| Mushrooms, by lb. or basket | 1 basket weighs 3 lbs. | | | | 1 lb. raw sliced tops and stems measures 7 C.; 2-½ C. sautéed weigh 1 lb. |
| Onions, by lb. | 4 to 6 medium per lb. | 3 to 3-½ oz. or ½ C. | 3 to 4 | 14 to 16 lbs. | 1 lb. yields 2-½ to 3 C. chopped; 1 C. chopped weighs 5 oz.; 1 C. sliced weighs 4 oz. |
| Parsley, by bunch | 1 bunch weighs 1 oz. | | | | 1 medium bunch yields ¼ C. finely chopped; 1 C. chopped weighs 3 oz. |
| Parsnips, by lb. | 3 to 4 medium per lb. | 2-½ to 3 oz. | 3 to 4 | 15 lbs. | |
| Peppers, single or by lb. | 5 to 7 per lb. | | | | 1 lb. yields 2 C. finely diced; 1 C. chopped weighs 5 oz. |
| Potatoes, sweet, by lb. | 3 medium per lb. | 3-½ to 4 oz. | 2-½ to 3 | 17 to 20 lbs. | |
| Potatoes, white by lb. | 3 medium per lb. | 4 to 4-½ oz. or ½ C. mashed or creamed | 2 to 3 | 15 to 20 lbs. | 1 lb. yields 2-¼ C. diced |
| by bushel | 1 bu. weighs 60 lbs. | 4 to 4-½ oz. or ½ C. | 2 to 3 | | |
| by bag | 1 bag weighs 50 lbs. | 4 to 4-½ oz. or ½ C. | 2 to 3 | | |
| Rutabagas, by lb. | 1 to 2 per lb. | 3 to 3-½ oz. or ½ C. | 2 to 2-½ | 20 to 25 lbs. | 1 lb. yields 1-½ C. mashed or 2-½ C. diced |
| Spinach, by bag or bushel | 10 or 20 oz. per bag | 3 to 3-½ oz. or ½ C. | 2-½ to 3 | 17 to 20 lbs. home-grown or 12 to 15 10-oz. bags cleaned | A 10 oz. bag yields 2 qts. raw, coarsely chopped for salad |
| Squash Summer, by lb. | | 2-½ to 3 oz. or ½ C. | 3 to 4 | 13 to 16 lbs. | |
| Winter, by lb. | | 3 oz. or ½ C. mashed | 2 | 25 to 30 lbs. | |
| Tomatoes, by lb., 8 lb. basket, or 10-lb. carton | 3 to 4 medium per lb. | 3 slices raw | 5 (sliced) | 10 lbs. for slicing | 1 lb. yields 2 C. diced or cut in wedges |
| Turnips, white, by lb. | | 3 oz. or ½ C. | 3 to 4 | 15 to 20 lbs. | |

**FRUITS***

| | | | | | |
|---|---|---|---|---|---|
| Apples by lb. | 2 to 3 medium per lb. | ½ C. sauce | | 15 to 20 lbs. for sauce or pie | 1 lb. before peeling yields 3 C. diced or sliced; 4-½ to 5 C. pared, diced, or sliced weigh 1 lb. |
| by pk. | 1 pk. weighs 12 lbs. | ½ C. sauce | | 15 to 20 lbs. | 1 pk. (12 lbs.) makes 4 to 5 pies, 4 to 5 qts. of sauce, 7 to 8 qts. of raw cubes |

Table C-1, continued

| Food and Purchase Unit | Amount per Unit | Approximate Serving Size | Servings per Pound (AP) | Amount to Buy for 50 Servings | Comments |
|---|---|---|---|---|---|
| **Apples (continued)** | | | | | |
| by bu. | 1 bu. weighs 48 lbs. | ½ C. sauce | | 15 to 20 lbs. | |
| by box | 1 box contains 80 to 100 large or 113 to 138 medium | ½ C. sauce | | 15 to 20 lbs. | |
| Bananas, by lb. or dozen | 3 to 4 medium per lb. | 1 small | 3 to 4 | 15 lbs. | 1 lb. yields 2 to 2-½ C. sliced thin or 1-¼ C. mashed; for 1 C. sliced or diced, use 1-⅓ medium; for 1 C. mashed, use 2-¼ medium |
| Cranberries, by lb. | 1 lb. measures 1 to 1-¼ qts. | ¼ C. sauce | 12 to 14 for sauce | 4 lbs. for sauce | 1 lb. makes 3 to 3-½ C. sauce or 2-¾ C. jelly |
| Grapefruit, by dozen, box, or half-box | 54 to 70 medium per box; 80 to 126 small per box | | | | 1 medium-small yields 10 to 12 sections or 1-¾ C. broken sections |
| Lemons, by dozen, box, or half-box | 210 to 250 large per box; 300 to 360 medium per box; 392 to 432 small per box | | | 25 to 30 lemons (1-¼ qts. juice) for 50 glasses of lemon-ade | 1 medium yields ¼ C. juice and 1 t. grated rind; 4 to 5 medium yield 1 C. juice |
| Oranges, by dozen, box, or half-box | 80 to 126 large per box; 150 to 200 medium per box; 216 to 288 small per box | ½ C. sections | | 40 to 50 oranges | Use medium oranges for table and salad; 1 medium yields 12 sections and ½ to ⅔ C. diced |
| **Peaches** | | | | | |
| by lb. | 3 to 5 per lb. | 3 oz. or ½ C. | 4 | 10 to 12 lbs. for slicing | 1 lb. yields 2 C. peeled and diced |
| by pk. | 1 pk. weighs 12-½ lbs. | 3 oz. or ½ C. | 4 | | |
| by ½ bu. | ½ bu. weighs 25 lbs. | 3 oz. or ½ C. | 4 | | |
| Pineapple, single | 1 medium weighs 2 lbs. | ½ C. cubed | | 5 medium | 1 medium yields 3 to 3-½ C. peeled and cubed |
| Rhubarb, fresh, by lb. | | ½ C. sauce | 5 | 10 lbs. | 10 lbs. yield 6 qts. sauce |
| Strawberries, by qt. | 1 qt. yields 3 C. hulled | ½ C. | | 10 to 13 qts. | 1 qt. yields 4 to 5 servings of fruit |
| | 1 qt. yields 1 pt. hulled and crushed | ⅓ C. for shortcake | | 8 to 10 qts. | 1 qt. yields 6 servings of sauce for shortcake |
| | | | | | |
| **STAPLES\*** | | | | | |
| Cocoa | 1 lb. measures 4 C.; 1 C. weighs 4 oz. | | | 2 C. (½ lb.) for 50 C. bev-erage (2-½ gals.) | |
| Rice | 1 lb. raw mea-sures 2-⅛ C. | 1 no. 16 or no. 12 scoop | 15 to 20 | 2-½ to 3 lbs. | 1 lb. cooked measures 1-¾ qts. |
| **Sugar** | | | | | |
| Cubes | 50 to 60 large or 100 to 120 small cubes per lb. | 1 large or 2 small | 50 to 60 | ¾ to 1 lb. | |
| Granulated | 1 lb. measures 2-⅛ C.; 1 C. weighs 7 oz. | 1-½ t. to sweeten coffee | 50 to 60 | ¾ to 1 lb. | |

*Table C-1, continued*

| Food and Purchase Unit | Amount per Unit | Approximate Serving Size | Servings per Pound (AP) | Amount to Buy for 50 Servings | Comments |
|---|---|---|---|---|---|
| **Bread, by loaf** | | | | | |
| White and whole wheat | 1-lb. loaf yields 18 slices | 1-½ slices to accompany meal | 12 | 4 loaves | |
| | 2-lb. club loaf yields 24 slices | 1-½ slices | 8 | 3 loaves | |
| | 2-lb. Pullman (sandwich) loaf yields 36 slices | 1-½ slices | 12 | 2 loaves | |
| Rye | 1-lb. loaf yields 17 slices | 1-½ slices | 11 | 4-½ loaves | |
| | 2-lb. short loaf yields 29 slices | 1-½ slices | 10 | 5 loaves | |
| | 2-lb. long loaf yields 36 slices | 1-½ slices | 12 | 2 loaves | |
| **Butter** | 1 lb. measures 2 C.; 1 oz. measures 2 T. | | 48 to 60 | 1 to 1-½ lbs. | Available in wholesale units cut into 48 to 90 pieces per lb.; 60 count gives average size cut |
| **Cheese** | | | | | |
| Brick | 1 brick weighs 5 lbs. | 1-oz. thin slices for sandwiches | 16 | 3-¼ lbs. for sandwiches | |
| | | 4/5-oz. cubes for pie | 20 | 2-½ lbs. for pie | |
| Cottage | 1 lb. measures 2 C. | no. 10 scoop (approximately ½ C.) | 8 to 9 | 6 lbs. | 1 lb. yields 12 to 13 of the no. 16 scoops and 25 of the no. 30 scoops |
| **Coffee** | | | | | |
| Ground | 1 lb. drip grind measures 5 C. | | | 1 lb. | Makes 50 C. when added to 2-½ gals. of water |
| Instant | | | | 2-½ C. | Add to 2-½ gals. of water |
| **Cream** | | | | | |
| Heavy (40 percent) to whip | | 1 rounded T. | | 1 pt. (yields 1 qt. whipped) | Doubles its volume in whipping |
| Light (20 percent) or top milk for coffee | 1 qt. yields 64 T. | 1-½ T. | | 1-¼ qts. | |
| **Fruit or vegetable juice** | 1 46-oz. can measures approximately 1-½ qts. | 4-oz. glass or ½ C. | | 4-⅓ 46-oz. cans (6-½ qts.) | |
| | 1 no. 10 can measures 13 C. or 3-¼ qts. | 4-oz. glass or ½ C. | | 2 no. 10 cans (6-½ qts.) | |
| **Fruits, dried** | | | | | |
| Prunes | 1 lb. contains 40 to 50 medium | 4 to 5 for stewed fruit | | 5 to 6 lbs. | |
| Honey | 1 lb. measures 1-⅓ C. | 2 T. | | 5 lbs. | |
| **Ice cream** | | | | | |
| Brick | 1-qt. brick cuts 6 to 8 slices | 1 slice | | 7 to 9 bricks | Available in slices individually wrapped |
| Bulk, by gals. | | no. 10 scoop | | 2 gals. | 1 gal. yields 25 to 30 servings |
| **Lemonade** | | 8-oz. glass (¾ C.) | | 2-½ gals. (25 to 30 lemons for 1-¼ qts. of juice) | |
| **Peanut butter** | 1 lb. measures 1-¾ C. | | | 4 lbs. for sandwiches | |
| **Potato chips** | 1 lb. measures 5 qts. | ¾ to 1 oz. | | 2 lbs. | |

*Table C-1, continued*

| Food and Purchase Unit | Amount per Unit | Approximate Serving Size | Servings per Pound (AP) | Amount to Buy for 50 Servings | Comments |
|---|---|---|---|---|---|
| Salad dressings Mayonnaise, by qt. | | 1 T. for salad | | 1 to 1-½ qts. for mixed salads; 3 to 4 C. for garnish | |
| French | | | | ¾ to 1 qt. | |
| Sandwiches | | | | | |
| Bread | 2 lb. (14-in.) loaf cut 30 to 35 medium or 35 to 40 very thin slices | 2 slices | 7 to 8 medium; 9 to 10 very thin | 3 loaves | |
| Butter, by lb. | | spread on 1 slice | | ¾ lb. | |
| | | spread on 2 slices | | 1-½ lbs. | |
| Fillings | | 2 T. or no. 30 scoop | | 1-¾ to 2 qts. | |
| | | 3 T. or no. 24 scoop | | 2-½ to 3 qts. | |
| Tea, iced | 1 lb. measures 6 C. | | | 3 oz. | Makes 50 glasses when added to 2-½ gals. water and chipped ice |
| Vegetables, dried | | | | | |
| Beans, navy | 1 lb. measures 2-½ C. | | | 5 to 6 lbs. | |

*From Marion Wood Crosby and Katharine W. Harris, Purchasing Food for 50 Servings, rev. ed., Cornell Extension Bulletin no. 803 (Ithaca: New York State College of Home Economics, 1963). Reprinted with permission of Cornell Cooperative Extension.*

*Note:* Can be used for hotel and restaurant food service.

## Table C-2. Egg Equivalency Table

Fresh or frozen:
1 whole egg. . . . . . . . . . . . . . . . . . . . . . . = 3 T.
8 whole eggs. . . . . . . . . . . . . . . . . . . . . = 1½ C.

Fresh or frozen:
16 egg whites. . . . . . . . . . . . . . . . . . . . = 1 pt.
24 egg yolks. . . . . . . . . . . . . . . . . . . . . = 1 pt.

Dried whole egg powder:
Sifted. . . . . . . . . . . . . . . . . . . . . . . ½ oz. or 2½ T.
+ Water. . . . . . . . . . . . . . . . . . . . . . . . . . . 2½ T.
= Number of eggs. . . . . . . . . . . . . . . . . . . . . 1

Dried whole egg powder:
Sifted. . . . . . . . . . . . . . . . . . . . . . . 4 oz. or 1⅓ C.
+ Water. . . . . . . . . . . . . . . . . . . . . . . . . . 1⅓ C.
= Number of eggs. . . . . . . . . . . . . . . . . . . . . 8

Dried whole egg powder:
Sifted. . . . . . . . . . . . . . . . . . . . . . . 6 oz. or 1 pt.
+ Water. . . . . . . . . . . . . . . . . . . . . . . . . . 1 pt.
= Number of eggs. . . . . . . . . . . . . . . . . . . . . 12

Dried whole egg powder:
Sifted. . . . . . . . . . . . . . . . . . . . . . 12 oz. or 1 qt.
+ Water. . . . . . . . . . . . . . . . . . . . . . . . . . 1 qt.
= Number of eggs. . . . . . . . . . . . . . . . . . . . . 24

*From Recipes and Menus for All Seasons (Chicago: John Sexton and Co., n.d.). Reprinted with permission.*

## Table C-3. Milk Conversion Table

Nonfat dry milk. . . . . . . . . . . . . . . . . . . . 13 oz.
+ Water. . . . . . . . . . . . . . . . . . . . . . . . . 7¾ pts.
= Liquid skim milk. . . . . . . . . . . . . . . . . . . . 1 gal.

Nonfat dry milk solids. . . . . . . . . . . . . . . . 1½ oz.
+ Water. . . . . . . . . . . . . . . . . . . . . . . . . 14½ oz.
= Liquid skim milk. . . . . . . . . . . . . . . . . . . . 1 lb.

Nonfat dry milk. . . . . . . . . . . . . . . . . . . . 3¼ oz.
Butter. . . . . . . . . . . . . . . . . . . . . . . . . . 1⅔ oz.
+ Water. . . . . . . . . . . . . . . . . . . . . . . . . . 1 qt.
= Whole milk. . . . . . . . . . . . . . . . . . . . . . . 1 qt.

Dry whole milk. . . . . . . . . . . . . . . . . . . . . 1 lb.
+ Water. . . . . . . . . . . . . . . . . . . . . . . . . 7¼ pts.
= Liquid whole milk. . . . . . . . . . . . . . . . . . . 1 gal.

Dry whole milk. . . . . . . . . . . . . . . . . . . . . 2 oz.
+ Water. . . . . . . . . . . . . . . . . . . . . . . . . 14 oz.
= Liquid whole milk. . . . . . . . . . . . . . . . . . . 1 lb.

Dry whole milk. . . . . . . . . . . . . . . . . . . . . 4½ oz.
Sugar. . . . . . . . . . . . . . . . . . . . . . . . . . 6½ oz.
+ Water. . . . . . . . . . . . . . . . . . . . . . . . . 5 oz.
= Sweetened condensed whole milk. . . . . . . . . 1 lb.

Nonfat dry milk solids. . . . . . . . . . . . . . . . 4 oz.
Sugar. . . . . . . . . . . . . . . . . . . . . . . . . . 7 oz.
+ Water. . . . . . . . . . . . . . . . . . . . . . . . . 5 oz.
= Sweetened condensed skim milk. . . . . . . . . 1 lb.

*From Recipes and Menus for·All Seasons (Chicago: John Sexton and Co., n.d.). Reprinted with permission.*

## Table C-4. Dipper Equivalency Measures

| Dipper Size | Equivalent |
| --- | --- |
| No. 8. | ½ C. or 8 T. |
| No. 10. | ⅖ C. or 6 T. |
| No. 12. | ⅓ C. or 5⅔ T. |
| No. 16. | ¼ C. or 4 T. |
| No. 20. | ⅕ C. or 3⅓ T. |
| No. 24. | ⅙ C. or 2⅔ T. |
| No. 30. | ⅛ C. or 2 T. |

*From Recipes and Menus for All Seasons (Chicago: John Sexton and Co., n.d.). Reprinted with permission.*

## Table C-5. Common Container Sizes

| Industry Term | Approximate Amount Contained | | | Principal Content | Approximate Number of Servings |
|---|---|---|---|---|---|
| | Net Weight | Fluid Measure | Cups | | |
| 8 oz. | 8 oz. | | 1 | Fruits, vegetables, specialties[a] for small families | 2 |
| Picnic | 10-½ to 12 oz. | | 1-¼ | Mainly condensed soups. Some fruits, vegetables, meat, fish, specialties[a] | 2 to 3 |
| 12 oz. (vacuum) | 12 oz. | | 1-½ | Principally for vacuum-pack corn | 3 to 4 |
| No. 300 | 14 to 16 oz. (14 oz. to 1 lb.) | | 1-¾ | Pork and beans, baked beans, meat products, cranberry sauce, blueberries, specialties[a] | 3 to 4 |
| No. 303 | 16 to 17 oz. (1 lb. to lb. 1 oz.) | | 2 | Principal size for fruits and vegetables. Some meat products, ready-to-serve soups, specialties[a] | 4 |
| No. 2 | 20 oz. (1 lb. 4 oz.) | 18 fl. oz. (1 pt. 2 fl. oz.) | 2-½ | Juices,[b] ready-to-serve soups, some specialties.[a] pineapple, apple slices. No longer in popular use for most fruits and vegetables | 5 |
| No. 2-½ | 27 to 29 oz. (1 lb. 11 oz. to 1 lb. 13 oz.) | | 3-½ | Fruits, some vegetables (pumpkin, sauerkraut, spinach and other greens, tomatoes) | 5 to 7 |
| No. 3 | 33 oz. (2 lbs. 1 oz.) | | 4 | Some juices | |
| No. 3 cylinder or 46 fl. oz. | 51 oz. (3 lbs. 3 oz.) | 46 fl. oz. (1 qt. 14 fl. oz.) | 5-¾ | Fruit and vegetable juices,[b] pork and beans. Institutional size for condensed soups, some vegetables | 10 to 12 |
| No. 5 | 56 oz. (3 lbs. 8 oz.) | | 7 | | |
| No. 10 | 6-½ lbs. to 7 lbs. 5 oz. | | 12 to 13 | Institutional size for fruits, vegetables, and some other foods | 25 |

*Notes:* Strained and homogenized foods for infants, and chopped junior foods for infants, and chopped junior foods, come in small jars and cans suitable for the smaller servings used. The weight is given on the label. Meats, poultry, and fish and seafood are almost entirely advertised and sold under weight terminology. The labels of cans or jars of identical size may show a net weight for one product that differs slightly from the net weight on the label of another product, due to the difference in the density of the food. An example would be pork and beans (1 lb.), blueberries (14 oz.), in the same size can.

[a] A specialty is usually a food combination such as macaroni, spaghetti, Spanish-style rice, Mexican-type foods, Chinese foods, tomato aspic, etc.

[b] Juices are now being packed in a number of can sizes.

*Sources:* National Canners Association; *Recipes and Menus for All Seasons* (Chicago: John Sexton and Co., n.d.).

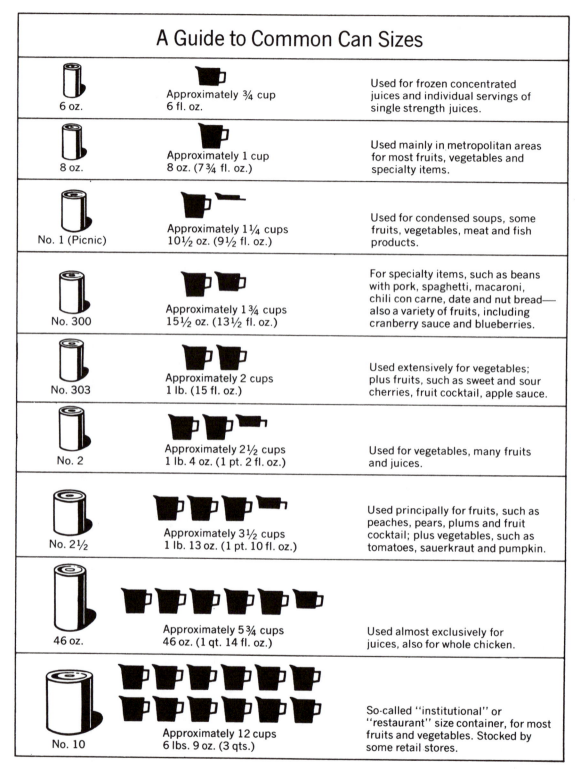

## A Guide to Common Can Sizes

| | | |
|---|---|---|
| 6 oz. | Approximately ¾ cup 6 fl. oz. | Used for frozen concentrated juices and individual servings of single strength juices. |
| 8 oz. | Approximately 1 cup 8 oz. (7¾ fl. oz.) | Used mainly in metropolitan areas for most fruits, vegetables and specialty items. |
| No. 1 (Picnic) | Approximately 1¼ cups 10½ oz. (9½ fl. oz.) | Used for condensed soups, some fruits, vegetables, meat and fish products. |
| No. 300 | Approximately 1¾ cups 15½ oz. (13½ fl. oz.) | For specialty items, such as beans with pork, spaghetti, macaroni, chili con carne, date and nut bread— also a variety of fruits, including cranberry sauce and blueberries. |
| No. 303 | Approximately 2 cups 1 lb. (15 fl. oz.) | Used extensively for vegetables; plus fruits, such as sweet and sour cherries, fruit cocktail, apple sauce. |
| No. 2 | Approximately 2½ cups 1 lb. 4 oz. (1 pt. 2 fl. oz.) | Used for vegetables, many fruits and juices. |
| No. 2½ | Approximately 3½ cups 1 lb. 13 oz. (1 pt. 10 fl. oz.) | Used principally for fruits, such as peaches, pears, plums and fruit cocktail; plus vegetables, such as tomatoes, sauerkraut and pumpkin. |
| 46 oz. | Approximately 5¾ cups 46 oz. (1 qt. 14 fl. oz.) | Used almost exclusively for juices, also for whole chicken. |
| No. 10 | Approximately 12 cups 6 lbs. 9 oz. (3 qts.) | So-called "institutional" or "restaurant" size container, for most fruits and vegetables. Stocked by some retail stores. |

**Figure C-1.  Average Container Sizes**

*From American Can Company, Greenwich, Connecticut*

## Table C-6. Food Serving Chart—Canned, Frozen, Preserved

### CANNED VEGETABLES

| Cans per Case and Container Size | Food | Style | Type | Approximate Net Weight | Range in Contents per Container | Suggested Portion per Serving | Approximate Portions per Container | Approximate Drained Weight | Miscellaneous Information |
|---|---|---|---|---|---|---|---|---|---|
| 6/5 squat | Asparagus | Colossal all-green spears | California | 4 lbs. 1 oz. | 50 to 60 | 2 spears | 25 to 30 | 2 lbs. 14 ozs. | |
| 6/5 squat | Asparagus | Mammoth large all-green spears | California | 4 lbs. 1 oz. | 85 to 95 | 3 to 4 spears | 21 to 34 | 2 lbs. 14 ozs. | |
| 6/5 squat | Asparagus | Blended mammoth large all-green spears | California | 4 lbs. 1 oz. | 80 to 85 | 3 to 4 spears | 20 to 26 | 2 lbs. 8 ozs. | About 25 percent tips |
| 6/10 | Asparagus | Cut, all-green | Michigan | 6 lbs. 5 ozs. | 300 to 375 | ½ C. | 24 | 3 lbs. 15 ozs. | |
| 6/5 squat | Asparagus | Colossal whole green-tipped and white | California | 4 lbs. 1 oz. | 50 to 60 | 3 to 4 spears | 12 to 15 | 2 lbs. 10 ozs. | |
| 6/5 squat | Asparagus | Mammoth whole green-tipped and white | California | 4 lbs. 1 oz. | 60 to 70 | 4 to 5 spears | 12 to 14 | 2 lbs. 14 ozs. | |
| 6/10 | Beans, green | Tiny whole | Northwest Blue Lake | 6 lbs. 5 ozs. | | ½ C. | 29 | 3 lbs. 13 ozs. | No. 1 sieve |
| 6/10 | Beans, green | Small whole | Northwest Blue Lake | 6 lbs. 5 ozs. | | ½ C. | 30 | 3 lbs. 13 ozs. | No. 2 sieve |
| 6/10 | Beans, green | Salad whole | Northwest Blue Lake | 6 lbs. 5 ozs. | 420 | 12 to 14 pieces | 30 to 35 | 3 lbs. 13 ozs. | No. 3 sieve |
| 6/5 squat | Beans, green | Whole vertical pack | Northwest Blue Lake | 4 lbs. | 200 | 10 to 12 pieces | 18 to 20 | 2 lbs. 8 ozs. | No. 4 sieve |
| 6/10 | Beans, green | French-style | Northwest Blue Lake | 6 lbs. 5 ozs. | | ½ C. | 30 | 3 lbs. 13 ozs. | |
| 6/10 | Beans, green | Cut | Northwest Blue Lake | 6 lbs. 5 ozs. | | ½ C. | 26 | 3 lbs. 15 ozs. | 1½-inch cuts, No. 3 sieve |
| 6/10 | Beans, green | Cut | Northwest Blue Lake | 6 lbs. 5 ozs. | | ½ C. | 26 | 3 lbs. 15 ozs. | No. 4 sieve |
| 6/10 | Beans, kidney | Dark red | Eastern Fordhook | 6 lbs. 12 ozs. | | ½ C. | 24 | 4 lbs. 12 ozs. | |
| 6/10 | Beans, lima | Garden run Fordhook | Eastern Fordhook | 6 lbs. 9 ozs. | | ½ C. | 24 | 4 lbs. 8 ozs. | Fresh |
| 6/10 | Beans, lima | Small green | Eastern Henderson Bush | 6 lbs. 9 ozs. | | ½ C. | 24 | 4 lbs. 8 ozs. | Fresh |
| 6/10 | Beans, lima | Medium green | Eastern Henderson Bush | 6 lbs. 9 ozs. | | ½ C. | 24 | 4 lbs. 8 ozs. | Fresh |
| 6/10 | Beans, oven-baked | | New England | 6 lbs. 14 ozs. | | ½ C. | 25 | 6 lbs. 14 ozs. | New England pack with salt pork |
| 6/10 | Beans, red | | Idaho Red | 6 lbs. 12 ozs. | | ½ C. | 24 | 5 lbs. 2 ozs. | |
| 6/10 | Beans, wax | Cut | King Horn Variety | 6 lbs. 5 ozs. | | ½ C. | 26 | 3 lbs. 15 ozs. | No. 3 sieve |
| 6/10 | Beets | Cubed | Eastern Detroit Red | 6 lbs. 8 ozs. | 400 to 450 | ½ C., 15 cubes | 26 to 30 | 4 lbs. 7 ozs. | ¾-inch cubes |
| 6/10 | Beets | Diced | Eastern Detroit Red | 6 lbs. 8 ozs. | | ½ C. | 27 | 4 lbs. 7 ozs. | |
| 6/10 | Beets | Julienne | Eastern Detroit Red | 6 lbs. 8 ozs. | | ½ C. | 30 | 4 lbs. 8 ozs. | |
| 6/10 | Beets | Sliced | Northwest Detroit Red | 6 lbs. 8 ozs. | 200 to 250 | ½ C., 10 slices | 20 to 25 | 4 lbs. 8 ozs. | |
| 6/10 | Beets, rosebud | Whole | Oregon Detroit Red | 6 lbs. 8 ozs. | Over 250 | 6 to 8 pieces | 30 to 40 | 4 lbs. 5 ozs. | |
| 6/10 | Cabbage, red | Sweet-sour | New York | 6 lbs. 3 ozs. | | ½ C. | 30 | 5 lbs. | |
| 6/10 | Carrots | Diced | Northwest Chantenay | 6 lbs. 9 ozs. | | ½ C. | 28 | 4 lbs. 8 ozs. | |
| 6/10 | Carrots | Julienne | Northwest Chantenay | 6 lbs. 9 ozs. | | ½ C. | 29 | 4 lbs. 6 ozs. | |
| 6/10 | Carrots | Quartered | Northwest Chantenay | 6 lbs. 9 ozs. | 86 | 3 pieces | 28 | 4 lbs. 6 ozs. | |
| 6/10 | Carrots | Small sliced | Northwest Chantenay | 6 lbs. 9 ozs. | 325 to 375 | 6 to 8 slices | 43 to 54 | 4 lbs. 3 ozs. | 1½ inch diameter |
| 6/10 | Carrots | Tiny whole | Northwest Chantenay | 6 lbs. 9 ozs. | Over 200 | 6 to 8 pieces | 30 to 35 | 4 lbs. 6 ozs. | |
| 6/10 | Carrots | Small whole | Northwest Chantenay | 6 lbs. 9 ozs. | Over 100 | 6 to 8 pieces | 24 to 30 | 4 lbs. 6 ozs. | |
| 6/10 | Celery | | California | 6 lbs. 2 oz. | | ½ C. | 23 | 4 lbs. 2 ozs. | Packed in brine |
| 6/10 | Corn, cream-style | Little kernel Country Gentleman | Midwest White | 6 lbs. 10 ozs. | | ½ C. | 25 | 6 lbs. 10 ozs. | |
| 6/10 | Corn, cream-style | Golden sweet | Midwest | 6 lbs. 10 ozs. | | ½ C. | 25 | 6 lbs. 10 ozs. | |
| 6/10 | Corn, whole grain | Golden sweet | Midwest | 6 lbs. 10 ozs. | | ½ C. | 26 | | |
| 6/10 | Hominy | Golden | Southern | 6 lbs. 9 ozs. | | ½ C. | 22 | 4 lbs. 1 oz. | |
| 6/10 | Kale | Chopped | Wisconsin | 6 lbs. 8 ozs. | | ½ C. | 23 | 3 lbs. 12 ozs. | |
| 6/10 | Mixed vegetables | | | | | ½ C. | 25 | 4 lbs. 1 oz. | Carrots, potatoes, celery, green beans, corn, peas, lima beans |
| 6/10 | Mustard greens | Chopped | Southern | 6 lbs. 2 ozs. | | ½ C. | 20 | 3 lbs. 12 ozs. | |
| 6/10 | Okra | Cut | Southern | 6 lbs. 3 ozs. | | ½ C. | 25 | 4 lbs. 1 oz. | |
| 6/10 | Onions | Tiny whole | Eastern | 6 lbs. 5 ozs. | Over 200 | 10 pieces | 20 | 4 lbs. | |
| 6/10 | Onions | Small whole | Eastern | 6 lbs. 9 ozs. | Over 100 | 5 pieces | 20 | 4 lbs. | |
| 6/10 | Peas, early June | Extra sifted | Wisconsin Alaska | 6 lbs. 9 ozs. | | ½ C. | 24 | | No. 2 sieve |
| 6/10 | Peas, early June | Sifted | Wisconsin Alaska | 6 lbs. 9 ozs. | | ½ C. | 24 | | No. 3 sieve |

*Table C-6 continued*

| Cans per Case and Container Size | Food | Style | Type | Approximate Net Weight | Range in Contents per Container | Suggested Portion per Serving | Approximate Portions per Container | Approximate Drained Weight | Miscellaneous Information |
|---|---|---|---|---|---|---|---|---|---|
| | | | **CANNED VEGETABLES** *(continued)* | | | | | | |
| 6/10 | Peas, alsweet | Sifted | Wisconsin Alsweet | 6 lbs. 9 ozs. | | ½ C. | 24 | | No. 3 sieve |
| 6/10 | Peas, telephone | Sweet | Wisconsin Sweet | 6 lbs. 9 ozs. | | ½ C. | 25 | | No. 5 sieve |
| 6/10 | Potatoes, white | Tiny whole | Midwest | 6 lbs. 6 ozs. | Over 150 | 6 pieces | 25 | 4 lbs. 6 ozs. | |
| 6/10 | Potatoes, white | Small whole | Midwest | 6 lbs. 6 ozs. | Over 100 | 4 pieces | 25 | 4 lbs. 6 ozs. | |
| 12/3 cyl. | Potatoes, sweet | Small whole | Louisiana yams | 3 lbs. 3 ozs. | 20 to 25 | 2 | 10 to 12 | 2 lbs. 3 ozs. | In heavy syrup |
| 6/10 | Sauerkraut | | Midwest | 6 lbs. 3 ozs. | | ½ C. | 37 | 5 lbs. | |
| 6/10 | Spinach | Leaf | California | 6 lbs. 2 ozs. | | ½ C. | 18 | 3 lbs. 12 ozs. | |
| 6/10 | Spinach | Sliced | California | 6 lbs. 2 ozs. | | ½ C. | 15 | 3 lbs. 12 ozs. | |
| 6/10 | Tomatoes | Italian-style | California | 6 lbs. 6 ozs. | 28 | 1 whole | 28 | 4 lbs. 4 ozs. | Trace of calcium chloride added |
| 6/10 | Tomatoes | Whole | Midwest | 6 lbs. 6 ozs. | 20 | 1 whole | 20 | 4 lbs. 8 ozs. | Trace of calcium chloride added |
| 6/10 | Tomato paste | Sweet | California blended, round and plum tomatoes | 6 lbs. 15 ozs. | | | 12 cups | 6 lbs. 15 ozs. | 30 percent solids |
| 6/10 | Tomato puree | Extra heavy | California | 6 lbs. 9 ozs. | | | 12 cups | 6 lbs. 9 ozs. | 1.07 specific gravity |
| 6/10 | Tomato puree | Superb | California | 6 lbs. 9 ozs. | | | 12 cups | 6 lbs. 9 ozs. | 1.06 specific gravity |
| 6/10 | Turnip greens | Chopped | Southern | 6 lbs. 2 ozs. | | ½ C. | 20 | 3 lbs. 12 ozs. | |
| | | | **DEHYDRATED VEGETABLES** | | | | | | |
| 6/1¾ # | Onions, white | Slices | | 1 lb. 12 ozs. | | | | | Yields 2½ gallons when reconstituted |
| 6/10 | Potatoes | Flakes | | 1 lb. 12 ozs. | | ½ C. | 90 | | |
| 6/10 | Potatoes | Instant | Powdered | 6 lbs. | | ½ C. | 112 | | |
| | | | **CANNED FRUITS** | | | | | | |
| 6/10 | Apple sauce | | New York State | 6 lbs. 12 ozs. | | ½ C. | 26 | 6 lbs. 12 ozs. | Heavy coarse finish |
| 6/10 | Apricots | Unpeeled halves | Blenheim | 6 lbs. 14 ozs. | 75 to 85 | 3 halves | 25 to 28 | 4 lbs. 2 ozs. | In syrup |
| 6/10 | Apricots | Whole peeled | Blenheim | 6 lbs. 14 ozs. | 40 to 50 | 2 pieces | 20 to 25 | 4 lbs. 4 ozs. | In syrup |
| 6/10 | Apricots | Sliced, peeled | Blenheim | 6 lbs. 14 ozs. | | ⅓ to ½ C. | 20 to 25 | 4 lbs. 2 ozs. | In syrup |
| 6/10 | Boysenberries | | California Genuine Variety | 6 lbs. 12 ozs. | | 12 berries | 26 | 3 lbs. 7 ozs. | In syrup |
| 6/10 | Cherries, bing | Unpitted | Pacific Northwest | 6 lbs. 12 ozs. | 220 | 11 cherries | 20 | 4 lbs. 5 ozs. | In syrup |
| 6/10 | Cherries, bing | Pitted | Pacific Northwest | 6 lbs. 14 ozs. | 300 to 350 | 11 cherries | 27 to 32 | 4 lbs. 2 ozs. | In syrup |
| 6/10 | Cherries, red | Pitted | Michigan Montmorency | 6 lbs. 14 ozs. | | ½ C. | 23 | 4 lbs. 12 ozs. | In syrup |
| 6/10 | Cherries, Royal Ann | Light sweet unpitted | Pacific Coast | 6 lbs. 12 ozs. | 250 to 300 | 11 cherries | 23 to 27 | 4 lbs. 2 ozs. | In syrup |
| 6/10 | Cranberry sauce | Home-style | Cape Cod or Wisconsin | 7 lbs. | | ¼ C. | 50 | | 2 ozs. or No. 48 souffle |
| 6/10 | Cranberry sauce | Strained | Cape Cod or Wisconsin | 7 lbs. | | ¼ C. | 50 | | 2 ozs. or No. 48 souffle |
| 6/10 | Figs | Whole | California Kadota | 7 lbs. | 70 to 90 | 3 pieces | 23 to 30 | 4 lbs. 4 ozs. | Slice of orange added in syrup |
| 6/10 | Fruit cocktail | | California Fancy | 6 lbs. 14 ozs. | | ⅓C. | 27 | 4 lbs. 8 ozs. | In syrup |
| 6/10 | Fruit for salad | | California Fancy | 6 lbs. 14 ozs. | | ½ C. | 20 | 4 lbs. 6 ozs. | Peach slices, pear slices, grapes, apricot halves, pineapple tidbits, maraschino cherries in syrup |
| 12/3 cyl. | Grapefruit | Segments | Florida | 3 lbs. 2 ozs. | 50 to 60 | 4 segments | 12 to 15 | 2 lbs. 1 oz. | In syrup |
| 12/3 cyl. | Grapefuit and orange | Segments | Florida | 3 lbs. 2 ozs. | 65 to 75 | 5 segments | 13 to 15 | 2 lbs. | In syrup |
| 6/10 | Grapes | Seedless | California Thompson | 6 lbs. 14 ozs. | | ½ C. | 22 | 4 lbs. 3 ozs. | In syrup |
| 12/3 cyl. | Orange | Segments | Florida Valencia | 3 lbs. 2 ozs. | 65 to 75 | 6 segments | 11 to 13 | 2 lbs. 1 oz. | In orange juice syrup |
| 6/10 | Orange, mandarin | Segments | Japanese | 6 lbs. 6 oz | 425 to 450 | ½ C. | 20 | 4 lbs. 3 oz. | In syrup |
| 6/10 | Peaches, ambrosia | Halves | Ambrosia yellow cling California | 6 lbs. 14 ozs. | 25 to 30 | 1 half | 25 to 30 | 4 lbs. 10 ozs. | In syrup |
| 6/10 | Peaches, ambrosia | Sliced | Ambrosia yellow cling California | 6 lbs. 12 ozs. | | 6 slices | 16 | 4 lbs. 10 ozs. | In syrup |
| 6/10 | Peaches, yellow cling | Diced | Midsummer yellow cling California | 6 lbs. 12 ozs. | | ½C. | 21 | 4 lbs. 5 ozs. | In syrup |

| | | | | | | | | | |
|---|---|---|---|---|---|---|---|---|---|
| 6/10 | Peaches, yellow cling | Halves | Midsummer yellow cling California | 6 lbs. 14 ozs. | 30 to 35 | 1 half | 30 to 35 | 4 lbs. 2 ozs. | In syrup |
| 6/10 | Peaches, yellow free | Halves | Yellow free Elberta California | 6 lbs. 14 ozs. | 25 to 30 | 1 half | 25 to 30 | | In syrup |
| 6/10 | Peaches, yellow free | Sliced | Yellow free Elberta California | 6 lbs. 14 ozs. | 150 | 6 slices | 25 | | In syrup |
| 6/10 | Pears, Bartlett | Halves, peeled | Pacific Northwest Bartlett | 6 lbs. 10 ozs. | 30 to 35 | 1 half | 30 to 35 | 4 lbs. 2 ozs. | In syrup |
| 6/10 | Pears, Bartlett | Halves, peeled | Pacific Northwest Bartlett | 6 lbs. 10 ozs. | 35 to 40 | 1 half | 35 to 40 | 4 lbs. 3 ozs. | In syrup |
| 6/10 | Pears, Bartlett | Halves, unpeeled | Pacific Northwest Bartlett | 6 lbs. 10 ozs. | 25 to 35 | 1 half | 25 to 35 | 3 lbs. 10 ozs. | In syrup |
| 6/10 | Pears, Bartlett | Diced | Pacific Coast Bartlett | 6 lbs. 10 ozs. | | ½ C. | 21 | 4 lbs. 9 ozs. | In syrup |
| 6/10 | Pears, Kieffer | Halves | Michigan Kieffer | 6 lbs. 10 ozs. | 40 to 50 | 2 halves | 20 to 25 | 3 lbs. 15 ozs. | In syrup |
| 6/10 | Pineapple | Crushed | Hawaiian Cayenne | 6 lbs. 12 ozs. | | ½ C. | 20 | 5 lbs. 5 ozs. | In syrup |
| 6/10 | Pineapple | Crushed | Hawaiian Cayenne | 6 lbs. 11 ozs. | | ½ C. | 18 | 4 lbs. 10 ozs. | In juice |
| 6/10 | Pineapple | Dessert cut | Hawaiian Cayenne | 6 lbs. 12 ozs. | 250 to 300 | 8 pieces | 31 to 37 | 4 lbs. 5 ozs. | In syrup |
| 6/10 | Pineapple | Sliced | Hawaiian Cayenne | 6 lbs. 13 ozs. | 52 | 1 slice | 52 | 4 lbs. 8 ozs. | In syrup |
| 6/10 | Pineapple | Sliced | Hawaiian Cayenne | 6 lbs. 13 ozs. | 66 | 1 slice | 66 | 4 lbs. 3 ozs. | In syrup |
| 6/10 | Pineapple | Tidbits | Hawaiian Cayenne | 6 lbs. 12 ozs. | 850 to 900 | ½ C. | 23 | 4 lbs. 12 ozs. | In syrup |
| 6/10 | Plums, Green Gage | Whole unpeeled | California | 6 lbs. 14 ozs. | 27 to 35 | 2 pieces | 13 to 17 | 3 lbs. 12 ozs. | In syrup |
| 6/10 | Plums, Green Gage | Whole peeled | California | 6 lbs. 14 ozs. | 27 to 35 | 2 pieces | 13 to 17 | 3 lbs. 12 ozs. | In syrup |
| 6/10 | Plums, prune | Whole unpeeled | Northwest Italian | 6 lbs. 14 ozs. | 60 to 70 | 3 pieces | 20 to 23 | 4 lbs. | In syrup |
| 6/10 | Prunes | Prepared | Santa Clara | 6 lbs. 14 ozs. | 150 to 160 | 5 pieces | 30 to 32 | 4 lbs. 7 ozs. | 40 to 50 cut out prunes per pound |
| 6/10 | Prunes | Ready-to-serve | San Jose | 7 lbs. | 110 to 115 | 4 to 5 pieces | 30 to 35 | 5 lbs. 2 ozs. | Water and sugar added |
| 6/10 | Rhubarb | | Michigan | 6 lbs. 9 ozs. | | ½ C. | 18 | 4 lbs. 1 oz. | U.S. certified food coloring added in syrup |

## VACUUM-PACKED SHELLED NUTS

| | | | | | | | | | |
|---|---|---|---|---|---|---|---|---|---|
| 6/3# | Almonds | Sliced | Blanched | 3 lbs. | 3 qts. | | | | |
| 12/1# | Almonds | Slivered | Blanched | 1 lb. | 1 qt. | | | | |
| 6/4# | Nut topping | | | 4 lbs. | 4 qts. | | | | Peanuts, cashews, almonds, pecans |
| 6/3# | Pecans | Halves | | 3 lbs. | 3 qts. | | | | |
| 6/3# | Pecans | Pieces | | 3 lbs. | 3 qts. | | | | |
| 6/2¾# | Walnuts | Halves and pieces | Light California | 2 lbs. 12 ozs. | 2¾ qts. | | | | |
| 12/1# | Walnuts | Halves and pieces | Light California | 1 lb. | 1 qt. | | | | |
| 12/1# | Walnuts, black | Kernels | Eastern | 1 lb. | 1 qt. | | | | |

## DRIED FRUITS

| | | | | | | | | | |
|---|---|---|---|---|---|---|---|---|---|
| 6/2# | Apple | Pie slices | Low moisture fruit | 2 lbs. | 1½ gal. | | 5—9-in. Pies | | Used 1 quart for each pie |
| 6/2½# | Apple | Sauce nuggets | Low moisture fruit | 2 lbs. 8 ozs. | 3¼ gals. | ½ C. | 104 | | |
| 30# Carton | Apricots | Dried | Blenheim | 30 lbs. | 2550 | 6 to 7 pieces | 364 to 425 | | |
| 6/10 | Apricots | Slices | Low moisture fruit | 3 lbs. 8 ozs. | 2¼ gals. | ½ C. | 72 | | |
| 30# Carton | Figs | Dried | Calimyrna jumbo | 30 lbs. | 702 | 3 pieces | 234 | | |
| 5# Bag | Figs | Dried | Calimyrna jumbo | 5 lbs. | 117 | 3 pieces | 39 | | |
| 6/10 | Fruit cocktail mix | | Low moisture fruit | 2 lbs. 12 ozs. | 2¼ gals. | ½ C. | 72 | | Maraschino cherries, apricots, peaches, apples, grapes |
| 30# Carton | Fruit | Dried | Mixed | 30 lbs. | 690 prunes 432 apricots 114 peaches 84 pears | 5 pieces | 264 | | Blenheim apricots, Lake County pears, Muir peaches, Santa Clara prunes |
| 30# Carton | Peaches | Dried | Muir | 30 lbs. | 1134 | 3 pieces | 378 | | |
| 30# Carton | Prunes | Dried | Santa Clara | 30 lbs. | 540 to 720 | 2 pieces | 270 to 360 | | Size 18/24 |
| 5# Can | Prunes | Dried | Santa Clara | 5 lbs. | 90 to 120 | 2 pieces | 45 to 60 | | Size 18/24 |
| 30# Carton | Prunes | Dried | Santa Clara | 30 lbs. | 600 to 900 | 3 pieces | 200 to 300 | | Size 20/30 |
| 5# Can | Prunes | Dried | Santa Clara | 5 lbs. | 100 to 150 | 3 pieces | 33 to 50 | | Size 20/30 |
| 30# Carton | Prunes | Dried | Santa Clara | 30 lbs. | 900 to 1200 | 4 pieces | 225 to 300 | | Size 30/40 |
| 5# Can | Prunes | Dried | Santa Clara | 5 lbs. | 150 to 200 | 4 pieces | 37 to 50 | | Size 30/40 |
| 30# Carton | Prunes | Dried | Santa Clara | 30 lbs. | 1200 to 1500 | 5 pieces | 240 to 300 | | Size 40/50 |
| 5# Can | Prunes | Dried | Santa Clara | 5 lbs. | 200 to 250 | 5 pieces | 40 to 50 | | Size 40/50 |

Table C-6, continued

| Cans per Case and Container Size | Food | Type | Style | Approximate Net Weight | Range in Contents per Container | Suggested Portion per Serving | Approximate Portions per Container | Approximate Drained Weight | Miscellaneous Information |
|---|---|---|---|---|---|---|---|---|---|
| **PREPARED PIE FILLINGS** | | | | | | | | | |
| 6/10 | Apples | Greenings | | 7 lbs. 4 ozs. | | | 3—9-in. Pies | | Apple slices, sugar, lemon juice and water. Used 1 quart for each pie. |
| 6/10 | Blueberry | Maine | | 7 lbs. 4 ozs. | | | 3—9-in. Pies | | Contains blueberries, sugar, lemon juice, starch, salt and water. Used 1 quart for each pie. |
| 6/10 | Cherry | Michigan | | 7 lbs. 8 ozs. | | | 3—9-in. Pies | | Contains cherries, cornstarch, sugar, lemon juice, food coloring and water. Used 1 quart for each pie. |
| 6/10 | Lemon | | | 7 lbs. 14 ozs. | | | 3—9-in. Pies | | Sugar, corn syrup, eggs, cereal, lemon juice, stabilizers, vegetable shortening, salt, fruit acid, lemon flavoring. Used 1 quart for each pie. |
| 6/10 | Peaches | Yellow cling | Sliced | 7 lbs. 4 ozs. | | | 3—9-in. Pies | | Freestone peaches, sugar, starch, lemon juice and water. Used 1 quart for each pie. |
| **PIE FILLINGS** | | | | | | | | | |
| 6/10 | Apples | York Imperial | Sliced | 6 lbs. 12 ozs. | | | 16½ C. | 6 lbs. 12 ozs. | No syrup |
| 6/10 | Apricots | Blenheim, Royal or Tilton | Unpeeled halves | 6 lbs. 10 ozs. | | | 11¾ C. | 6 lbs. 10 ozs. | Preheated solid pack pie apricots, no syrup |
| 6/10 | Blackberries | Washington State Evergreen | | 6 lbs. 7 ozs. | | | 12½ C. | 4 lbs. 15 ozs. | Packed in water |
| 6/10 | Black raspberries | Michigan | | 6 lbs. 6 oz. | | | 8 C. | 3 lbs. 3 ozs. | Packed in water |
| 6/10 | Blueberries | Maine or Canada Genuine Variety | | 6 lbs. 6 ozs. | | | 9¾ C. | 3 lbs. 12 ozs. | Packed in water |
| 6/10 | Boysenberries | California or Oregon | | 6 lbs. 7 ozs. | | | 6¾ C. | 3 lbs. 6 ozs. | Packed in water |
| 6/10 | Cherries, red sour | Michigan or Wisconsin Montmorency | Pitted | 6 lbs. 7 ozs. | | | 11¾ C. | 4 lbs. 7 ozs. | Packed in water |
| 6/10 | Gooseberries | Northwest or Michigan | | 6 lbs. 5 ozs. | | | 11¾ C. | 3 lbs. 13 ozs. | Packed in water |
| 6/10 | Mincemeat | Olde English | | 7 lbs. 12 ozs. | | | 13½ C. | 7 lbs. 12 ozs. | Contains raisins, evaporated apples, sugar, boiled cider, candied fruits, beef suet, cider vinegar, spices |
| 6/10 | Peaches, yellow cling | Midsummer or Phillips yellow cling California | Halves or slices | 6 lbs. 8 ozs. | | | 14 C. | 6 lbs. 3 ozs. | Preheated solid pack pie peaches, no syrup |
| 6/10 | Pumpkin | California | | 6 lbs. 10 ozs. | | | 14 C. | 6 lbs. 10 ozs. | Dry pack |
| **SPICED FRUITS** | | | | | | | | | |
| 6/10 | Apples, spiced | Jonathan | Rings | 6 lbs. 10 ozs. | 70 to 80 | 1 ring | 70 to 80 | 3 lbs. 13 ozs. | Colored, unpeeled, cored in heavy syrup |
| 6/10 | Apricots, spiced | California Blenheim | Whole peeled | 6 lbs. 14 ozs. | 35 to 40 | 1 | 35 to 40 | 4 lbs. 4 ozs. | Pit loosened in extra heavy syrup |
| 6/10 | Cantaloupe, preserved | | Cubed | 8 lbs. | 214 | 2 | 107 | 5 lbs. 11 ozs. | In heavy syrup |
| 6/10 | Crab Apples, spiced | Michigan Hyslop | Whole | 6 lbs. 10 ozs. | 50 to 60 | 1 | 50 to 60 | 4 lbs. 1 oz. | Colored red, cored in heavy syrup |
| 6/10 | Honeydew melon, preserved | | Cubed | 8 lbs. | 226 | 2 | 113 | 5 lbs. 13 ozs. | In heavy syrup |
| 12/5 | Kumquats, preserved | Florida | Whole | 3 lbs. 8 ozs. | 70 to 75 | | 70 to 75 | 2 lbs. 8 ozs. | In syrup |
| 6/10 | Peaches, yellow cling, spiced | California | Whole | 6 lbs. 14 ozs. | 25 to 30 | 1 | 25 to 30 | 4 lbs. 10 ozs. | Pit loosened in extra heavy syrup |
| 6/10 | Pears, Bartlett cinnamon-flavored | California | Halves | 6 lbs. 12 ozs. | 25 to 30 | 1 | 25 to 30 | 3 lbs. 10 ozs. | Colored red in extra heavy syrup |

| | | | | | | | | | |
|---|---|---|---|---|---|---|---|---|---|
| 6/10 | Pears, Bartlett peppermint-flavored | Halves | California | 6 lbs. 12 ozs. | 25 to 30 | 1 | 25 to 30 | 3 lbs. 10 ozs. | Colored green in extra heavy syrup |
| 6/10 | Pears, Kieffer, spiced | Whole | Michigan | 6 lbs. 10 ozs. | 40 to 50 | 1 | 40 to 50 | 3 lbs. 15 ozs. | Colored red in heavy syrup |
| 6/10 | Pears, Seckel, spiced | Whole | New York Seckel | 6 lbs. 12 ozs. | 70 to 80 | 1 | 70 to 80 | 4 lbs. 9 ozs. | In extra heavy syrup |
| 6/5 | Prunes, spiced | Whole | D'Agen | 3 lbs. 4 ozs. | 62 | 1 | 62 | 2 lbs. 10 ozs. | Sometimes available in No. 10 cans |
| 6/10 | Watermelon, preserved | Cubed | | 8 lbs. | 194 | 2 | 97 | 5 lbs. 9 ozs. | |
| | | | **FRUIT JUICES, NECTARS, AND BEVERAGE BASES** | | | | | | |
| 4/1 gal. | Apple | Cider | | 1 gal. | | 4 oz. | 32 | | |
| 12/46 oz. | Apple | Juice | Unsweetened | 46 oz. | | 4 oz. | 11½ | | |
| 12/46 oz. | Cherry | Juice | Red | 46 oz. | | 4 oz. | 11½ | | Sugar added |
| 4/1 gal. | Cranberry | Juice | Cocktail | 1 gal. | | 4 oz. | 32 | | Sugar added |
| 12/46 oz. | Grape | Juice | Concord | 46 oz. | | 4 oz. | 11½ | | Sugar added |
| 12/46 oz. | Grape | Juice | Concord | 46 oz. | | 4 oz. | 11½ | | Unsweetened |
| 12/46 oz. | Grapefruit | Juice | Texas or Florida | 46 oz. | | 4 oz. | 11½ | | Unsweetened |
| 12/46 oz. | Orange | Juice | Florida Valencia | 46 oz. | | 4 oz. | 11½ | | Unsweetened |
| 12/46 oz. | Orange and grapefruit | Juice | Florida | 46 oz. | | 4 oz. | 11½ | | Sugar added |
| 12/46 oz. | Pineapple | Juice | Hawaiian | 46 oz. | | 4 oz. | 11½ | | Unsweetened |
| 12/46 oz. | Prune | Juice | | 46 oz. | | 4 oz. | 11½ | | Unsweetened juice of dried prunes |
| 12/46 oz. | Tangarine | Juice | Florida | 46 oz. | | 4 oz. | 11½ | | Sugar added |
| 6/10 | Tomato | Juice | Eastern or California | 3 qts. | | 4 oz. | 24 | | |
| 12/46 oz. | Tomato | Juice | Eastern or California | 46 oz. | | 4 oz. | 11½ | | |
| 12/46 oz. | Vegetable | Juice | Eastern | 46 oz. | | 4 oz. | 11½ | | |
| 12/46 oz. | Apricot | Nectar | California | 46 oz. | | 4 oz. | 11½ | | Sweetened |
| 12/46 oz. | Boysenberry | Nectar | Northwest | 46 oz. | | 4 oz. | 11½ | | Sugar added |
| 12/46 oz. | Loganberry | Nectar | | 46 oz. | | 4 oz. | 11½ | | Sweetened |
| 12/46 oz. | Peach | Nectar | California Elberta | 46 oz. | | 4 oz. | 11½ | | Sugar added |
| 12/46 oz. | Pear | Nectar | California | 46 oz. | | 4 oz. | 11½ | | Sugar added |
| 12/1 qt. | Punch | Beverage base | Oahu | | | 8 oz. | 27 | | Pineapple juice, orange juice, apricot nectar, loganberry nectar |
| 4/1 gal. | Punch | Beverage base | Oahu | | | 8 oz. | 96 | | Pineapple juice, orange juice, apricot nectar, loganberry nectar |
| 12/1 qt. | Syrup | Beverage base | Concord Grape | | | 8 oz. | 28¼ | | |
| 12/1 qt. | Syrup | Beverage base | Lemonade | | | 8 oz. | 24 | | Sugar, water, corn syrup, concentrated lemon juice, lemon oil, ascorbic acid, certified artificial color, and 1/10 of 1 percent benzoate of soda |
| 12/1 qt. | Syrup | Beverage base | Refresh-O-Orange Press | | | 8 oz. | 30 | | |
| | | | **PICKLES** | | | | | | |
| 6/10 | Pickles | Sweet, circles | Kurley Kut (serrated) | 3 qts. | 360 to 400 | 3 | 120 to 133 | | 1½-inch diameter |
| 6/10 | Pickles | Sweet | Miniature | 3 qts. | 425 | 2 to 3 | 130 | | About 1½-inch length |
| 6/10 | Pickles | Sweet | Tiny | 3 qts. | 230 to 240 | 2 | 125 | | About 1¾-inch length |
| 6/10 | Pickles | Sweet | Midget | 3 qts. | 160 to 165 | 2 | 80 | | About 2-inch length |
| 6/10 | Pickles | Sweet, chips | Twentieth-century cross cuts | 3 qts. | 461 | 3 to 4 | 150 | | Small-type pickle, 1¼-inch diameter |
| 6/10 | Pickles | Sweet | Quartered stix | 3 qts. | 170 to 180 | 2 | 75 to 80 | | |
| 6/10 | Pickles | Sweet | Tidbits | 8 lbs. | 315 to 320 | 1 oz. | 88 | | Watermelon, cantaloupe, Burr gherkin halves, pickle rings, tiny sweet gherkins, diced red peppers |
| 6/10 | Pickles | Sweet | Mixed | 3 qts. | 357 | 1 oz. | 70 | | 70 percent cut mixed pickles, 20 percent cauliflower, 10 percent onions |
| 6/10 | Cucumber | Sweet, circles | Cross cut | 3 qts. | 225 to 235 | 2 to 3 | 110 to 120 | | |
| 6/10 | Pickles | Sweet | Whole No. 60 | 3 qts. | 115 to 120 | 1 to 2 | 58 to 112 | | |
| 6/10 | Pickles | Sweet, whole | Small No. 36 | 3 qts. | 55 to 60 | 1 | 55 to 60 | | About 3-inch length |
| 6/10 | Pickles | Home-style | Circles | 3 qts. | 390 | 4 | 95 to 98 | | Fresh cucumber pickles, bread-and-butter style |

*Table C-6, continued*

### PICKLES *(continued)*

| Cans per Case and Container Size | Food | Style | Type | Approximate Net Weight | Range in Contents per Container | Suggested Portion per Serving | Approximate Portions per Container | Approximate Drained Weight | Miscellaneous Information |
|---|---|---|---|---|---|---|---|---|---|
| 6/10 | Pickles | Home-style | Quartered. stix | 3 qts. | 140 to 150 | 2 | 70 to 75 | | Bread-and-butter style |
| 6/10 | Pickles | Dill. sweet | Circles, cross cuts | 3 qts. | 280 to 300 | 2 to 3 | 140 to 150 | | |
| 6/10 | Pickles | Dill. genuine | Circles | 3 qts. | 225 to 235 | 2 | 110 to 115 | | |
| 6/10 | Pickles | Dill. genuine | Whole. No. 18 | 3 qts. | 32 to 35 | ⅓ | 75 to 80 | | About 3½-inch length |
| 6/10 | Pickles | Dill. genuine | Whole. No. 12 | 3 qts. | 20 to 24 | ¼ | 80 to 90 | | About 4-inch length |
| 6/10 | Pickles | Dill. genuine | Whole. No. 18. garlic-flavored | 3 qts. | 30 to 35 | ¼ | 80 to 90 | | About 3½-inch length |

### OLIVES

| Cans per Case and Container Size | Food | Style | Type | Approximate Net Weight | Range in Contents per Container | Suggested Portion per Serving | Approximate Portions per Container | Approximate Drained Weight | Miscellaneous Information |
|---|---|---|---|---|---|---|---|---|---|
| 4/1 gal. | Olives | Colossal | Queen. plain | 5 lbs. 8 ozs. | 180 to 190 | 1 | 180 to 190 | | Imported Spain. Size: 60-60 |
| 4/1 gal. | Olives | Jumbo | Queen. plain | 5 lbs. 12 ozs. | 200 | 1 | 200 | | Size: 70-80 |
| 4/1 gal. | Olives | Mammoth | Queen. plain | 5 lbs. 12 ozs. | 220 | 1 | 220 | | Imported Spain. Size: 80-100 |
| 4/1 gal. | Olives | Giant | Queen. plain | 5 lbs. 12 ozs. | 250 | 1 | 250 | | Size: 90-110 |
| 4/1 gal. | Olives | Large | Queen. plain | 5 lbs. 4 ozs. | 280 | 1 to 2 | 140 to 280 | | Imported Spain. Size: 100-110 |
| 4/1 gal. | Olives | Medium | Queen. plain | 5 lbs. | 330 | 2 to 3 | 110 to 165 | | Size: 130-150 |
| 4/1 gal. | Olives | Fancy. pitted | Queen. plain | 5 lbs. 12 ozs. | 260 | 1 | 260 | | Size: 90-100 |
| 4/1 gal. | Olives | Colossal | Queen. stuffed | 5 lbs. 14 ozs. | 200 | 1 | 200 | | Imported Spain stuffed with bright red Spanish pimiento. Size: 70-80 |
| 4/1 gal. | Olives | Jumbo | Queen. stuffed | 6 lbs. | 225 | 1 | 225 | | Size: 80-90 |
| 4/1 gal. | Olives | Mammoth | Queen. stuffed | 5 lbs. 12 ozs. | 250 | 1 | 250 | | Imported Spain stuffed with bright red pimiento. Size: 90-100 |
| 4/1 gal. | Olives | Large | Queen. stuffed | 5 lbs. 12 ozs. | 300 | 1 to 2 | 150 to 200 | | Imported Spain stuffed with bright red pimiento. Size: 100-130 |
| 4/1 gal. | Olives | Medium | Queen. stuffed | 5 lbs. 4 ozs. | 330 | 2 to 3 | 110 to 165 | | Size: 130-150 |
| 4/1 gal. | Olives | Medium | Manzanilla. stuffed | 5 lbs. 12 ozs. | 700 | 3 to 4 | 175 to 233 | | Size: 240-260 |
| 4/1 gal. | Olives | Small | Manzanilla. stuffed | 5 lbs. 2 ozs. | 800 to 822 | 4 to 5 | 160 to 200 | | Imported Spain. Size: 300-320 |
| 6/10 | Olives | Super colossal | Ripe | 4 lbs. | 128 | 1 | 128 | | Sevilliano variety |
| 6/10 | Olives | Colossal | Ripe | 4 lbs. | 152 | 1 | 152 | | |
| 6/10 | Olives | Large | Ripe | 4 lbs. | 404 | 1 to 2 | 202 to 404 | | |
| 6/10 | Olives | Medium | Ripe | 4 lbs. 2 ozs. | 460 | 2 to 3 | 153 to 230 | | Mission variety |
| 6/10 | Olives | Medium | Ripe. pitted | 3 lbs. 4 ozs. | 480 | 1 to 2 | 240 to 480 | | |
| 24/5½ oz. | Olives | Medium | Ripe. pitted | 5½ oz. | 50 to 52 | 1 to 2 | 26 to 52 | | |

### DESSERT POWDER BASES

| Cans per Case and Container Size | Food | Style | Type | Approximate Net Weight | Range in Contents per Container | Suggested Portion per Serving | Approximate Portions per Container | Approximate Drained Weight | Miscellaneous Information |
|---|---|---|---|---|---|---|---|---|---|
| 6/10 | Dessert powder | Gelatin | | 5 lbs. 4 ozs. | | 4 oz. | 128 | | Flavors: apple, wild cherry, citrus, grape, lemon, lime, melba, orange, black raspberry, red raspberry, strawberry. Dissolved in 3½ gals. of water |
| 12/2¾ | Dessert powder | Gelatin | | 1 lb. 8 ozs. | | 4 oz. | 32 | | Flavors: apple, wild cherry, citrus, grape, lemon, lime, melba, orange, black raspberry, red raspberry, strawberry. Dissolved in 1 gal. of water |
| 6/10 | Dessert powder | | | 5 lbs. | | 4 oz. | 70—½ C. | | Flavors: butterscotch, chocolate, coconut, vanilla. Makes 6—9 in. pies. Used 2 gals. of water |

| | | | | | | | | | |
|---|---|---|---|---|---|---|---|---|---|
| 6/10 | Dessert powder | | Lemon | 5 lbs. 8 ozs. | | 4 oz. | 70—½ C. | | Makes 6—9 in. pies. Used 2 gals. of water |
| 12/2½ | Dessert powder | | | 1 lb. 6 ozs. | | 4 oz. | 20—½ C. | | Flavors: butterscotch, chocolate, coconut, vanilla. Makes 2—9 in. pies Used 2¼ qts. of water |
| 12/2½ | Dessert powder | | Lemon | 1 lb. 8 ozs. | | 4 oz. | 20—½ C. | | Makes 2—9 in. pies. Used 2¼ qts. of water |
| 12/2½ | Dessert powder | Blancmange | Mix 'n serve | 1 lb. 4 ozs. | | 4 oz. | 30—½ C. | | Flavors: chocolate, coconut. Used 2½ qts. of water |
| 12/2½ | Dessert powder | Blancmange | Mix 'n serve | 1 lb. 8 ozs. | | 4 oz. | 30—½ C. | | Flavors: butterscotch, vanilla. Used 3 qts. of water |
| | | | | **SEAFOODS** | | | | | |
| 24/303 | Clams | No. 1 Little Neck | Whole | 1 lb. 4 ozs. | 16 Whole<br>1¾ Cups | | | 8 oz. | Liquor—1½ C. |
| 24/2 | Clams | No. 2 Little Neck | Whole | 1 lb. 4 ozs. | 66 Whole<br>1 Cup | | | 10 oz. | Liquor— ½C. |
| 12/5 Tall | Clams | | Chopped or minced | 3 lbs. 3 ozs. | 4 Cups | | | 1 lb. 7 ozs. | Liquor—3½ C. |
| 24/1 | Crab meat | King | Imported Japan | 13 oz. | B & F—3½Cups<br>C—2¾ Cups | 2 oz.<br>4 oz. | 6½<br>3½ | 10 oz. | Liquor—½ C. |
| 12/2½ | Fish flakes | Pollack | | 2 lbs. | 5¾ Cups | | | | Liquor—1¼ C. |
| 24/1 | Lobster | | Imported Canada | 10 oz. | B & F—2½Cups<br>C—2¼ Cups | 2 oz.<br>4 oz. | 5<br>2½ | | Liquor—½ C. |
| 48/1 | Salmon | Sockeye | Fancy Red Alaska | 1 lb. | B & F—2¼ Cups<br>C—2 Cups | 2 oz.<br>(⅓—½ C.)<br>4 oz.<br>(⅔—¾ C.) | 5<br><br>2½ | | Liquor—½C.<br>Color—deep red.<br>Small firm flakes |
| | | | | **CONDENSED SOUPS** | | | | | |
| 6/10 | Chicken | Broth | | 3 qts. | | 8 oz. - 1C. | 24+ | | Chicken broth, hydrolized wheat protein, chicken fat, and fresh vegetable flavoring |
| 12/5 | Chicken | Broth | | 3 lbs. 2 oz. | | 8 oz. - 1C. | 12+ | | |
| 12/5 | Beef | Bouillon | | 3 lbs. 2 oz. | | 8 oz. - 1C. | 12 | | Beef stock, parsnips, carrots, beef extract, onions, and seasonings |
| 12/5 | Tomato | Bouillon | | 3 lbs. 2 oz. | | 8 oz. - 1C. | 12+ | | Tomato juice, sugar, salt, beef extract, vegetable oil, onion powder, and spices |
| 12/5 | Chicken | Chowder | | 3 lbs. 2 oz. | | 8 oz. - 1C. | 12 | | Chicken broth, potatoes, carrots, chicken, celery, cornstarch, onions, peas, corn, tomatoes, red peppers, and seasonings |
| 12/5 | Clam | Chowder | Manhattan | 3 lbs. 2 oz. | | 8 oz. - 1C. | 12 | | Potatoes, clams, carrots, clam juice, tomato paste, red peppers, onions, celery, parsley flakes, and seasonings |
| 12/5 | Clam | Chowder | New England | 3 lbs. 2 oz. | | 8 oz. - 1C. | 12 | | Clams, potatoes, onions, and seasonings |
| 12/5 | | Chowder | Red Snapper | 3 lbs. 2 oz. | | 8 oz. - 1C. | 12 | | Potatoes, red snappers, tomatoes, carrots, onions, clam juice, corn, celery, red peppers, rice |
| 12/5 | Asparagus, Bean, Beef, Celery, Chicken, Chicken-Rice, Mushroom, Pea, Pepper-Pot, Tomato, Vegetable | Soup | | 3 lbs. 2 oz. | | 8 oz. - 1C. | 12 | | According to recipe |

*Table C-6 continued*

| Cans per Case and Container Size | Food | Style | Approximate Net Weight | Suggested Portion Per Serving | Approx. Portions Per Container | Miscellaneous Information |
|---|---|---|---|---|---|---|
| **JAMS** | | | | | | |
| 6/10 | Apple | Butter | 7 lbs. 8 oz. | No. 45 souffle, 1 oz. | 120 | Made from evaporated apples |
| 6/4 3/4# | Cherry, Grape, Damson plum, Plum | Jam | 4 lbs. 12 oz. | No. 45 souffle, 1 oz. | 76 | Made from fresh fruits and juices |
| **JELLIES** | | | | | | |
| 6/4½# | Apple, Grape, Black Raspberry, Cherry, Currant, Elderberry, Mint, Plum, Quince, Strawberry | Jelly | 4 lbs. 8 oz. | No. 45 souffle, 1 oz. | 72 | Made from fresh fruits and juices |
| 6/10 | Apple, Grape | Jelly | 8 lbs. | No. 45 souffle, 1 oz. | 128 | |
| **PRESERVES** | | | | | | |
| 6/10 | Peach, Plum, Strawberry | Preserves | 8 lbs. 4 oz. | No. 45 souffle, 1 oz. | 132 | Made from fresh fruits and juices |
| 6/4 3/4# | Apricot, Blackberry, Cherry, Grape, Elberta Peach, Orange, Pineapple, Pine Apricot, Plum, Raspberry, Strawberry | Preserves | 4 lbs. 12 oz. | No. 45 souffle, 1 oz. | 76 | |

# Appendix D
# 1,001 Items for Menu Writers

As we mentioned in Chapter 7, the menu is a vital marketing tool for a restaurant. Changes in menu items and prices to meet the changing tastes of your clientele require a lengthy list of menu selections. The following list of 1,001 items is a handy reference for menu writing. Although this might appear to be an exhaustive list, it can in fact be extended indefinitely if you use your imagination.

## Beef

1. Roast Prime Rib of Beef, Yorkshire Pudding
2. London Broil (Sliced Flank Steak), Bordelaise, Potatoes au Gratin, Creamed Carrots and Peas
3. French Beef Stew Smothered in Burgundy Wine, Parsley Potato
4. Browned Corned Beef Hash, Poached Egg, Spiced Peach
5. Boiled Beef Dumplings with Horseradish Sauce
6. Beef Goulash en Casserole, Hungarian Style, Spaetzels Sauté
7. Yankee Pot Roast, Macaroni au Gratin
8. Yankee Pot Roast with Corn Fritters
9. Beefsteak Pie, Family Style
10. Porterhouse Steak with Baby Artichokes, Pickled Walnuts
11. Pepper Steak, Cabaret Style en Casserole, Fried Tomatoes, German Fried Potatoes
12. Old-Fashioned Pounded Steak with Bacon
13. Corned Beef and Eggs Pancake Style with French-Fried Potatoes
14. Braised Smoked Beef Tongue with Red Wine Cabbage
15. T-Bone Steak with Lemon Sauce, Mustard Pickles
16. Hanna Hash Browned, Poached Eggs, Mixed Salad
17. Smothered Swiss Steak with Diced (Baked) Celery, Potatoes and Cubed Tomatoes
18. Diced Roast Beef, Southern Style, Fried Bananas, Sweet Potato, Poached Egg
19. Larded Beef a la Mode with Red Wine Sauce, Marrow Dumplings, Young Vegetables
20. Tomato Filled with Chopped Beef, Mushroom Gravy, and Asparagus Tips

21. Devilled Ribs of Beef, Regency Sauce, Vegetables Matigon
22. Chopped Corned Beef Sandwich with Cole Slaw and Russian Dressing, Sliced Bananas and Oranges with Cookie
23. Minute Steak, Sherry Wine Sauce, Celery Heart
24. Table d'Hote Dinner: Swiss Steak with Brown Gravy
25. Broiled Hamburgers Wrapped in Bacon, Baked Bananas, French-Fried Onions, Creamed Mushrooms, Tomato and Lettuce Salad, French Dressing
26. Baked Corned Beef Hash, Fried Sweet Potatoes
27. Braised Beef Tenderloin Tips on Toast, Brussels Sprouts, French-Fried Potatoes
28. Baked Meat Ball a la Creole with Fluffy Mashed Potatoes
29. Swedish Meat Balls, Stewed Tomatoes, Creamed Whipped Potatoes
30. Boiled Smoked Beef Tongue, Buttered Spinach, Steamed Potato, Hot Corn Muffin
31. Tender Country Fried Cube Steak, Stewed Tomatoes, Fluffy Mashed Potatoes
32. Fried Baby Beef Liver with Onions or Bacon, French-Fried Potatoes
33. Swiss Steak in Natural Sauce, Young Stringless Beans, Oven-Browned Potato
34. Hungarian Beef Goulash and Spaetzels
35. German Pot Roast with Sugar Corn Fritters
36. Roast Beef Hash, Southern Style, Banana Fritter
37. Diced Tenderloin Steak with Peppers and Mushrooms, Hashed Brown Potatoes
38. Grilled Salisbury Steak, Creole Eggplant and Tomato
39. Broiled Sirloin Steak, Baked Potato, Cauliflower with Cheese Sauce, Baked Tomato Stuffed with Mushrooms
40. Steak and Kidney Pie, Parsley Buttered Potatoes,
41. New England Boiled Dinner (Corned Beef and Salt Pork with Cabbage, Turnips, Carrots, and Potatoes), Apple, Celery, and Nut Salad
42. Filet Mignon, French-Fried Onions, Baked Banana, Buttered Fresh Spinach, Jellied Fruit Salad, Cream Cheese Dressing
43. Broiled Chopped Steak, Baked Potato, Creamed Mushrooms, Buttered Brussels Sprouts, Orange and Grapefruit Salad, French Dressing
44. Beef Goulash with Vegetables, Fried Tomato, Spiced Baked Prunes, Endive, Egg Yolk Grated, Mayonnaise Dressing
45. Beefsteak Sandwich, Sliced Bermuda Onion, Grilled Tomatoes, Fried Mushrooms, Romaine, Chiffonade Dressing
46. Braised Shortribs of Beef, Buttered Lima Beans, Cauliflower, Tomato Sauce, Mashed Turnip, Cucumber Salad, Sour Cream Dressing
47. Broiled Beef Tenderloin, Lattice Potatoes, Buttered Spinach, Diced Summer Squash, Beef Salad, Sour Cream Dressing
48. Chutney Beef Loaf with Mushroom Sauce, Buttered New Asparagus, Steamed Potatoes, Hot Spiced Red Cabbage, Green Pepper and Cheese Salad
49. Creamed Chipped Beef, Baked Potatoes, Buttered Green Beans, Fried Vegetable Marrow, Tomato and Pineapple Salad, French Dressing
50. Beef Steak and Mushroom Pie, Mashed Potatoes, Fried Eggplant, Hot Slaw, Hearts of Lettuce, Thousand Island Dressing
51. Roast Fillet of Beef, Mushroom Sauce, Buttered Lima Beans,

Broiled Tomatoes, Buttered Brussels Sprouts, Orange and White Grape Salad, French Dressing

52. Cold Roast Beef, Potato Salad, Baked Stuffed Tomato, Scalloped Cabbage, Chicory Salad, French Dressing

53. Poached Eggs on Roast Beef Hash, Hot Slaw, Pickled Beets, French-Fried Onions, Hearts of Lettuce, Roquefort Cheese Dressing

54. Sliced Cold Beef Tongue, Creamed Potatoes (Hot), Wilted Raw Spinach Salad, Baked Stuffed Onions (Hot)

## Veal

55. Fried Veal Steak, Hashed Brown Potatoes, Lettuce and Tomato Salad

56. Baked Veal Loaf with Italienne Spaghetti, Combination Salad, French Dressing

57. Fried Calf Brain, Tomato Sauce, Hashed Brown Potatoes, Mixed Vegetable Salad

58. Baked Veal Birds with Celery Dressing

59. Roast Stuffed Shoulder of Veal with Cauliflower and Potatoes

60. Roast Leg of Veal with Celery Dressing

61. Roast Veal with Sherry Wine Sauce, French-Fried Potatoes and a Head Lettuce Salad

62. Roast French Veal Loaf with Mushroom Sauce

63. Roast Leg of Veal, Wild Rice Stuffing, Spiced Apricot

64. Scaloppine of Veal with Mushrooms and Wine Sauce

65. Veal Chops a la Marengo

66. Fricandeau of Milk-Fed Veal, Noodles, and Prunes

67. Veal Loaf, Vegetable Sauce with Shredded Lettuce, Cabbage and Apple Salad, Mashed Potatoes au Gratin

68. Roast Leg of Veal with Dill Dressing, Glazed Carrots

69. Broiled Veal Chop, Baked Bananas, Broccoli with Hollandaise Sauce, Baked Tomato Stuffed with Corn

70. Veal Rolls, Spiced Peaches, Creamed Potatoes, Buttered Green Beans, Fried Tomatoes, Fruit Salad, Boiled Dressing

71. Curry of Veal with Rice, Buttered Green Beans, Baked Tomatoes, Glazed Apricots, Date, Orange, and Endive Salad, French Dressing

72. Calf Liver Cakes with Bacon, Lyonnaise Potatoes, Sauté Pineapple, Buttered Carrots, Cucumber Salad, French Dressing

73. Breaded Veal Cutlet (Wiener Schnitzel), Tomato Sauce, Sauerkraut, German Fried Potatoes, Stuffed Apricot Salad

74. Veal Loaf, Macaroni and Cheese, Baked Tomatoes, Buttered Brussels Sprouts, Pineapple, Apple, and Celery Salad, Mayonnaise Dressing

75. Grilled Calf's Liver and Bacon, Hashed in Cream Potatoes, Sauté Pineapple, Fried Onions, Tomatoes Stuffed with Cucumber, French Dressing

76. Sweetbread Cutlet, Mushroom Sauce, Watermelon Pickle, Buttered New Peas, Cauliflower au Gratin, Orange, Grapefruit, and Grape Salad, French Fruit Dressing

77. Roast Veal, Brown Gravy, Brandied Peaches, Mashed Potatoes, Broccoli Hollandaise, Orange Sherbet, Tomato, Green Pepper and Celery Salad, French Dressing

78. Baked Veal Loaf, Broiled Tomatoes, Corn Pudding, Glazed Apricots, Hearts of Lettuce, Chopped Pickle

79. Broiled Sweetbreads and Bacon, Creamed Potatoes, Fried Mushrooms, Glazed Peach, Asparagus Tips in Tomato (small) Salad, Mayonnaise Dressing
80. Breaded Veal Cutlet, Spaghetti, Buttered Spinach, Globe Artichoke, Hollandaise

## Pork

81. Grilled Pork Tenderloin Steak, Spiced Crabapples, American Fried Potatoes
82. Old-style Smoked Sausage, Fried Hominy, Stewed Apples
83. Southern Pit Barbecue Sandwich on Bun, New Fall Cabbage Salad
84. Boiled Boneless Ham Hocks, Buttered Lima Beans,
85. Roast Loin of Pork, Spiced Crab Apples, Fried Sweet Potatoes, Sliced Tomatoes
86. Pan-fried Country Sausage, Pineapple and Apple Salad, American Fried Potatoes
87. Stuffed Pork Tenderloin, Candied Sweet Potatoes, Buttered Peas
88. Boiled Fresh Spareribs, Fancy Wisconsin Sauerkraut, Steamed Potato, Hot Corn Muffins
89. Grilled Sausages with Glazed Apples, Baked Stuffed Potato, Brussels Sprouts, Hollandaise Sauce, Tomato, Cucumber and Onion Salad, French Dressing
90. Broiled Pork Tenderloin, Maraschino Cherry Sauce
91. Pork Chop Sauté, Hot Stewed Apple
92. Assorted Cold Sausages, Combination Salad, Sweet Pickles
93. Broiled Pork Chops, Applesauce, New String Beans
94. Pork Tenderloin Sauté Country Style, Pineapple Fritter, Sweet Potatoes

95. Country Sausage Patties with Grilled Pineapple Ring, Whipped Potatoes and Wax Beans in Cream
96. Pork Sausage on Mashed Potatoes, Fried Apples, Buttered Carrots
97. Smoked Farm Sausage with Sauerkraut or Lentils, Sweet and Sour
98. Pork Chop Glacé, Apple Cakes, French-Fried Potatoes
99. Oven-baked Pork Chop, Waldorf Salad, Green Peas and Carrots
100. Braised Loin of Pork, Orange Sauce, Mashed Potatoes
101. Little Pig Sausages, Scrambled Eggs, and French-Fried Potatoes
102. Braised Pork Shoulder with Sauerkraut, Mashed Potatoes and Gravy
103. Braised Loin of Pork, Stuffed with Apple and Prunes
104. Stuffed Baked Apple with Sausage Meat, French-Fried Potatoes, Buttered Spinach, Hot Spiced Cabbage, Lettuce and Tomato Salad, French Dressing
105. Broiled Pork Tenderloin, Pepper Relish, Delmonico Potatoes, Apple Rings, Fried Eggplant, Orange and Onion Ring Salad, French Dressing
106. Baked Pork Chop, Applesauce, Lyonnaise Potatoes, Hot Spiced Beets, Buttered Broccoli, Grapefruit, Avocado Salad, French Dressing
107. Philadelphia Scrapple, Apple Butter, Pot Cheese, Fresh Vegetable Salad
108. Boiled Pickled Pigs Feet, Boiled Potatoes, Sauerkraut, Buttered Beets, Lettuce, Russian Dressing
109. Baked Pork and Beans, Brown Bread, Fried Apples, Pickled Beets, Hot Slaw, Lettuce, Russian Dressing
110. Spareribs, Sauerkraut, Dill Pickles, Mashed Potatoes, Buttered Green Beans, Orange and Prune Salad, French Dressing
111. Stuffed Pork Tenderloin, Warm

Spiced Applesauce, Delmonico Potatoes, Baked Beets, French-Fried Onions, Grapefruit and Orange Salad, French Fruit Dressing

112. Baked Stuffed Pork Chop, Sweet Potato Croquette, Succotash, Buttered Beets, Tomato and Grapefruit Salad, French Dressing

113. Roast Loin of Pork, Onion Dressing, Cinnamon Apple Rings, Baked Stuffed Sweet Potato, Buttered Green Beans, Jellied Tomato Salad

114. Broasted Pork Chops, Applesauce, Boiled Potato, New Green Peas, Hearts of Lettuce, Thousand Island Dressing

115. Barbecued Back Ribs, German Fried Potatoes, Green Beans with Slivered Almonds, Mixed Green Salad, Vinaigrette Dressing

## Lamb and Mutton

116. Spring Lamb Stew with Drop Dumplings and Fresh Vegetables

117. Spring Lamb, Virginia Ham, Navy Bean Salad Nicoise

118. Broiled Lamb Chop with Sauté Hawaiian Pineapple

119. English Lamb Chop Platter Bacon, Pickled Walnut, Fried Tomato, au Gratin Potatoes

120. English Mutton Chop, Fresh Mushrooms and Bacon

121. Grilled Lamb Chop with Ring of Pineapple Glacé

122. Stuffed Breast of Lamb with Pickled Crabapple

123. Boneless Devilled Breast of Lamb Polonaise with Spaghetti and Fresh Applesauce

124. Pan-Fried Lamb Cake, Pineapple Ring, Fresh String Beans

125. Broiled Lamb Chops and Vegetable Grill, Melon Balls in Lime Jelly

126. Pickled Lamb's Tongue, Vinaigrette Sauce, and Potato Salad

127. Grilled English Mutton Chop, Stripped with Bacon, Fresh Mushrooms Sauté on Toast, Idaho Baked Potato

128. Baby Lamb Hash with Eggplant en Bordure

129. Spring Lamb Steak Sauté with Bananas

130. Ragout of Spring Lamb with Fresh Vegetables

131. Two Lamb Chops, Pineapple Salad, Peas, Baked Idaho Potato

132. Curry of Spring Lamb Rajah Benares, Curried Rice with Raisins, New String Beans

133. Broiled Lamb Chop with Orange and Mint Relish, Baked Tomato, Pear au Gratin, Cucumber Salad, Sour Cream Dressing

134. Lamb Stew (Potatoes, Carrots, Celery, and Onions) Tea Biscuit, Prune Stuffed with Cottage Cheese Salad

135. Roast Leg of Lamb, Brown Gravy, Potatoes au Gratin, Buttered New Asparagus, Diced Summer Squash, Pineapple Mint Salad

136. Shepherd's Pie, Green Peas, Cauliflower Polonaise, Buttered Beets, Stuffed Peach Salad (Cream Cheese)

137. Stuffed Shoulder of Lamb, Green Peas with Mint, Braised Carrots, Green Beans, Hollandaise Sauce, Grapefruit and Cherry Salad, French Fruit Dressing

138. Broiled Lamb Chop, au Gratin Potatoes, Baked Stuffed Tomato, Sauté Pineapple with Mint Jelly in Center, Ginger Pear Salad

139. Roast Leg of Lamb, Dressing, Browned Potatoes, Buttered Carrots, Green Beans, Hollandaise Sauce, Grapefruit and Cherry Salad, French Fruit Dressing

140. Lamb Hash, Fried Hominy, Turnip Greens, Sauté Pineapple, Carrot, Banana, and Peanut Salad

141. Roast Leg of Lamb, Mint Apples,

Buttered New Peas, Creamed Cauliflower, Broiled Tomatoes, Orange and Date Salad, French Dressing

142. Broiled Lamb Chop, Currant Jelly, Banana Fritter, Lemon Sauce, Buttered Green Peas, Braised Carrots, Mint Jelly Salad with Diced Celery on Lettuce

143. Lamb Croquettes, Brown Gravy, Green Pepper Stuffed with Macaroni, au Gratin, Baked Carrots, Buttered Green Beans, Pear, Cream Cheese, Bar le Duc Dressing

144. Baked Breast of Lamb with Celery and Onion Stuffing, Baked Banana, Buttered Brussels Sprouts, Creamed Lima Beans, Jellied Raw Carrots and Orange Salad

## Chicken

145. Pan-Baked Chicken with Mushrooms, Buttered Baked Yam, Broiled Peach

146. Creamed Chicken and Hot Cheese Puff Sandwich, Waffle Potatoes, Pineapple Salad

147. Fried Half Spring Chicken, Banana Fritter, Long Branch Potatoes and New Asparagus

148. Chicken Cutlet, Celery Sauce

149. Sliced Capon with Mushrooms and Poached Eggs a la Reine au Gratin

150. Paprika Chicken en Casserole

151. Spring Chicken Platter with Bacon, Corn Fritter, Potato Croquette, Cream Sauce

152. Plantation Chicken Shortcake with Hot Corn Bread, Tender Slices of Chicken and a Delicious Hot Chicken Sauce Flavored with Smithfield Ham, Candied Sweet Potatoes, Cabbage Salad

153. Emince of Chicken au Curry Indienne, New Peas, Steamed Rice

154. Casino Special Creamed Chicken Sandwich, Fried Noodles

155. Curried Chicken with Rice and Shredded Fresh Coconut

156. California Chicken-Fried Steak

157. Sliced Breast of Chicken, Spiced Crabapples

158. Chicken Pot Pie, Family Style, with Carrots, Peas, Potato and Dumplings

159. Pan-fried Half Spring Chicken, Pineapple Fritters, and Shoe-String Potatoes

160. Hot Creamed Chicken and Sweetbreads in Puff Shell with Salad of Fresh Fruit

161. Chicken Cutlet, Mushroom Sauce, New Peas

162. Chicken Shortcake with Cauliflower, Pickled Beets, Sliced Tomatoes

163. French Chicken Loaf, Fresh Mushroom Sauce, New String Beans

164. Creamed Chicken and Mushrooms with Waffles

165. Half Spring Chicken Fried in Butter, Fig Fritters a la Crawford

166. Roast Capon, Giblet Sauce, Apricot Compote

167. Fried Breast of Chicken and Grilled Ham with Pineapple Ring

168. Hot Creamed Chicken in Puff Shell with Blushing Pear and Marron Salad

169. Baked Tomato Filled with Chicken and Mushrooms, Chicken Gravy and French-Fried Potatoes

170. Chicken Sauté with Fine Herbs and Rhine Wine, Served en Casserole

171. Boneless Chicken and Fresh Vegetables, en Casserole

172. Minced Chicken, Paprika and Rice Valencienne

173. Molded Chicken Salad on Sliced Pineapple

174. Hot Chicken Loaf, Chicken Gravy, Fresh String Beans

175. Fried Boneless Breast of Chicken with Ham, Peas, and Candied Sweet Potatoes

176. Sliced Breast of Chicken with As-

paragus Salad and Tomato Aspic

177. Chicken a la King on Toast, Brussels Sprouts, Snowflake Potatoes
178. Creamed Chicken on Toasted Noodles, Served with Parisian Potatoes and Buttered Fresh Asparagus Tips
179. Broiled Chicken Leg with Bacon, Sausages, Candied Sweet Potatoes, Creamed Spinach
180. Chicken Shortcake Delmonico
181. Chicken Croquettes (2) with Mushroom Sauce, Succotash, Sweet Potato
182. Hot Chicken Tamales, Mexican Sauce
183. Chicken Croquettes with Pimiento Cream Sauce, Potato Chips, and Fresh String Beans
184. Baked Chicken Loaf with Mushrooms and Shredded Almonds
185. Chicken Gumbo with Snickerdoodle (Raisin Coffee Cake)
186. Sliced Chicken on a Bed of Rice Covered with Chicken Gravy en Casserole
187. Chicken Fritters with Bacon, Cream Sauce, Mashed Potatoes, Summer Squash
188. Waffles with Creamed Chicken
189. Breast of Chicken on Virginia Ham, Sweet Potato Puff, Creamed Mushrooms, Buttered Green Beans, Avocado and Grapefruit Salad, French Dressing
190. Roast Stuffed Chicken, Cranberry and Orange Relish, Mashed Potatoes, Baked Winter Squash, Buttered Spinach, Tomato and Lettuce Salad, French Dressing
191. Roast Capon, Onion Dressing, Potato Balls, Parsley Butter, Stuffed Mushrooms, Baked Squash, Apple and Celery Salad, Boiled Dressing
192. Fried Chicken, Pickled Peaches, Sweet Potato Waffle, Buttered Green Beans, Creamed Mushrooms, Grapefruit and Cherry Salad, French Dressing
193. Roast Capon, Ripe Olives, Celery

Dressing, Steamed Rice Carrots O'Brien, Sliced Radishes on Watercress
194. Fried Chicken, Spiced Watermelon Relish, Creamed Baked Potatoes, Glazed Onions, Buttered Beets, Orange and Pear Salad, French Fruit Dressing
195. Chicken Cutlets, Mushroom Sauce, Buttered Lima Beans, Baked Stuffed Tomatoes, Creamed Onions, Jellied Pineapple and Cranberry Salad on Lettuce
196. Broiled Chicken, New Potatoes and Peas in Cream, Buttered Asparagus, Fried Eggplant, Fruit Salad with Honey and Sour Cream Dressing
197. Individual Chicken Pie with Cranberry Sauce, Corn on the Cob, Diced Summer Squash Glazed Onions, Orange and Banana Salad
198. Chicken Livers and Bacon en Brochette, Potatoes au Gratin, Buttered Onions, Baked Tomatoes, Apple and Celery Salad, Mayonnaise
199. Chicken Dumpling, Buttered New Peas, Broiled Tomato, Baked Banana, Currant Jelly, Cantaloupe and Mint Salad, French Fruit Dressing
200. Chicken Cutlets, Cranberry and Orange Relish, Buttered Green Peas, Baked Stuffed Tomato, Broiled Mushrooms, Julienne Celery, Cucumbers, and Pimiento Salad, French Dressing
201. Fried Chicken Sandwich, Currant Jelly, Buttered Green Beans, Glazed Pineapple, Broiled Tomato, Watercress, French Dressing
202. Creamed Chicken on Rice Cakes, Steamed Whole Tomatoes, Parsley Butter Sauce, Buttered Green Beans, Orange and Raisin Salad, French Dressing
203. Cold Chicken Loaf, Stuffed Olives, Potato Chips, Baked Tomato

Stuffed with Celery (Hot), Buttered Asparagus, Grapefruit and Strawberry Salad, French Fruit Dressing

204. Fricassee of Chicken with Biscuit, Corn Sauté, Fried Eggplant, Diced Buttered Carrots, Melon Ball Salad, French Fruit Dressing

205. Chicken Creole, Steamed Rice, Buttered Green Beans, Pineapple Fritter, Lemon Sauce, Lettuce, Chiffonade Dressing

206. Chicken Shortcake, Buttered Green Peas, Fried Mushrooms, Sauté Pineapple, Romaine Salad, Chiffonade Dressing

207. Tomato Stuffed with Chicken Salad, Ripe and Queen Olives, Potato Chips, Buttered New Asparagus, Baked Banana with Orange Sauce, Lettuce, Roquefort Cheese Dressing

208. Individual Chicken Pot Pie, Buttered New Peas, Broiled Tomatoes, Julienne Carrots, Jellied Cranberry and Apple Salad

209. Chicken Timbale, Buttered French Asparagus, Lattice Potatoes, Buttered Beets, Watercress, Orange, and Grapefruit Salad, French Dressing

210. Spring Chicken Baked in Cream, Served with Noodles Polonaise

211. Julienne of Chicken in Fricassee Sauce over Crisp Pecan Waffle

212. Disjointed Fried Chicken Maryland Style, with Corn Fritters and Cream Gravy

213. Half Chicken Sautéed in White Wine, Mt. Royal (Baked in Cocotte with Baby Carrots, Tiny Onions, and Parisienne Potatoes)

214. Casserole of Chicken Breast Sauté Caruso (Sautéed in White Wine with Egg Noodles, Mushrooms and Foie Gras)

215. Breast of Chicken Bostonian (Sautéed in White Wine served on Crisp Waffle with Lobster Garnish)

216. Breast of Chicken Chablis, Beacon Hill (Baked to a Golden Brown in Casserole with Egg Noodles and Mushrooms Parmesan)

217. New England Baked Half Chicken Glazed with Whole Cranberries

218. Orange Batter-Fried Chicken with Cream Gravy and Mandarin Garnish

219. Oven-Fried Crumbed Chicken on Saffron Rice, Creamed Pan Gravy

220. Lemon Broiled Chicken with Spiced Peach Garnish

221. Breast of Young Chicken Cordon Bleu

222. Philadelphia Chicken Leg Mixed Grill, Herbed Tomato

223. Baked Broiler-Chicken with Honey-Drizzled (Potato) Chip Coating

224. Boneless Breast of Chicken Hawaiian with Baked Banana

225. Boneless Breast of Young Capon Kiev

226. Boneless Breast of Chicken with Wild Rice, Sauce Supreme

227. Breast of Chicken Madeira with Bouquets of Fresh Vegetables

228. Chicken Cacciatore over Hot Green Noodles

229. Pan-fried Chicken Livers on Toasted French Bread with Chive Butter and Grilled Tomatoes

230. Cassolette of Baked Chicken and Noodles, Sauce Supreme and Mushrooms

231. Braised Chicken Leg with Vegetables, Folies Bergeres, Sauce Veloute

232. A Casserole of Young Chicken Baked with Rice, Spanish Style

233. Sliced Breast of Chicken and Virginia Ham Sauté, Sauce Supreme

234. Emince of Chicken and Oysters in Cream on French Toast

235. Chicken and Pineapple in Sauce Supreme over Noodles and Almonds

236. Curry of Chicken Indienne on Saf-

fron Rice

237. Southern Ham and Chicken Sweet Potato Pie with Jellied Cranberry Salad
238. Chinese Chicken Breasts (Julienne of Chicken Breasts Sauté with Water Chestnuts, Bamboo Shoots, Chinese Style, Served with Rice)
239. Baked Chicken Hash in Fresh Avocado, Pineapple Garnish
240. Brunswick Chicken Stew (With Corn, Onions, Salt Pork, Tomatoes, Potatoes, and Lima Beans)

## Duck and Goose

241. Roast Young Duck with Celery Dressing, Cranberry Sauce, Escalloped Sweet Potatoes and Apples
242. Supreme of Duck, Spiced Orange, Cauliflower, and Candied Sweet Potatoes
243. Roast Duck Legs, Apple and Raisin Dressing, Giblet Sauce
244. Roast Duck, Apple and Prune Stuffing
245. Mallard Duck in Casserole, Fresh Mushrooms, Port Wine Sauce
246. Filet of Duckling, Fruit Macedoine
247. Roast Stuffed Duckling with Pickled Fruit
248. Stewed Duckling, Cherries and Pineapple
249. Roast Fresh-killed Baby Duckling, New String Beans in Butter, Whole Glazed Apple, Fried Sweet Potatoes
250. Cold Roast Duck, Candied Sweet Potatoes, Orange and Onion Salad
251. Baked Domestic Duck, Dressing, Orange Relish
252. Roast Duck, Apple Stuffing, Fried Sweet Potatoes, Hot Spiced Red Cabbage, Buttered Green Beans, Jellied Orange Salad
253. Roast Duck, Chestnut Stuffing,

Rice Croquettes, Currant Jelly, Buttered Spinach, Stuffed Onions, Red Apple Salad, Boiled Dressing
254. Roast Goose, Sage Dressing, Potato Puff, Glazed Apples, Hot Spiced Beets, Grapefruit and Celery Salad, French Dressing
255. Roast Stuffed Young Watertown Goose with Sweet Pickle, Pork Dressing and Applesauce
256. Barbecued Young Duckling served with Tart Apple-Berry Sauce
257. Broiled Ginger Duck with Kumquats, Saffron Rice
258. Honey-Glazed Duckling with Plum Sauce
259. Braised Apple Stuffed Duckling with Montmorency Cherries
260. Julienne of Cape Cod Duckling with Sautéed Mushrooms and Orange in a Rice Ring
261. Braised Duckling a l'Orange, Sweet Potato Croquettes
262. Roast Long Island Duckling with Apples and Sauerkraut
263. Salmis of Duckling in Red Wine on a Bed of Wild Rice
264. Braised Young Duckling a la Stroganoff on Brown Rice

## Squab, Pheasant, Quail, and Guinea Hen

265. Roast English Pheasant, Bread Crumbs and Bread Sauce
266. Whole Roast Pheasant, Champagne Kraut (Served for Two)
267. Quail in Cocotte with Pineapple
268. Guinea Hen Leg Mixed Grill
269. Grilled Boned Squab Chicken with Banana and Pineapple
270. Roast Stuffed Quail, Wild Rice Croquette
271. Barbecued Broiled Squab on Toast, Spiced Crabapple
272. Grilled Royal Squab on Toast,

Rasher of Bacon, Wild Rice, Glazed Figs
273. Whole Stuffed California Squab, Texas Figs
274. Grilled Royal Squab on Toast, Orange Basket

## Turkey

275. Roast Young Indiana Turkey, Oyster Dressing, Cranberry Sauce, Candied Sweet Potatoes, Celery, and Olives
276. Turkey Cutlets (2) with Creamed Succotash
277. Roast Turkey, Chestnut Stuffing, Giblet Gravy, Baked Bananas with Cranberry Sauce, Buttered Brussels Sprouts, Mashed Yellow Turnips, Jellied Pineapple and Grated Raw Carrot Salad
278. Turkey Cutlets (2) Olé, Jardinere
279. Hot Turkey Hash with Poached Eggs, Plum Butter, and Toasted Rolls
280. Creamed Spring Turkey Hash, Small Oyster Plant Fritter
281. Creamed Turkey Flakes and Mushrooms in Patty Shell
282. Curried Turkey Legs with Pineapple
283. Turkey a la King with Waffle
284. Combination Turkey Fritters, Sliced Canadian Bacon, Fried Apples and Country Gravy
285. Creamed Sliced Turkey a la King with Rice Pilau
286. Turkey Cutlets, Cauliflower, Potato Cake
287. Skillet Barbecued Small Turkey with Mushrooms and Olives
288. Oven-Fried Baby Turkey with Pan Gravy Piquante
289. Broiled Young Turkey with Rosemary and Whole Cranberries
290. Emince of Turkey and Mushrooms with Water Chestnuts on Chinese Noodles, Cashew Nut Garnish
291. Fillet of Turkey Breast Cordon Bleu, Sauce Supreme
292. Sliced Breast of Turkey on Buttered Noodles, Fricassee Sauce
293. Migonettes of Turkey in Sweet Sour Sauce, Served with Chinese Cabbage, Celery and Pineapple, Garnish of Macadamia Nuts
294. Turkey Divan, Parisienne Slices of Turkey on Broccoli, Mornay Baked to a Bubbling Brown
295. Fried Turkey Turnovers Served with Old-Fashioned Cream Gravy
296. Baked Turkey Hash en Cocotte Topped with Poached Egg
297. Curried Turkey Amandine on Egg Noodles Polonaise
298. Emince of Turkey Baked in Cream with Spaghetti, Mornay
299. Turkey Scaloppine in Marsala Wine with Fresh Mushroom Slices
300. Turkey and Shrimp Orientale (Diced Turkey and Baby Shrimp Combined in a Soy Sauce with Pineapple Chunks and Bamboo Shoots, Served with Rice)
301. Fillet of Turkey Baked in Cream, Served with Sweet Potato Glacé
302. Baked Devilled Turkey Leg with Spiced Crabapple
303. Roast Native Turkey with Cornbread Dressing, Giblet Gravy, and Whole Cranberry Sauce
304. Sliced White Meat of Turkey and Country Ham, Chablis Sauce

## Ham

305. Virginia Ham Baked in Cider with Greens
306. Roast Prime Ham in Sherry Wine, Pan Cream Gravy, Candied Yams
307. Poached Egg Hollandaise on Sautéed Ham with Green Peas

308. Fried Sugar-Cured Ham with Plain Spinach and Fried Banana
309. Grilled York Ham Steak, Applesauce, Candied Sweet Potatoes
310. Roast Fresh Jersey Ham Glacé, Applesauce, Winekraut, Puree Potatoes
311. Baked Spiced Berkshire Ham, Wine Sauce, Spiced Pear
312. Baked Sugar-Cured Ham, Pineapple Sauce
313. Boiled Virginia Ham and Cabbage
314. Roast Fresh Ham, Baked Apple Stuffed with Raisins, Scalloped Potatoes, Glazed Beets, Buttered Spinach, Cabbage and Pimiento Salad, French Dressing
315. Broiled Ham Steak, Fried Sweet Potatoes, Buttered Spinach, Creamed Mushrooms, Egg and Green Pepper Salad
316. Baked Ham, Mustard Sauce, Candied Sweet Potatoes, Globe Artichokes, Hollandaise Sauce, Scalloped Cabbage, Pineapple, Marshmallow Salad, Boiled Dressing
317. Ham Cutlets, Horseradish Sauce, Scalloped Potatoes, Glazed Pineapple, Hot Cabbage with Sour Cream, Melon Ball Salad, French Fruit Dressing
318. Broiled Ham Steak, Colbert Sauce, Puree of Fresh Broccoli, Fried Sweet Potatoes
319. Ham Baked in Cream, Baked Stuffed Sweet Potato with Pineapple, Buttered Asparagus, Beet Greens, Jellied Tomato Salad
320. Ham Loaf, Scalloped Sweet Potatoes with Apples, Buttered New Cabbage, Fried Eggplant, Escarole, Chiffonade Dressing
321. Scalloped Ham and Potatoes, Buttered Spinach, Fried Summer Squash, Pineapple and Cream Cheese Salad, Mayonnaise Dressing
322. Frizzled Ham, Corn Fritters, But-

tered Brussels Sprouts, Baked Tomatoes, Broiled Peach, Chicory, Chiffonade Dressing
323. Cold Baked Ham, Baked Beans (Hot), Steamed Brown Bread, Sliced Tomatoes, Cabbage Salad, Boiled Dressing
324. Baked Ham Loaf, Mustard Sauce, Breaded Noodles, Buttered Spinach with Egg, Glazed Apples, Escarole, Pimientos, French Dressing
325. Baked Ham with Cider Sauce, Baked Banana, Corn Sauté, Broccoli with Hollandaise Sauce, Jellied Raw Spinach and Carrot Salad
326. Ham Loaf, Mustard Sauce, Candied Sweet Potatoes, Buttered Spinach, Cauliflower au Gratin, Lettuce, Russian Dressing
327. Baked Ham, Raisin Sauce, Scalloped Sweet Potatoes and Apples, Buttered Asparagus, Celery au Gratin, Orange and Pear Salad, French Dressing
328. Candied Virginia Ham, Cider Sauce, Creamed Spinach
329. Roast Spiced Ham, Cumberland Sauce, and Kadota Figs
330. Mousselines of Virginia Ham, Paprika, Creamed Spinach
331. Baked Sugar-Cured Ham, Honey Sauce, Candied Sweet Potatoes, Pineapple and Apple Salad
332. Baked Ham and Spiced Raisins
333. Cold Ham Loaf, Potato Salad, Butter Pickles
334. Fried Slices of Virginia Ham and Oysters with Brown Rice
335. Roast Sweet Pickled Ham, Champagne Sauce
336. Hawaiian Ham Steak, Pineapple Glacé
337. Baked Sugar-Cured York Ham, Cider Sauce, Braised Red Cabbage
338. Ham Steak Fried with Honey, Baked Squash, Heart of Lettuce, Thousand Island Dressing
339. Broiled Sliced Virginia Ham,

French Pancake

340. Virginia Ham Steak, Pineapple and Sweet Potatoes, Champagne Sauce
341. Baked Sugar-Cured Ham, Fruit Sauce, New Spinach, and Parsley Boiled Potato
342. Boiled Ham with Sauerkraut, Crabapple

## Bacon

343. Canadian Bacon and Baked Eggs
344. Broiled Bacon, Sweet Potato Croquette, Glazed Apple Rings, Buttered Spinach, Lettuce and Tomato Salad, French Dressing
345. Broiled Canadian Bacon, Baked Bananas, French Pancakes, Currant Jelly, Sweet Gherkins, Celery and Apple Salad, Mayonnaise Dressing
346. Broiled Bacon, Baked Stuffed Tomato, Potato Chips, Devilled Eggs on Spinach, Apple and Celery Salad, Mayonnaise Dressing
347. Broiled Bacon, Spiced Peaches, French Pancakes, Orange Sauce, Baked Tomato Stuffed with Corn and Green Peppers, Pear and Ginger Salad

## Fish and Seafood

348. Broiled Bluefish with Baked Stuffed Potato and Pickled Beets
349. Scalloped Oysters, Cole Slaw, Browned New Potato
350. Clam Fritters with Cole Slaw Salad
351. Barbecued Oysters
352. Crab Flakes and Shrimp, Russian Dressing, Cole Slaw
353. Omelette with Creamed Oysters
354. Breaded Oysters, Tartar Sauce, French-Fried Potatoes, Sliced Tomatoes

355. Fresh Crab Salad in Avocado Half with Bran Muffins
356. Six Broiled Oysters (in Shell) Topped with Crabmeat
357. Creamed Cod Fish with Sliced Eggs on Toast
358. Baked Fresh Mackerel, White Wine Sauce with Mushrooms, Potato Duchesse
359. Melted Cheese over Fresh Crab on Toast
360. Broiled Shad Roe, Bacon
361. Panned Oysters with Waffle
362. Broiled Fresh Swordfish Steak with Anchovy Butter
363. Colorado Brook Trout Sautéed in Butter with Toasted Almonds
364. Broiled Halibut Steak with Scallops and Pineapple en Brochette
365. Fresh Jumbo Shrimp and Rice in Casserole, Louisiana Style
366. Ocean Fresh Codfish Baked in White Wine with Tomato, Onion and Green Pepper Slices
367. Fluffy New England Codfish Balls with Spicy Tomato Sauce and Poached Egg
368. Fillet of Sole Marguery in White Wine with Mushrooms, Shrimp, and Oysters
369. Individual Casserole of Baked Tuna and Egg Noodles Topped with Tomato and Parmesan Cheese
370. Golden Brown Tuna Croquettes with Tangy Olive Sauce
371. Spaghetti with Minced Clam and Shrimp Sauce Topped with Parmesan Cheese
372. Baked Salmon Loaf with Shrimp and Egg Sauce
373. Old New England Yankee Oyster Pie with Flaky Pastry Crust
374. Finnan Haddie Delmonico with French-Fried Potatoes
375. Codfish Cakes and Fried Salt Pork, Boston Baked Beans
376. Oyster Crab Patty, Newburg Sauce
377. Marinated Herring in Sour Cream
378. Omelettte with Diced Shad Roe

and Peppers

379. Young Codfish Breaded Sauté, Mustard Sauce, Hashed Brown Potatoes, Brussels Sprouts
380. Lobster and Shrimps, Bordelaise, Rice Timbale
381. Stuffed Tomato with Crab Flake and Caviar
382. Devilled Clam Petite, Fried Tomato, French-Fried Potatoes
383. Broiled Fresh Haddock, Mustard and Egg Sauce, Parsley Potato
384. Salmon Croquettes, Cream Sauce, Buttered Broccoli
385. Jumbo White Fish Sauté with Toasted Almonds and Small Chef's Salad
386. Oyster Omelette with Green Beans and Pineapple Salad, Hot Bread
387. Baked Fresh White Fish Stuffed a la Creole with Beet and Horseradish Salad
388. Crab Flakes with Green Peppers on Toast
389. Crabmeat Casserole with Mushrooms, Hard-Boiled Eggs and Chopped Green Peppers
390. Baked Homemade Egg Noodles, Fresh Shrimp a la Creole au Gratin
391. Seafood in French Pancake
392. Baked Weakfish Portugaise
393. Three Fried Oysters, Relish, French-Fried Potatoes, Baked Beans
394. Crabmeat a la Maryland
395. Fresh Shrimps Creole on Toast with Steamed Rice
396. Brochette of Oysters and Shrimps, Evangeline
397. Broiled Oysters on Toast, Bacon, Lattice Potatoes, Baked Tomato Stuffed with Celery
398. Oyster Shortcake, Buttered Green Peas, Grilled Mushrooms
399. Baked Macaroni and Oysters, Grilled Tomatoes, Buttered Green Beans
400. Scalloped Tuna Fish, Lyonnaise Potatoes, Buttered Beets
401. Baked Stuffed Fillet of Haddock, Hashed Brown Potatoes, Stewed Tomatoes
402. Fish Hash, Pickled Beets, Cole Slaw
403. Finnan Haddie Baked in Cream, Baked Potato, Pickled Beets
404. Scalloped Oysters, Potato Chips, Broiled Tomatoes
405. Cold Poached Salmon with Mayonnaise, Devilled Egg, Cucumber Stuffed with Anchovy, Tomato Stuffed with Vegetable Salad
406. Lobster and Mushrooms au Gratin, Buttered Asparagus, Julienne Potatoes
407. Oysters, Scallops and Mushrooms en Casserole
408. Tuna Fish Timbale, Cream Sauce, Buttered Green Peas, Stuffed Mushrooms
409. Broiled Pompano, Parsley Butter Sauce, Baked Potato, Okra Sauté
410. Crabmeat Chow Mein, Fried Noodles
411. Broiled Shad Roe, Creamed Potatoes, Buttered Asparagus
412. Creamed Salt Codfish, Baked Potato, Pickled Beets, Hot Corn Bread
413. Poached Flounder on Spinach, Cheese Sauce
414. Baked Fillet of Flounder, Mushroom Stuffing, Oyster Sauce, Glazed Onions
415. Baked Fillet of Haddock, Cheese Sauce, French-Fried Potatoes, Buttered Asparagus
416. Steamed Halibut, Lobster Sauce, Stuffed Baked Potato, Buttered Brussels Sprouts
417. Mackerel Baked in Milk, Boiled New Potatoes, Fried Eggplant
418. Broiled Sardines on Toast, Lemon, Creamed Asparagus, Cole Slaw
419. Tuna Fish Loaf, Olive Sauce, Lattice Potatoes, Broiled Tomatoes
420. Broiled Oysters on Toast, Creamed Celery, Bacon
421. Shrimps in Curry Sauce, Boiled Rice, Chutney
422. Baked Whitefish, Butter Sauce, Po-

tato Puff, Fried Tomatoes

423. Broiled Kippered Herring, Butter Sauce, Boiled Potatoes, Pickled Eggs

424. Grilled Sea Trout, Duchesse Potatoes, Red Cabbage

425. Broiled Weakfish, Hashed Brown Potatoes, Scalloped Tomatoes

426. Boiled Salt Mackerel, German Fried Potatoes (Breakfast or Lunch)

427. Fried Perch, Parsley Buttered Potatoes, Tomato Stuffed with Cole Slaw

428. Broiled Halibut, Anchovy Butter, au Gratin Potatoes, Buttered Spinach

429. Baked Red Snapper with Tomato Sauce, Mashed Potato, Glazed Onions

430. Broiled Scrod, Potato Croquette, Diced Yellow Turnips

431. Devilled Crab, Tartar Sauce, Julienne Potatoes, Sliced Tomatoes

432. Broiled Lobster, Saratoga Potatoes, Cucumber Salad, Sour Cream Dressing

433. Baked Salmon, Egg Sauce, Mashed Potatoes, Buttered Carrots and Peas

434. Baked Fillet of Cod, Oyster Stuffing, Delmonico Potatoes, Buttered Corn, Dill Pickles

435. Baked Pike with Onion Stuffing, Buttered Green Beans, French-Fried Potatoes

436. Broiled Sea Bass, Parsley Butter, Baked Stuffed Potato, Spiced Beets

437. Fried Smelts, Tartar Sauce, Delmonico Potatoes, Buttered Broccoli

438. Finnan Haddie au Gratin, Baked Potato, Buttered Green Beans

439. Baked Bluefish, Parsley Butter Sauce, Lyonnaise Potatoes, Harvard Beets

440. Poached Salmon Steak, Creamed New Potatoes, Buttered Spinach

441. Fillet of Haddock, Baked with Cheese Sauce, Parsley Buttered Potatoes, Grilled Tomatoes

442. Broiled Halibut Steak, Spanish Sauce, Duchesse Potatoes, Fried Egg Plant

443. Baked Stuffed Fillet of Haddock, French-Fried Onions, Creole Rice

444. Baked Tomato Stuffed with Tuna Fish, Potato Chips, Broccoli with Hollandaise Sauce, Sweet Pickles

445. Crabmeat a la King in Patty Shell, Potato Croquette, Broiled Tomato

446. Broiled Mackerel, Lemon Butter, Gaufrette Potatoes, Cauliflower au Gratin, Sliced Cucumbers, Catsup Dressing

447. Broiled Swordfish, Egg Sauce, Olivette Potatoes, Buttered Green Beans

448. Baked Salmon Loaf, Cream Sauce with Olives, Potato Nests with Green Peas, Radish Roses

449. Curried Shrimp, Steamed Rice, Buttered Green Beans, Pepper Relish

450. Sautéed Fillet of Flounder, Lemon Butter, Delmonico Potatoes, Buttered Brussels Sprouts, Pickled Beets

451. Codfish Cake with Poached Egg, Tomato Sauce, Buttered Green Beans, Cabbage Salad

452. Broiled Spanish Mackerel, Lemon Butter Lyonnaise Potatoes, Buttered Asparagus

453. Scrambled Eggs with Shad Roe, Hashed Brown Potatoes, Cornsticks (Breakfast or Lunch)

454. Tuna Fish Timbale, Caper Sauce, Creamed New Potatoes, Buttered Peas, Grated Raw Carrot and Cabbage Salad

455. Baked Tomatoes Stuffed with Crabmeat, Lattice Potatoes, Broccoli Hollandaise

456. Baked Bluefish with Oyster Stuffing, Parsley Buttered Potatoes, Hot Spiced Beets

457. Scallops a la King, Potato Croquettes Sliced Fresh Tomatoes on Lettuce
458. Fried Scallops, Tartar Sauce, Grilled Tomatoes, Buttered Green Beans
459. Baked Oysters Casino, French-Fried Potatoes, Broccoli Hollandaise
460. Planked Shad, Mashed Potato Nests with Green Peas, Baked Bananas
461. Lobster Cutlets with Mushroom Sauce, Scalloped Potatoes, Buttered Asparagus
462. Broiled Oysters on Toast, Bacon, Lattice Potatoes, Baked Tomato Stuffed with Celery
463. Oyster Shortcake, Buttered Green Peas, Grilled Mushrooms
464. Baked Macaroni and Oysters, Grilled Tomatoes, Buttered Green Beans
465. Scalloped Tuna Fish, Lyonnaise Potatoes, Buttered Beets
466. Fish Hash, Pickled Beets, Cole Slaw
467. Broiled Fillet of Haddock, Lemon Butter, Parisienne Potatoes, Sour Red Cabbage
468. Lobster and Mushrooms au Gratin, Julienne Potatoes, Buttered Asparagus
469. Oysters, Scallops and Mushrooms en Casserole, Baked Potato
470. Tuna Fish Timbale, Cream Sauce, Buttered Green Peas, Stuffed Mushrooms
471. Fillet of Cod, Baked with Tomato Sauce, Lattice Potatoes, Glazed Onions, Pepper Relish
472. Fried Shad Roe, Creamed Potatoes, Baked Bananas with Lemon
473. Creamed Salt Cod Fish, Baked Potato, Pickled Beets, Hot Corn Bread
474. Poached Flounder on Spinach, Cheese Sauce, French-Fried Onions
475. Baked Fillet of Flounder, Mushroom Stuffing, Oyster Sauce, Glazed Onions
476. Poached Halibut, Lobster Sauce, Stuffed Baked Potato, Buttered Asparagus
477. Fillet of Haddock Sauté, Cucumber Hollandaise Sauce, Baked Stuffed Potato, Buttered New Peas
478. Mackerel Baked in Milk, Boiled New Potatoes, Fried Eggplant
479. Creamed Shrimp and Mushroom Patty, Broiled Tomato, Sauté Pineapple
480. Broiled Swordfish, Lemon Butter, Parsley New Potatoes, Baked Stuffed Tomato
481. Fried Fillet of Sole, Tartar Sauce, Buttered Lima Beans, Lettuce and Tomato Salad, French Dressing
482. Fried Cod Fish Cakes, Tomato Sauce, Buttered Green Beans, Scalloped Cabbage
483. Baked Lake Trout, Boiled New Potatoes, Broccoli Hollandaise
484. Broiled Salmon Steak, Glazed Pineapple Ring, Green Peas, Potato Soufflé
485. Broiled Butterfish, French-Fried Potatoes, Sliced Cucumbers on Watercress, French Dressing
486. Stewed Carp with Mushrooms, Carrots, Onions, and Potatoes
487. Fried Frog Legs, Creamed Potatoes, Buttered Asparagus
488. Broiled Stuffed Pickerel, Boiled Potatoes, Buttered Onions, Tomato and Lettuce Salad
489. Fried Porgies, Baked Potato, Scalloped Celery and Potatoes
490. Fried Whiting, Spaghetti with Tomato Sauce, Buttered Asparagus
491. Lake Perch Sauté Meuniere, Browned Potatoes, Buttered Carrots
492. Fried Whitefish with Parsley Potatoes, New Green Peas, Creole Celery
493. Whitefish Cutlets Sauté with Mushroom Sauce, Baked Stuffed Potato,

Broiled Tomatoes

494. Broiled Red Snapper, Lemon Butter, Buttered Brussels Sprouts, Boiled Potato, Mixed Green Salad, Dressing
495. Broiled Grouper, Glazed Pineapple Ring, au Gratin Potatoes, Steamed Broccoli, Sliced Tomatoes and Onions, Vinaigrette Dressing
496. Blackened Grouper, Creole Sauce, French-Fried Potatoes, Spinach, Cole Slaw
497. Fillet of Flounder Stuffed with Crabmeat, Parsley Potato, Buttered Green Beans, Head Lettuce with Thousand Island Dressing
498. Fillet of Scrod Sauté, Tartar Sauce, Green Pasta, Steamed Wax Beans, Romaine Salad with Caesar Dressing
499. Broiled Mahi Mahi, Tomato Sauce, Spiced Pineapple Ring, Hashed Brown Potatoes, Peas and Carrots
500. Broiled Shark Steak, Lemon Sauce, Long Branch Potatoes, Fried Okra, Sliced Beefsteak Tomatoes on Lettuce
501. Poached Monk Fish, Drawn Butter, O'Brien Potatoes, Buttered Broccoli, Greek Salad with Feta Cheese

## Egg Dishes

502. Shirred Eggs, Boulangere with Sausage and Fresh Mushrooms
503. Poached Eggs Anna Held (Toast, Sliced Chicken, Poached Eggs, Cream Sauce au Gratin)
504. Poached Eggs on Fish Cake, Newburg Sauce, Asparagus Tips in Butter
505. Shirred Eggs with Swiss Cheese and Stewed Tomatoes
506. Creamed Eggs and Devilled Smithfield Ham on Toast
507. Scrambled Eggs with Kippered Herring

508. Poached Eggs Alsacienne (Poached on Sauerkraut with Liver Paste and Madeira Sauce
509. Shirred Eggs with Crab Flakes in Cream
510. Scrambled Eggs with Tomato Sauce
511. Scrambled Eggs with Anchovy Toast
512. Scrambled Eggs with Creamed Mushrooms
513. Scrambled Eggs with Stuffed Mushrooms
514. Scrambled Eggs with Creamed Sweetbreads
515. Scrambled Eggs with Shad Roe
516. Scrambled Eggs with Rice and Bacon
517. Mint Jelly Omelette, French-Fried Potatoes, Toast
518. Red Currant Jelly Omelette with Pear Fritter
519. Stuffed Eggs a la Russe, Cole Slaw
520. Omelette with Preserved Apricots
521. Scrambled Eggs with Shad Roe, Mixed Salad
522. Scrambled Eggs Country Style on Toast with Fillet of Anchovies, Creamed Succotash, Fried Hominy
523. Eggs Benedict
524. Swiss Cheese Omelette
525. Omelette with Stewed Cherries, Crabapple
526. Omelette Confiture with Glass of Sherry
527. Scrambled Eggs, Broiled Chicken Livers, Potato Pancake
528. Shirred Eggs with Lamb Kidneys
529. Curry of Eggs with Rice, Mushrooms, and Mango Chutney
530. Shirred Eggs with Creamed Finnan Haddie
531. Egg Pancake with Fresh Rhubarb Compote
532. Shirred Eggs with Virginia Ham and Pineapple
533. Stuffed Eggs with Crabmeat, Russian Dressing
534. Scrambled Eggs with Shad Roe and

Peppers, Carrots and Peas, Parsley Potato

535. Moulded Egg Ring Filled with Sweetbreads and Mushrooms
536. Potato and Egg Salad with Smoked Fillets of Herring
537. Chef's Salad with Anchovies and Sliced Hard-Boiled Eggs
538. Stuffed Egg and Jellied Perfection Salad with Rye Bread
539. An Individual Casserole of Devilled Eggs in Cheese Sauce with Shrimp and Mushrooms
540. Tartlets of Poached Eggs Baltimore with Corn Sauté and Hollandaise Sauce
541. A Pair of Eggs Shirred with Sugar-Cured Ham and Sweet Potatoes
542. An Individual Casserole of Mushroom-Stuffed Eggs in Cream Sauce with Parmesan Cheese
543. Poached Fresh Country Eggs on Wild Rice with a Tangy Tomato Sauce
544. Poached Eggs Florentine on Buttered Fresh Spinach Topped with Cheese Sauce
545. Poached Eggs Benedict on Toasted English Muffin with Country Ham or Canadian Bacon, Hollandaise Sauce
546. Golden French Omelette with Asparagus, Sauce Mornay
547. Western Omelette with a Medley of Diced Country Ham, Bell Pepper and Onion
548. Creamy Scrambled eggs with Sautéed Chicken Livers and Sliced Fresh Mushrooms
549. Shirred Eggs with Tiny Chicken Croquettes and Fresh Tomato
550. Omelette with Diced Bacon, Ham, Peppers, and Onions

## Cheese

551. Cottage Cheese, Prunes and Shredded Carrots, Peanut Butter Sandwich
552. American Cheese, Liver Sausage with Saratoga Chips
553. Cream Cheese on Toast, Currant Jelly, Bacon Strips
554. Canapé of Anchovy, Melted Swiss Cheese, Bacon
555. English Rarebit with Poached Egg and Bacon, Buttered English Muffin
556. Cheese Rarebit on Toast with Broiled Bacon, Tomato Slices, and a Fresh Purple Plum Salad
557. Buttered Egg Noodles with Cheese Fondue and Grilled Bacon
558. Welsh Rarebit on Toast with Pineapple Ring, Green Olives and Radishes
559. A Baked Cheese and Noodle Ring with a Center of Creamed Sweetbreads and Chicken and a Frozen Fruit Salad
560. Cheese Blintzes, Sour Cream Dressing
561. Baked Macaroni and Cheese, Red Cabbage, String Beans
562. Pot Cheese and Sour Cream with Chives and Boiled Potato
563. Cheese Omelette with French-Fried Potatoes
564. Grilled Cheese and Candied Pineapple Sandwich (Open)
565. French Pancake Filled with Cottage Cheese and Raisins, French-Fried Sweet Potato, Buttered New String Beans

## Vegetable Dishes

566. Fresh Vegetable Plate with Fried Egg
567. Kaldoma (Stuffed Cabbage Swed-

ish Style) with Mashed Potatoes and Fresh Cranberry Sauce

568. Chilled Tomato Filled with Seafood Salad, Cream Cheese Sandwich
569. Grilled Tomato with Sauté Mushroom Caps, Asparagus Hollandaise, and a Waldorf Salad
570. Stuffed Eggplant a l'Ancienne, Mushroom Sauce, Lima Beans
571. French Vegetable Plate with Green Beans, Harvard Beets, French-Fried Eggplant
572. Tiny Artichoke and Mushrooms, Mornay, Grilled Eggplant
573. Baked Stuffed Green Pepper, Creamed Potatoes
574. Baked Tomatoes with Vermicelli Parmesan
575. Raw Vegetable Lunch (Grated Carrots, String Beans, Chopped Celery, Sliced Tomatoes, and Julienne of Lettuce
576. Fresh Vegetable Dinner with Capon Croquette
577. Assorted Vegetable Salad Plate with Sardine and Hard-Cooked Egg
578. Vegetable Plate with Tomato Slices, Green Onions, Radishes, Celery, Devilled Egg, Swiss and American Cheese
579. Creamed Mushrooms on Toast, Grilled Tomato
580. Salad Plate Italian Garden: Lettuce, Asparagus, Artichoke, Avocado, Cheese
581. Creamed Fresh Mushroom Patty, Stuffed Celery, and Ripe Olives
582. Jellied Tomato Ring with Celery Mayonnaise, Cottage Cheese, and Chives
583. Braised Stuffed Cabbage, Family Style, Brown Gravy
584. A Plate of Hot Vegetables with a Glass of Apple Cider
585. Buttered Asparagus, Spiced Red Cabbage, Scalloped Potatoes, Buttered Carrots
586. Dandelion Greens, Parsley Buttered New Potatoes, Buttered Beets, Creamed Carrots
587. Asparagus au Gratin, Mashed Rutabagas, Buttered Endive, Pineapple Fritter, Spiced Red Cabbage
588. Asparagus Hollandaise, Glazed Onions, Creamed Mushrooms, Buttered Beets, Fried Apples
589. Artichoke (Globe) Hollandaise, Young Onions in Cream, Spiced Red Cabbage
590. Asparagus Hollandaise, Rice Cake, Hot Slaw, Buttered Green Beans, Glazed Apples
591. Vegetable Plate with Escalloped Corn, Brussels Sprouts, Buttered Beets, Hashed Brown Potatoes
592. Iceberg Head Lettuce, Devilled Eggs, Sliced Red Ripe Tomatoes, Wafers and Butter
593. Buttered Kale, Creole Rice, Diced Beets, Mashed Turnip
594. Stuffed Baked Potato, Glazed Onions, Fried Eggplant, Diced Carrots, Buttered Green Beans, Hot Spiced Beets
595. Sweet Potato Waffle, Scalloped Cabbage, Broiled Tomato, Buttered Green Beans, Glazed Pineapple, Buttered Spinach
596. Buttered Broccoli, Hot Spiced Beets, Buttered Endive, Broiled Tomato, Glazed Apples, Baked Beans
597. Asparagus au Gratin, Sour Red Cabbage, Pineapple Fritter, Mashed Rutabagas
598. Baked Onion au Gratin, Apple Fritter, Buttered Spinach, Candied Sweet Potatoes, Creamed Carrots
599. Asparagus Hollandaise, Buttered Beets, Buttered Kale, Diced Carrots, Fried Mushrooms, Macaroni and Cheese
600. Dandelion Greens, Glazed Pineapple, Spaghetti with Mushrooms

## Pancakes and Waffles

601. Grilled Country Ham and Broiled Tomato on Crisp Golden Waffle Topped with Cheese Sauce
602. Rolled Delicate Pancakes Stuffed with Diced Smoked Ham and Sautéed Mushrooms Topped with Rarebit Sauce
603. Lazy-Dazy Pancakes with Creamy Cottage Cheese, Spiced Peach, and Hot Fruit Sauce (arrange dollar-sized pancakes petal fashion around a mound of cottage cheese for a "daisy")
604. Folded Golden Brown Pancakes with Apricot Jam (strawberry, pineapple, plum or other flavored jams may be substituted)
605. Old-Fashioned Chicken Fricassee on Crisp Southern Waffle
606. Fresh Blueberry Pancakes with Crisp Bacon, Whipped Butter and Pure Vermont Maple Syrup
607. Golden Brown Almond-Rice Pancakes with Plantation Creamed Chicken (creamed tuna or salmon may be substituted)
608. Crisp Cinnamon-Nut Waffle with Grilled Canadian Bacon and Hot Apple Sauce
609. Cottage Cheese Filled Pancakes and Sour Cream and Red Caviar
610. Rolled Pancakes with Chopped Beef and Mushrooms in Sour Cream, Tomato Slices
611. Crisp Golden Waffle with Maple Butter and Crisp Bacon or Fresh Strawberries
612. Delicate Thin Pancakes with Maple Butter and Crisp Bacon or Fresh Strawberries
613. Crisp Golden Waffle with Creamed Chipped Beef and Mushrooms

## Miscellaneous

614. Old-Fashioned Potato Pancakes with Crisp Bacon and Hot Cinnamon Applesauce
615. Hawaiian Style Broiled Ham with Corn Fritters and Maple Syrup
616. Glazed Baked Ham Loaf with Green Gage Plum Sauce
617. Individual Casserole of Mushroom Chop Suey with Steamed Rice and Crisp Noodles
618. Golden Brown Apple Fritters with Maple Syrup and Country Sausage
619. A Plate of Garden Fresh Vegetables with Poached Egg and Rarebit Sauce. Note: A timbale of garden spinach, Harvard beets, lemon-buttered broccoli, grilled tomato and Vichy carrots
620. Baked Macaroni and Cheese en Casserole Topped with Grilled Tomato
621. Golden French Toast with Grilled Tomato Slices and Stuffed Mushroom Bonnets
622. Spaghetti with Marinara Sauce Topped with Romano Cheese
623. Baked Hamburger Pinwheel with Mushroom Gravy. Note: Green or Spinach Spaghetti or Noodles may be used
624. Old-Fashioned Corned Beef Hash with Poached Egg
625. Savory Hamburger Pot Pie with Sliced Fresh Mushrooms
626. Baked Italian Lasagna with Ground Beef and Ricotta Cheese in Tomato Sauce
627. Individual Casserole of Baked Corn Pudding with Grilled Tomato and Canadian Bacon

## Money-Making Sandwiches

628. Open-faced Tomato, Cheese, and Bacon Sandwich on Toast, Ripe Olives
629. Chicken Sandwich Supreme au Gratin, Spiced Peach
630. Hot Baked Ham Sandwich with Fruit and Raisin Sauce, French-Fried Sweet Potatoes, and Mustard Pickle
631. Fresh Seafood Newburg Sandwich with French-Fried Potatoes and Green Peas (Use cut-up shrimp, halibut, and sea scallops)
632. French-Toasted Ham and Cheese Sandwich with Green Onions and Crisp Radishes
633. French-Fried Fillet of Sole on Toasted Roll, Cole Slaw, Sliced Tomato, and Tartar Sauce
634. Hot Roast Turkey Sandwich, Giblet Gravy, and Whole Cranberry Sauce
635. Shrimp Rarebit Sandwich, Tomato Wedge and Celery Hearts
636. An Open Sandwich of Baked Ham with Chicken Hash au Gratin on Toast, Glazed Pineapple Ring
637. Baked Ham and Asparagus on Toasted English Muffin with Cheese Sauce, Hard-Cooked Egg Garnish
638. Fried Oysters on Toast with French-Fried Potatoes, Sliced Tomatoes, Cole Slaw and Ketchup
639. Broiled Frankfurters on Toasted Roll with Cheese Sauce, Tomato Wedges, and Pickle Chips
640. Fried Boneless Chicken Leg on Toast with Pineapple Cole Slaw
641. Open Chopped Chicken Sandwich Baked with Sliced Pineapple and American Cheese, Spiced Crabapple
642. Argentine Grill: Turkey, Bleu Cheese, Tomato, and Bacon on Toast
643. Horizon Special: Turkey, Tomato, Lettuce, Hard-Boiled Egg, and Bacon Served Open-faced on Toast
644. Monte Cristo: 3-Decker, Deep-Fried, Chicken, Ham and Swiss Cheese
645. Camelot: Open-faced, Turkey, Tomato, Shredded Lettuce, Bacon and Thousand Island Dressing
646. Golden Gate Chicken Sandwich: Open-faced, Chicken, Avocado, Tomato on Lettuce, Russian Dressing
647. Hot Ham and Turkey Sandwich Princess: Open Ham and Turkey Topped with Green Asparagus Spears and Cheese Sauce
648. Turkey Sandwich Grill: Chopped Turkey and Pickle Relish Salad Topped with Grated Cheddar Cheese, Broiled and Served Open with Grilled Tomato Slices and Crisp Bacon
649. French-Toasted Turkey Sandwich: Served with Orange-Cranberry Relish
650. Suzie Wong's Delight: Combine Slices of Turkey Breast with Boiled Ham in a Rolled Sandwich—Sliced and Dipped in Egg Batter and Fried in Deep Fat—Garnish with Lettuce, Tomato, and Watercress
651. Turkey Hamburger on a Bun with Whole Cranberry Sauce
652. Seafarer's Hero: A Crusty French Bread Sandwich of Sardines, Tomato, Hard-Cooked Egg and Romaine served with a Cucumber Wedge and Lemon
653. Biloxi Twist Shrimp Sandwich: A Bountiful Portion of Gulf Shrimp on Toast with Crisp Slaw Topped with Pineapple Twist and Ripe Olive. Served with a Piquante Cocktail Sauce
654. Beefeaters's Favorite: A Generous Portion of Thinly Sliced Roast Beef on Buttered Rye Bread. Served with Crisp Cole Slaw, Dill Pickle, and Radish Rose

655. Nut Bread, Cream Cheese, and Minted Melon
656. Cream Cheese and Anchovies on Rye Bread
657. Graham Date Bread with Prune Cream Cheese
658. Nut Bread, Cream Cheese, and Orange Marmalade
659. Gorgonzola, Cream Cheese, Smoked Beef, and Horseradish Served on Toasted Wheat Bread
660. Melted Cheese and Grilled Hawaiian Pineapple, Bacon Served Open-faced on Rye with Pickle Chips
661. Cold Roast Pork with Raspberry Jelly and Tomato on White Bread
662. Chicken Club: Double-decked Toasted White Bread with Breast of Chicken, Bacon, Lettuce and Tomato
663. White House: Chopped Chicken and Baked Ham on Buttered White Bread Served with Sweet Relish
664. Student Sandwich: Baked Ham, Peanut Butter on White Bread with Lettuce, Tomato and Spiced Pear
665. Toasted Minced Tongue and Bacon Sandwich
666. Sliced Breast of Turkey, Virginia Ham, and Swiss Cheese Double-decked Served with Cole Slaw and Russian Dressing
667. Fried Salami and Egg, Pancake Style on Pumpernickle
668. Pounded Steak Sandwich, French-Fried Potatoes
669. Bacon, Lettuce, and Tomato Served on Toasted White Bread
670. Manhattan: Baked Ham, Swiss Cheese, Lettuce on Rye Served with Red Beet Salad
671. Coffee Shop Club: Chopped Virginia Ham, Lettuce, Tomato, Melted Cheese, Currant Jelly Served Open-faced
672. Smoked Liver Sausage Sandwich with Kosher Dill Pickle
673. Hot Creamed Chicken and Noodle Sandwich on Toast, Potatoes, and Country Gravy
674. Hot Prime Ribs of Beef Served Open-faced with Mashed Potatoes and Gravy
675. Sliced Ham and Fried Egg with Sliced Breast of Chicken Served Double-Decked on Toast

## Salad Combinations

676. Stuffed Prunes and Cottage Salad, French Dressing
677. Fresh Fruit Salad with Almond Cream Dressing and Toasted Vienna Coffee Cake
678. Fruit Salad with Strawberry, Mayonnaise
679. Fruit Salad with Chicken Salad Sandwich
680. Diced Roman Beauty Apple, Crisp Texas Celery, Chopped Walnuts, Preserved Plum, California Peach, Chilled Lettuce
681. Banana Filled with Fresh Fruit Salad and Pecan Muffins
682. Fresh Fruit Plate with Cottage Cheese, Sherbet, Finger Sandwiches
683. Jellied Cantaloupe Salad
684. Grapefruit and Orange Sections Arranged on Sliced Pineapple, Garnished with Rosettes of Cream Cheese and Maraschino Cherries, Served with Creamed Mayonnaise
685. Orange and Prune with Cream Cheese
686. Lettuce, Diced Apples, Pineapple, Pears, Celery, Mixed with Creamed Cottage Cheese and Served with French Dressing
687. Cantaloupe Filled with Fresh Fruit Salad, Cream Dressing
688. Apricot and Frozen Fruit Salad, Toasted Pecan Loaf
689. Fresh Peach Salad with Raspberry Cream Dressing and Cream Cheese and Nut Sandwich

690. Hawaiian Fruit Plate
691. Log Cabin Banana and Nut Salad, Cream Dressing, Wafers
692. Charm House Frozen Fruit Salad, Whipped Cream Dressing with Minced White Meat of Chicken Sandwiches
693. Sliced Fresh Pineapple with Cream Cheese and Pimiento Ball on Crisp Lettuce, French Dressing, Toast and Jelly
694. Cantaloupe Ring Filled with Fresh Fruits, Waffle Potato
695. Salad Bowl with Shredded Summer Sausage
696. Chicken Salad with Pineapple Rings
697. Chicken Salad Heaped on Pineapple Halves, Garnished with Cheese and Nut Balls, Served with Mayonnaise
698. Combination Salad Plate: Center of Chicken or Fresh Shrimp, on Large Plate, Surrounded with Fresh Fruits and Vegetables on Bed of Lettuce, Served with Hot Breads
699. Cold Sliced Chicken with Fresh Fruit Salad
700. Ham Cones Filled with Potato Salad
701. Bombay Salad: Chicken, Fresh Coconut, Rice and Relish, Chutney-French Dressing
702. Shredded Chicken and Vegetables, Lorenzo Dressing
703. Grapefruit, Orange and Stuffed Date Salad with Melba Toast
704. Health Salad: Chopped Raw Cabbage, Carrots and Pineapple
705. Asparagus Salad, French Ketchup Dressing, Prune Bread Toast
706. Chef's Salad Bowl with Crab Flakes, Lemon Cream Dressing
707. Chilled Tomato Stuffed with Chicken Salad, Golden Brown Toast
708. Tuna and Avocado with Nut Sandwiches
709. Assorted Salad Plate: Chicken Salad, Potato Salad, Fruit Salad, and Vegetable Salad in Individual Lettuce Cups
710. Kit Kat Special: Crisp Lettuce, Fresh Tomato, Caviar, Chopped Celery, Shredded Green Peppers, Anchovies, Cucumbers, Shallots, Sliced Egg

## Appetizers

711. Coupé of Fresh Fruit with Melon Balls
712. Oysters on Half-Shell Dressed with Red Caviar, Fresh Ground Horseradish
713. Half Grapefruit with Mandarin Oranges
714. A Variety of Fresh Seafoods with Avocado Slices
715. Fruit Juice Shrub with Sherbet
716. Chilled Tomato Juice with Stuffed Celery
717. Broiled Pink Grapefruit with Minted Coconut
718. Seasonal Melon with Lime
719. A Wreath of Fresh Grapefruit and Apples, Tokay
720. Melon Ring with Macedoine of Fresh Fruit
721. Mulled Cranberry Juice Cocktail
722. Herring in Sour Cream, Apple Slices
723. Pink Grapefruit Grenadine
724. A Coquille of Seafood Salad with Avocado Slices
725. Fresh Fruit in Orange Cup
726. Pink Grapefruit au Pomeganate
727. Frosty Tomato Juice with Chived Cheese and Crackers
728. Oysters on the Half Shell with Caviar
729. Shrimp Cocktail en Coquille
730. Hot Mushroom Caps with Crabmeat a l'Aurore

731. Fresh Shrimp in Jellied Tomato Ring
732. Devilled Eggs with Red Caviar
733. Hearts of Artichoke with Anchovy Fillets Vinaigrette
734. Fruit Cup with Raspberry Sherbet
735. Cranberry Shrub
736. Shrimp Platter with Stuffed Celery and Red Sauce
737. Honey-Broiled Grapefruit
738. A Cup of Autumn Fruits with Port
739. Cherrystone Calms on the Half-Shell
740. Baked Stuffed Oysters with Crabmeat Mornay
741. Jumbo Shrimps on Tomato Slice, Russian Dressing
742. Chilled Fresh Apple Cider
743. Vermont Maple-Glazed Grapefruit
744. Supreme of Autumn Fruits, Cranberry Sherbet
745. Potted Baby Shrimps in Garlic Butter
746. Blue Point Oysters on the Half-Shell
747. Coquille of Scalloped Oysters
748. Fresh Shrimp Cocktail, Remoulade and Red Sauces
749. Cape Cod Cocktail (Cranberry and Orange Juices)
750. Tomato and Clam Juice Cocktail
751. Broiled Grapefruit with Sherry
752. Herring in Cream, MacIntosh Slices
753. Supreme of Autumn Fruits Topped with Orange Sherbet
754. Hot Crabmeat Canapé
755. Alaskan King Crabmeat Canapé, Russian Dressing
756. Cherrystone Clams Served on Crushed Ice
757. Shrimp and Grapefruit Sections, Piquante Sauce
758. Curried Stuffed Eggs, Shredded Lettuce
759. Tomato Filled with Salmon Flakes
760. Poached Apple with Chicken Liver Pâté

761. Baked Coquille of Crabmeat
762. Melon Decorated with Fresh Fruit
763. Herbed Tomato Juice with Cheese Sticks
764. Coquille of Baked Scallops au Gratin
765. V-8 Cocktail with Cheese Straws
766. Fresh Curried Seafood on Tomato Slice
767. Coquille of Scalloped Oysters
768. Shrimp Mayonnaise with Avocado
769. Honey-Grilled Grapefruit
770. Clamato Juice Cocktail with Lemon
771. Shrimp Bowl with Cocktail Sauce
772. Sweet Apple Cider with Cinnamon Sticks
773. Coquille of Shrimps on Crushed Ice, Stuffed Celery, Remoulade and Cocktail Sauces
774. Fresh Autumn Fruit Ambrosia
775. Supreme of Autumn Fruits Topped with Orange Sherbet
776. Broiled Fresh Cape Scallops in Sweet Butter
777. Supreme of Fresh Seafood on Ice
778. Broiled Grapefruit with Maple Syrup
779. Coupé of Fresh Fruits, Elegante
780. Man-Sized Shrimp Cocktail, Sauce Oscar
781. Medley of Fresh Mixed Fruits in Kirsch
782. Norwegian Sardines on Lettuce, Lemon Wedge
783. Parfait of Shrimp, Sauce Rosé
784. Liver Pâté on a Bed of Watercress Madeira
785. Small Tomato Stuffed with Shrimp a la Russe
786. Minted Honeydew Slices with Lime
787. Hearts of Artichoke and Tomato Vinaigrette
788. Frosted Cranberry Juice Cocktail
789. Supreme of Strawberries and Pineapple
790. A Cut of Cantaloupe with Fresh Fruits

791. Supreme of Fresh Fruits, Strawberry Garnish
792. Pickled Pink Eggs and Asparagus Vinaigrette
793. Herring and Apple Canapé
794. Avocado Boat with Fresh Strawberries, Honey Dressing
795. Pineapple Boat with Fresh Fruit and Sherbet
796. Chunks of Alaskan King Crab, Remoulade Sauce
797. Pink Grapefruit with Grapes
798. Panned Crab with Almonds on Melba Toast
799. Sliced Eggs on Artichoke Heart, Vinaigrette
800. Stuffed Devilled Eggs with Anchovies on Shredded Lettuce
801. Half Grapefruit with Shrimp Cocktail Garniture
802. Italian Artichoke Cup Filled with Fresh Crabmeat on Sliced Tomato
803. Iced Honeydew, Fresh Lime
804. Small Tomato Stuffed with Shrimp Salad, Sliced Hard-Cooked Egg
805. Louisiana Shrimp on Pink Grapefruit Slices a la Russe
806. Honeydew Melon with Smoked Salmon
807. Stuffed Cherry Tomatoes with Shrimp Salad and Caviar
808. Coronets of Cantaloupe with Lime
809. Devilled Egg Molded in Tomato Aspic
810. Baby Shrimp on Ice
811. Fresh Seafood in Aspic Ring, Curried Mayonnaise
812. Stewed Prunes in Port Wine
813. Supreme of Fresh Fruit Ambrosia
814. Apricot Nectar Frappé
815. A Salad of Crabmeat and Shrimp on Pineapple Ring
816. Hot Broiled Tuna Canapé with Cheese and Tomato
817. Supreme of Strawberry and Pineapple
818. Hot Broiled Mushrooms Stuffed with Crabmeat Mornay

819. Liver Pâté on Pineapple Ring
820. Brochette of Chicken Livers, Water Chestnuts, and Bacon
821. A Coquille of Seafood Salad with Pineapple
822. Fresh Strawberries with Powdered Sugar
823. Sliced Bananas in Cream
824. Baked Rhubarb and Pineapple
825. Stuffed Eggs with Fresh Asparagus Vinaigrette
826. Smoked Salmon with Chopped Hard-Cooked Eggs and Onions
827. Chopped Chicken Livers with Pimiento Chopped Hard-Cooked Egg and Onion on Lettuce
828. Hot Crabmeat Canapé Topped with Anchovy
829. Coquille of Seafood in White Wine, Gratinee
830. Casserole of Shrimp in Beer
831. Chilled Melon with Prosciutto
832. Baked Oysters on the Half-Shell
833. Broiled Mediterranean Scampi en Brochette with Garlic Butter
834. Lobster Cocktail on Ice with Stuffed Celery Lemon and Two Sauces
835. Potted Shrimp Old Norfolk
836. Anchovy Canapé—Minced Anchovies and Hard-Boiled Eggs on Buttered Toast
837. Anchovy Tartines—Circles of Brown Bread Spread with Anchovy Paste, Decorated with Sliced Gherkins
838. Anchovies aux Olives—Anchovy Toast Garnished with Sliced Stuffed Olives
839. Bouchees of Chicken with Truffles
840. Bouchees of Oysters
841. Bouchees a la Reine—Filled with Diced Tongue, Chicken, Truffles, and Mushrooms in Sauce Supreme
842. Bouchees a la Strasbourg—Filled with Foie Gras and Mushrooms
843. Hard-Boiled Egg Stuffed with Caviar
844. Lamb Kidney Paste Seasoned with Butter, Cayenne, Salt, and Lemon

Juice on Toast

845. Minced, Seasoned Lobster Meat on Buttered Toast

846. Cocktail Sausages with Red Sauce

## Soups

847. Cream of Mushroom with Watercress
848. Consommé Madrilene
849. Tomato Bouillon with Rice
850. Cream of Peanut Soup
851. Clear Turtle Soup
852. Old-Fashioned Tomato Soup
853. Cream of Chicken Soup
854. Oyster Bisque
855. Old-Fashioned Chicken Noodle Soup
856. Cream of Tomato Soup Sprinkled with Parsley
857. Clear Beef Broth
858. Cream of Corn Chowder
859. Spiced Tomato Bisque, Whipped Cream
860. Old-Fashioned Beef Vegetable Soup
861. New England Clam Chowder
862. Manhattan Clam Chowder
863. Old-Fashioned Chicken and Corn Soup
864. Mushroom Consommé
865. Cream of Corn Soup
866. Hearty Beef Soup with Spring Vegetables
867. Snapper Soup with Dry Sack Sherry
868. Chilled Fresh Cucumber Soup
869. Chilled Danish Fruit Soup
870. Shrimp Bisque
871. Chicken a la Reine
872. Chicken Broth with Rice
873. Cream of Fresh Asparagus Soup
874. French Onion Soup with Croutons
875. Consommé with Fresh Spring Vegetables
876. Hot Vichyssoise with Fresh Dill

877. Cold Vichyssoise
878. Steaming Onion Soup with Cheese
879. Essence of Tomatoes Madrilene
880. Fresh Mushroom Bisque
881. Ruby Consommé Topped with Chived Whipped Cream
882. Black Bean Soup Laced with Sherry
883. Hot Tomato Bouillon with Sour Cream
884. Cream of Watercress Soup
885. Gaspacho
886. Cream of Cheese Soup
887. Potage Basque (Barley Soup)
888. Chilled Tea House Orange Soup
889. Chilled Duchess Soup
890. Chilled Curry Soup
891. Cold Strained Gumbo
892. Split Pea Soup
893. Lentil Soup with Frankfurter Slices
894. Chicken Gumbo Soup
895. She-Crab Soup
896. Dutch Potato Soup
897. Rice Soup Florentine
898. Bouillabaisse
899. Consommé with Vermicelli
900. Old-Fashioned Navy Bean Soup

## Desserts

901. Hot Fresh Apple Pie with Cider Sauce
902. Pumpkin Pie with Whipped Cream
903. Angel Food Cake with Peppermint Stick Ice Cream
904. Mixed Fresh Fruit Ambrosia
905. Fruit Jello with Whipped Cream
906. Flaming English Plum Pudding with Brandy and Hard Sauce
907. North Pole Snowball, Fudge Sauce
908. Lemon Sherbet with Menthe Parfait
909. Buch de Noel (Christmas Log)
910. Nut-Glazed Pumpkin Pie
911. Danish Apple Cake, Whipped Cream
912. Southern White Fruit Cake

913. Hot Mincemeat Pie, Brandy Sauce
914. Peppermint Stick Parfait
915. Pumpkin Chiffon Pie with Pecans
916. Egg Nog Tortoni
917. Biscuit Tortoni
918. Flaming Cranberries Jubilee
919. Egg Nog Ice Cream
920. Hot Fresh Apple Pie with Cheddar Cheese
921. Pistachio Ice Cream with Raspberry Sherbet
922. Winter Pear Baked in Maple Syrup
923. Rum Butter Parfait
924. New England Walnut Torte, Whipped Cream
925. Baked Indian Pudding with Vanilla Ice Cream
926. Orange Chiffon Cake with Coffee Ice Cream
927. Jellied Ambrosia with Whipped Cream
928. Cranberry and Orange Sherbet with Old-Fashioned Sugar Cookies
929. Baked Roman Beauty Apple, Whipped Cream
930. Maple-Rum-Nut Parfait
931. Pumpkin Custard Pie with Whipped Cream and Candied Ginger
932. Baked Apple Dumpling, Rum Butter Sauce
933. New England Black Walnut and Molasses Pie, Whipped Cream
934. Hot Gingerbread Topped with Soft Ice Cream
935. Brandied Mincemeat Tart
936. Walnut-Stuffed Baked Apples
937. Wine Jello with Soft Custard Sauce
938. Poached Bartlett Pear, Cinnamon Whipped Cream
939. Baked Apple Stuffed with Nuts and Raisins
940. Spiced Autumn Pears in Port
941. Ginger Bavarian Cream with Foamy Sauce
942. Golden Nut Brownies a la Mode
943. Mincemeat Ice Cream, Homemade Gingersnaps
944. Chocolate Layer Cake

945. Grape Jello Chantilly
946. Double Chocolate Sundae with Salted Peanuts, Whipped Cream
947. Baked Apple Dumpling, Rum Butter Sauce
948. Hot Ginger Bread Topped with Vanilla Ice Cream
949. Baked Apple Dumpling, Currant-Cider Sauce
950. Southern Pecan Pie, Chantilly
951. Chocolate Nut Sundae
952. Grapes in Jelly with Custard Sauce
953. Old-Fashioned Fresh Strawberry Shortcake
954. Fresh Peach Pie
955. Cherry Pie
956. Chocolate Chiffon Pie
957. Lemon Chiffon Pie
958. Frozen Ice Cream Pie with Strawberry Sauce
959. Chocolate Fudge Cake
960. Marble Layer Cake
961. Fresh Peach Sundae
962. Fresh Strawberry Tart
963. Frozen Profiteroles au Chocolat
964. Chocolate Eclair
965. Napoleon Slice
966. French Buttercream Pastry
967. French Cream Horn
968. Palm Leaf Toasts
969. Cheese Cake with Strawberry Sauce
970. Cheese Cake with Cherry Sauce
971. Chocolate Chip Cheese Cake
972. Angel Food Cake a la Mode, Melba Sauce
973. Red Cherry Lattice-top Tartlett
974. Pecan Snowball with Fudge Sauce
975. Lattice Rhubarb Tartlett
976. Key Lime Pie
977. Chocolate, Marshmallow Nut Sundae
978. Creme de Menthe Parfait
979. Frozen Raspberry Angel Food
980. Hot Fudge Puff Chantilly
981. Peanut Brittle Chiffon Pudding
982. Old-Fashioned Bread Pudding
983. A Wedge of Fresh Pineapple with Creme de Menthe

984. Compote of Fresh Fruit with Sauternes
985. Chocolate Pistachio Parfait
986. Baked Caramel Custard
987. Rice Pudding
988. Peppermint Stick Ice Cream Roll
989. Carrot Cake
990. Cherry Jubilee Meringue
991. Date-Nut Torte with Ice Cream, Butterscotch Sauce
992. Fresh Rhubarb and Apple Pie
993. Chocolate Chiffon Pie
994. Old-Fashioned Deep-Dish Blueberry Pie
995. Old-Fashioned Deep-Dish Strawberry Shortcake
996. Frozen Eclair, Raspberry Sauce
997. Fresh Lime Meringue Pie
998. Banana Caramel Cream Pie
999. Boston Cream Pie, Melba Sauce
1000. Hazelnut Cream Pie
1001. Chocolate Chip Pie with Almond Crust

## All-Time Best Sellers

*Prime Rib of Beef*—The all-time *best seller* dinner entrée in restaurants and banquets.

*Pot Roast of Beef*—The number one best seller at banquet luncheons and number two behind Prime Rib at dinner.

*Lamb Stew*—Believe it or not, it is the banquet luncheon best seller in Hawaii.

*Apple Pie with Rat (Cheddar) Cheese*—The best seller luncheon dessert.

*Double Rich Ice Cream*—The best seller dinner dessert in restaurants.

*Breaded Veal Cutlet*—The best seller at "Club Luncheons" in hotels.

*Coupé of Fresh Fruit with Melon Balls*—Tops the list of best seller appetizers at banquet functions.

*Old-Fashioned Beef Vegetable Soup*—Perhaps it is not a sophisticated choice, but it is the best seller soup.

*Hot Kosher Corned Beef on Dark Rye* and *French Dip*—In bars that serve sandwich luncheons, these two items tie for best seller.

*Roast Cornish Game Hen*—Politicians who have a lot of speaking engagements are said to be on the "Chicken and Peas" circuit. They eat very well because this is the best seller of Roast Chicken items.

*Best Seller (Easter)*—Baked Sugar-Cured Ham with Orange Wheels.

*Best Seller (Mothers' Day)*—Pan-Roasted Spring Chicken, Maryland Style, Sauce Supreme.

*Best Seller (Thanksgiving Day)*—Roast Tom Turkey with Chestnut-Sage Dressing.

*Best Seller (Christmas Day)*—Prime Ribs of Beef, Yorkshire Pudding.

*Beef.* In America's steak houses, Prime Rib is still the first choice of the guests; however, in the steak line, men favor the hearty Boneless Strip Sirloin Steak at 12 to 13 ounces. Women customers choose the Fillet Mignon with Bernaise Sauce. The size can be as small as 6 ounces and is seldom larger than 8 ounces. The Sirloin Butt Steak is presented as the "House Favorite Steak" in many restaurants.

*Veal.* In Italian restaurants, Scaloppine of Veal, Marsala, is the favorite in this meat category.

In family restaurants, Calf's Liver with Bacon tops the list of veal favorites. Actually few veal dishes are featured in these restaurants.

In French restaurants, Les Mignons de Veau Savoyarde avec les Pates Fraiches (Thick slices of Veal Tenderloin topped with Cheese and Fresh Pasta) is a regular feature and a popular choice.

*Pork.* Broiled Pork Chops, Baked Pork Chops, Broasted Pork Chops, all accompanied by a variety of apple (Applesauce, Cinnamon Apple, Spiced Apple Rings, etc.). Take your pick from these hearty items.

*Lamb.* The Double French Lamb Chops with Mint Sauce is a favorite alternative to the Prime Rib or Steak in American signature restaurants. A Single Lamb Chop is a popular suggestion as a low-calorie diet luncheon. In New England, Roast Leg of Lamb is offered at many dinner parties at home.

*Poultry.* Kentucky Fried Chicken has made its title selection the largest selling poultry item in the United States and perhaps the world. Breast of Chicken Cordon Bleu and Kiev made as convenience entrées have found great favor as banquet selections, and Breast of Chicken on Ham Slice with Sauce Supreme is the leading poultry dish in signature restaurants.

*Fish.* The best sellers in this category vary with the different geographical regions of the United States. Boston Scrod or Schrod (if cut from a small cod it is spelled Scrod; if from a small haddock it is spelled Schrod) is the favorite in New England. In the southeast it is Red Snapper or Grouper, depending on availability. Snapper Throats is a favorite luncheon item in Mobile, Alabama, and New Orleans. In Dairyland, U.S.A., and the Bread Basket of our country, Walleyed Pike has mouths watering. Chicago opts for Lake Whitefish. On the west coast, the Petrale Sole is first choice. On the Fourth of July in Boston, not to have Fresh Salmon and Fresh Peas is unpatriotic bordering on criminal.

*Other Seafood.* Again, there are regional favorites. Maine Lobster would very likely be a national favorite if there were availability and the price was not nearly a day's wages. Regional pride might keep shrimp a favorite in the Gulf of Mexico area despite the above assertion. Blue Crab in Baltimore and Dungeness Crab in San Francisco are the popular choices in these great cities. Oysters are the most universally eaten shellfish.

*Salads.* The most popular entrée salad at ladies' luncheons is the Chef's Salad. This has taken many forms but the classic Chef's Salad is composed of lettuce, radishes, tomato, julienne breast of chicken, ham, and cheese, with slices of hard-cooked egg. Dressing can vary. A Fruit Plate with a center of Cottage Cheese or Sherbet with Finger Sandwiches is a summer favorite at resort hotels.

The most widely eaten side salad is the Mixed Green. Lack of imagination on the part of both restaurateurs and guests is probably as responsible for the popularity of this selection as desires of taste. The Waldorf Salad is a favorite side salad of fruit.

*Sandwich.* Thanks to McDonald's, Burger King, Big Boy, and company, the Hamburger is the most widely eaten sandwich in the world. It also is a leading luncheon item on the menus of family restaurants. It is difficult to find a menu without some form of hamburger (ground beef) present—Hamburger Steak, Salisbury Steak, Swedish Meat Balls, and so on. There are a couple of other sandwiches that merit "honorable mention." The BLT (Bacon, Lettuce, and Tomato) ranks high in the selection of female office workers at luncheon. A bit upscale from the BLT is the Club Sandwich. A favorite low-priced sandwich is the Grilled Cheese Sandwich. In France or Quebec it is popular as the "Croque Monsieur."

*Desserts.* Apple Pie and Ice Cream are the perennial favorites, but for variety check above where we have listed 101 desserts.

## Summary

In the authors' nearly one hundred years' experience in the food service industry, the above "best sellers" stand out as leaders year in and year out. The challenge of people coming into the industry is to create items that can compete for popularity with these favorites.

# A Glossary for Menu Writers

**A la.**   In the style or fashion of.

**A la broche.**   Cooked on a skewer.

**A la carte.**   Meal chosen item by item. Each item is prepared to order and priced separately.

**A la goldenrod.**   Chopped, hard-cooked egg whites in cream sauce. Grated egg yolks serve as a garnish.

**A la king.**   Contains a thick cream sauce with egg yolks, pimientoes, and mushrooms.

**A la mode.**   Literally in the fashion of. With reference to pie, topped with ice cream; to beef, larded and braised.

**Ambrosia.**   Cold dessert of fruits, usually bananas, shredded coconuts, and oranges.

**Anchovy.**   Small fish of the herring family, usually salted and pickled. Often used as an appetizer garnish.

**Antipasto.**   Italian hors d'oeuvres, appetizer, or relish served as a first course.

**Apple strudel.**   Dessert of rolled dough on which apples, sugar, cinnamon, butter, and sometimes almonds are spread.

**Aspic.**   Clear jelly made from meat, fish, poultry, or vegetable stock.

**Au beurre..**   Cooked with butter.

**Au gratin.**   Topped with cheese and browned off.

**Au jus.**   Served with natural juices or gravy.

**Au naturel.**   Natural or plain cooking.

**Baba au rhum.**   Individual molded yeast cake soaked in a rum-sugar solution.

**Baked Alaska.**   Solid frozen brick of ice cream on cake, covered with meringue and oven browned quickly.

**Bavarian cream.**   Either whipped cream or a thick custard mixed with gelatin to which a variety of fruits and liqueurs may be added, shaped in fancy molds.

**Bechamel.**   Thick white sauce of butter, flour, and milk and seasoned with onion, spices, and carrots.

**Bill of fare.**   The menu list of food selections.

**Bisque.**   Thick, creamy seafood soup or stew. May also be a frozen dessert with nuts.

**Bordelaise.**   Food items flavored with Bordeaux wine. Also a brown sauce with beef marrow containing *mirepoix* (carrots, celery, onions, and seasoning).

**Borsch (also spelled Borsheh, Bortch, Bortsch, Borscht).**   Russian soup made of beef stock, beets, tomatoes, seasoning, and served with sour cream.

**Boston cream pie.**   Sponge cake of two layers filled with thick cream or custard. Served in pie-shaped pieces. Variations may be white or chocolate layer cake with chocolate or other fillings.

**Bouillabaisse.** Five or six varieties of fish cooked with white mushrooms. White wine is added before serving. The broth and fish are often served separately.

**Bouillon.** Clear soup made from meat, fish, or vegetable.

**Brochette.** Meat roasted on a spit.

**Brown Betty.** Apple pudding with bread crumbs, spices, and sweetening, served with either lemon sauce or whipped cream.

**Brunswick stew.** Chicken or veal with corn, onion, salt pork, tomatoes, potatoes, and lima beans. In the South, rabbit is often used in place of the chicken or veal.

**Cabinet pudding.** Gelatin, milk, eggs, and macaroon, in a mold with whipped cream.

**Cafe au kirsch.** Coffee with kirschwasser liqueur.

**Cafe au lait.** Coffee with scalded milk.

**Cafe brule.** After-dinner coffee with brandy and whipped cream.

**Cafe diable.** Hot black coffee with brandy and a twist of orange rind.

**Cafe noir.** Black coffee.

**Cafe royale.** Coffee with cognac.

**Camembert.** Soft, full-flavored cheese.

**Canapé.** An appetizer made of fried or toasted bread spread with anchovies, pastes, eggs, cheese, or other savory foods.

**Caper.** Pickle bud of a prickly shrub grown in California and the Mediterranean region.

**Carte du jour.** Menu of the day.

**Caviar.** Eggs of the sturgeon, slightly salted and pressed.

**Chantilly-consommé.** Chicken broth with diced chicken, chervil, peas, and shredded lettuce. Sauce cold—mayonnaise with lemon juice and whipped cream; sauce hot—bechamel blended with whipped cream; soup—cream soup with pureé of peas and lettuce.

**Charlotte russe.** Thin sponge cake or split lady fingers line a mold, its center filled with sweetened, flavored whipped cream and gelatin.

**Chateaubriand.** Thick tenderloin steak served with brown or Spanish sauces, garnished with parsley.

**Cheddar cheese.** Hard, smooth yellow cheese.

**Chiffonade.** Shredded green vegetables used for soups and salads. Salad—shredded romaine, lettuce, chicory, escarole, sliced cucumbers, and quartered tomatoes. Served with French dressing.

**Chili con carne.** Finely ground meat, beef, or pork that has been fried with chili powder, then simmered with tomatoes and kidney beans.

**Chives.** Plant of the onion and leek family with a delicate flavor, used in salads, soups, and garnishes.

**Chutney.** A relish, sweet or sour, served with curried dishes.

**Cobbler.** Baked of sugar, butter, eggs, and milk; filled with fruit, with rich biscuit toppings.

**Cocktail.** An appetizer; may be fruit, juice, shellfish, or alcoholic beverage.

**Compote.** A mixture of fruit stewed in syrup.

**Consommé.** A clear soup made with meat, poultry, game, or fish stock.

**Corned beef.** Pickled beef, usually the brisket.

**Cottage pudding.** Baked pudding of milk, butter, sugar, eggs. Served with a hot sauce.

**Creole sauce.** Sauce prepared with green peppers, tomatoes, and onions; soup and fish a la creole use the same ingredients.

**Crepe suzette.** Thin, fried pancakes rolled and served with a rich, orange, flaming sauce.

**Croquettes.** Mixture of chopped and cooked foods, shaped, rolled in egg and bread crumbs, and fried.

**Croutons.** Small cubes of fried or toasted bread served with salad or soup.

**Curry.** Spiced yellow powder used as a seasoning.

**Cutlet.** Small piece of meat, usually veal, cut from the leg; also a mixture, usually of fish or meat, shaped and cooked like a meat cutlet.

**Deep-dish pie.** A meat or fruit pie with pastry top, baked in a deep dish.

**Demitasse.** A small (half) cup of strong black coffee, served without cream or sugar at the end of the meal; also literally a half cup.

**Denver sandwich.** Finely chopped ham and beaten egg, fried.

**Devilled.** Highly seasoned with powdered mustard and cayenne pepper, chopped or ground, and mixed.

**Drawn butter.** Melted seasoned butter. Drawn buttersauce—butter, flour, and salt.

**Duchesse potatoes.** Mashed potatoes seasoned with butter and egg yolk, piped on a baking sheet, and browned in the oven.

**Eclair.** Pastry shell filled with custard or whipped cream, and iced with chocolate or caramel.

**En brochette.** Cooked and served on a skewer.

**En casserole.** Served in the dish in which it is cooked.

**En coquille.** Cooked and served in a shell.

**Enchiladas.** Mexican dish of tortillas filled with a tomato sauce, shredded lettuce, and meat; folded over and served hot with grated cheese on top.

**Entasse.** Served in a cup.

**Entrée.** Today used to mean the main dishes on a menu; formerly, a light dish served before the roast or main meat course.

**Espagnole sauce.** Brown sauce of butter, flour, and meat juice. Salad—shredded lettuce, string beans, tomatoes, onions, and pimientos, French dressing.

**Filet.** A cut of tenderloin of beef, veal, mutton, or pork; also fish served boneless.

**Filet Mignon.** Tenderloin of beef.

**Fines herbes.** A combination of fresh herbs—finely chopped parsley, chervil, tarragon, and spring onions—used in salads and sauces.

**Flambé.** Served with flaming brandy or other liqueur.

**Foie gras.** Goose liver.

**Forcemeat.** Finely chopped or strained meat, poultry, fish, game, or liver, seasoned with herbs.

**Frappé.** Iced.

**Fricassee.** Poultry or veal cut into small pieces, cooked and served in white gravy.

**Galantine.** Molded roll of meat, poultry, or game. Stuffed with forcemeat and coated with sauce or aspic.

**Goulash (Hungarian).** A beef stew simmered with onions, sweet paprika, and other seasonings. Usually served with noodles.

**Grenadin.** Small slices of meat, usually veal.

**Grenadine.** Syrup of pomegranates or red currants used in mixed drinks.

**Guacamole:** A paste of avocado mashed with onions, garlic juice, and chopped tomatoes. Used on toasted tortillas as an appetizer or with chopped lettuce as a salad or dip.

**Gumbo.** Okra; also soup of veal stock, okra, tomatoes, green peppers, and seasonings.

**Hollandaise sauce.** Sauce made with yolk of egg, butter, and lemon juice.

**Hors d'oeuvres.** Appetizers made from scores of different combinations of delicacies and tidbits: for example, toast spread with anchovies, caviar, tiny herring, mushrooms, scallions, or sardine paste.

**Indian pudding.** Slowly baked dessert of corn meal, milk, brown sugar, eggs, raisins, and seasonings.

**Irish stew.** Lamb, carrots, turnips, potatoes, onions, and seasonings; may be served with dumplings or biscuit.

**Julienne.** Vegetables cut into fine matchlike strips; also a clear soup with vegetables cut julienne style.

**Kippered.** Any fish split, salted, and smoked.

**Kirschwasser.** A liqueur of fermented cherries. Used as flavoring for desserts.

**Kosher meat.** Meat taken from animals that have been slaughtered in accordance with requirements of the orthodox Jewish faith.

**Limburger.** A semi-hard, rich, odorous, cheese.

**London broil.** Broiled flank steak, sliced across the grain, and served on toast with a brown sauce.

**Lyonnaise.** Cooked with onions.

**Macedoine.** Mixture of fruit or vegetables, cut small.

**Maitre d'hotel.** Head of the catering department; head of the food service. Also a butter sauce with lemon juice, parsley, and sometimes with worcestireshire sauce; also potatoes cooked in skin, peeled, cut in slices, covered with hot milk, and sprinkled with parsley and nutmeg.

**Marengo.** A garnish used with chicken that includes crayfish.

**Marinade.** To pickle.

**Marinate.** To season with a mixture of oil and vinegar.

**Marmite.** A clear broth containing small pieces of meat and vegetables served in an earthenware pot.

**Mayonnaise.** A basic cold, white emulsified sauce of egg yolk, oil, vinegar or wine, or lemon juice.

**Medallion.** Small cuts of beef or pork tenderloin; or small round bits of foie gras.

**Melba sauce.** Raspberry puree flavored with a liqueur; strawberries are sometimes substituted for raspberries.

**Melba toast.** Thin sliced bread baked in an oven or toasted under a slow grill; very brittle.

**Meringues.** Shells made of egg whites and sugar, served with ice cream, fruit, or sauce.

**Minestrone.** A thick Italian vegetable and pasta soup.

**Mock turtle soup.** Made of veal stock with diced calves' heads, with carrots, onions, turnips, and spices.

**Mongol soup.** Puree of peas, consommé julienne, and puree of tomatoes.

**Mornay.** Cream Sauce with cheese.

**Mousse.** Usually a frozen dessert of whipped cream, gelatin, and flavorings; also an entrée chicken, veal, or fish whipped with cream to form a froth.

**Mulligatawny soup.** Thin highly seasoned soup with veal, onions, carrots, tomatoes, peppers, and curry powder.

**Neopolitan ice cream.** Brick ice cream in three colors or flavors.

**Napoleons.** Strips made of puff pastry with custard or cream filling, topped with icing.

**Nesselrode.** A frozen pudding of sweetened chestnuts, fruit, and cream.

**Newburg.** A rich sauce of egg yolk and cream, flavored with sherry wine.

**O'Brien potatoes.** Diced green peppers, pimientos, and onions in hashed cream potatoes.

**Omelet.** An egg dish made from beaten eggs that may be filled with cheese, meats, or other seasonings.

**Oysters Rockefeller.** Oysters on the half shell with a sauce of onion, celery, crumbs, seasonings, and pureed spinach; browned in the oven or under the broiler.

**Papillote.** Meat or fish cooked and served in paper casings.

**Parfait.** Ice cream served in tall, slender glasses with fruit or sauces and whipped cream; formerly, a dessert made from mousse (whipped cream sweetened and flavored).

**Peach melba.** Ice cream on half peach with melba (raspberry) sauce.

**Perigueux.** A sauce made with truffles.

**Petits fours.** Small decorated cakes.

**Pilaf (Pilaff, Pilau, and Pilaw):** A rice dish sometimes cooked with fish, meat, or fowl.

**Piquant.** Dishes that are highly seasoned and stimulating.

**Pot pie.** Stew of chicken, beef, or other meats cooked and served in a casserole with a pastry lid.

**Praline.** Candy made from pecans, maple sugar or syrup, and cream; often made with brown sugar.

**Provencal:** Dishes prepared with garlic and olive oil; sometimes using tomatoes.

**Puree:** Pulp or paste of vegetable or fruit; also a thick soup.

**Quenelles:** Forcemeat of different kinds composed of fish, poultry, meat, or game, shaped into tiny balls or dumplings; used for garnishes.

**Quiche Lorraine.** Pie dough lined with bacon, filled with small thin slices of Swiss cheese, covered with custard, and seasoned with nutmeg; baked and served hot.

**Ragout.** Thick savory brown stew.

**Ramekin.** A small cheese tartlet served as an appetizer; also a shallow baking dish.

**Ravigote butter.** Fresh butter mixed with essence of parboiled herbs.

**Ravioli.** A pasta stuffed with ground meat, cheese, or vegetables; served with tomato or meat sauce.

**Roquefort cheese.** Semi-hard white crumbly, cheese streaked with green mold.

**Roux.** Flour stirred into butter to thicken; used to thicken sauces and soups.

**Russian dressing.** Like thousand island dressing with finely chopped chives, pickled beets, parsley, olives, and caviar.

**Saffron.** Thistle of crocuslike flower grown in southern Europe. Used in rice dishes, buns, fish, and fried dishes; gives a yellow color.

**Saratoga chips.** Thinly sliced potatoes, deep fat fried (potato chips).

**Scallopine.** Cutlet pounded very thin, sautéed.

**Scotch broth.** Made with lamb or mutton, barley, carrots, and onions.

**Shallot.** A variety of the onion family.

**Shish kebab.** Lamb or other meat or fish roasted on a skewer together with onions, tomatoes, and other vegetables.

**Smorgasbord.** An assortment of appetizers, hors d'oeuvres, meats, salads, and hot dishes.

**Soufflé.** Food well beaten and made light by the addition of egg whites; puffs up when baked.

**Squab.** Young pigeon, usually best at four weeks of age, weighing from 3/4 to 1¼ pounds.

**Table d'hote.** Fixed-price meal.

**Tartar sauce.** Mayonnaise with finely chopped gherkins, capers, parsley, shallots, and tarragon.

**Terrine.** Earthenware pot or jar; also (de Foie Gras) jars of imported goose liver.

**Thermidor.** Cooked lobster removed from the shell and mixed with white wine, egg yolk, and white sauce; it is replaced in the shell and browned under a broiler.

**Timbale.** Pastry mold for a variety of fillings.

**Tortillas.** Mexican dish made from a batter of flour, eggs, and baking powder; rolled thin, cut into rounds, and deep fried.

**Truffle.** A black fungus grown underground, used chiefly for decoration.

**Tutti-frutti.** Mixture of fruit and nuts.

**Veloute.** Basic rich white sauce consisting of white roux and chicken stock.

**Vichyssoise.** Soup consisting of potatoes, onions, leeks, chicken stock, and cream; served hot or cold.

**Vinaigrette sauce.** Oil, vinegar, yolk of hard-boiled eggs, gherkins, capers, and shallots.

**Vol-au-vent.** Puff pastry usually filled with creamed foods.

**Welsh rarebit.** Cooked cheese, butter, beer, and eggs, flavored with Worcestershire sauce and served on toasted bread.

**Wiener schnitzel.** Thinly sliced veal, breaded with egg and bread crumbs, pan fried, and served with anchovy fillet and slice of lemon.

**Yorkshire pudding.** Flour, milk, eggs, beaten well and then baked in a very hot oven; served with roast beef.

# Index